Architecture and Science

Architecture and Science

Giuseppa Di Cristina

WILEY-ACADEMY

Acknowledgement

Special thanks are due to Giovanni Narici of Editrice Libreria Dedalo, Rome, Italy, for the idea that inspired these compilations.

Page 2: Peter Eisenman, Rebstock Park, Frankfurt, view of the model

First published in Great Britain in 2001 by
WILEY-ACADEMY

a division of
JOHN WILEY & SONS LTD
Baffins Lane
Chichester
West Sussex PO19 1UD

ISBN 0-471-49722-3

Other Wiley Editorial Offices
New York • Weinheim • Brisbane • Singapore • Toronto

Cover design: Mario Bettella, Klára Smith

Layout and Prepress: ARTMEDIA PRESS Ltd, London

Printed and bound in Italy

Contents

Stephen Perrella with Rebecca Carpenter The Möbius House Study

THE TOPOLOGICAL TENDENCY IN ARCHITECTURE

Giuseppa Di Cristina

The articles in this volume concern, directly or indirectly, the topological approach in architecture which has developed progressively throughout the last decade. This has produced an alternative to the logic of conflict and contradiction explored by Deconstructivist architects: flexible, curvilinear, pliant architectures that meet the requirements of design tactics of fluidity, viscosity and connection. Even the Deconstructivists, who express the differences and heterogeneity of the physical and cultural contexts of our age by means of formal strategies of the discontinuous, the fragmented, the diagonal, juxtaposition and opposition – in other words through formal conflicts – have begun to search for an alternative way of responding to the complexity of the contemporary world. They have approached this through the logic of curvilinearity and pliancy, which is capable of embodying in a fluid manner disparate elements and differences within heterogeneous continuous systems.

The tactic of mixing, in a continuous and cohesive way, different forces internal and external to the architectural object in accordance with a logic of 'gratification' rather than conflict, has resulted in the adoption of pliant systems – that is, flexible and changing systems – in response to the various contextual, programmatic, structural and other requirements of the project. These pliant and fluid 'new architectures' tend to constitute an inclusive and organic environment. Their purpose is to model the conditions that constitute the dynamics of the urban context, from which a new urban life emerges. Thus the art of architecture becomes the capacity to give life to an interconnected series of factors (form, technology, functional programme, physical and cultural context, purchasers, market, utilisation) in the way of a global architectural practice that, according to Michael Speaks, results in a new practice of urbanism.[1]

The sensitivity for curved and bent lines is connected, then, to the will to construct fluid spaces by means of continuous, while at the same time differentiated, systems that are capable of embodying the various contextual factors in the development of form dynamically and in a cohesive manner. In fact, these fluid connections through pliant systems describe a viscous space that is capable of complex deformations and has the capacity to change in response to heterogeneous and differentiated contexts.

The articles that are included here bear witness to the interweaving of this architectural neo-avant-garde with scientific mathematical thought, in particular topological thought: although no proper theory of topological architecture has yet been formulated, one could nevertheless speak of a topological tendency in architects at both the theoretical and operative levels. The breaking down of the fences between the different circles of disciplines has fostered an interdisciplinary attitude – or rather a 'transdisciplinary' one – that tends to transpose concepts and notions from one field of thought and human activity to another. This produces a mixture of ideas and visions of a kind that determines a transversal and metamorphic condition which Marcos Novak defines by the term *transmodernity*. In particular,

developments in modern geometry or mathematics, perceptual psychology and computer graphics have an influence on the present formal renewal of architecture and on the evolution of architectural thought.

In the framework of geometry or modern mathematics topology[2] proves useful for architecture both as a conceptual resource and as an operative technique. The *Folding in Architecture* issue of *Architectural Design* in 1993 was dedicated to the topological turning point of the curvilinear, pliant and flexible 'new architecture' of the end of the 20th century.[3] Jeffrey Kipnis, Greg Lynn, Peter Eisenman and Bahram Shirdel are among the architect-theoreticians who accept topology as a cultural and scientific resource of folded, curved, undulated and twisted architectures. They are concerned with the dynamic aspects of topological geometry – that is, with the more general processes of *continuous transformation*.

Topology, also called the 'geometry of the rubber sheet', admits all possible transformations of a figure drawn on a rubber sheet when the sheet is manipulated in every possible way without tears or rents. A topological transformation, or *homeomorphism*, of one figure into another is determined by a bi-univocal and bi-continuous correspondence between the points of the respective figures. Topological transformations are the more general continuous transformations[4] that maintain the geometrical properties of the connection and vicinity of the points of the figure (so that near points continue to remain near and far-off points continue to be far away).

Thus topology considers objects as elastic bodies liable to continuous transformations that change their form; and figures that can be transformed into one another by means of a process of continuous transformation, avoiding cuts and tears, are topologically equivalent. This means that from the topological point of view there is no difference between a circumference and an ellipse, a triangle and a square, just as there is also no difference between a sphere, a cube, a cylinder and a cone. By virtue of this we can conceive figures as the products of the transformation of other figures. Topological geometry is therefore a flexible and dynamic system that is capable of curving, folding or twisting by means of continuous transformations. Accordingly, the pliant and curvilinear architectures are understood and practised as being the result of processes of manipulation and deformation of form itself, by means of continuous nonlinear transformations. Folds and curves are the forms of nonlinearity, the mathematical significance of which is illustrated by Peter T Saunders[5] and included in this volume.

The architectural theory of the fold, which has the topological notion of transformation as a conceptual resource, also ties up with the philosophy of Gilles Deleuze, thus associating the logic of pliancy with his idea of complexity and vicissitude. As Greg Lynn writes,[6] the etymology of complexity is connected with the word *plexus*, meaning fold, and the concept of complexity may be traced back to the complications of a plexus; complexity thus refers to something folded

Jeffrey Kipnis in collaboration with Philip Johnson, Briey Intervention

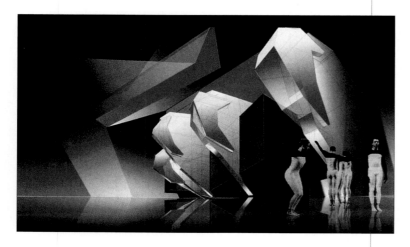

Bahram Shirdel, Nara Convention Hall

back several times in an intricate whole which cannot be reduced to mathematical exactness but is traced back to a rigorous probability; contained within folds and curves are areas of proximity that are areas of potential, unforeseen and accidental events. What most interests architects who theorise about the logic of curvilinearity and pliancy is the meaning of 'event', 'evolution' and 'process', that is, of the *dynamism* that is innate in the fluid and flexible configurations of what is now called *topological architecture*.

Architectural topology means the *dynamic variation* of form facilitated by computer-based technologies, computer-assisted design and animation software. The *topologising* of architectural form according to dynamic and complex configurations leads architectural design to a renewed and often spectacular plasticity, in the wake of the Baroque and of organic Expressionism.

The dynamic variation of form expresses evolution and continuous progress; seen in this way, architectural form is considered in its generative aspects and on the basis of the forces determining it. Topology is attractive to certain contemporary architects because it concerns, precisely, the dynamics of form, with important consequences for both the design process and the form constructed: according to a topological approach, the design process is characterised by techniques that produce the 'deformation' and 'emergence' of form; the latter is conceived of not as a presupposition – a basic datum – but as the outcome of a process of transformation, from which it emerges.

As Brian Massumi explains,[7] form is generated by a movement that exceeds it. It is no longer a matter of assuming that the pre-existing forms of the Platonic world are at the origin of the design process; using the topological approach the architect is responsible for a continuous conformative development from which form is drawn. Massumi defines transformation as a sort of 'superfigure' characterised by the continuity of the transformation;[8] this superfigure is a kind of figure that is shared by a family of topologically equivalent figures. It is, as it were, a continuous and multiple figure, the nature of which is vectorial, that is, transitional and dynamic, in relation to its duration. This superfigure is not determined, but is determinable; it exceeds the actuality of every figure emerging. So the form concerns a condition of emergence from a process of continuous variation and corresponds to the actuality of what has emerged.

But the greatest novelty of the contemporary architectural avant-garde lies not so much in its increasingly surprising and strange formal aspect – many architectures of the past anticipated the formal revolution of the present day; think of the Baroque or the works of the German Expressionists, or those of Gaudí, Kiesler, Pietilä or Goff – but in the instruments used in its designs. As Michael Speaks points out, referring to the American avant-garde,[9] the novelty concerns not so much architectural forms as the forms of architectural practice. That is, the techniques that are used to generate architectural forms through processes of computer-assisted dynamic modelling, which also have recourse to the use of animation software as in the case of Greg Lynn, and the use of geometrical and mathematical models of deformation like those of the well-known biologist D'Arcy W Thompson[10] and the French topologist mathematician René Thom, author of *Stabilité structurelle et morphogenèse* in which he introduced his 'catastrophe theory'.[11] The topologising of architecture is therefore a progressively developing tendency, thanks to the growing presence of computer technology; the malleability of form facilitated by the available technologies fosters the development of a topological architecture of change and variation of form.

Interest in this tendency is inspired not only by the opportunities for formal renewal, and the novelty of the techniques of generation of form, provided by sophisticated computer programs. Also, and above all, it is inspired by the spatial exploration of architecture which the present-day electronic media make possible. Considering architecture in its 'interiority' and assuming space as its essential content,[12] for architects a powerful focus of interest is, then, the idea of topological 'space', in the sense of a dynamic, heterogeneous and differentiated space, as an alternative to the traditional concept of the metric, quantitative, infinite and homogeneous space of the Euclidean and Cartesian geometries.

The dynamic system of transformations implies a field of external forces that weigh on the bodies and deform them. The forms of change are an expression of the action of vectors that bring about deformations and bending. Accordingly, architectural space generated by configurations under tension is characterised as a dynamic field with directions and trajectories; this vectorial space is a qualitative space of variation. The free and changing forms, made possible by the flexibility of topological geometry, express the plastic and elastic forces of material subjected to deformation and variation. They denote the energetic density of space, considered not as an incorporeal ether but as a material field crossed by flows of energy. And all of this, for architecture, is not merely an expressive or metaphorical question of some other condition. The dynamism that signifies in physical terms a spatial-temporal variation is inherent in the curving and bending forms of the built object.

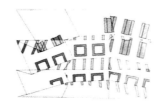

As Peter Eisenman argues,[13] the bends, the folds and the cusps present in curvilinear architecture are *singularities* that constitute topological 'events'. They are the points at which changes occur and, since the events imply the dimension of time, the singularities – the event-points – create the pluridimensional nature of space, as space-time consists of four dimensions. The architecture of folds and of cusps thus implies a temporal modulation together with the continuous variation of space, which produces dynamism. Accordingly, the dynamism is due not to the movement of the observer, but to the modification of the very form of the object so that it is capable of revealing a temporal action. Thus the architectural object takes the form of an *object event*; it is no longer defined by an essential form, but by the continuous development of the form that signifies event.

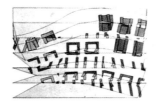

According to Eisenman, in architecture the fold permits the achieving of the condition of becoming in the declinations of involve-evolve, envelop-develop, compress-explode and contract-dilate, to which the conformative actions of infolding and unfolding correspond more precisely. The topological space of this architecture of action, as Stephen Perrella writes, 'differs from Cartesian space in that it imbricates temporal events-within form'.[14] From this point of view, by means of the topological approach the dynamic result is not limited to the mere architectural expression of the idea of transformation and movement, in which the dynamic 'effect' is connected with the tension contained in the configuration and the dynamic quality of configuration is understood as an expression of forces present in the spatial field. Rather, it takes place 'really' in the spatial-temporal variation that is implicit in nonlinear formal developments.

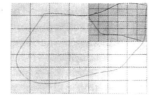

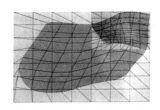

This line of reasoning may constitute a first resolution of the theoretical problem of establishing whether forms that result from dynamic processes of topologising are still dynamic when they are constructed architecture. However, according to a certain criticism, architecture designed by means of topological procedures of deformation and emergence of form is not effectively topological because it is an end product extracted from an animated process which is interrupted; that is, the form obtained when the process is interrupted is ultimately

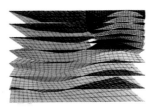

Peter Eisenman, Rebstock, concept drawings

Greg Lynn, Stranded Sears Tower, model view

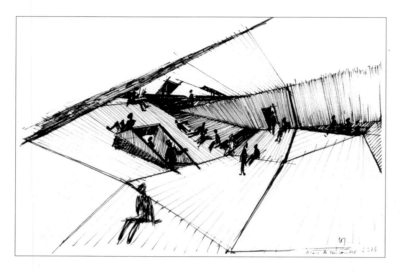

Claude Parent, Espace de Rencontre

a static figure. In other words, the techniques of topological design, based on continuity and movement, are betrayed by the fixity of their end product. As Michael Speaks states,[15] one of the questions Jeffrey Kipnis asked Greg Lynn concerns the reason why architecture itself is not animate: when movement is interrupted and transformation becomes form, architecture does not move and it becomes static.

Others argue that when the configurative movement is interrupted the constructed form no longer renders perceptible the very process that generated it.[16] The question is therefore whether the change, the event – the potential exceeding of actuality which is expressed in the transition from one form to another, and which Brian Massumi refers to as the meaning of 'virtual' in the architectural context (so that constructed form is virtuality becoming actual)[17] – may still be reread in the form emerging from the process of transformation when the latter is interrupted. Massumi, when he too raises this question, wonders where the virtuality (in the sense described above) is in the end product, and what trace of it remains in the concrete form that becomes actual as a residue of the process; in a word, what is the relationship between the constructed form that emerges from its generative process and the process itself?

In the face of this problem, Greg Lynn retorts that architecture should not be understood as a static form but rather as a stable one

which, if it has been temporally bent, implies movement without actually moving;[18] the reason lies precisely in Eisenman's reasoning regarding singularities, mentioned above. Brian Massumi seeks a way out of this impasse by considering the aspect of perception and experience of the constructed form. According to Massumi, in the constructed form the virtuality may leave traces as 'effects' of perception through the various sensorial modalities, in a condition of interaction between subject and object. The experience of things implies a transformation that involves not only movement and sight, but all the other senses (touch, hearing and smell); in other words, the topologising of form, which takes place in every experience, involves the union of the senses (synaesthesia), and forms emerge from the perceptual experience. In the actuality of what is constructed the transformability of form, its topological dimension which contains virtuality – continuous variation, becoming, event – consists of a flowing of human experience. In fact, Massumi writes:

> We ourselves – as spatially located forms in regular interaction with other forms, as embodied subjects in reciprocity with objects – must be co-occurrences with depth and boundary, co-emergences of concretion and stoppage, companion arrests, fall-out of the befallen. 'We' ourselves are stoppage events in the flow of experience.[19]

Thus our very existence is a topological transformation and constructed forms act as catalysers of perceptual events. So Massumi's maxim, according to which the virtuality of the changing nature of form exceeds its actuality, joins up once more with concrete architecture and its stable forms if we consider the human experience of the constructed form as being capable of restituting the dynamism that is otherwise lost with the interruption of the conformative process. According to Massumi, for architecture to join up with the virtual again, taking into consideration man's experiential dimension means aspiring to 'building the insensible'. And, reversing this reasoning, he notes that the method of topological design that uses digital techniques of deformation and animation merely repeats what our bodies experience in space by means of movement – their ability to extract forms from movement.

From this second point of view the topological figure corresponds to the form of experience, and the experiential effects of dynamism are called 'hyperfigure' or 'hyperspace'. The effects are real but they are not part of the formal definition of the concrete figure. Rather, they are the product of the experience of this; they are extraformal. Hyperspace in this context does not refer literally to the mathematical meaning of space as having more than three dimensions, but is used in an existential sense to indicate an experiential surplus connected with the dynamic effects of spatial configurations, so that experience itself may be defined as a hyperdimensional reality. Thus the space of experience is a topological space that may be defined in existential terms as a hyperspace of transformation.

Within the framework of the existential conception of transformation we also find the theory of hypersurface that was formulated by Stephen Perrella.[20] He uses the term hypersurface not in the proper mathematical meaning of a surface in hyperspace which accordingly has more than three dimensions, but in a translated sense in the cultural/existential meaning of a complex hybridisation of the classic dualities of thought. Hypersurface is a reconsideration of culturally instituted dichotomic relationships (interior/exterior, subject/object, form/image, structure/ornament, ground/building), not as separate and opposed entities but as transversally constituted conditions or 'planes of immanence'. That is, as entities infused into one another in which there is no longer any clear distinction between the binary terms.

Topology, in so far as it represents a passing from one element to the other with continuity, without any clear limit between them, is thus linked with Perrella's notion of hypersurface. A hypersurface is the topology of an interstitial terrain between binary oppositions that flow transversally in an interweaving of associations. And the topological surfaces that curve and bend above and within themselves in intricate and complex configurations fulfil the condition of hypersurface. The topological transformation of the fold, for example, makes it possible to articulate the surface in such a way that there is no longer any clear distinction between interior and exterior: the space caught between the folds is neither internal nor external, or else it is both, thus corresponding to a field of 'spatial indecision'.

The collapse of the traditional dualisms also refers to the phenomenological philosophy of Heidegger and to the thoughts of Deleuze, according to which everything is connected prior to divisions and subject and object are therefore also fundamentally linked. For example, in the case of the Fresh Water Pavilion in Neeltje Jans in The Netherlands, designed by Nox Architects, the topological perception of this 'liquid architecture' is that of a continuous whole in which there is no difference between the floor and the ceiling, no opposition between the horizontal and the vertical, and no distinction between form and deformation. Instability is the building's underlying characteristic and the subject's every action is based on this; he is induced to react with his own body, to interact with the object. The topological deformations of the building activate a field of forces that do not merely remain contained in the form, but stimulate how the human body with which the building interrelates acts. Such interactivity is not obtained solely through 'motion geometry', but also through technologies that activate sensor devices of various kinds (luminous, visual, sound) with which the beneficiary interacts; and at that point the categories of the real and the virtual, of the material and the immaterial, are no longer in opposition.

In the proposal of the 'oblique' by Claude Parent, the architectural volume is broken down into inclined planes that cross and intersect, abolishing the notion of enclosure connected with volume and, accordingly, with the distinction between internal and external; the limit of enclosure is exceeded in favour of continuity between interior and exterior: '... enclosure is not formulated architecturally by a specific element but becomes virtual, imprecise, indecisive.'[21] Stephen Perrella and Rebecca Carpenter's study of the Möbius House, which made use of membrane-diagrams generated by animated sequences of bending, represents the search for a post-Cartesian dwelling that, as the authors themselves write, 'is neither an interior space nor an exterior form. It is a transversal membrane that reconfigures binary notions of interior/exterior into a continuous, interwrapping median – it is a hypersurface'.[22]

In the new meaning of hypersurface, 'hyper' no longer has the mathematical meaning of 'higher' but has instead acquired the existential sense of 'altered'; and hyper does not truly relate to the surface, but is a new reading that describes a complex condition within architectural surfaces. Thus architecture of the hypersurface is the incommensurate action of human activity on a material topology. The condition of hypersurface is a condition of 'flux'. Hyper suggests an existential phenomenology of the subject-beneficiary and surface implies the new condition of an object in relation to a subject. The term hypersurface indicates the condition in which the two polarities of subjectivity and objectivity become dynamic and mix. The hypersurface is the exchange between human action and material and, more generally, it signifies any set of relationships which behave as exchange systems. This displacement and reinterpretation of the

meaning of the mathematical term hypersurface are motivated by the attempt to superimpose existential sensibility on mathematical abstraction, in order to merge the ideal abstraction with the world of life and to contaminate ideals that can no longer maintain their purity, shifting them to a more material realm. In this way the abstraction of mathematical hyperdimensions is transferrred to the lived-in cultural context; if there are 'dimensional' constructions in the abstract mathematical space, in cultural terms we have 'existential configurations'. Thus hypersurfaces are events linked with experiencing the phenomenology of space-time; the architecture of hypersurface is linked with interest in forms of experience, in the lived world and in the activities of daily life.

Following this last line of reasoning which, like the others in this essay, emerges from the articles gathered in this volume, we could add that the bridge between the ideal abstraction of mathematics and the lived world to which architecture belongs may be sought within topology itself, if the topology is considered in its widest meaning rather than the partial one of continuous transformation to which the theory of architectural neo-avant-garde is mainly linked.

Van Berkel & Bos, Pavilion, Milan Triennale

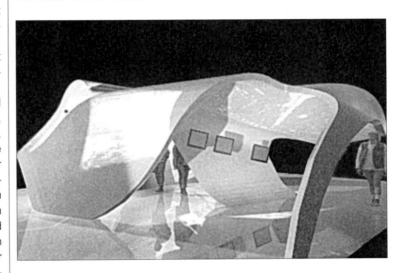

As Marcos Novak points out,[23] topology does not mean curved surfaces, as is currently held, but is precisely the study of the geometrical properties that remain unchanged when figures undergo continuous transformations, including those that are so far-reaching that the figures lose all their metrical and projective properties. Topological properties are therefore those properties that do not change as a result of more general geometrical transformations – for example, when figures are subjected to bending or stretching without cuts or tears. They are qualitative, nonmetrical properties that concern the more general and fundamental characteristics of space. They are the properties of spatial relationship – the relationships of proximity or closeness, of interior-exterior, of openness-enclosure, of connection-separation, of continuous-discontinuous, of apertures-intact solids . . .

Topological notions concern the essential aspects of figures and define the spatial relationships established between things. So topological means not only dynamic, with reference to the more general processes of continuous transformation – topological transformations. It also means qualitative, with reference to topological properties – the relational aspects of figures and space. In the first meaning, topological pertains to movement and duration, the vectorial space of the transposition of points. In the second, it pertains to all figures including Euclidean ones – as Novak appropriately remarks, 'A cube is not less topological than a blob' – and is a geometry that is implicit in all things, found in all cases of constructed reality. Topology in the sense of dynamic agrees well with the digital architecture of curvilinear and folded forms, while topology in the sense of qualitative and relational may be attributed not only to the architecture of waves and folds, but to all the architecture we contemplate, interpret and carry out from the topological, relational point of view.

The very architecture of topological deformations, over and above any attempts at formal and spatial dynamism, goes beyond the defined form and reveals the qualitative space of spatial relationships. And the topological space, that of spatial relations, is directly connected to man's existential dimension. In fact, according to studies in psychology, and above all those of the celebrated Swiss psychologist Jean Piaget,[24] the topological properties of space are connected with man's sensible experience; our actions and our experiences of the physical environment comprise a spatial dimension according to the properties of vicinity, opening, interior, etc, so topological concepts are also existential concepts. That is to say, topological space corresponds to the space of existence. The topological properties listed earlier are therefore not abstract spatial notions but refer to man in his environment, and they concern the position and

Marcos Novak, Warp Map

relationship between things as much as they do the relationship between man and things. If the essential character of things is topological, and the topological corresponds to the space of experience, we could say that the topological point of view is 'really abstract' and that architectural space topologically interpreted in the relational sense corresponds to a kind of applied abstraction.

Within the framework of topological space conceived of as a space of relationships it is therefore possible to get beyond certain dichotomies, like those of space/mass and subject/object. Space as this relational concept might be considered not as an incorporeal ether, a vacuum to be filled with objects or contained within masses, as traditional thought has it, but as a *material* field generated by the reciprocal relationships of objects. Space is, accordingly, a field in which there is no opposition between space and mass **and** space is not the negative of mass, just as mass is a space in so far as it is in its turn a series of related material elements. No contraposition or complementarity exists between object and space: an object is an object if it is considered as an element of a larger spatial whole, but in itself it is a space if it is considered as a whole that consists of related

elements. In the material meaning of space it might be considered that there is no opposition between a solid and a void, but space may be interpreted as a solid endowed with intervals or interstices.

Thereafter, spatial relations are equally concerned with the object and the subject, which are not opposed and distant but form part of a single reality. Our bodies and our senses are involved in the relational interplay of things, and a body is an element that moves, and is situated in the midst of objects. It establishes a variety of relationships with the objects in addition to those that already exist between the objects alone. We therefore bring about relationships of positions among things as well as our position in relation to these. If we too form part of the relational structure that generates space, then we continuously modify this with our bodies in a system of interaction between subject and object.

These last considerations mean that in addition to the topological tendency in architecture producing change of form – to which the articles in this volume above all refer – there is a further topological tendency which may be found and theorised in architectural space interpreted and understood as a space of relationship.

Notes

1 See Michael Speaks, 'It's Out There …', p 184.

2 The official birth of topology occurred in 1895 with the publication of the French mathematician Jules-Henri Poincaré's *Analysis Situs*. However the term topology was used for the first time in 1847 by JB Listing in the title of his *Vorstudien zur Topologie*, and problems concerning topology are discussed in the works of the mathematicians Leonhard Euler (1707–83), August Ferdinand Möbius (1790–1868) and Georg Cantor (1845–1918).

3 In the United Kingdom, Brutalism legitimated the assumption of an informal organisation of space, making explicit reference to a more advanced mathematical conception like that offered by topology: in 1955 Reyner Banham wrote of the project the Smithsons entered in the competition for the University of Sheffield extension: '… it can be demonstrated that this is subordinate to a composition, but no longer based on the geometry of rule and compass that still underpins so many architectural compositions, but rather based on an intuitive topological sensitivity.' The quotation is from Francesco Tentori's 'Phoenix Brutalism' in *Zodiac*, no 18 (1969), pp 32–3.

4 Topological transformations also include the various 'groups of geometrical transformation' (isometric transformations or isometries, similar transformations or similarities, affinities, projective transformations or projectivities, and nonlinear transformations).

5 Peter T Saunders, 'Nonlinearity, p 110.

6 Greg Lynn, 'Architectural Curvilinearity', p 26.

7 Brian Massumi, 'Sensing the Virtual, Building the Insensible', p 198.

8 Massumi, 'Strange Horizon', p 190.

9 Speaks, op cit.

10 The best-known chapter in D'Arcy W Thompson's celebrated book *Growth and Form* (1917) concerns the 'theory of transformations' which, with the famous diagrams of transformation (the Cartesian transformations) provides a geometrical description of the deformations of morphological types present in nature; although Thompson does not quote topology, his dissertation on the transformation of forms is substantially inspired by it.

11 According to Thom's catastrophe theory a natural process occurs in conformity with a dynamic model which is described as a field characterised by the presence of limit states, known as 'attractors', towards which the system evolves. For each attractor A the sum total of trajectories of the field that tend towards A forms a domain of space called 'the basin' of attractor A. Several separate attractors are in competition. The basins that relate to the different attractors are separated by the so-called 'surfaces of catastrophe' – 'crest line' or 'crash wave' 'hypersurfaces'. These separating surfaces have a qualitative (topological) structure and there are seven types, for which Thom provides the algebraic model and the geometrical pattern. The types are: the fold, the cusp, the swallowtail, the butterfly, the hyperbolic umbilicus, the elliptic umbilicus and the parabolic umbilicus. The fold and the cusp, recurrent in architectural forms, thus correspond to topological continuums that describe two of the seven elementary catastrophes which correspond, according to Thom's theory, to phases of transition – sudden changes in the processes of natural evolution, both inanimate and living.

12 Space, which architectural theory has considered to be the essential content of architecture only since the end of the 19th century, today represents the fundamental event in present-day architectural experimentation which seeks to go beyond Euclidean geometry and Cartesian space in favour of new spatial ideas.

13 Peter Eisenman, 'Folding in Time', p 50.

14 Stephen Perrella, 'Hypersurface Theory: Architecture><Culture', p 138.

15 Speaks, op cit.

16 Ibid.

17 Massumi, 'Sensing the Virtual, Building the Insensible', op cit.

18 Speaks, op cit.

19 Massumi, 'Sensing the Virtual, Building the Insensible', op cit.

20 Perrella, op cit.

21 Claude Parent, 'The Oblique Function Meets Electronic Media', p 160.

22 Stephen Perrella with Rebecca Carpenter, 'The Möbius House Study', p 158.

23 Marcos Novak, 'Transarchitectures and Hypersurfaces', p 152.

24 Jean Piaget studied babies' interest in space and showed that the early comprehension of space is intuitive and corresponds to the topological properties of space; so the topological space corresponds to the intuitive, existential space.

KENNETH POWELL
UNFOLDING FOLDING

During the last quarter of a century the certainties which appeared to underlay the hegemony of modernism in architecture have been under constant attack, so that what seemed beyond question – a set of immutable 'truths' – is now largely discredited. The Modern Movement was born at the CIAM Congress of 1928, when Corbusier and Gropius hammered out a persuasive, but essentially exclusive programme for architectural revolution.

Revolutionaries often end up as tyrants What began as a liberating force became a rigid orthodoxy. In a recent exposé of the failings of the 'functionalist' gospel (*AA Files*, Autumn, 1992) Colin St John Wilson quotes Alvar Aalto to the effect that 'one of the ways to arrive at a more and more humanely built environment is to expand the concept of the 'Rational'. Aalto is identified – with Wright, Asplund, Scharoun and others – as part of 'the other tradition' of modern architecture.

Venturi's *Complexity and Contradiction* (1966) stands at the head of a series of key texts which undermined homogeneity and orthodoxy in favour of an honest acceptance of the discontinuity and disjunction which are part of all human life More recently, Deconstruction has been seen as a basis for the revival of the humane art of architecture With a strong philosophical base the Deconstructivist 'movement' (if ever such) was libertarian, permissive, dynamic, but rooted in the conflict which its adherents have seen as the dominant characteristic of modern urban life. As Mark Wigley put it, Deconstructivist architecture is 'devious' and 'slippery' – and disturbing. It had to disturb, to be subversive, in order to break the hold of the old order.

Deconstruction has done its job. Its jagged discordancies were shocking enough. But five years ago, when the work of seven allegedly Deconstructivist architects was shown at MOMA in New York,

none of those represented (with the exception of Frank Gehry) had built on any scale. Now all are building extensively. The new architecture of the end of the 20th century faces the problem of reconciling (as Greg Lynn suggests) the opposing goals of conflict and contradiction and of unity and reconstruction. In practice, architecture cannot be engaged in a process of permanent revolution. It has practical and formal, as well as speculative and philosophical ends to pursue.

The work reviewed here has significance as the product of a generation of architects who had previously espoused Deconstruction but now seek to address issues (especially those related to the life of the city) In which confrontation cannot be all. They have taken up the challenge of making their architecture a power on the streets, not just in the gallery and the pages of the specialist journals.

Peter Eisenman is a key figure in all this. His definition of 'weak form' paved the way for a flexible and flowing, soft edged approach to architectural design Eisenman now seeks a new philosophical basis for an architecture which, were it not for the inescapable Wrightian overtones, one might categorise as 'organic'

On reflection, 'organic' is not so inappropiate as an adjective where the projects included are concerned. Just as Baroque architecture grew out of an age of conflict and violence and yet was characterised by its richly decorative, highly expressive sense of conviction. the new expressive architecture of today s moving towards a sculptural drama which is powerfully present in projects such as that of Bahram Shirdel for the Nara Convention Center ('a complex spatial unity guided by the theme of the symbiosis of history and the future'), Eisenman's Wexner Center and Emory University Arts Center, and a number of recent and forthcoming schemes by

Frank Gehry. (In this respect, the Vitra Museum was a harbinger of things to come) There are no obvious historical references to suggest a borrowing from the Baroque. yet there are uncanny links.

In particular, as Baroque architects transformed Rome and Prague, while respecting the existing form of those cities, the new organic architects of the 1990s are passionate urbanists. Urban transformation without violent upheaval is perhaps the central theme of their work. All these architects question the relevance of post-modernist and classicist formulae for urban survival/revival, while maintaining their defiance of the old modernism

Seen in this light, the new architecture which has evolved out of the Deconstructivist episode is vastly important for its celebration of diversity. Post-Modernism rediscovered the city but its analysis of urban form and urban life, largely in the theory of collage, has proved inadequately retrograde Gehry, Eisenman. Shirdel and others are seeking for nothing less than a reinstatement of the expressive power of architecture which underlies its cultural and social role. Lynn's project for 'reconfiguring' the Sears Tower as part of the fabric of Chicago reflects a desire for unity and harmony through rich diversity.

This issue explores just one theme, one approach to a new pliant, flowing architecture. It is an approach that has already produced rich rewards. Yet it is merely a start. Architects, confident in their role as social artists in the best sense, will increasingly reject the old constraints in favour of an inclusive and organic way of designing which is in tune with the man-made and natural world. These projects are far from being a re-run of history: they could play a part in making history.

Carsten Juel-Christiansen, The Passage

JEFFREY KIPNIS
TOWARDS A NEW ARCHITECTURE

'Well, I stand up next to a mountain,
and I chop it down with the edge of my
hand.
Then I pick up all the pieces and make an
island,
might even make a little sand.' *Jimi Hendrix*

Over the last few years, a few projects by a
handful of architects have broached
discussions of a New Architecture. The
themes of this discussion are only now
coming into sufficient focus to allow for the
preliminary efforts to articulate some of
them in this volume. Before we turn our
attention to that specific task, however, let
us consider for a moment what is at stake in
the endeavour.

'A New Architecture'. Today one whispers this phrase with trepidation and
embarrassment, perhaps for good reason.
True enough, most New Architectures are
so ill-conceived that they are stillborn or die
a merciful death early in infancy. But the
prognosis is poor even for those with the
strength to survive their hatching, for the
majority of these are killed by a well coordinated, two-pronged attack.

There are several variations, but the
general schema of this attack is well-
known: first, critics from the right decry the
destabilising anarchism of the New Architecture and the empty egotism of its
architects; then, critics from the left rail
against the architecture as irresponsible
and immoral and the architects as corrupt
collaborationists. Sapped by this onslaught, the eviscerated remainders are
quickly mopped up by historians, with their
uncanny ability to convince us that the
supposed New Architecture is actually not
new at all and that it was in fact explored
with greater depth and authenticity in
Europe some time ago.[1]

Today, historians and critics alike
proselytise upon the creed that there is
nothing new that is worthwhile in architecture, particularly no new form. Their doxol-
ogy is relentless, 'praise the past, from
which all blessings flow.' Thus, we retreat
from the new and have become ashamed to
look for it. I have colleagues who comb

drafts of their work before publication in
order to replace the word 'new' as often as
possible; I have done it myself. As a result,
PoMo, whose guiding first principle is its
unabashed and accurate claim to offer
nothing new, has become the only architecture to mature over the last 20 years.

'Nonsense!' It will be argued. 'During the
same period a flourishing revival of the
avant-garde has developed' and fingers
will point to MOMA's Decon exhibition and
to the buildings of Eisenman, Gehry,
Libeskind, Tschumi, Koolhaas, Hadid and
others. Yet, upon closer examination, it is
not more accurate to say that these works
have been executed under the auspices of
an implicit contract of disavowal. In other
words, is it not the case that these designs
are celebrated as auratic, signature
buildings of interest only for their
irreproducible singularity, rather than as
sources of new principles for a general
architectural practice. In that sense, the
discipline of architecture has recognised
them as exotic, precisely so as to suppress
their contribution to a New Architecture.

Yet within these disparate works are
insights that might well contribute to
formulating a framework for a New Architecture: one that promises both formal
vitality and political relevance. Consider the
work of Daniel Libeskind, for example. From
his *Chamber Works* to his recent projects in
Germany and elsewhere, one finds a
sustained, penetrating critique of the axis
and its constellation of linear organisations.
Considering the political, social and spatial
history of the axis in architecture and
urbanism, this is no minor issue. Yet, very
little on this subject can be found in the
critical literature treating these projects.
Instead, Libeskind is configured as an
avatar of the esoteric and the status and
power of the axis in quotidian architectural
practice, so thoroughly re-thought in his
projects, is left unquestioned.

On the surface, our retreat from the New
seems both historically and theoretically
well-informed. Towards its utopian aspirations, architectural Modernism sought to
overthrow obsolete spatial hierarchies and

establish a new and more democratic,
homogeneous space. However well-
meaning this goal was, insofar as its search
for the New was implicated in an Enlighten-
ment-derived, progressivist project, it was
also implicated in the tragedies that
resulted. The instrumental logic of architectural Modernism's project of the new
necessarily calls for erasure and replacement, of Old Paris by Le Corbusier, for
example.

In the name of heterogeneity, post-
modern discourse has mounted a critique
of the project of the new along several
fronts. It has demonstrated both the
impossibility of invention *tabula rasa* and
the necessity to celebrate the very differences Modernism sought to erase. Its own
version of the search for the New, a giddy
logic of play, of reiteration and recombination, of collage and montage, supplants
Modernism's sober, self-serious search for
the Brave New. In Post-Modernism's play,
history regains renewed respect, though on
different terms. Rejected as the linear,
teleological process that underwrites its
own erasure and replacement, history is
now understood as the shapeless well of
recombinatorial material; always deep,
always full, always open to the public.

In Post-Modernism's most virulent
practices, those that use reiteration and
recombination to insinuate themselves into
and undermine received systems of power,
a relationship to the New is maintained that
is optimistic and even progressive, albeit
not teleologically directed. In such post-
modern practices as deconstruction, the
project of the new is rejected. New intellectual, aesthetic and institutional forms, as
well as new forms of social arrangements,
are generated not by proposition but by
constantly destabilising existing forms.
New forms result as temporary
restabilisations, which are then
destabilised. Accelerated evolution
replaces revolution, the mechanisms of
empowerment are disseminated,
heterogeneous spaces that do not support
established categorical hierarchies are
sought, a respect for diversity and differ-

ence is encouraged. Far from being nihilistic, Post-Modernism in this conception is broadly affirmative.

Unfortunately, however, Post-Modernism's critique of the politics of erasure/replacement and emphasis on recombination have also led to its greatest abuse, for it has enabled a reactionary discourse that re-establishes traditional hierarchies and supports received systems of power, such as the discourse of the nothing new employed by Ronald Reagan and Margaret Thatcher for their political ends and by Prince Charles, Roger Scruton and even Charles Jencks to prop up PoMo.

I believe, therefore, that it is not Post-Modernism itself, but another, more insidious pathology, a kind of cultural *progeria*, that underlies our current withdrawal from the New. The symptoms of this disorder were first diagnosed by Nietzsche and have been thoroughly analysed more recently by Roberto Unger.[2] Briefly, it manifests itself as a rationale which holds that the catalogue of possible forms (in every sense of the word form: institutional, social, political and aesthetic) is virtually complete and well-known. We may debate the relative merits of this form or that, but we will no longer discover nor invent any new forms. This position is far from the suppositions of post-modern combinatorics.

Is it possible that 'Westernity' as a cultural experiment is finished and, put simply, that we are old? Only in that context could our current, excessive veneration for the received catalogue of forms be valid. Frankly, I cannot believe that in the short span of our history we have experimented with and exhausted the possibilities of form. It seems to me that every indication today is to the contrary; whether one considers the political transformations in Eastern Europe or the technological transformations that characterise today's society. The building of the catalogue of available forms, aesthetic forms, institutional forms and of forms of social arrangement, has only just begun.

I have already indicated some of the broader criteria for a New Architecture. If it is not to repeat the mistakes of Modernism, it must continue to avoid the logic of erasure and replacement by participating in recombinations. As far as possible, it must seek to engender a heterogeneity that resists settling into fixed hierarchies. Furthermore, it must be an architecture, ie, a proposal of principles (though not prescriptions) for design. Finally, it must experiment with and project new forms.

The first two of these criteria, already belong to architectural Post-Modernism. However, the last two criteria – the call for principles and the projection of new forms – detach fundamentally the theorisation of a New Architecture from Post-Modernism proper, however much it draws upon the resources of the latter.

Indicative of that detachment is the degree to which some New Architecture theorists, notably Sanford Kwinter and Greg Lynn, have shifted their attention from post-structural semiotics to a consideration of recent developments in geometry, science and the transformations of political space, a shift that is often marked as a move from a Derridian towards a Deleuzian discourse.[3]

In these writings, the Deleuzian cast is reinforced with references to Catastrophe Theory – the geometry of event-space transformations – and to the new Biology. Not only are geometry and science traditional sources par excellence of principles and form for architecture, but, more importantly, the paramount concern of each of these areas of study is morphogenesis, the generation of new form. However provocative and invaluable as resources these studies in philosophy or science are, it must be said that neither provide the impetus for a New Architecture, nor the particulars of its terms and conditions. Rather, these have grown entirely out of architectural projects and developments within the discipline of architecture itself.

One contributing factor to the search for a New Architecture is the exhaustion of collage as the prevailing paradigm of architectural heterogeneity. In order to oppose Modernism's destituting proclivity for erasure and replacement, Post-Modernism emphasised grafting as the recombinatorial instrument of choice. The constellation of collage, in all its variations,[4] offered the most effective model of grafting strategies. From Rowe to Venturi to Eisenman,[5] from PoMo to the deconstructivists, collage has served as the dominant mode of the architectural graft. There are indications, however, to suggest that collage is not able to sustain the heterogeneity architecture aspires to achieve. In lieu of the meticulous study necessary to support this claim, allow the suggestion of two of its themes, the first, historical, and the second, theoretical. First, post-modern collage is an extensive practice wholly dependent on effecting incoherent contradictions within and against a dominant frame. As it becomes the prevailing institutional practice, it loses both its contradictory force and its affirma-

tive incoherence. Rather then destabilising an existing context, it operates more and more to inscribe its own institutional space. The only form collage produces, therefore, is the form of collage.

Secondly, and perhaps more importantly, collage is limited to a particular order of semiotic recombinations. Each element in a collage, even in the aleatoric process-collages of dada, must be known and rosterable in its own right. Thus, although collage may engender new compositions as well as shifts, slips, accidents and other chimeral effects, the long-term effect of collage is to valorise a finite catalogue of elements and/or processes.

Collage is only able to renew itself by constantly identifying and tapping into previously unrostered material. Thus, collage can never be projective. The exhaustion of collage derives from the conclusion that the desire to engender a broadly empowering political space in respect of diversity and difference cannot be accomplished by a detailed cataloguing and specific enfranchisement of each of the species of differentiation that operate within a space. The process is not only economically and politically implausible, it is theoretically impossible.[6] If collage is exhausted as a recombinatorial strategy – a matter still debated[7] – then the problem becomes one of identifying grafts other than collages. The key distinction from collage would be that such grafts would seek to produce heterogeneity within an intensive cohesion rather than out of extensive incoherence and contradiction.[8]

In a lecture delivered in 1990 to the ANYONE conference in Los Angeles, the neo-modern social theorist Roberto Mangeiberra Unger took issue with current post-modern practices in architecture, primarily in terms of what he saw as the 'ironic distancing' effected by both PoMo and Deconstructivist architecture. At the conclusion of his lecture, he outlined five criteria that any New Architecture seeking to contribute to a non-hierarchical, heterogeneous political space must meet.

According to Unger, such an architecture must be *vast* and *blank*, it must *point* and be *incongruous* and *incoherent*.[9] It is not clear from the lecture how Unger intended his criteria to be interpreted, but I was struck by the degree to which, with one exception, they lent themselves to a discourse on grafting alternatives to collage. Particularly interesting to me was how well these criteria read as generalisations of the spacial/formal project of

Modernism outlined in Le Corbusier's points. Where Le Corbusier's points are directed towards producing a broadly democratic space by achieving homogeneity, Unger's are directed towards a similar political goal by achieving a spatial heterogeneity that does not settle into stable alignments or hierarchies. I interpret and modify Unger's criteria as follows: (i) Vastness – negotiates a middle-ground between the homogeneity of infinite or universal space and the fixed hierarchies of closely articulated space. Recognising the necessity of finitude for heterogeneity, vastness seeks sufficient spatial extension to preclude the inscription of traditional, hierarchical spatial patterns. Design implication: generalisation of free-plan to include disjunction and discontinuity; extension of free plan to 'free-section'; emphasis on residual and interstitial spaces. (ii) Blankness – extrapolates the Modernist project of formal abstraction understood as the suppression of quotation or reference through the erasure of decoration and ornament to include canonic form and type. By avoiding formal or figural reference, architecture can engage in unexpected formal and semiotic affiliations without entering into fixed alignments. Design implication: generalisation of free-facade to free-massing. (iii) Pointing – architecture must be projective, ie, it must point to the emergence of new social arrangements and to the construction of new institutional forms. In order to accomplish this, the building must have a point, ie, project a transformation of a prevailing political context. The notion of pointing should not be confused with signifying, and in fact is a challenge to the determined structure of the signifier/signified, whether monosemic or polysemic. The indeterminacy of pointing shifts the emphasis from the formation of stable alignments and/or allegiances to the formation of provisional affiliations. (iv) Incongruity – a requirement to maintain yet subvert received data, including, for example, the existing site as a given condition and/or the programme brief. Maintenance and subversion are equally important; either alone leads inexorably to spatial hypostatisation. Design implication: a repeal of the architectural postulates of harmony and proportion, structural perspicuity and system co-ordination (eg, among plan, section and facade, or between detail and formal organisation). (v) Intensive Coherence – in fact, Unger stresses the necessity for incoherence, understood as a repeal of the

architectural postulate of unity or wholeness. However, because incoherence is the hallmark of post-modern collage, I suggest as an alternative, a coherence forged out of incongruity. Intensive coherence implies that the properties of certain monolithic arrangements enable the architecture to enter into multiple and even contradictory relationships. It should not be confused with Venturi's notion of the 'difficult whole', in which a collage of multiplicity is then unified compositionally.

At the beginning of this essay, I noted that a handful of recent projects offer specific terms and conditions for a New Architecture. While, in general, these projects show a shift away from a concern for semiotics towards a concern for geometry, topology, space and events, in my view, they subdivide broadly into two camps, which I term DeFormation and InFormation. DeFormation, the subject of this volume, seeks to engender shifting affiliations that nevertheless resist entering into stable alignments. It does so by grafting abstract topologies that cannot be decomposed into simple, planar components nor analysed by the received language of architectural formalism.

The strategy of InFormation, of which Koolhaas' Karlsruhe and Tschumi's Le Fresnoy are exemplary cases, is to form a collecting graft, usually by encasing disparate formal and programmatic elements within a neutral, modernist monolith. The resultant incongruous, residual spaces are then activated with visual layering, programmatic innovation, technological effects and events.

Although both evolve from the same problem, the architectures of DeFormation and InFormation are by no means simply collaborative. In general, both agree on certain architectural tactics that can be understood in terms of Unger's criteria (as modified). Both, for example, rely on such devices as box-within-box sections with an emphasis on interstitial and residual spaces (vast, incongruous); also, both deploy monolithic forms and avoid any obvious applied ornament or figurative reference (blank, intensive cohesion).

Yet the tensions between them are pronounced. While DeFormation emphasises the role of new aesthetic form and therefore the visual in the engenderment of new spaces, InFormation de-emphasises the role of aesthetic form in favour of new institutional form, and therefore of programme and events. The event-spaces of new geometries tend to drive the former,

while the event-spaces of new technologies occupy the latter.

One of the pervasive characteristics of InFormation is its unapologetic use of the orthogonal language of Modernism. When post-modernist architecture first emerged, the formal language of Modernism was simply condemned as oppressive and monotonous – recall Venturi's 'Less is a bore'. Subsequently, that critique was deepened as architects and theorists demonstrated that, far from being essentialist, the language of Modernism constituted a sign-system. Once the demonstration that architecture was irreducibly semiotic was complete, the essentialist justification for the austere language of Modernism dissolved and the door opened to the use of any and all architectural signs in any and every arrangement.

InFormation posits that the exhaustion of collage is tantamount to a rendering that is irrelevant of all aesthetic gestures.[10] The architectural contribution to the production of new forms and the inflection of political space therefore can no longer be accomplished by transformations of style. Furthermore, InFormation argues that the collective architectural effect of the orthogonal forms of Modernism is such that it persists in being Blank; often stressing that blankness by using the forms as screens for projected images. Pointing is accomplished by transformations of institutional programmes and events. For, DeFormation, on the other hand, architecture's most important contribution to the production of new forms and to the inflection of political space continues to be aesthetic. Far from being Blank, DeFormation perceives the modernist language of InFormation as nothing less than historical reference and the use of projected images no more than applied ornament. Instead, DeFormation searches for Blankness by extending Modernism's exploration of monolithic form, while rejecting essentialist appeal to Platonic/Euclidean/Cartesian geometries. Pointing is accomplished in the aesthetics; the forms transform their context by entering into undisciplined and incongruous formal relationships. InFormation sees the gestured geometries of DeFormation as predominantly a matter of ornament style.

To examine the design consequences of these issues, let us look at a brief comparison of Tschumi's InFormation at Le Fresnoy with Shirdel's DeFormation at Nara. The National Center for Contemporary Arts at Le Fresnoy offered a perfect circumstance in which to reconsider the graft. In his description of the problem, Tschumi was specific in outlining the various possibilities. Since many of the existing structures were in disrepair, a return to an erase-and-replace approach was perfectly plausible. On the other hand, the quality of the historical forms and spaces at Le Fresnoy also suggested a renovation/restoration approach à la Collage. Tschumi eschews both, however, and envelops the entire complex within a partially enclosed modernist roof to create a cohesive graft. The graft does not produce a collage; rather than creating compositionally resolved collection of fragments, the roof reorganises and redefines each of the elements into a blank, monolithic unity whose incongruity is internalised. Tschumi sutures together the broad array of resulting spaces with a system of catwalks and stairs, visually interlacing them with cuts, partial enclosures, ribbon windows and broad transparencies. Wherever one is in the complex, one sees partial, disjointed views of several zones from inside to outside at the same time.

Like the visual effects, the role of programming in this project concerns the production of space as much, if not more than, the accommodation of function. As far as possible, Tschumi programmes all the resultant spaces, even treating the tile roofs of the old building as a mezzanine. Where direct programming is not possible, he elaborates the differential activation in material/events. In the structural trusses of the new roof, he projects videos as an architectural material in order to activate those residual spaces with events.

The result is a project which promises a spatial heterogeneity that defies any simple hierarchy: a collection of differentiated spaces capable of supporting a wide variety of social encounters without privileging or subordinating any. Le Fresnoy undermines the classical architectural/political dialectic between hierarchical heterogeneity and homogeneity and points to a potentially new institutional/architectural form.

Like Tschumi at Le Fresnoy, Shirdel also uses a collecting-graft to unify an incongruous, box-in-box section in his project for the Nara Convention Center. Unlike Tschumi, however, he shapes the form and internal structure of the graft by folding a three-bar parti with two complex regulating line geometries. The first geometry involutes the exterior of the building into an abstract, non-referential monolith whose form flows into the landscaping of the site. The second

geometry has a similar effect on the major structural piers that hold the three theatres (each one a box whose form is determined simply by exigent functional requirements) suspended in section.

The internal and external geometries connect in such a way that 'major' space of the complex is entirely residual, an alley, so to speak, rived in the provisional links between two invaginated geometries. The residual-space effect is reinforced by the fact that all of the explicit programme of the building is concentrated in the theatres and lobbies that float as objects above and away from the main space. In a sense, Shirdel's attitude towards programme is the opposite of Tschumi's. Although the building functions according to its brief, there is no architectural programme other than the function, no informing choreography nor any use of technology to activate spaces. Shirdel's computer renderings of Japanese dancers performing in eerie isolation in the emptied, residual space underline the point. The entire issue of spatial heterogeneity rests in the aesthetics of the form and in the opposition between unprogrammed event and function. In passing, it is worth noting that the risk of proposing that the dominant (and most expensive) space of a building be nothing other than residual space should not be underestimated.

I pursue the development of DeFormation in greater detail below and will have occasion to return to the Shirdel Nara project. However, I believe that the brief comparison above, is sufficient to indicate both the similarities and divergences in the routes that are being mapped by InFormation and DeFormation towards a New Architecture.

DeFormation[11]

As is always the case in architectural design theory, Deformation is an artifact, a construction of principles that have emerged after the fact from projects by diverse architects that were originally forged with different intentions and under different terms and conditions. Thus, strictly speaking, there are no DeFormationist architects (yet), just as there were no Mannerist or Baroque architects. It is a minor point, perhaps too obvious to belabour; yet as we move towards a development of principles and a technical language with which to articulate them, we must be cautious not to allow these prematurely to circumscribe and regulate a motion in design whose fertility derives as

much from its lack of discipline as from its obedience to policy. If there is a DeFormation, it has only just begun.

Much has been written and no doubt more will be written that consigns the work of DeFormation (and InFormation) to this or that contemporary philosopher, particularly Gilles Deleuze. It cannot be denied that a powerful consonance exists between the field of effects sought by these architectures and various formulations of Deleuze and Guattari in *A Thousand Plateaus* or by Deleuze in *Le Pli*. The sheer number of terms that the architectural literature has borrowed from the Deleuzian discourse (affiliation, pliancy, smooth and striated space, etc) not to mention such fortuities as the shared thematisation of folding, testify to the value of this correspondence. However, for all of the profitability of this dialogue there are costs to which we should be attentive. In general, obligating any architecture to a philosophy or theory maintains a powerful but suspect tradition in which architecture is understood as an applied practice. In that tradition, the measure of architectural design is the degree to which it exemplifies a theory or philosophy, rather than the degree to which it continuously produces new architectural effects; as a consequence, the generative force of design effects in their own right are subordinated to the limited capacity of architecture to produce philosophical (or theoretical) effects.

In his reading of Leibniz in *Le Pli*, Deleuze stages his meditation on the fold in part on an interpretation of the space of Baroque architecture, thus it might be assumed that Baroque architecture stands as a paradigm of the architectural effects of the fold. Such an assumption, however careless, would be fair and would underwrite the configuration of DeFormation as nothing more than a neo-Baroque.

Now, though Deleuze's reading of Baroque architecture is adequate to exemplify his thought on the fold, it is by no means an adequate reading of the architectural effects of the Baroque. Baroque architecture is no more able to realise the contemporary architectural effects of the fold than Leibniz's philosophy is able to realise the contemporary philosophical effects of Deleuze's thought. In other words, Deleuze's philosophy is no more (merely) neo-Leibnizian than DeFormation is (merely) neo-Baroque.

However much Deleuze's philosophy profits from the generative effects of Leibniz's texts, its payoff, ie, what it has new to say, does not rest on the accuracy of its scholarly recapitulation of Leibniz's philosophy; rather, it rests primarily on the differences between what Deleuze writes and what Leibniz writes. On this point, I believe Deleuze (and Leibniz!) would agree. In the same way, the interest of DeFormation does not rest on its recapitulation of Baroque themes, but primarily on the differences it effects with the Baroque and its other predecessors.

But perhaps, the dearest cost to which we must be attentive is the degree to which formulating DeFormation in terms of a Deleuzian language belies the independent development of the (consonant ideas within) architecture. No doubt this development, more a genealogy than a history, lacks the grace and pedigree that it would obtain from architecture conceived as applied philosophy. Yet, the halting, circuitous pathways of DeFormation's evolution – here lighting on cloth folds depicted in a painting by Michelangelo, there on train-tracks, here a desperate attempt to win a competition, there a last-minute effort to satisfy a nervous client, and always drawing upon the previous work of others – not only bears a dignity all its own, but also materially augments the substance of the philosophy.

Allow me then, to retrace some of these paths, collecting my effects along the way. Neither arbitrarily nor decisively, I begin with three contemporaneous projects: Shirdel and Zago's Alexandria Library Competition entry, Eisenman's Columbus Convention Center and Gehry's Vitra Museum.[12]

For a number of years beginning in the early 1980s, Bahram Shirdel, in association with Andrew Zago, pursued an architecture which he termed black-stuff. Ironic as the term may first appear, black-stuff is quite an accurate name for the effects Shirdel sought to achieve. Rejecting the deconstructivist themes of fragments, signs, assemblages and accreted space, Shirdel pursued a new, abstract monolithicity that would broach neither reference nor resemblance. Shirdel was interested in generating disciplined architectural forms that were not easily decomposable into the dynamics of point/line/plane/volume of modern formalism. We will come to refer to these forms in terms of anexact geometries and non-developable surfaces, but Shirdel's black-stuff set the stage for the Deformationist principle of non-referential, monolithic abstraction we have already discussed.

To generate these forms, Shirdel developed a technique in which he would begin with one or more recognisable figure(s) whose underlying organisation possessed the desired internal complexity. Then, in a series of steps, he mapped the architectural geometry of these figures in meticulous detail, carefully abstracting or erasing in each progressive step aspects of the original figure that caused it to be referential or recognisable – a process I termed disciplined relaxation at the time. Similar processes appear in the discussion of the Gehry and Eisenman projects to follow.

The culmination of the black-stuff investigations was the Shirdel/Zago entry premiated in the Alexandria Library competition, a design that evolved from a disciplined relaxation of a painting of folded cloth by Michelangelo. In that figure of the fold, Shirdel found precisely the formal qualities he sought. Although the final form shows no obvious traces of the original painting, relationships among surface, form and space are captured in the architecture.

Shortly after the Alexandria competition, Peter Eisenman entered a limited competition against Holt, Henshaw, Pfau and Jones, and Michael Graves[13] to design a convention centre for Columbus, Ohio. Because the City of Columbus framed the opening of the centre in terms of its quintcentennial celebration of Christopher Columbus' first voyage, Eisenman's initial strategy was to design a collage project based on the nautical architecture of the Santa Maria. With only three weeks remaining in the 12-week competition period, Eisenman learned that Graves, too, was basing his design on a nautical theme. Anxious to win the competition, (he had only just opened his own office) Eisenman took the extreme risk of abandoning nine weeks of work and shifting to an entirely different scheme, taking a moment to send Graves a postcard of a sinking ship en passant.

The new scheme was based on the notion of 'weak form' Eisenman had only just begun to formulate.[14,15] Working from two oddly similar diagrams, one of a fibre-optics cable cross-section and the other of the train-track switching system that once occupied the site in Columbus, Eisenman produced the winning design: a monolithic box knitted out of vermiform tendrils. The likeness shared by the two diagrams is important to note, for in that weak resemblance, Eisenman first saw the potential of weak form.

Although similar in many respects, the Eisenman weak-form projects are different

from Shirdel's black-stuff in one aspect that is of fundamental significance to the principles of DeFormation. Eisenman also attempts to achieve an abstract monolith free of explicit reference. But while the black-stuff projects were intended to be radically other, Eisenman's notion of weakness requires the form to retain a hint of resemblance, so that it might enter into unexpected relationships, like the one that connects the two diagrams.

True enough, once alerted, one is quite able to read both the train-truck and fibre optic diagrams in the convention centre form. However, the most surprising weak link occurs when the scheme is placed on the site. As is to be expected, the design addressed many traditional architectural relationships to the site; such as reinforcing the street edge and negotiating a severe scale transition. On the other hand, almost as if it had been planned from the beginning, the braided forms of Eisenman's project connected the mundane three-storey commercial buildings across to street from centre to the complex highway system interchange behind it. Though entirely unplanned, this connection has the effect of transforming the prevailing architectural logic of the site.

Borrowing from Deleuze, DeFormation refers to these tentative formal links with contingent influences as affiliations, and engendering affiliations is the foremost mechanism by which DeFormation attempts to Point. Affiliations are distinct from traditional site relations in that they are not pre-determined relationships that are built into the design, but effects that flow from the intrinsic formal, topological or spatial character of the design.

Typically, one identifies important site influences such as manifest or latent typological/morphological diagrams, prevailing architectural language, material, detailing or the like, and incorporates some or all of these influences into a design, often by collage. Such relationships are not affiliations, but alignments and serve to reinforce the dominant architectural modes governing a context.

Affiliations, on the other hand, are provisional, ad hoc links that are made with secondary contingencies that exist within the site or extended context. Rather than reinforcing the dominant modes of the site, therefore, affiliations amplify suppressed or minor organisations that also operate within the site, thereby re-configuring the context into a new coherence. Because they link disjoint, stratified organisations into a coherent heterogeneity, the effect of such affiliations is termed 'smoothing.'[16,17]

In order to complete our initial survey of affiliative effects, we must pick up a few threads from Frank Gehry at Vitra. Gehry's design process, not unrelated to Shirdel's disciplined relaxation and Eisenman's weakening, involves incessant modelling and remodelling an initial figure or set of figures. Though he distorts and deforms the figures towards architectural abstraction, Gehry is even more concerned than Eisenman to preserve a representational heritage in the design.

Gehry's Vitra commission called for a site masterplan, a chair assembly factory, and a museum for the furniture collection. In the preliminary design, Gehry simply aligned the new factory with the factory buildings previously on the site, while his Museum, a geometer's Medusa, stood in stark contrast. Though Gehry reduced the difference to some extent by surfacing the Museum in white plaster, so as to relate to the factory buildings; nevertheless, as a graft on the site, the form of the Museum installed the familiar disjunctive incoherence I have associated with collage. The client, fearful of employees' complaints that all of the design attention was being invested in the Museum and none in the workplace, asked Gehry as an afterthought to enliven the new factory building. In response, Gehry appended some circulation elements that reiterated the stretched and twisted tentacles of the museum to the two corners of the new factory nearest the Museum.

The architectural effect was dramatic, for like the Eisenman Convention Center, the additions knit affiliative links between the factory buildings and the museum, smoothing the site into a heterogeneous, but cohesive whole. However, unlike the Convention Centre, the staircases entered the site as a field rather than as an object – pointing to the possibility of intensive coherence generating a smoothing effect at an urban scale. From this perspective, the circulation additions contribute as much to the architecture of DeFormation as the Museum itself.

Because other genealogies tracing through other projects can also be drawn, it cannot be said that DeFormation is born from these three projects, two of the key principles of DeFormation are in place. In summary, these are: (i) an emphasis on abstract, monolithic architectural form that broaches minimal direct references or resemblance and that is alien to the dominant architectural modes of a given site; (ii)

the development of smoothing affiliations with minor organisations operating within a context that are engendered by the intrinsic geometric, topological and/or spatial qualities of the form. However, before we examine the discussions that have developed around these issues, the evolution of one last principle must be traced.

As Bahram Shirdel and I analysed these and related projects, we noticed that, for all of their other movements, they tend to leave the classical congruity between massing and section largely intact. As a result, the skin of the building continues to be partitioned into the familiar programme-driven hierarchies of major, minor and service spaces implied by the massing. The issue, as we saw it, was to avoid both the continuous, homogenous space of the free plan and the finite, hierarchical space of more traditional sectional strategies.

Several projects suggested different ways to approach the problem of section. Among the more influential of these were Eisenman's Carnegie Mellon research institute, the Nouvel/Starck entry for the Tokyo Opera House competition and Koolhaas' Bibliothèque de France. In the Eisenman scheme, essentially a chain of pods, a large sculptural object whose form was congruent with the pod, floated concentrically within each pod; in effect rendering the primary space of the building interstitial. The striking Nouvel/Starck Opera House was noteworthy for the way its theatre was embedded as in incongruent object into the urban object massing. In his competition entry for the Bibliotheque de France, a seminal example of Information, Koolhaas achieved an extreme detachment of sectional space from the massing. Bahram Shirdel, Andrew Zago and I formed a partnership in order to continue to develop methods for generating affiliative, monolithic forms and, as well, to develop these sectional ideas. Our Event-Structure entry for the Place Jacques Cartier-Montreal competition, for example, called for a large DeFormed envelope within which three independently DeFormed theatres floated as sectional objects. As in InFormation, every surface, including the outside and inside of both the exterior envelope and the floating theatres was programmed. Our goal was to render all of the spaces in the building interstitial and/or residual and to activate them into a non-hierarchical differential structure. However, the formal similarity between the two systems, the envelope and the sectional object-theatres, resulted in spaces that

were less interstitial than homogeneous.[18]

Our subsequent design for the Scottish National Museum competition produced somewhat more interesting results. The typical section of such museums partitions the space into well-defined compartments determined by the categories of the different collections. In order to counter this alignment between form and programme, we devised a section and circulation system in which elements of differing collections would enter into various and shifting associations as one moved through the museum. The effect of encouraging provisional, weak-links among the items in the collection was further augmented with a series of windows calculated to frame objects in the urban setting as if they were objects within the collection. Finally, two of the major lobes of the building itself stood as objects within the basement galleries.

The section/circulation system was embedded within a three-lobed, articulated monolith. Though conspicuously alien to the classical language and other dominant architectural influences of the site, the geometry of the massing took good advantage of several subordinate organisations within both Edinburgh and the larger context of Scotland to extend the production of affiliative effects. A catalogue of over two-dozen of these relationships generated by Doug Graf, an architectural theorist specialising in formal relations, was included with the competition submission.[19] As we and others worked on similar problems, the two major sectional themes of DeFormation began to emerge. First, as far as possible, the section space of the building should not be congruent with the internal space implied by the monolith. Secondly, wherever possible, residual, interstitial and other artifactual spaces should be emphasised over primary spaces. Because the box-within-box section is effective at producing both of these effects, it is often the tactic of choice, though by no means the only one possible. The impetus to programmatic saturation so central to InFormation plays a much less significant role in DeFormation.

With these sectional themes, the last of the preliminary principles of DeFormation is in place. Yet, we should not prematurely draw the conclusion that DeFormation is complete and that a prescription for its architecture written. Indeed, though paradigmatic building projects such as Eisenman's Max Reinhardthaus[20] or Shirdel's Nara Convention Hall can be identified, the internal debates among these and other related projects assure us that there are principles and projects to follow. The most interesting of these debates revolve around design techniques for producing smoothing affiliations.[21] Because such affiliations require that loose links be made among dominant and contingent organisations operating within a context, some architects work by identifying examples of both types of organisation and then drive the design towards their connection, while others rely entirely on the intrinsic contextual affiliations engendered by the Eisenman Convention Center or the Shirdel, Zago, Kipnis Scottish National Museum are examples of the latter; in each case, most of the links were unplanned and occurred only after grafting the project to the site.

Shoei Yoh's Odawara Sports Complex, on the other hand, is a conspicuous case of the former. Shoei Yoh designed the complex's roof by mapping a detailed study of a variety of contingent forces confronting the roof such as snow loads into a structural diagram. He fine-tuned the mapping by abandoning the coarse, triangulated structural geometries that generalise force diagrams, choosing instead to use computer-generated structural analysis that resolves force differentials at an ultrasensitive scale. The unusual undulating form of the roof resulted. This process, enables Shoei Yoh to avoid the pitfalls of stylistic necessities of the project. As computer aided manufacturing techniques proliferate, such approaches which maximise efficient use of material will no doubt enjoy favour.

Undoubtedly, such an approach to contingency is attractive; yet, questions arise. At the very least, these processes threaten to turn DeFormation into a single theme architecture based on a search for contingent influences, much as Arnold Schoenberg's dodecaphonic theories of atonal music composition resulted in a decade during which serious music composers devoted all of their attention to finding new tone rows. As Greg Lynn quipped, 'soon we'll be designing form based on the air turbulence generated by pedestrians walking near the building.' More significant, however, is the degree to which such processes are actually aligning, rather than affiliative. It seems to me that by predetermining the contingent influences to be addressed, the process simply redefines the dominant architectural influences on the site. The test of whether or not the results are DeFormative, therefore, will not

depend on the success of the project in embodying responses to those influences, but on the other contingent effects it continuously generates.

If embodying effects into the design a priori is problematic, then the central issue for DeFormation design technique becomes the elucidation of methods that generate monolithic, non-representational forms that lend themselves well to affiliative relationships a posteriori. If all that were required was gesture and articulation, then the problem would pose no particular difficulty and could be saved by employing familiar expressionist techniques. Yet, the DeFormationist principle of minimal representation also prohibits explicit reference to Expressionist architecture, much as it criticises InFormation for its explicit reference to formalist Modernism. I have already mentioned a group of related techniques that start with a complex figure or set of figures and then move these towards non-representational abstraction while preserving the intrinsic complexity. These techniques have stimulated investigations into a variety of methods for accomplishing that movement towards non-representation; for example, including the study of camouflage methods, experimenting with computer 'morphing' programmes that smoothly transform one figure into another, or employing topological meshing techniques such as splines, NURBS, etc, that join the surfaces delimited by the perimeters of disjoint two-dimensional figures into a smoothed solid. Because these methods often yield anexact geometries and non-developable surfaces, other architects have turned their attention to these areas of study. Anexact geometry is the study of non-analytic forms (ie, forms that are not describable by an algebraic expression) yet that show a high degree of internal self-consistency. Non-developable surfaces cannot be flattened into a plane.

As far as I am concerned, it is in the context of the development of architectural technique rather than as applied philosophy that the issue of the fold in DeFormation is best understood. Clearly, the initial figure and transforming process in any DeForming technique does not in itself guarantee the results, nevertheless, both of these mainly contribute to the effective properties of the results. It has occurred to many architects that the fold as a figure and folding as a transformative process offered many advantages, long before any of these persons ever heard of Le Pli or paid any attention to the diagrammatic folds found in

Lacan or René Thom's Catastrophe Theory.

Neither pure figure nor pure organisation, folds link the two; they are monolithic and often non-representational, replete with interstitial and residual spaces, and intrinsic to non-developable surfaces. As a process exercised in a matrix such as urban site, folding holds out the possibility of generating field organisations that negotiate between the infinite homogeneity of the grid and the hierarchical heterogeneity of finite geometric patterns, an effect which Peter Eisenman employs in his housing and office park in Rebstock, Germany.[22] Finally, when exercised as a process on two or more organisations simultaneously, folding is a potential smoothing strategy.

All of these aspects of the fold are related to architectural effects. Although they may be attracted to the underlying work, none of the architects who make use of Thom's fold diagrams, for example, make any claim, as far as I know, to inscribing the four-dimensional event space that the diagrams depict for mathematicians in the resultant architecture; any more than any architect claims to be inscribing the effects of Descartes' philosophy when they employ a cartesian grid. And, fortunately, there do not seem to be too many persons suffering from a radical mind/body split walking around mid-town Manhattan. In both cases, architects employ these diagrams for the architectural effects they engender.

As is typical of Eisenman, both the Rebstock Park and the Alteka Tower are driven more by folding as a process than by any particular fold as a diagram or spatial organisation. In the former, Eisenman inscribes an initial parti derived from the modern housing schemes of Ernst May on the site. Then, operating strictly in the representational field of drawing, he projects the both extended site and the parti into the respective figures formed by the boundaries of these two sites. The resulting drawings create the representational illusion that these two organisations have been folded. This drawing, neither axonometric, nor perspective or fold, is than massed as the project. Through this process, he attempts to transform the modern, axonometric space characteristic of the original scheme into a visual space that hovers between an axonometric and a perspectival space with multiple vanishing points. The figure of the fold, a quotation of sections cut through a Thomian diagram, appears on the tops of the building to effect the weak, cross-disciplinary links of which

Eisenman is so fond.[23] Similarly, the Alteka tower begins with the high-rise type and folds it in a process reminiscent of *origami* in order to deform the type and to produce multiple residual spaces.

Many diagrams such as those depicting Lacan's 'mirror state' or parabolic umbilic fold and the hyperbolic umbilic fold associated with Thom's Catastrophe Theory, have attracted architectural interest for several reasons. In order to avoid the pitfalls of expressionist processes, such diagrams offer a level of discipline to the work. Using these diagrams as a source of regulating lines, so to speak, allows the architect to design with greater rigour. As Le Corbusier writes, 'The regulating line is a guarantee against wilfulness.' Moreover, as stated, such diagrams are neither purely figural nor purely abstract. They therefore hold the potential to generate weak, resemblance effects. Finally, the multiple and disjoint formal organisations that compose these compound diagrams themselves have many of the desired spatial characteristics described previously on sections.

A more sophisticated use of these diagrams as regulating lines can be found in Shirdel's Nara Convention Center. To better understand the role of the diagrams in this project, it is necessary to examine its design process in greater detail. Rather than beginning with a typological or formal parti, Shirdel initiated the design for the Hall by grafting a carefully excerpted portion of the Scottish National Museum project to the site. He chose a portion of the museum where two independent lobes of the museum joined obliquely and were subtending a constricted, interstitial space. Transferred to Nara, this graft had the advantage of already being incongruent but coherent, an after-effect of excerpting the connection between the two disjoint lobes. Shirdel reinforced this effect by using the resultant interstitial space as the main entry-way into the new building.

Studying the famous Todai-ji temple in Nara, Shirdel found the temple space dominated by three figures: a giant central Buddha and two smaller flanking attendant figures. Stimulated by this analysis, Shirdel decided to encase each of the Hall's three theatres in objects that would float in the section. The forms of these theatre-objects were determined simply by functional exigencies. Other than their patinated copper cladding, chosen to link the sectional objects to the figures in the temple, the theatres were entirely undesigned.

Visitors to the Todai-ji temple encounter the Buddha figures frontally; a classical arrangement that emphasises the subject/object relationship between the two. Shirdel, on the other hand, arranged his three sectional objects axially. Visitors entering the Convention Hall confront nothing but empty space – the enormous mass of the three theatres hovering off to the side. In order to design the envelope of the Hall and to configure the main entry as residual space, Shirdel uses two folds. First, he reconfigured the massing of the original graft with a Thomian diagram of a hyperbolic umbilic fold, extending this fold into the surrounding landscape so as to smooth the connection of the building with its immediate site. Then, he shaped the concrete piers holding up the three theatres and the lobby of the small music theatre according to the parabolic umbilic fold. As a result, the main space of the Hall is the residual space between the topology of these two folds, an effect that the constricted entry-way again reinforces. Shirdel's scheme introduces into Nara an entirely new form in both the architectural and institutional sense. More interestingly, it effects its affiliations spatially as well as formally. At the level of a building, it accomplishes the effects that the preliminary principles of DeFormation seek to engender. I also believe that it meets the five criteria for a New Architecture, ie, that it Points, that it is Blank, Vast, Incongruent and Intensively Coherent.

Whether or not DeFormation and /or InFormation mature into a New Architecture, remains to be seen. Certainly, the rate of realisation for DeFormation is not yet as promising as it is for InFormation and not sufficient for either to develop or evolve. Yet, I believe it can be said with some confidence that at least these architectures have broached the problem of the New and thus offer a measure of optimism. But, the critics and historians have not begun to circle them in earnest. Yet.

Notes

1   Historians may note similarities in the work included in this volume to the spatial character of Baroque architecture and/or to the formal character of German Expressionism. I predict their observations will conclude that none of the architects or theorists working in this area are aware of these similarities. Because the writings and projects are not salted with analyses of Borromini, Guaranini and Bernini or references to Finsterlin, the Tauts, Polzig, Haring, Mendelsohn, Scharoun, Steiner, etc, it will be assumed the work is conducted in blissful ignorance of these similarities.

This first conclusion is necessary to support the second, namely that the similarities are far more important than the differences. Thus, recalling Marx, they will argue that the second instance is but a parody of the tragic profundity of the first; (a tautological argument, since the first instance establishes the terms and conditions of similarity. By coincidence, this argument also happens to support the capitalisation of their professional activities). However interesting and worthy of study the similarities are, greater stakes are found in the differences: historians will again miss the point.

2   Cf, Unger, RM, *Knowledge and Politics,* Free Press, New York, 1979; Unger, RM, *Social Theory,* Cambridge University Press, 1987.

3   Other post-structural architectural theorists, notably Jennifer Bloomer and Robert Somol, have appealed to the writings of Deleuze and Guattari, though to different ends.

4   'Collage' is used here as a convenient, if coarse umbrella term for an entire constellation of practices, eg bricolage, assemblage and a history of collage with many important distinctions and developments. This argument is strengthened by a study of the architectural translations of the various models of collage and its associated practices. As we proceed further into the discussion of affiliative effects below, one might be inclined to argue that surrealist collage, with its emphasis on smoothing the seams of the graft, might provide an apt model. Though there is merit in this position, it seems to me that so-called seamlessness of surrealist collage, like all collages, acts actually to emphasise by irony the distinct nature of the elements of the collage and therefore the incoherent disjunctions at work.

A better model might be Jasper John's cross-hatch paintings, prints and drawings. Though these works certainly employ many techniques associated with collage, their effect is quite different. In them non-ideal, grid-like organisations are materialised by grafting elements whose form is disjoint from the overall organisation. Moreover, in some of these works, other cloud-like shapes entirely outside of the dominant formal/tonal language are built up of the medium itself and camouflaged within the work. For me, these paintings are good examples of a cohesive heterogeneity engendered out of an intensive coherence in the elements themselves.

5   For example the Wexner Center for the Visual Arts and his 'scaling' projects eg, 'Romeo and Juliet.'

6   Clearly, the economic and political difficulties that result from a model of heterogeneity based on rostering definable species of difference I have associated with collage have broad implications across many institutional frontiers. In the recent US presidential election, for example, a key issue in the election was the widely felt frustration over the number of officially recognised special interest groups (now numbering in the thousands) seeking

to influence decisions by federal government. However cynical one may be about this situation, it is an inevitable consequence of a social arrangement that attempts to negotiate the classical conflict between individual and community and to achieve a democracy by offering the right to adequate voice and recognition of differences, ie, democracy through extensive incoherence. Models of heterogeneity achieved through intensive coherence would need not only to rethink the individual/community conflict, but ultimately to rethink the entire notion of a democracy achieved by systems of rights.

7 Cf, Robert Somol, 'Speciating Sites', in *Anywhere*, Davidson, ed, Rizzoli, 1992.

8 To be sure, we have already seem possibilities for such grafts, eg, in the work of Hejduk or Rossi. It is entirely unpersuasive to account with the logic of collage for the effects of Aldo Rossi's incongruous grafts of received institutions with his catalogue of autonomous architectural forms or for the effects of Hejduk's mytho-poetic, scenographic urban grafts.

9 See Unger, 'The Better Futures of Architecture', in *Anyone* Davidson, ed, Rizzoli, 1991.

10 Rem Koolhaas stresses this point in his short programme for the recent Shinkenchiku Housing competition, entitled, 'No Style'. cf JA 7.

11 Many of the ideas introduced in the second part of this text grew out of discussions I have enjoyed with Greg Lynn and Sanford Kwinter as well as from their writings. That I do not cite these writings in particular in this text is merely a testimony to how thoroughly it is suffused with their influence. Cf, Greg Lynn, 'Inorganic Bodies', *Assemblage 19*, or Sanford Kwinter in the *Journal of Philosophy and the Visual Arts*, Vol 2, Benjamin, ed. For related issues, see *Incorporations*, Crary and Kwinter, eds, UrZone Press, New York, 1992.

12 In order to achieve some focus, in this account I stress DeFormation primarily as a matter of building design and touch on urban issues only as they arise in that context. Several projects have attempted to extend the themes I here identify with DeFormation to urban design, such as Eisenman's office and housing park in Rebstock and the Shirdel, Zago, Kipnis project for the central business district of Montreal. There are also projects incorporating the themes of InFormation such as Koolhaas' Lille and La Defense or Tshcumi's Chartres. I will attempt a treatment of these works in another setting.

13 For a discussion of these three projects, see my 'Freudian slippers, or what were we to make of the Fetish', in *The Fetish*, Lynn, Mitchell and Whiting, Princeton Architectural Press, Princeton, 1992.

14 For a discussion of Eisenman's weak form projects, see my 'A Matter of Respect', in the *A+U* special edition on Eisenman, January, 1990.

15 One of the most fascinating aspects of Peter Eisenman's design career is his uncanny ability to derive an entire architectural design thesis from a key word or phrase happened upon in his reading of criticism or philosophy. While not underestimating the significance of this eventual arrival at some understanding of the source of the term in question, the fact of the matter is that Eisenman's design inventions virtually always evolve form his initial reaction to what he sees as the architectural implication of the term or phrase, loosened from its original discursive context. Whether it was Chomsky's 'deep structure', Derrida's 'trace', Mandelbrot's 'fractal scaling', or Vattimo's 'weak', Eisenman's architectural derivations have much more to do with his stimulated intuition of potential architectural effects than with embodying the original philosophical effect in question. Eisenman's 'deep structure', 'trace', 'scaling' and 'weak form' therefore have little to do with the philosophy, but much to do with architecture. This comment is by no means meant to disparage. Indeed, to the contrary – insofar as Eisenman's work has at one and the same time maintained a dialogue with philosophical discourse while loosening the domain of architectural effects from and exemplifying/embodying obligation to philosophical effects may be its most important contribution. The conspicuous absence of this issue from the critical literature on Eisenman's work – including my own – testifies to an institutional need for critical literature to maintain a metaphysic of embodiment at any cost, even at the cost of paying attention to the architecture.

16 Camouflage is often cited as a paradigm of affiliations that smooth. Effective camouflage such as 'dazzle painting' is often entirely different from the prevailing influences of the operative context and almost always outside of the dominant modes of the primary discipline (ie, of clothing design or the surface treatment of ships or planes). Yet the effect of camouflage is to smooth the disjoint relationship between site and interloper into another context.

17 Though the discussion of affiliation to this point emphasises form-to-form effects, a meditation on the weak-links of affiliative effects also undermines the most pre-eminent of strongly aligned relations in architecture is the correlation between form and programme. 'Form follows function', is, of course, the declaration par excellence of an alignment between architectural design and programme. Yet, does a close attention to the history of architecture actually sustain that position? I believe a careful reading of that history would require a negative answer to the question.

Throughout its history, the relationship between form and programme has been far more affiliative than aligned, a fact to which the endless numbers of reprogrammings more than testify (houses to museums, fascist headquarters to state treasury facilities, fire stations to Ghostbuster's offices ad infinitum). This is not to say that there is no relationship between form and function, but that the relationship is in its essence weak. It is the affiliative character of the form/programme relationship that allows Rossi to produce his typological grafts and Tschumi to theorise about dis-cross and trans-programming. After all, has the design of any building significant to architectural history ever achieved its status due to how well it functioned? But the most glaring case of form/programme affiliation is to be found in the house, for no one ever lives in a house according to its architectural programme. Can a theory of strong alignment between form and programme account for reading in the bathroom or eating in the livingroom, or for the particular pleasures of having sex anywhere but the bedroom? No doubt it was out of a frustration over the failure of affiliations to congeal into alignments that drove Mies van der Rohe to nail down the furniture. The affiliative nature of the relationship between form and programme accounts in the large part for DeFormation's relative complacency vis a vis InFormation on the issue of programme.

18 For additional discussion of the Shirdel, Zago, Kipnis Place Jacques Event Structure project, see *L'Arca*, December 1991, no 55.

19 For additional discussion of the Shirdel, Zago Kipnis project for the Scottish National Museum, see *ANYWHERE*, Rizzoli, 1992.

20 A mixed-use office tower in Berlin. Though unavailable for publication at this time, the Max Reinhardthaus project is scheduled to be published in *ANYWHERE*.

21 To state that the most interesting discussions in architecture revolve around design technique, is, to me, virtually a tautology. The most interesting aspect of any and every study of architecture – historical, theoretical or otherwise – is its consequence for current design technique.

22 For more on the Rebstock project see R Somol, 'Accidents Will Happen', *A+U* September 1991 and John Rajchman, 'Perplications', the catalogue essay for the *Unfolding Frankfurt* exhibition, Aedis Gallery, Ernst & Sohn, Verlag, 1991. For Eisenman on folding see 'Visions Unfolding', *Incorporations*, Crary and Kwinter, eds, UrZone Books, 1992. An earlier version is in *Domus*, June 1992.

23 In his studio at the Ohio State University, Eisenman and his students began to develop the implications of the initial Rebstock folding for the building sections and to study its capacity to interlace disjoint organisations. I intend to treat this work and further developments of the scheme in more detail in my forthcoming treatment on InFormation and DeFormation urban design.

The illustrations with this article are of the *Briey Intervention,* a project by Jeffrey Kipnis in consultation with Philip Johnson. Project Architect: Matt Geiser; Producers: Don Bates, Ken Rabin; Construction Supervisor: Greg Skogland; Computer drawings: *Modelling on the Form Z*

GREG LYNN
ARCHITECTURAL CURVILINEARITY
The Folded, the Pliant and the Supple

For the last two decades, beginning with Robert Venturi's *Complexity and Contradiction in Architecture*,[1] and Colin Rowe and Fred Koetter's *Collage City*,[2] and continuing through Mark Wigley and Philip Johnson's *Deconstructivist Architecture*, architects have been primarily concerned with the production of heterogeneous, fragmented and conflicting formal systems. These practices have attempted to embody the differences within and between diverse physical, cultural and social contexts in formal conflicts. When comparing Venturi's *Complexity and Contradiction* or *Learning from Las Vegas* with Wigley and Johnson's *Deconstruction Architecture* it is necessary to overlook many significant and distinguishing differences in order to identify at least one common theme.

Both Venturi and Wigley argue for the deployment of discontinuous, fragmented, heterogeneous and diagonal formal strategies based on the incongruities, juxtapositions and oppositions within specific sites and programmes. These disjunctions result from a logic which tends to identify the potential contradictions between dissimilar elements. A diagonal dialogue between a building and its context has become an emblem for the contradictions within contemporary culture. From the scale of an urban plan to a building detail, contexts have been mined for conflicting geometries, materials, styles, histories and programmes which are then represented in architecture as internal contradictions. The most paradigmatic architecture of the last ten years, including Robert Venturi's Sainsbury Wing of the National Gallery, Peter Eisenman's Wexner Center, Bernard Tschumi's La Villette park or the Gehry House, invests in the architectural representation of contradictions. Through contradiction, architecture represents difference in violent formal conflicts.

Contradiction has also provoked a reactionary response to formal conflict. Such resistances attempt to recover unified architectural languages that can stand against heterogeneity. Unity is constructed through one of two strategies: either by reconstructing a continuous architectural language through historical analyses (Neo-Classicism or Neo-Modernism) or by identifying local consistencies resulting from indigenous climates, materials, traditions or technologies (Regionalism). The internal orders of Neo-Classicism, Neo-Modernism and Regionalism conventionally repress the cultural and contextual discontinuities that are necessary for a logic of contradiction. In architecture, both the reaction to and representation of heterogeneity have shared an origin in contextual analysis. Both theoretical models begin with a close analysis of contextual conditions from which they proceed to evolve either a homogeneous or heterogeneous urban fabric. Neither the reactionary call for unity nor the avant-garde dismantling of it through the identification of internal contradictions seems adequate as a model for contemporary architecture and urbanism.

In response to architecture's discovery of complex, disparate, differentiated and heterogeneous cultural and formal contexts, two options have been dominant; either conflict and contradiction or unity and reconstruction. Presently, an alternative smoothness is being formulated that may escape these dialectically opposed strategies. Common to the diverse sources of this post-contradictory work – topological geometry, morphology, morphogenesis, Catastrophe Theory or the computer technology of both the defence and Hollywood film industry – are characteristics of smooth transformation involving the intensive integration of differences within a continuous yet heterogeneous system. Smooth mixtures are made up of disparate elements which maintain their integrity while being blended within a continuous field of other free elements.

Smoothing does not eradicate differences but incorporates[3] free intensities through fluid tactics of mixing and blending. Smooth mixtures are not homogeneous and therefore cannot be reduced. Deleuze describes smoothness as 'the continuous variation' and the 'continuous development of form'.[4] Wigley's critique of pure form and static geometry is inscribed within geometric conflicts and discontinuities. For Wigley, smoothness is equated with hierarchical organisation: 'the volumes have been purified – they have become smooth, classical – and the wires all converge in a single, hierarchical, vertical movement.'[5] Rather than investing in arrested conflicts, Wigley's 'slipperiness' might be better exploited by the alternative smoothness of heterogeneous mixture. For the first time perhaps, complexity might be aligned with neither unity nor contradiction but with smooth, pliant mixture.

Both pliancy and smoothness provide an escape from the two camps which would either have architecture break under the stress of difference or stand firm. Pliancy allows architecture to become involved in complexity through flexibility. It may be possible to neither repress the complex relations of differences with fixed points of resolution nor arrest them in contradictions, but sustain them through flexible, unpredicted, local connections. To arrest differences in conflicting forms often precludes many of the more complex possible connections of the forms of architecture to larger cultural fields. A more pliant architectural sensibility values alliances, rather than conflicts, between elements. Pliancy implies first an internal flexibility and second a dependence on external forces for self-definition.

If there is a single effect produced in architecture by folding, it will be the ability to integrate unrelated elements within a new continuous mixture. Culinary theory has developed both a practical and precise definition for at least three types of mixtures. The first involves the manipulation of homogeneous elements; beating, whisking and whipping change the volume but not the nature of a liquid through agitation. The second method of incorporation mixes two or more disparate elements; chopping, dicing, grinding, grating, slicing, shredding and mincing eviscerate elements into fragments. The first method agitates a single uniform ingredient, the second eviscerates disparate ingredients. Folding, creaming and blending mix smoothly multiple ingredients 'through repeated gentle overturnings without stirring or beating' in such a way that their individual characteristics are maintained.[6] For instance, an egg and chocolate are folded together so that each is a distinct layer within a continuous mixture.

Folding employs neither agitation nor evisceration but a supple layering. Likewise, folding in geology involves the sedimentation of mineral elements or deposits which become slowly bent and compacted into plateaus of strata. These strata are compressed, by external forces, into more or less continuous layers within which heterogeneous deposits are still intact in varying degrees of intensity.

A folded mixture is neither homogeneous, like whipped cream, nor fragmented, like chopped nuts, but smooth and heterogeneous. In both cooking and geology, there is no preliminary organisation which becomes folded but rather there are unrelated elements or pure intensities that are intricated through a joint manipulation. Disparate elements can be incorporated into smooth mixtures through various manipulations including fulling:

'Felt is a supple solid product that proceeds altogether differently, as an anti-fabric. It implies no separation of threads, no intertwining, only an entanglement of fibres obtained by fulling (for example, by rolling the block of fibres back and forth). What becomes entangled are the microscales of the fibres. An aggregate of intrication of this kind is in no way homogeneous; nevertheless, it is smooth and contrasts point by point with the space of fabric (it is in principle infinite, open and uninhibited in every direction; it has neither top, nor bottom, nor centre; it does not assign fixed or mobile elements but distributes a continuous variation).'[7]

The two characteristics of smooth mixtures are that they are composed of disparate unrelated elements and that these free intensities become intricated by an external force exerted upon them jointly. Intrications are intricate connections. They are intricate, they affiliate local surfaces of elements with one another by negotiating interstitial rather than internal connections. The heterogeneous elements within a mixture have no proper relation with one another. Likewise, the external force that intricates these elements with one another is outside of the individual elements control or prediction.

Viscous Mixtures

Unlike an architecture of contradictions, superpositions and accidental collisions, pliant systems are capable of engendering unpredicted connections with contextual, cultural, programmatic, structural and economic contingencies by vicissitude. Vicissitude is often equated with vacillation, weakness[8] and indecisiveness but more importantly these characteristics are frequently in the service of a tactical cunning.[9] Vicissitude is a quality of being mutable or changeable in response to both favourable and unfavourable situations that occur by chance. Vicissitudinous events result from events that are neither arbitrary nor predictable but seem to be accidental. These events are made possible by a collision of internal motivations with external forces. For instance, when an accident occurs the victims immediately identify the forces contributing to the accident and begin to assign blame. It is inevitable however, that no single element can be made responsible for any accident as these events occur by vicissitude; a confluence of particular influences at a particular time makes the outcome of an accident possible. If any element participating in such a confluence of local forces is altered the nature of the event will change. In *A Thousand Plateaus*, Spinoza's concept of 'a thousand vicissitudes' is linked with Gregory Bateson's 'continuing plateau of intensity' to describe events which incorporate unpredictable events through intensity. These occurrences are difficult to localise, difficult to identify.[10] Any logic of vicissitude is dependent on both an intrication of local intensities and the exegetic pressure exerted on those elements by external contingencies. Neither the intrications nor the forces which put them into relation are predictable from within any single system. Connections by vicissitude develop identity through the exploitation of local adjacencies and their affiliation with external forces. In this sense, vicissitudinous mixtures become cohesive through a logic of viscosity.

Viscous fluids develop internal stability in direct proportion to the external pressures exerted upon them. These fluids behave with two types of viscidity. They exhibit both internal cohesion and adhesion to external elements as their viscosity increases. Viscous fluids begin to behave less like liquids and more like sticky solids as the pressures upon them intensify. Similarly, viscous solids are capable of yielding continually under stress so as not to shear.

Viscous space would exhibit a related cohesive stability in response to adjacent pressures and a stickiness or adhesion to adjacent elements. Viscous relations such as these are not reducible to any single or holistic organisation. Forms of viscosity and pliability cannot be examined outside of the *vicissitudinous* connections and forces with which their deformation is intensively involved. The nature of pliant forms is that they are sticky and flexible. Things tend to adhere to them. As pliant forms are manipulated and deformed the things that stick to their surfaces become incorporated within their interiors.

Curving away from Deconstructivism

Along with a group of younger architects, the projects that best represent pliancy, not coincidentally, are being produced by many of the same architects previously involved in the valorisation of contradictions. Deconstructivism theorised the world as a site of differences in order that architecture could represent these contradictions in form. This contradictory logic is beginning to soften in order to exploit more fully the particularities of urban and cultural contexts. This is a reasonable transition, as the Deconstructivists originated their projects with the internal discontinuities they uncovered within buildings and sites. These same architects are beginning to employ urban strategies which exploit discontinuities, not by representing them in formal collisions, but by affiliating them with one another though continuous flexible systems.

Just as many of these architects have already been inscribed within a Deconstructivist style of diagonal forms, there will surely be those who would enclose their present work within a Neo-Baroque or even Expressionist style of curved forms. However, many of the formal similitudes suggest a far richer 'logic of curvilinearity'[11] that can be characterised by the involvement of outside forces in the development of form. If internally motivated and homogeneous systems were to extend in straight lines, curvilinear developments would result from the incorporation of external influences. Curvilinearity can put into relation the collected projects in this publication, Gilles Deleuze's *The Fold: Leibniz and the Baroque* and René Thom's catastrophe diagrams. The smooth spaces described by these continuous yet differentiated systems result from curvilinear sensibilities that are capable of complex deformations in response to programmatic, structural, economic, aesthetic, political and contextual influences. This is not to imply that intensive curvature is more politically correct than an uninvolved formal logic, but rather, that a cunning pliability is often more effective through smooth incorporation than contradiction and conflict. Many cunning tactics are aggressive in nature. Whether insidious or ameliorative these kinds of cunning connections discover new possibilities for organisation. A logic of curvilinearity argues for an active involvement with external events in the folding, bending and curving of form.

Already in several Deconstructivist projects are latent suggestions of smooth mixture and curvature. For instance, the Gehry House is typically portrayed as representing materials and forms already present within, yet repressed by, the suburban neighbourhood: sheds, chain-link fences, exposed plywood, trailers, boats and recreational vehicles. The house is described as an 'essay on the convoluted relationship between the conflict within and between forms . . . which were not imported to but emerged from within the house.'[12] The house is seen to provoke conflict within the neighbourhood due to its public representation of hidden aspects of its context. The Gehry House violates the neighbourhood from within. Despite the dominant appeal of the house to contradictions, a less contradictory and more pliant reading of the house is possible as a new organisation emerges between the existing house and Gehry's addition. A dynamic stability develops with the mixing of the original and the addition. Despite the contradictions between elements possible points of connection are exploited. Rather than valorise the conflicts the house engenders, as has been done in both academic and popular publications, a more pliant logic would identify, not the degree of violation, but the degree to which new connections were exploited. A new intermediate organisation occurs In the Gehry House by vicissitude from the affiliation of the existing house and its addition. Within the discontinuities of Deconstructivism there are inevitable unforeseen moments of cohesion.

Similarly, Peter Eisenman's Wexner Center is conventionally portrayed as a collision of the conflicting geometries of the campus, city and armoury which once stood adjacent to the site. These contradictions are represented by the diagonal collisions between the two grids and the masonry towers. Despite the disjunctions and discontinuities between these three disparate systems, Eisenman's project has suggested recessive readings of continuous non-linear systems of connection. Robert Somol[13] identifies such a system of Deleuzian rhizomatous connections between armoury and grid. The armoury and diagonal grids are shown by Somol to participate in a hybrid L-movement that organises the main gallery space. Somol's schizophrenic analysis is made possible by, yet does not emanate from within, a Deconstructivist logic of contradiction and conflict. The force of this Deleuzian schizo-analytic model is its ability to maintain multiple organisations simultaneously. In Eisenman's project the tower and grid need not be seen as mutually exclusive or in contradiction. Rather, these disparate elements may be seen as distinct elements co-present within a composite mixture. Pliancy does not result from and is not in line with the previous architectural logic of contradiction, yet it is capable of exploiting many conflicting combinations for the possible connections that are overlooked. Where *Deconstructivist Architecture* was seen to exploit external forces in the familiar name of contradiction and conflict, recent pliant projects by many of these architects exhibit a more fluid logic of connectivity.

Immersed in Context

The contradictory architecture of the last two decades has evolved primarily from highly differentiated, heterogeneous contexts within which conflicting, contradictory and discontinuous buildings were sited. An alternative involvement with heterogeneous contexts could be affiliated, compliant and continuous. Where complexity and contradiction arose previously from inherent contextual conflicts, present attempts are being made to fold smoothly specific locations, materials and programmes into architecture while maintaining their individual identity.

This recent work may be described as being compliant; in a state of being plied by forces beyond control. The projects are formally folded, pliant and supple in order to incorporate their contexts with minimal resistance. Again, this characterisation should not imply flaccidity but a cunning submissiveness that is capable of bending rather than breaking. Compliant tactics, such as these, assume neither an absolute coherence nor cohesion between discrete elements but a system of provisional, intensive, local connections between free elements. Intensity describes the dynamic internalisation and incorporation of external influences into a pliant system. Distinct from a whole organism – to which nothing can be added or subtracted – intensive organisations continually invite external influences within their internal limits so that they might extend their influence through the affiliations they make. A two-fold deterritorialisation, such as this, expands by internalising external forces. This expansion through incorporation is an urban alternative to either the infinite extension of International Modernism, the uniform fabric of Contextualism or the conflicts of Post-Modernism and Deconstructivism. Folded, pliant and supple architectural forms invite exigencies and contingencies in both their deformation and their reception.

In both *Learning from Las Vegas* and *Deconstructivist Architecture*, urban contexts provided rich sites of difference. These differences are presently being exploited for their ability to engender multiple lines of local connections rather than lines of conflict. These affiliations are not predictable by any contextual orders but occur by vicissitude. Here, urban fabric has no value or meaning beyond the connections that are made within it. Distinct from earlier urban sensibilities that generalised broad formal codes, the collected projects develop local, fine grain, complex systems of intrication. There is no general urban strategy common to these projects, only a kind of tactical mutability. These folded, pliant and supple forms of urbanism are neither in deference to nor in defiance of their contexts but exploit them by turning them within their own twisted and curvilinear logics.

The Supple and Curvilinear

1 supple\ *adj* [ME *souple*, fr OF, fr L *supplic-*, *supplex* submissive, suppliant, lit, bending under, fr *sub* + *plic-* (akin to *plicare* to fold) - more at PLY] 1a: compliant often to the point of obsequiousness b: readily adaptable or responsive to new situations 2a: capable of being bent or folded without creases, cracks or breaks: PLIANT b: able to perform bending or twisting movements with ease and grace: LIMBER c: easy and fluent without stiffness or awkwardness.[14]

At an urban scale, many of these projects seem to be somewhere between contexturalism and expressionism. Their supple forms are neither geometrically exact nor arbitrarily figural. For example, the curvilinear figures of Shoei Yoh's roof structures are anything but decorative but also resist being reduced to a pure geometric figure. Yoh's supple roof structures exhibit a logic of curvilinearity as they are continuously differentiated according to contingencies. The exigencies of structural span lengths, beam depths, lighting, lateral loading, ceiling height and view angles influence the form of the roof structure. Rather than averaging these requirements within a mean or minimum dimension they are precisely maintained by an anexact yet rigorous geometry. Exact geometries are eideric; they can be reproduced identically at any time by anyone. In this regard, they must be capable of being reduced to fixed mathematical quantities. Inexact geometries lack the precision and rigor necessary for measurement.

Anexact geometries, as described by Edmund Husserl,[15] are those geometries which are irreducible yet rigorous. These geometries can be determined with precision yet cannot be reduced to average points or dimensions. Anexact geometries often appear to be merely figural in this regard. Unlike exact geometries, it is meaningless to repeat identically an anexact geometric figure outside of the specific context within which it is situated. In this regard, anexact figures cannot be easily translated.

Jeffrey Kipnis has argued convincingly that Peter Eisenman's Columbus Convention Center has become a canonical model for the negotiation of differentiated urban fringe sites through the use of near figures.[16] Kipnis identifies the disparate systems informing the Columbus Convention Center including: a single volume of inviolate programme of a uniform shape and height larger than two city blocks, an existing fine grain fabric of commercial buildings and network of freeway interchanges that plug into the gridded streets of the central business district. Eisenman's project drapes the large rectilinear volume of the convention hall with a series of supple vermiforms. These elements become involved with the train tracks to the north-east, the highway to the south-east and the pedestrian scale of High Street to the west. The project incorporates the multiple scales, programmes and pedestrian and automotive circulation of a highly differentiated urban context. Kipnis' canonisation of a form which is involved with such specific contextual and programmatic contingencies seems to be frustrated from the beginning. The effects of a pliant urban mixture such as this can only be evaluated by the connections that it makes. Outside of specific contexts, curvature ceases to be intensive. Where the Wexner

Center, on the same street in the same city, represents a monumental collision, the Convention Center attempts to disappear by connection between intervals within its context; where the Wexner Center destabilises through contradictions the Convention Center does so by subterfuge.

In a similar fashion Frank Gehry's Guggenheim Museum in Bilbao, Spain covers a series of orthogonal gallery spaces with flexible tubes which respond to the scales of the adjacent roadways, bridges, the Bilbao River and the existing medieval city. Akin to the Vitra Museum, the curvilinear roof forms of the Bilbao Guggenheim integrate the large rectilinear masses of gallery and support space with the scale of the pedestrian and automotive contexts.

The unforeseen connections possible between differentiated sites and alien programmes require conciliatory, complicit, pliant, flexible and often cunning tactics. Presently, numerous architects are involving the heterogeneities, discontinuities and differences inherent within any cultural and physical context by aligning formal flexibility with economic, programmatic and structural compliancy. A multitude of *pli* based words – folded, pliant, supple, flexible, plaited, pleated, plicating, complicitous, compliant, complaisant, complicated, complex and multiplicitous to name a few – can be invoked to describe this emerging urban sensibility of intensive connections.

The Pliant and Bent

pliable\ *adj* [ME fr *plier* to bend, fold-more at PLY] 1a: supple enough to bend freely or repeatedly without breaking b: yielding readily to others: COMPLAISANT 2: adjustable to varying conditions: ADAPTABLE *syn* see PLASTIC *ant* obstinate.[17]

John Rajchman, in reference to Gilles Deleuze's book *Le Pli* has already articulated an affinity between complexity, or *plex*-words, and folding, or plic-words, in the Deleuzian paradigm of 'perplexing plications' or 'perplication'.[18] The plexed and the plied can be seen in a tight knot of complexity and pliancy. Plication involves the folding in of external forces. Complication involves an intricate assembly of these extrinsic particularities into a complex network. In biology, complication is the act of an embryo folding in upon itself as it becomes more complex. To become complicated is to be involved in multiple complex, intricate connections. Where Post-Modernism and Deconstructivism resolve external influences of programme,

use, economy and advertising through contradiction, compliancy involves these external forces by knotting, twisting, bending and folding them within form.

Pliant systems are easily bent, inclined or influenced. An anatomical 'plica' is a single strand within multiple 'plicae'. It is a multiplicity in that it is both one and many simultaneously. These elements are bent along with other elements into a composite, as in matted hair(s). Such a bending together of elements is an act of multiple plication or multiplication rather than mere addition. Plicature involves disparate elements with one another through various manipulations of bending, twisting, pleating, braiding and weaving through external force. In RAA Um's Croton Aqueduct project a single line following the subterranean water supply for New York City is pulled through multiple disparate programmes which are adjacent to it and which cross it. These programmatic elements are braided and bent within the continuous line of recovered public space which stretches nearly 20 miles into Manhattan. In order to incorporate these elements the line itself is deflected and reoriented, continually changing its character along its length. The seemingly singular line becomes populated by finer programmatic elements. The implications of *Le Pli* for architecture involve the proliferation of possible connections between free entities such as these.

A plexus is a multi-linear network of interweavings, intertwinings and intrications; for instance, of nerves or blood vessels. The complications of a plexus – what could best be called complexity – arise from its irreducibility to any single organisation. A *plexus* describes a multiplicity of local connections within a single continuous system that remains open to new motions and fluctuations. Thus, a plexial event cannot occur at any discrete point. A multiply plexed system – a complex – cannot be reduced to mathematical exactitude, it must be described with rigorous probability. Geometric systems have a distinct character once they have been plied; they exchange fixed co-ordinates for dynamic relations across surfaces.

Alternative types of transformation

Discounting the potential of earlier geometric diagrams of probability, such as Buffon's *Needle Problem*,[19] D'Arcy Thompson provides perhaps the first geometric description of variable deformation as an instance of discontinuous morphological development. His cartesian deformations, and their use of flexible topological rubber sheet geometry, suggest an alternative to the static morphological transformations of autonomous architectural types. A comparison of the typological and transformational systems of Thompson and Rowe illustrates two radically different conceptions of continuity. Rowe's is fixed, exact, striated, identical and static, where Thompson's is dynamic, anexact, smooth, differentiated and stable.

Both Rudolf Wittkower – in his analysis of the Palladian villas of 1949[20] – and Rowe – in his comparative analysis of Palladio and Le Corbusier of 1947[21] – uncover a consistent organisational type: the nine-square grid. In Wittkower's analysis of 12 Palladian villas the particularities of each villa accumulate (through what Edmund Husserl has termed variations) to generate a fixed, identical spatial type (through what could best be described as phenomenological reduction). The typology of this 'Ideal Villa' is used to invent a consistent deep structure underlying Le Corbusier's Villa Stein at Garche and Palladio's Villa Malcontenta. Wittkower and Rowe discover the exact geometric structure of this type in all villas in particular. This fixed type becomes a constant point of reference within a series of variations.

Like Rowe, Thompson is interested in developing a mathematics of species categories, yet his system depends on a dynamic and fluid set of geometric relations. The deformations of a provisional type define a supple constellation of geometric correpondences. Thompson uses the initial type as a mere provision for a dynamic system of transformations that occur in connection with larger environmental forces. Thompson's method of discontinuous development intensively involves external forces in the deformation of morphological types. The flexible type is able to both indicate the general morphological structure of a species while indicating its discontinuous development through the internalisation of heretofore external forces within the system.[22] For instance, the enlargement of a fish's eye is represented by the flexing of a grid. This fluctuation, when compared to a previous position of the transformational type, establishes a relation between water depth and light intensity as those conditions are involved in the formal differences between fish. The flexing grid of relations cannot be arrested

at any moment and therefore has the capacity to describe both a general type and the particular events which influence its development. Again, these events are not predictable or reducible to any fixed point but rather begin to describe a probable zone of co-present forces; both internal and external. Thompson presents an alternative type of inclusive stability, distinct from the exclusive stasis of Rowe's nine-square grid. The supple geometry of Thompson is capable of both bending under external forces and folding those forces internally. These transformations develop through discontinuous involution rather than continuous evolution.

The morphing effects used in the contemporary advertising and film industry may already have something in common with recent developments in architecture. These mere images have concrete influences on space, form, politics and culture; for example, the physical morphing of Michael Jackson's body, including the transformation of his form through various surgeries and his surface through skin bleaching and lightening. These physical effects and their implications for the definition of gender and race were only later represented in his recent video *Black & White*. In this video multiple genders, ethnicities and races are mixed into a continuous sequence through the digital morphing of video images. It is significant that Jackson is not black *or* white but black *and* white, not male *or* female but male *and* female. His simultaneous differences are characteristic of a desire for smoothness; to become heterogeneous yet continuous. Physical morphing, such as this, is monstrous because smoothness eradicates the interval between what Thompson refers to as discriminant characteristics without homogenising the mixture. Such a continuous system is neither an assembly of discrete fragments nor a whole.[23] With Michael Jackson, the flexible geometric mechanism with which his video representation is constructed comes from the same desire which aggressively reconstructs his own physical form. Neither the theory, the geometry or the body proceed from one another; rather, they participate in a desire for smooth transformation. Form, politics and self-identity are intricately connected in this process of deformation.

A similar comparison might be made between the liquid mercury man in the film *Terminator 2* and the Peter Lewis House by Frank Gehry and Philip Johnson. The Hollywood special effects sequences allow

the actor to both become and disappear into virtually any form. The horror of the film results not from ultra-violence, but from the ability of the antagonist to pass through and occupy the grids of floors, prison bars and other actors. Computer technology is capable of constructing intermediate images between any two fixed points resulting in a smooth transformation. These smooth effects calculate with probability the interstitial figures between fixed figures. Furthermore, the morphing process is flexible enough that multiple between states are possible. Gehry's and Johnson's Peter Lewis House is formulated from multiple flexible forms. The geometry of these forms is supple and can accommodate smooth curvilinear deformation along their length. Not only are these forms capable of bending to programmatic, structural and environmental concerns, as is the roof of Shoei Yoh's roof structures, but they can deflect to the contours and context of the site, similar to Peter Eisenman's Columbus Convention Center and RAA Um's Croton Aqueduct project. Furthermore, the Lewis House maintains a series of discrete figural fragments – such as boats and familiar fish – within the diagrams of D'Arcy Thompson, which are important to both the morphing effects of Industrial Light and Magic and the morphogenetic diagrams of René Thom, Gehry's supple geometry is capable of smooth, heterogeneous continuous deformation. Deformation is made possible by the flexibility of topological geometry in response to external events, as smooth space is intensive and continuous. Thompson's curvilinear logic suggests deformation in response to unpredictable events outside of the object. Forms of bending, twisting or folding are not superfluous but result from an intensive curvilinear logic which seeks to internalise cultural and contextural forces within form. In this manner events become intimately involved with particular rather than ideal forms. These flexible forms are not mere representations of differential forces but are deformed by their environment.

Folding and other catastrophes for architecture

3 fold vb [ME *folden*, fr. OE *foaldan*; akin to OHG *faldan* to fold, Gk di *plasios* twofold] vt 1: to lay one part over another part, 2: to reduce the length or bulk of by doubling over, 3: to clasp together: ENTWINE, 4: to clasp or em-brace closely: EMBRACE, 5: to bend (as a rock) into folds 6: to incorporate (a food ingredient) into a mixture by repeated gentle overturnings without stirring or beating, 7: to bring to an end.[24]

Philosophy has already identified the displacement presently occurring to the Post-Modern paradigm of complexity and contradiction in architecture, evidenced by John Rajchman's *Out of the Fold* and *Perplications*. Rajchman's text is not a manifesto for the development of new architectural organisations, but responds to the emergence of differing kinds of complexity being developed by a specific architect. His essays inscribe spatial innovations developed in architecture within larger intellectual and cultural fields. Rajchman both illuminates Peter Eisenman's architectural practice through an explication of *Le Pli* and is forced to reconsider Deleuze's original argument concerning Baroque space by the alternative spatialities of Eisenman's Rebstock Park project. The dominant aspect of the project which invited Rajchman's attention to folding was the employment of one of René Thom's catastrophe diagrams in the design process.

Despite potential protestations to the contrary, it is more than likely that Thom's catastrophe nets entered into the architecture of Carsten Juel-Christiansen's Die Anhalter Faltung, Peter Eisenman's Rebstock Park, Jeffrey Kipnis' Unite de Habitation at Briey installation and Bahram Shirdel's Nara Convention Hall as a mere formal technique. Inevitably, architects and philosophers alike would find this in itself a catastrophe for all concerned. Yet, their use illustrates that at least four architects simultaneously found in Thom's diagrams a formal device for an alternative description of spatial complexity. The kind of complexity engendered by this alliance with Thom is substantially different than the complexity provided by either Venturi's decorated shed or the more recent conflicting forms of Deconstructivism. Topological geometry in general, and the catastrophe diagrams in particular, deploy disparate forces on a continuous surface within which more or less open systems of connection are possible.

'Topology considers superficial structures susceptible to continuous transformations which easily change their form, the most interesting geometric properties common to all modification being studied. Assumed is an abstract material of ideal deformability which can be deformed, with the exception of disruption.'

These geometries bend and stabilise with viscosity under pressure. Where one would expect that an architect looking at catastrophes would be interested in conflicts, ironically, architects are finding new forms of dynamic stability in these diagrams. The mutual interest in Thom's diagrams points to a desire to be involved with events which they cannot predict. The primary innovation made by those diagrams is the geometric modelling of a multiplicity of possible co-present events at any moment. Thom's morphogenesis engages seemingly random events with mathematical probability.

Thom's nets were developed to describe catastrophic events. What is common to these events is an inability to define exactly the moment at which a catastrophe occurs. This loss of exactitude is replaced by a geometry of multiple probable relations. With relative precision, the diagrams define potential catastrophes through cusps rather than fixed co-ordinates. Like any simple graph, Thom's diagrams deploy X and Y forces across two axes of a gridded plane. A uniform plane would provide the potential for only a single point of intersection between any two X and Y co-ordinates. The supple topological surface of Thom's diagrams is capable of enfolding in multiple dimensions. Within these folds, or cusps, zones of proximity are contained. As the topological surface folds over and into itself multiple possible points of intersection are possible at any moment in the Z dimension. These co-present Z-dimensional zones are possible because the topological geometry captures space within its surface. Through proximity and adjacency various vectors of force begin to imply these intensive event zones. In catastrophic events there is not a single fixed point at which a catastrophe occurs but rather a zone of potential events that are described by these cusps. The cusps are defined by multiple possible interactions implying, with more or less probability, multiple fluid thresholds. Thom's geometric plexus organises disparate forces in order to describe possible types of connections.

If there is a single dominant effect of the French word *pli*, it is its resistance to being translated into any single term. It is precisely the formal manipulations of folding that are capable of incorporating manifold external forces and elements within form, yet *Le Pli* undoubtedly risks being translated into architecture as mere folded figures. In architecture, folded forms risk quickly becoming a sign for catastrophe. The success of the architects who are folding should not be based on their ability to represent catastrophe theory in architectural form. Rather, the topological geometries, in connection with the probable events they model, present a flexible system for the organisation of disparate elements within continuous spaces. Yet, these smooth systems are highly differentiated by cusps or zones of co-presence. The catastrophe diagram used by Eisenman in the Rebstock Park project destabilises the way that the buildings meet the ground. It smooths the landscape and the building by turning both into one another along cusps. The diagrams used by Kipnis in the Briey project, and Shirdel in the Nara Convention Hall, develop an interstitial space contained simultaneously within two folded cusps. This geometrically blushed surface exists within two systems at the same moment and in this manner presents a space of co-presence with multiple adjacent zones of proximity.

Before the introduction of either Deleuze or Thom to architecture, folding was developed as a formal tactic in response to problems presented by the exigencies of commercial development. Henry Cobb has argued in both the *Charlottesville Tapes* and his *Note on Folding* for a necessity to both dematerialise and differentiate the massive homogeneous volumes dictated by commercial development in order to bring them into relation with finer grain heterogeneous urban conditions. His first principle for folding is a smoothing of elements across a shared surface. The facade of the John Hancock Tower is smoothed into a continuous surface so that the building might disappear into its context through reflection rather than mimicry. Any potential for replicating the existing context was precluded by both the size of the contiguous floor plates required by the developer and the economic necessity to construct the building's skin from glass panels. Folding became the method by which the surface of a large homogeneous volume could be differentiated while remaining continuous. This tactic acknowledges that the existing fabric and the developer tower are essentially of different species by placing their differences in mixture, rather than contradiction, through the manipulation of a pliant skin.

Like the John Hancock Building, the Allied Bank Tower begins with the incorporation of glass panels and metal frames into a continuous folded surface. The differentiation of the folded surface, through the simultaneous bending of the glass and metal, brings those elements together on a continuous plane. The manipulations of the material surface proliferate folding and bending effects in the massing of the building. The alien building becomes a continuous surface of disappearance that both diffracts and reflects the context through complex manipulations of folding. In the recent films *Predator* and *Predator II*, a similar alien is capable of disappearing into both urban and jungle environments, not through cubist camouflage[25] but by reflecting and diffracting its environment like an octopus or chameleon. The contours between an object and its context are obfuscated by forms which become translucent, reflective and diffracted. The alien gains mobility by cloaking its volume in a folded surface of disappearance. Unlike the 'decorated shed' or 'building board' which mimics its context with a singular sign, folding diffuses an entire surface through a shimmering reflection of local adjacent and contiguous particularities. For instance, there is a significant difference between a small fish which represents itself as a fragment of a larger fish through the figure of a large eye on its tail, and a barracuda which becomes like the liquid in which it swims through a diffused reflection of its context. The first strategy invites deceitful detection where the second uses stealth to avoid detection. Similarly, the massive volume of the Allied Bank Tower situates itself within a particular discontinuous locale by cloaking itself in a folded reflected surface. Here, cunning stealth is used as a way of involving contextual forces through the manipulation of a surface. The resemblance of folded architecture to the stealth bomber results not from a similarity between military and architectural technologies or intentions but rather from a tactical disappearance[26] of a volume through the manipulation of a surface. This disappearance into the fold is neither insidious nor innocent but merely a very effective tactic.

Like Henry Cobb, Peter Eisenman introduces a fold as a method of disappearing into a specific context. Unlike Cobb, who began with a logic of construction, Eisenman aligns the fold with the urban contours of the Rebstock Park. The repetitive typologies of housing and office buildings are initially deployed on the site in a more or less functionalist fashion; then a topological net derived from Thom's Butterfly net is aligned to the perimeter of the site and pushed through the typological bars. This procedure differentiates the uniform bars in response to the global morphology of the site. In this manner the manifestation of the fold is in the incorpora-

tion of differences – derived from the morphology of the site – into the homogeneous typologies of the housing and office blocks. Both Eisenman's local differentiation of the building types by global folding, and Cobb's local folding across constructional elements which globally differentiates each floor plate and the entire massing of the building are effective. Cobb and Eisenman 'animate' homogeneous organisations that were seemingly given to the architect – office tower and *siedlung* – with the figure of a fold. The shared principle of folding identified by both Eisenman and Cobb, evident in their respective texts, is the ability to differentiate the inherited homogeneous organisations of both Modernism (Eisenman's *seidlung*) and commercial development (Cobb's tower). This differentiation of known types of space and organisation has something in common with Deleuze's delimitation of folding in architecture within the Baroque. Folding heterogeneity into known typologies renders those organisations more smooth and more intensive so that they are better able to incorporate disparate elements within a continuous system. Shirdel's use of Thom's diagrams is quite interesting as the catastrophe sections do not animate an existing organisation. Rather, they begin as merely one system among three others. The convention halls float within the envelope of the building as they are supported by a series of transverse structural walls whose figure is derived from Thom's nets. This mixture of systems, supported by the catastrophe sections, generates a massive residual public space at the ground floor of the building. In Shirdel's project the manipulations of folding, in both the catastrophe sections and the building envelope, incorporate previously unrelated elements into a mixture. The space between the theatres, the skin and the lateral structural walls is such a space of mixture and intrication.

With structure itself, Chuck Hoberman is capable of transforming the size of domes and roofs through a folding structural mechanism. Hoberman develops adjustable structures whose differential movements occurs through the dynamic transformation of flexible continuous systems. The movements of these mechanisms are determined both by use and structure. Hoberman's structural mechanisms develop a system of smooth transformation in two ways. The Iris dome and sphere projects transform their size while maintaining their shape. This flexibility of size within

the static shape of the stadium is capable of supporting new kinds of events. The patented tiling patterns transform both the size and shape of surfaces, developing local secondary pockets of space and enveloping larger primary volumes.

So far in architecture, Deleuze's, Cobb's, Eisenman's and Hoberman's discourse inherits dominant typologies of organisation into which new elements are folded. Within these activities of folding it is perhaps more important to identify those new forms of local organisation and occupation which inhabit the familiar types of the Latin cross church, the *siedlung*, the office tower and the stadium, rather than the disturbances visited on those old forms of organisation. Folding can occur in both the organisations of old forms and the free intensities of unrelated elements, as is the case with Shirdel's project. Likewise, other than folding, there are several manipulations of elements engendering smooth, heterogeneous and intensive organisation.

Despite the differences between these practices, they share a sensibility that resists cracking or breaking in response to external pressures. These tactics and strategies are all com*pli*ant to, com*plic*ated by, and com*plic*it with external forces in manners which are: submissive, suppliant, adaptable, contingent, responsive, fluent, and yielding through involvement and incorporation. The attitude which runs throughout this collection of projects and essays is the shared attempt to place seemingly disparate forces into relation through strategies which are externally plied. Perhaps, in this regard only, there are many opportunities for architecture to be effected by Gilles Deleuze's book *Le Pli*. The formal characteristics of pliancy – anexact forms and topological geometries primarily – can be more viscous and fluid in response to exigencies. They maintain formal integrity through deformations which do not internally cleave or shear but through which they connect, incorporate and affiliate productively. Cunning and viscous systems such as these gain strength through flexible connections that occur by vicissitude. If the collected projects within this publication do have certain formal affinities, it is as a result of a folding out of formalism into a world of external influences. Rather than speak of the forms of folding autonomously, it is important to maintain a logic rather than a style of curvilinearity. The formal affinities of these projects result from their pliancy and ability to deform in response to particular contingencies. What is being asked in different ways by the group of architects and theorists in this publication is: How can architecture be configured as a complex system into which external particularities are already found to be plied?

Notes

1 Venturi, Robert *Complexity and Contradiction in Architecture* (New York: Museum of Modern Art Papers on Architecture, 1966).

2 Two ideas were introduced in this text that seem extremely relevant to contemporary architecture: typological deformation and the continuity between objects and contexts. Both of these concepts receded when compared with the dominant ideas of *collision cities* and the dialectic of urban *figure/ground* relationships. Curiously, they illustrate typological deformations in both Baroque and early modern architecture: 'However, Asplund's play with assumed contingencies and assumed absolutes, brilliant though it may be, does seem to involve mostly strategies of response; and, in considering problems of the object, it may be useful to consider the admittedly ancient technique of deliberately *distorting* what is also presented as the *ideal* type. So the reading of Saint Agnese *continuously fluctuates between* an interpretation of the building as *object* and the building as *texture* . . . Note this type of strategy combines local concessions with a declaration of independence from anything local and specific.' p77.

3 See Sanford Kwinter and Jonathan Crary 'Foreword' *Zone 6: Incorporations* (New York: Urzone Books, 1992), pp12-15.

4 Deleuze, Gilles *A Thousand Plateaus: Capitalism and Schizophrenia* (Minneapolis: University of Minnesota Press, 1987), p478.

5 Wigley, Mark *Deconstructivist Architecture*, p15.

6 Cunningham, Marion *The Fannie Farmer Cookbook*, 13th edition (New York: Alfred A Knopf, 1990) pp41-47.

7 Deleuze, Gilles *Plateaus*, pp475-6.

8 An application of vicissitude to Kipnis' logic of undecidability and weak form might engender a cunning logic of non-linear affiliations. This seems apt given the reference to both undecidability and weakness in the definition of vicissitudes.

9 Ann Bergren's discussions of the *metis* in architecture is an example of cunning manipulations of form. For an alternative reading of these tactics in Greek art also see Jean-Pierre Vernant.

10 Deleuze, *Plateaus*, p256.

11 This concept has been developed by Leibniz and has many resonances with Sanford Kwinter's discussions of biological space and epigenesis as they relate to architecture and Catherine Ingraham's logic of the swerve and the animal lines of beasts of burden.

12 Wigley, Mark *Deconstructivist Architecture*, p22.

13 See 'O-O' by Robert Somol in the *Wexner Center for the Visual Arts* special issue of *Architectural Design* (London: Academy Editions, 1990).

14 *Webster's New Collegiate Dictionary* (Springfield, Mass: G&C Merriam Company, 1977), p1170.

15 Husserl, Edmund '*The Origin of Geometry*' *Edmund Husserl's Origin of Geometry: An Introduction* by Jacques Derrida (Lincoln: University of Nebraska Press, 1989).

16 See *Fetish* edited by Sarah Whiting, Edward Mitchell & Greg Lynn (New York: Princeton Architectural Press, 1992), pp158-173.

17 *Webster's*, p883.

18 Rajchman identifies an inability in contexualism to 'Index the complexifications of urban space'. Rajchman, John, 'Perplications: On the Space and Time of Rebstock Park,' *Unfolding Frankfurt* (Berlin: Ernst & Sohn Verlag, 1991), p21.

19 A similar exchange, across disciplines through geometry, occurred in France in the mid-18th century with the development of probable geometries. Initially there was a desire to describe chance events with mathematical precision. This led to the development of a geometric model that subsequently opened new fields of study in other disciplines. The mathematical interests in probability of the professional gambler Marquis de Chevalier influenced Comte de Buffon to develop the geometric description of the *Needle Problem*. This geometric model of probability was later elaborated in three-dimensions by the geologist Dellese and became the foundation for nearly all of the present day anatomical descriptions that utilise serial transactions: including CAT scan, X-Ray and PET technologies. For a more elaborate discussion of these exchanges and the impact of related probable and anexact geometries on architectural space refer to my forthcoming article in *NY Magazine no 1* (New York: Rizzoli International, 1993).

20 Wittkower, Rudolf, *Architectural Principles in the Age of Humanism* (New York: WW Norton & Co 1971).

21 Rowe, Colin *Mathematics of the Ideal Villa and Other Essays* (Cambridge: MIT Press, 1976).

22 For an earlier instance of discontinuous development based on environmental forces and co-evolution, in reference to dynamic variation, see William Bateson, *Materials for the Study of Variation: Treated with Especial Regard to Discontinuity in the Origin of Species* (Baltimore: John Hopkins University Press, 1894).

23 Erwin Panofsky has provided perhaps the finest example of this kind of heterogeneous smoothness in his analyses of Egyptian statuary and the Sphinx in particular: 'three different systems of proportion were employed – an anomaly easily explained by the fact that the organism in question is not a homogeneous but a heterogeneous one.'

24 *Webster's*, p445.

25 In Stan Allen's introduction to the work of Douglas Garofalo forthcoming in *assemblage 19* (Cambridge, Mass: MIT Press, 1992) a strategy of camouflage is articulated which invests surfaces with alternatives to the forms and volumes they delimit. The representation of other known figures is referred to as a logic of plumage. For instance, a butterfly wing representing the head of a bird invites a deceitful detection. This differs from the disappearance of a surface by stealth which resists any recognition.

26 This suggests a reading of Michael Hays' text on the early Mies van der Rohe Friedrichstrasse Tower as a tactic of disappearance by proliferating cacophonous images of the city. Hays' work on Hannes Meyer's *United Nations Competition Entry* is perhaps the most critical in the reinterpretation of functional contingencies in the intensely involved production of differentiated, heterogeneous yet continuous space through manipulations of a surface.

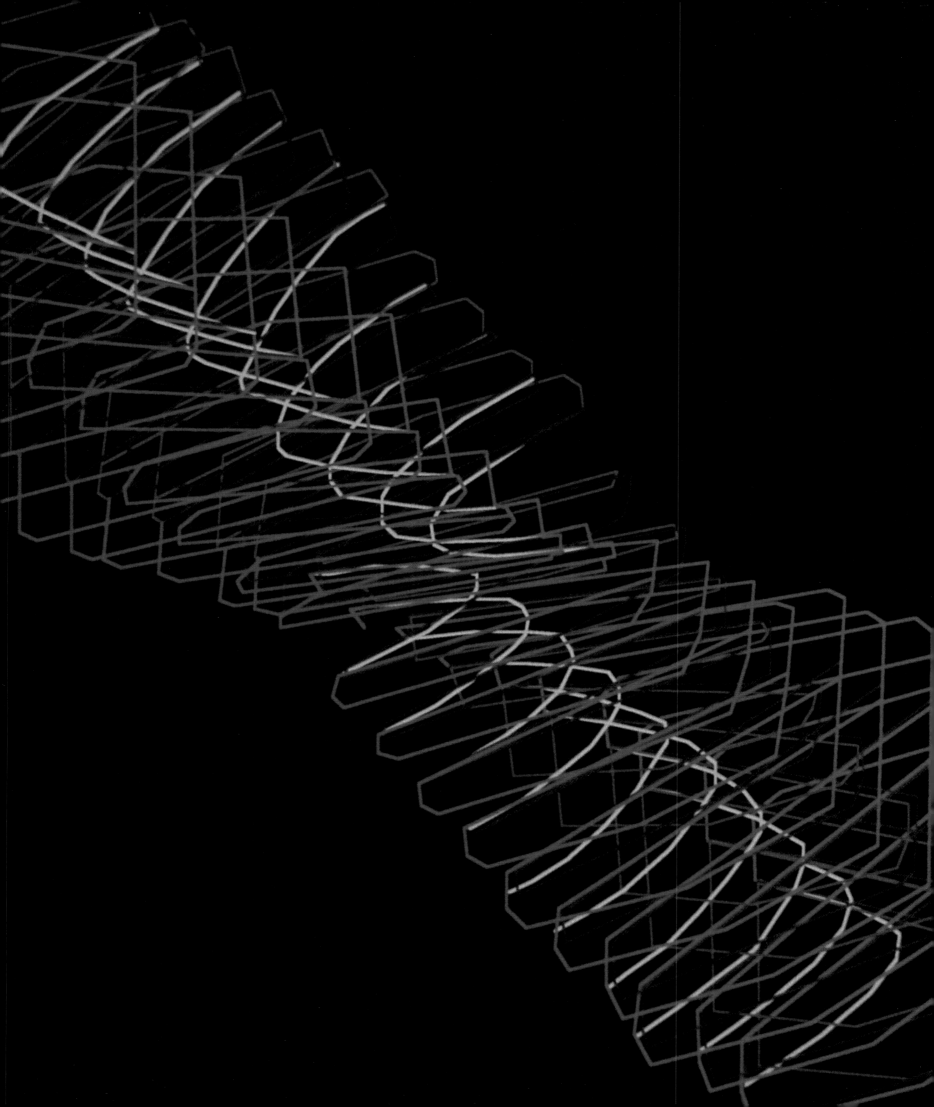

JOHN RAJCHMAN
OUT OF THE FOLD

What might architecture and urbanism make of the concept of the fold today – to what new places might they still take it?

The concept is a very old one. And yet, one cannot say that it is a concept traditional to philosophy, even though as an etymological matter it is parent, in European languages, of many concepts that are: 'explication' and 'implication', 'perplexity' and 'complexity', for example, derive from it. As such, it has a long history. The Greek root, to do with weaving, recurs in the *symploke* or weaving-together of discourse that Plato describes in the *Sophist*; but it is through Latin that words like 'implicate', 'explicate' and 'replicate' enter French, and in a slightly different way, English. Already we find Plotinus speaking of a great 'Complicatio' of the One in all that is. Much later, rather independently, we find references to the fold in Heidegger and, of course, in Mallarmé.

Perhaps the most intricate and extensive contemporary treatment of the concept is to be found in Gilles Deleuze's book, *Le Pli* (The Fold) that advances a new perspective on Leibniz and the Baroque. But then, Deleuze has a special view of what philosophical concepts are: they are *monsters*. They *show* (*montre*) things which, since they can't yet be said, appear incongruous or untimely. Deleuze wishes to restore to concepts in philosophy a dimension, not of logical possibility or necessity, but of logical *force* – the manner in which such concepts expose new 'enfoldings' or 'implications' that are yet to be 'unfolded' or 'explicated'; the manner in which they instigate new unanticipated possibilities in the midst of things, without predetermining or prefiguring the outcome; the manner in which they thus take a given conceptual space elsewhere, out from itself.

In fact, one may read Deleuze as offering an original image of conceptual space itself as something 'pliable' or ever susceptible of being folded, unfolded and refolded anew. Thus he writes of the bifurcations, the openings and closings, the surfaces, intervals, heights and depths of conceptual space, and of the manner in which thought 'orients' itself within that space. He thereby offers a different image of conceptual space from Frege (a philosophical concept is not a function mapping a range onto a domain) and from the austere Wittgenstein, whose image of the purity and simplicity of elements Adolf Loos found so appealing.

For Deleuze, conceptual space is not divided up by sets of discrete elements, nor given through a Unity or Totality of parts; and its aim is not to 'represent' or 'depict' the world by ordered combinations of such elements, any more than it is to 'express' the unity of such parts. Indeed, the world itself is not 'all that is the case' (as Wittgenstein took it to be) for it includes an undepictable anterior element out of which new kinds of things can happen, new concepts emerge – the space where unforeseen things 'take place'.

Conceptual space is thus neither timeless nor time-bound, but implies a peculiar type of temporality that Deleuze tries to unfold from 19th-century thought: from Proust's notion of a 'complicated time' (that still is connected to the Cathedral); from Bergson's notion of 'virtuality' (in which we can in retrospect see a relation to 'motion pictures'); and especially from Nietzsche's notion of the 'untimely' (which Deleuze sees Foucault as introducing into the archival study of history). At the end of the century, Frege had focused on the problem of numbers and sets. However, with the concept of the fold, Deleuze's philosophical imagination is drawn rather to mathematicians like René Thom and Benoît Mandelbrot, whose topographies suggest resonances with other domains, other spaces.

Fold-words – words with *plic-* and *plex-* – do of course also enjoy a prominent role in the discourses of architecture and of urbanism. Perhaps there is no word used more frequently than 'complexity'; and for Wolf Prix of Coop Himmelblau, architecture is a key art of the 90s because it must deal at once with social, economic and formal complexities. But 'complexity' has not always been so central a concept, and an important date for its emergence is provided by a work that for many marked a turning-point in architecture and architectural discourse: *Complexity and Contradiction in Architecture* of 1966. In this book, Robert Venturi drew on a vocabulary that had been elaborated by the Anglo-American New Critics, and was unaware that during the same years Deleuze was elaborating in France a different kind of vocabulary, a logic of 'difference and repetition', on which he would later draw in his own discussion of Mannerism and the Baroque in *Le Pli*. This other logic would be taken up some years later in architecture: For example, in his *Manhattan Transcripts* Bernard Tschumi would appropriate from Deleuze the notion of 'disjunctive synthesis', that in turn would lead to Derrida's reference to the fold in his essay on 'Maintaining Architecture'. However, out of the fold there may yet arise other possibilities, other ramifications; and some implications and complications of the concept may be traced along these four lines: multiplicity, chance, orientations and manners.

Multiplicity

The *pli*-word of which Deleuze is fond of above all others, and through whose eyes he sees all others is the word 'multiple'. On the first page of his book he declares: 'The multiple is not only what has many parts, but what is folded in many ways'. In Deleuze's philosophy, the multiple comes first before the One. States of affairs are never unities or totalities but are rather, 'multiplicities' in which there have arisen foci of unification or centres of totalisation. In such 'multiplicities' what counts is not the elements or the terms but what is in between them, their intervals or 'disparities'. Multiplicity thus involves a peculiar sort of complexity – a complexity in divergence – where it is not a matter of finding the unity of a manifold but, on the contrary, of seeing unity as a holding-together of a prior virtual dispersion. This sort of complexity does not consist in the One that is said in many ways, but rather in the fact that each thing may always diverge onto others, as in the ever-forking paths in Borges' fabled garden. A 'multiple' fabric is therefore one that can never be completely unfolded or definitively explicated, since to unfold or explicate it is only to fold or complicate it anew. Thus the multiple is not fragments or ruins of a lost or absent Whole, but the potentiality for divergence within any given unity. In this manner, the concept of complexity is freed from the logic of contradiction or opposition and connected instead to a logic of intervals: it becomes a matter of a 'free' differentiation (not subordinated to fixed analogies or categorical identities) and a 'complex' repetition (not restricted to the imitation of a pre-given model, origin or end).

Such a notion of 'complexity in divergence' differs from Venturi's notion of a contradictory or 'difficult' whole, just as it involves a strange, invisible, groundless depth; unlike the 'ground' in Colin Rowe's picture of Cubist collage and Gestaltist perception. For, Venturi would reduce complexity to a given totality and simplicity of compositional elements, and Rowe would reduce depth to the simultaneity of figure and ground. In this way they would eliminate just that which makes complexity multiple and divergent, and just what makes depth intensive and ungrounded. For them, architectural or urban vision remains fundamentally a matter of discovering an imperceptible unity in a perceptible diversity of elements. Deleuze suggests another kind of vision: one that tries to find the 'signs' of an imperceptible 'disparation' in what presents itself as a perceptual totality – the vision of an intensive 'multiplexity' in the midst of things.

Chance
For Deleuze, there is thus a folding of things that is prior to design or principle and that subsists as a potential complication in them. As such, the fold is connected to a notion of chance and necessity, which Deleuze formulates in his study of Nietzsche by saying: 'Nietzsche identifies chance with multiplicity . . . What Nietzsche calls *necessity* (destiny) is thus never the abolition but rather the combination of chance itself.'

Such views belong to a more general 'erosion of determinism' in which a Laplacian image of the universe as a sort of clock wound up by God opens onto a stochastic, unpredictable universe, where the laws of complex forms are not determined by those of simpler ones, but come into existence as those complex forms are created in the history of the universe: the universe as a great casting of the dice, the

patterns of which, upon falling, would assume a kind of necessity. For Peirce, as for Nietzsche, this new territory of chance opened up new sorts of philosophical questions. For, as Ian Hacking has argued, these two philosophers help to distinguish a 'bifurcation' in the new territory, dividing along the lines of two concepts of chance; one 'tamed', the other 'untamed'. In this way, we see how statiticians and dadaists came to populate the same conceptual and social world.

In Deleuze, we find a similar distinction between 'sedentary' and 'nomadic' views of chance. Pascal, in his wager, exemplifies the first, since he plays the game of chance according to pre-existent categorical rules that define probabilities which allow one to calculate gains and losses. But Nietzsche and Mallarmé play the game in another way: the table itself bursts open and becomes part of a larger, more complex game that always includes the possibility of new rules, so that in making each move one must affirm all of chance at once. And as the game of 'nomadic' distributions replaces the game of categorical ones, chance ceases to be tamed or hypothetical, and becomes free and imperative.

For Deleuze, the fold therefore involves the subsistence of a virtual space of chance in the organisation of design and of programme. And perhaps one might argue that this nomadic or untamed kind of chance was something that a certain heroic ambition in architecture and urbanism, and a certain image of the architect or the planner as a sort of master-builder, tried unsuccessfully to eliminate: the spaces of 'envelopment' in development, the spaces of virtual 'diagrammatisation' in plans and plannings. The question then arises of how and where such spaces might be discovered in another way than through the sense of omnipotence (and dejection) that comes from the desire to eliminate them.

Orientations
Heights and depths, ups and downs – these belong to what Deleuze terms the 'ascensional psychism' that Plato helped introduce into philosophy with his proverbial stories of the soul con-verting, reorienting itself out of the cave towards the light. What Socrates' suicide shows, he suggests, is the depressive side of such celestial orientation along a vertical axis. Deleuze wants to propose a different way of orienting oneself in thought: it would not be a matter of turning or looking up to the heights above things, any more than of

delving down into the formless *bas* beneath them, but of looking along the surfaces, in their intervals and midsts for what yet may happen, coming thus to see that 'the most profound is the skin'. *The Logic of Sense* offers many perspectives on this place where sense and non-sense would meet and where new, unforeseen things might happen. And, for Deleuze, this 'mid-place', this '*mi-lieu*', is precisely where folding occurs: 'Things and thoughts grow or grow up through the midst (*milieu*), and it is there that one has to be, it is always there that things are folded (*que ça se plie*).'

Through his notion of the *milieu*, Deleuze would deliver us from a 'linear' picture of time, proceeding from beginnings to endings as in a story or *histoire*. The midst is rather where beginnings are recast and new endings opened up in our stories; a *milieu* always interrupts the calm narrative of things, exposing a prior complexity and complication in them. And conversely, in the intervals in the midst of things there always subsists the chance for the sort of free self-complication of a space that instigates without prefiguring.

For Deleuze, events never happen out of a tabula rasa, but come out of complications, out of the fold; and time occupies a 'complicated' rather than a linear or circular space: it lies at the intersection of multiple lines that can never be disentangled in a single transparent plane given to a fixed external eye.

Thus Deleuze sees Leibniz as introducing a new 'regime of light', different from the Cartesian regime of the clear and the distinct: a baroque regime where things can be continuous even though they are distinct, and where what is clear or clarified is only a region within a larger obscurity, as when figures emerge from the 'dark background' in the paintings of Tintoretto or El Greco. For Leibniz's 'windowless monads' illuminate or clarify only singular districts in the dark complexities of the world that is expressed in them; and Leibniz becomes a perspectivist philosopher where things themselves are points of view on the world they express. Yet Leibniz retains the meta-principle that God selects this world as best, and that everything that happens is thus 'compossible' in that world. Deleuze considers Nietzsche to take things further: whereas for Leibniz, things are points of view on the same city, for Nietzsche, each point of view is a different city, resonating through its divergences with others, such that *his* principle was 'always another city in the city'.

Manners

We ourselves are folded beings, for there is a sense in which we never stop folding, unfolding, refolding our lives; and we are 'complicated' beings before we are logical ones, following out our 'life plans' within the spaces in which they can be expected to occur. When Deleuze says we are each of us plural or multiple, he doesn't mean that we are many things or have many egos, but that we are 'folded' in many entangled, irregular ways, none the same, and that this 'multiplicity' goes beyond what we can predict or be aware of: we are 'folded' in body and soul in many ways and many times over, prior to our being as 'subjects', as masters and possessors of what happens to us in our lives. Each of us is thus 'multiplicitous'; but not because we divide into distinct persons or personalities looking for a unity, lost or supposed, and not because our brains are programmed by several helpfully interacting cognitive 'modules'. It is rather that our modes of being are 'complicated' and 'unfold' in such a way that we can never be sure just what manners our being will yet assume.

Sartre saw the being of the other, of *autrui*, as this ungraspable gaze that captures and involves one in a violent struggle for recognition. But Deleuze, who admired Sartre, thought we should see *autrui* rather as the 'expression' of enfolded or implicated possibilities that don't yet exist outside the expression, but that may be unfolded or explicated through those 'encounters' that release them; and it is thus that they determine the points from which one can 'look' and be 'looked at', or the terrains in which struggles of gazes can transpire. 'The other' is thus not a subject any more than it is an object for one; it is rather the existence of multiple unrealised possibilities that go beyond the subject and that come to be expressed through what Deleuze called 'signs', in his study of Proust. In this book, Deleuze underscores that at least in the Proustian universe such involuntary 'signs' of enfolded possibilities are far richer in love and jealousy than they are in the friendship and goodwill that attracted those ancient Greek philosophers, who tried to make 'recognition among subjects' seem more important to our manners of being than 'encounters' among different worlds of possible complication. Conversely, to put 'encounters' before 'recognitions' is to see that there is something of which the body is yet capable, just as there are always states of the soul or mind that go beyond what one may be conscious of: that is, using Spinoza's word, what Deleuze calls *affects*. Our enfoldings and unfoldings 'affect' us before we re-collect them in the planned spaces of our purposeful undertakings. And if we can today re-read Spinoza and Leibniz as 'expressionist' philosophers, it is because, unlike Descartes' view of the mechanical or robotic body, they thought of body and soul as 'expressions' of the same thing: of entangled, enfolded manners or modes of our being, themselves as splendidly impersonal as the 'it' in 'it's raining'. Thus they thought that the soul is not 'in' the body, any more than it is 'above' it, but that it is rather 'with' it, accompanying it along the bifurcating paths of its distinctive manners of being.

It is this 'expressionist' construal of the philosophical theme of 'manners' or 'modes' of being that Deleuze connects, in *Le Pli*, to 'Mannerism' and the Baroque, and so reads the interior and exterior of Baroque architecture in terms of the Leibnizian theme of the windowless monad, and the harmonies of body and soul. And yet, Deleuze thinks, our own moment of complication requires another kind of expression. For we no longer have use for a principle of pre-established harmony; we have passed from the notion of the best compossible world to the possibility of a 'chaosmotic' one, in which our 'manners' ever diverge into new complications.

For Deleuze, the fold thus involves an 'affective' space from which the diverging manners of our being come and go, of which one may ask whether it will discover an architectural expression. The modernist 'machines for living' sought to express a clean efficient space for the new mechanical body; but who will invent a way to express the affective space for this other multiplicitous one?

What then might architecture make of this contemporary philosophy of the fold? Perhaps it is too soon to say, for it is a matter of new connections and of the creation of spaces in which such connections might acquire their vitality. It is a matter of the *force* of the concept in its encounter with architects.

Axonometric view of the René Thom Catastrophe Section drawn by Jeffrey Kipnis

GILLES DELEUZE
THE FOLD - LEIBNIZ AND THE BAROQUE
The Pleats of Matter

The Baroque refers not to an essence but rather to an operative function, to a trait. It endlessly produces folds. It does not invent things: there are all kinds of folds coming from the East, Greek, Roman, Romanesque, Gothic, Classical folds. . . Yet the Baroque trait twists and turns its folds, pushing them to infinity, fold over fold, one upon the other. The Baroque fold unfurls all the way to infinity. First, the Baroque differentiates its folds in two ways, by moving along two infinities, as if infinity were composed of two stages or floors: the pleats of matter, and the folds in the soul. Below, matter is amassed according to a first type of fold, and then organised according to a second type, to the extent its part constitutes organs that are 'differently folded and more or less developed'. [1] Above, the soul sings of the glory of God inasmuch as it follows its own folds, but without succeeding in entirely developing them, since 'this communication stretches out indefinitely'. [2] A labyrinth is said, etymologically, to be multiple because it contains many folds. The multiple is not only what has many parts but also what is folded in many ways. A labyrinth corresponds exactly to each level: the continuous labyrinth in matter and its parts, the labyrinth of freedom in the soul and its predicates. [3] If Descartes did not know how to get through the labyrinth, it was because he sought its secret of continuity in rectilinear tracks, and the secret of liberty in a rectitude of the soul. He knew the inclension of the soul as little as he did the curvature of matter. A 'cryptographer' is needed, someone who can at once account for nature and decipher the soul, who can peer into the crannies of matter and read into the folds of the soul. [4]

Clearly the two levels are connected (this being why continuity rises up into the soul). There are souls down below, sensitive animal; and there even exists a lower level in the souls. The pleats of matter surround and envelop them. When we learn that souls cannot be furnished with windows opening onto the outside, we must first, at the very least, include souls upstairs,

reasonable ones, who have ascended to the other level ('elevation'). It is the upper floor that has no windows. It is a dark room or chamber decorated only with a stretched canvas 'diversified by folds,' as if it were a living dermis. Placed on the opaque canvas, these folds, cords or springs represent an innate form of knowledge, but solicited by matter they move into action. Matter triggers 'vibrations or oscillations' at the lower extremity of the cords, through the intermediary of 'some little openings' that exist on the lower level. Leibniz constructs a great Baroque montage that moves between the lower floor, pierced with windows, and the upper floor, blind and closed, but on the other hand resonating as if it were a musical salon translating the visible movements below into sounds up above. [5]

It could be argued that this text does not express Leibniz's thought, but instead the maximum degree of its possible conciliation with Locke. The text also fashions a way of representing what Leibniz will always affirm: a correspondence and even a communication between the two levels, between the two labyrinths, between the pleats of matter and the folds in the soul. A fold between the two folds? And the same image, that of veins in marble, is applied to the two under different conditions. Sometimes the veins are the pleats of matter that surround living beings held in the mass, such that the marble tile resembles a rippling lake that teems with fish. Sometimes the veins are innate ideas in the soul, like twisted figures or powerful statues caught in the block of marble. Matter is marbled, of two different styles.

Wölfflin noted that the Baroque is marked by a certain number of material traits: horizontal widening of the lower floor, flattening of the pediment, low and curved stairs that push into space; matter handled in masses or aggregates, with the rounding of angles and avoidance of perpendiculars; the circular acanthus replacing the jagged acanthus, use of limestone to produce spongy, cavernous shapes, or to constitute a vortical form always put in motion by

renewed turbulence, which ends only in the manner of a horse's mane or the foam of a wave; matter tends to spill over in space, to be reconciled with fluidity at the same time fluids themselves are divided into masses. [6]

Huygens develops a Baroque mathematical physics whose goal is curvilinearity. With Leibniz the curvature of the universe is prolonged according to three other fundamental notions: the fluidity of matter, the elasticity of bodies and the motivating spirit as a mechanism. First, matter would clearly not be extended following a twisted line. Rather, it would follow a tangent. [7] But the universe appears compressed by an active force that endows matter with a curvilinear or spinning movement, following an arc that ultimately has no tangent. And the infinite division of matter causes the compressive force to return all portions of matter to the surrounding areas, to the neighbouring parts that bathe and penetrate the given body, and that determine its curvature. Dividing endlessly, the parts of matter form little vortices in a maelstrom, and in these are found even more vortices, even smaller, and even more are spinning in the concave intervals of the whirls that touch one another.

Matter thus offers an infinitely porous, spongy or cavernous texture without emptiness, caverns endlessly contained in other caverns: no matter how small, each body contains a world pierced with irregular passages, surrounded and penetrated by an increasingly vaporous fluid, the totality of the universe resembling 'a pond of matter in which there exist different flows and waves'. [8] From this, however, we could not conclude, in the second place, that even the most refined matter is perfectly fluid and thus loses its texture (according to a thesis that Leibniz imputes to Descartes). Descartes' error probably concerns what is to be found in different areas. He believed that the real distinction between parts entailed separability. What specifically defines an absolute fluid is the absence of coherence or cohesion; that is, the separability of parts, which in fact applies only to a passive and abstract matter.[9] According to Leibniz, two parts of really distinct matter can be inseparable, as shown not only by the action of surrounding forces that determine the curvilinear movement of a body, but also by the pressure of surrounding forces that determine its hardness (coherence, cohesion) or the inseparability of its parts. Thus it must be stated that a body has a degree of hardness as well as a degree of fluidity, or that it is essentially elastic, the elastic force of bodies being the expression of the active compressive force exerted on matter. When a boat reaches a certain speed a wave becomes as hard as a wall of marble. The atomistic hypothesis of an absolute hardness and the Cartesian hypothesis of an absolute fluidity are joined all the more because they share the error that posits separable minima, either in the form of finite bodies or in infinity in the form of points (the Cartesian line as site of its points, the analytical punctual equation).

This is what Leibniz explains in an extraordinary piece of writing: a flexible or an elastic body still has cohering parts that form a fold, such that they are not separated into parts of parts but are rather divided to infinity in smaller and smaller folds that always retain a certain cohesion. Thus a continuous labyrinth is not a line dissolving into independent points, as flowing sand might dissolve into grains, but resembles a sheet of paper divided into infinite folds or separated into bending movements, each one determined by the consistent or conspiring surrounding. 'The division of the continuous must not be taken as that of sand dividing into grains, but as that of a sheet of paper or of a tunic in folds, in such a way that an infinite number of folds can be produced, some smaller than others, but without the body ever dissolving into points or minima'.[10] A fold is always folded within a fold, like a cavern in a cavern. The unit of matter, the smallest element of the labyrinth, is the fold, not the point which is never a part, but a simple extremity of the line. That is why parts of matter are masses or aggregates, as a correlative to elastic compressive force. Unfolding is thus not the contrary of folding, but follows the fold up to the following fold. Particles are 'turned into folds,' that a 'contrary effort changes over and again'.[11] Folds of winds, of waters, of fire and earth, and subterranean folds of veins of ore in a mine. In a system of complex interactions, the solid pleats of 'natural geography' refer to the effect first of fire, and then of waters and winds on the earth; and the veins of

metal in mines resemble the curves of conical forms, sometimes ending in a circle or an ellipse, sometimes stretching into a hyperbola or a parabola.[12] The model for the sciences of matter is the 'origami', as the Japanese philosopher might say, or the art of folding paper.

Two consequences result that provide a sense of the affinity of matter with life and organisms. To be sure, organic folds have their own specificity, as fossils demonstrate. But on the one hand, the division of parts in matter does not go without a decomposition of bending movement or of flexions. We see this in the development of the egg, where numerical division is only the condition of morphogenic movements, and of invagination as a pleating. On the other hand, the formation of the organism would remain an improbable mystery, or a miracle, even if matter were to divide to infinity into independent points. But it becomes increasingly probable and natural when an infinity of indeterminate states is given (already folded over each other), each of which includes a cohesion at its level, somewhat like the improbability of forming a word by chance with separate letters, but with far more likelihood with syllables or inflections.[13]

In the third place, it is evident that motivating force becomes the mechanism of matter. If the world is infinitely cavernous, if worlds exist in the tiniest bodies, it is because everywhere there can be found 'a spirit in matter,' which attests not only to the infinite division of parts but also to progressivity in the gain and loss of movement all while the conservation of force is realised. The matter-fold is a matter-time; its characteristics resemble the continuous discharge of an 'infinity of wind-muskets'.[14] And there still we can imagine the affinity of matter for life insofar as a muscular conception of matter inspires force in all things. By invoking the propagation of light and 'the explosion into luminosity', by making an elastic, inflammable, and explosive spirit from animal spirits, Leibniz turns his back on cartesianism. He renews the tradition of Van Helmont and is inspired by Boyle's experimentation.[15] In short, to the extent that folding is not opposed to unfolding, such is also the case in the pairs tension-release and contraction-dilation (but not condensation-rarefaction, which would imply a void).

The lower level or floor is thus also composed of organic matter. An organism is defined by the endogenous folds, while inorganic matter has exogenous folds that

are always determined from without or by the surrounding environment. Thus, in the case of living beings, an inner formative fold is transformed through evolution, with the organism's development. Whence the necessity of a preformation. Organic matter is not, however, different from inorganic matter (here, the distinction of a first and a second matter is irrelevant). Whether organic or inorganic, matter is all one; but active forces are not the only ones exerted upon it. To be sure, these are perfectly material or mechanical forces, where indeed souls cannot be made to intervene: for the moment, vitalism is a strict organism. Material forces, which account for the organic fold, have only to be distinguished form the preceding forces, and be added to it; they must suffice, where they are exerted, to transform raw matter into organic matter. In contrast to compressive or elastic forces, Leibniz calls them 'plastic forces'. They organise masses but, although the latter prepare organisms or make them possible by means of motivating drive, it is impossible to go from masses to organisms, since organs are always based on these plastic forces that preform them, and are distinguished from forces of mass, to the point where every organ is born from a pre-existing organ.[16] Even fossils in matter are not explained by our faculty of imagination: when, for example, we see that the head of Christ we fancy in the spots on a wall refers to plastic forces that wind through organisms that already exist.

If plastic forces can be distinguished, it is not because living matter exceeds mechanical processes, but because mechanisms are not sufficient to be machines. A mechanism is faulty not for being too artificial to account for living matter, but for not being mechanical enough, for not being adequately machined. Our mechanisms are in fact organised into parts that are not in themselves machines, while the organism is infinitely machined, a machine whose every part or piece is a machine, but only 'transformed by different folds that it receives'.[17] Plastic forces are thus more machinelike than they are mechanical, and they allow for the definition of Baroque machines. It might be claimed that mechanisms of inorganic nature already stretch to infinity because the motivating force is of an already infinite composition, or that the fold always refers to other folds. But it requires that each time, an external determination, or the direct action of the surroundings, is needed in order to pass from one level to another; without this we would have to stop, as with our mechanisms. The living organism, on the contrary, by virtue of preformation has an internal destiny that makes it move from fold to fold, or that makes machines from machines all the way to infinity. We might say that between organic and inorganic things there exists a difference of vector, the latter going toward increasingly greater masses in which statistical mechanisms are operating, the former toward increasingly smaller, polarised masses in which the force of an individuating machinery, an internal individuation, is applied. Is this Leibniz's premonition of several aspects that will come true only much later?[18] No doubt, for Leibniz, internal individuation will only be explained at the level of souls: organic interiority is only derivative, and has but one container of coherence or cohesion (not of inherence or 'inhesion'). It is an interiority of space, and not yet of motion; also, an internalisation of the outside, an invagination of the outside that could not occur all alone if no true interiorities did not exist *elsewhere*. It remains the case that the organic body thus confers an interior on matter, by which the principle of individuation is applied to it: whence the figure of the leaves of a tree, two never being exactly alike because of their veins or folds.

Folding-unfolding no longer simply means tension-release, contraction-dilation, but enveloping-developing, involution-evolution. The organism is defined by its ability to fold its own parts and to unfold them, not to infinity, but to a degree of development assigned to each species. Thus an organism is enveloped by organisms one within another (interlocking of germinal matter), like Russian dolls. The first fly contains the seeds of all flies to come, each being called in its turn to unfold its own parts at the right time. And when an organism dies, it does not really vanish, but folds in upon itself, abruptly involuting into the again newly dormant seed by skipping all intermediate stages. The simplest way of stating the point is by saying that to unfold is to increase, to grow; whereas to fold is to diminish, to reduce, to 'withdraw into the recesses of a world'.[19] Yet a simple metric change would not account for the difference between the organic and the inorganic, the machine and its motive force. It would fail to show that movement does not simply go from one greater or smaller part to another, but from fold to fold. When a part of a machine is still a machine, the smaller unit is not the same as the whole. When Leibniz invokes Harlequin's layers of

clothing, he means that his underwear is not the same as his outer garments. That is why metamorphosis or 'metaschematism' pertains to more than mere change of dimension: every animal is double – but as a heterogeneous or heteromorphic creature, just as the butterfly is folded into the caterpillar that will soon unfold. The double will even be simultaneous to the degree that the ovule is not a mere envelope but furnishes one part whose other is in the male element.[20] In fact, it is the inorganic that repeats itself, with a difference of proximate dimension, since it is always an exterior site which enters the body; the organism, in contrast, envelops an interior site that contains necessarily *other* species of organisms, those that envelop in their turn the interior sites containing yet other organisms: 'Each portion of matter may be conceived as a garden full of plants, and as a pond full of fish. But every branch of each plant, every member of each animal, and every drop of their liquid parts is in itself likewise a similar garden or pond.'[21] Thus the inorganic fold happens to be simple and direct, while the organic fold is always composite, alternating and indirect (mediated by an interior surrounding).[22]

Matter is folded twice, once under elastic forces, a second time under plastic forces, but one is not able to move from the first to the second. Thus the universe is neither a great living being, nor is it in itself an Animal: Leibniz rejects this hypothesis as much as he rejects that of a universal Spirit. Organisms retain an irreducible individuality, and organic descendants retain an irreducible plurality. It remains that the two kinds of force, the two kinds of folds – masses and organisms – are strictly co-extensive. There are no *fewer* living beings than parts of inorganic matter.[23] Clearly an exterior site is not a living being; rather, it is a lake, a pond or a fish hatchery. Here the figure of the lake or pond acquires a new meaning, since the pond – and the marble tile – no longer refer to elastic waves that swim through them like inorganic folds, but to fish that inhabit them like organic folds. And in life itself the inner sites contained are even more hatcheries full of other fish: a 'swarm'. Inorganic folds of sites move between two organic folds. For

Leibniz, as for the Baroque, the principles of reason are veritable cries: Not everything is fish, but fish are teeming everywhere . . . Universality does not exist, but living things are ubiquitous.

It might be said that the theory of preformation and duplication, as observations made through the microscope confirm, has long been abandoned. The meaning of development or evolution has turned topsy-turvy since it now designates *epigenesis* – the appearance of organs and organisms neither preformed nor closed one within the other, but formed from something else that does not resemble them: the organ does not arch back to a pre-existing organ, but to a much more general and less differentiated design.[24] Development does not go from smaller to greater things through growth or augmentation, but from the

The Baroque House (an allegory)

Closed private room, decorated with a 'drapery diversified by folds'

Common rooms, with 'several small openings' the five senses

general to the special, through differentiations of an initially undifferentiated field either under the action of exterior surroundings or under the influence of internal forces that are directive, directional, but that remain neither constituitive nor preformative. However, insofar as preformism exceeds simple metric variations, it tends to be aligned with an epigenesis, to the extent that epigenesis is forced to hold to a kind of virtual or potential preformation. The essential is elsewhere; basically, two conceptions share the common trait of conceiving the organism as a fold, an orginary folding or creasing (and biology has never reflected this determination of living matter, as shown nowadays with the fundamental pleating of globular protein). Preformism is the form in which this truth of the 17-century is perceived through the first microscopes. It is hardly surprising that from then on the same problems are found in the sense of epigenesis and preformation.

Thus can all types of folding be called modifications or degrees of developments of a same Animal in itself? Or are there types of irreducible foldings, as Leibniz believes in a preformist perspective and as Cuvier and Baër also contend from an epigenic standpoint? [25] Certainly a great opposition subsists between the two points of view. With epigenesis the organic fold is produced, is unearthed, or is pushed up from a relatively smooth and consistent surface. (How could a redoubling, an invagination or an intubation be prefigured?) Now with preformism an organic fold always ensues from another fold, at least on the inside from a same type of organisation: every fold originates from a fold, *plica ex plica*. If Heideggerian terms can be used, we can say that the fold of epigenesis is an *Einfalt*, or that it is the differentiation of an undifferentiated, but that the fold from preformation is a *Zweifalt*, not a fold in two – since every fold can only be thus – but a 'fold-of-two', an *entre-deux*, something 'between' in the sense that a difference is being differentiated. From this point of view we cannot be sure if preformism does not have a future.

Masses and organisms, masses and living beings thus fill the lower level. Why then is another story needed, since sensitive or animal souls are already there, inseparable from organic bodies? Each soul even seems apt to be localised in its body, this time as 'point' in a droplet, that subsists in a part of the droplet when the latter is divided or diminished in volume: thus, in death the soul remains right where it was, in a part of the body, however reduced it may be. [26] Leibniz states that the point of view is in the body.[27] Surely everything in the body works like a machine, in accordance with plastic forces that are material, but these forces explain everything except for the variable *degrees of unity* to which they bring the masses they are organising (a plant, a worm, a vertebrate. . .) Plastic forces of matter act on masses, but they submit them to real unities that they take for granted. They make an organic synthesis, but assume the soul as the *unity of synthesis*, or as the 'immaterial principle of life'. Only there does an animism find a connection with organicism, from the standpoint of pure unity or of union, independently of all causal action. [28] It remains that organisms would not on their account have the causal power to be folded to infinity, and of

surviving in ashes, without the unity-souls from which they are inseparable, and which break away from Malebranche: not only is there a preformation of bodies, but also a pre-existence of souls in fertile seeds. [29] Life is not only everywhere, but souls are everywhere in matter. Thus, when an organism is called to unfold its own parts, its animal or sensitive soul is opened onto an entire theatre in which it perceives or feels according to its unity, independently of its organism, yet inseparable from it.

But – and here is the whole problem – what happens with bodies, from the time of Adam's seed that envelops them, that are destined to become humans? Juridically, one might say that they carry in a nutshell 'a sort of sealed act' that marks their fate. And when the hour comes for them to unfold their parts, to attain a degree of organic development proper to man, or to form cerebral folds, at the same time their animal soul becomes reasonable by gaining a greater degree of unity (mind): 'The organised body would receive at the same time the disposition of the human body, and its soul would be raised to the stage of a reasonable soul, but I cannot decide here if it occurs through an ordinary process or an extraordinary work of God.' [30] Then in every event this becoming is an elevation, an exaltation: a change of theatre, of rule, of level or of floors. The theatre of matter gives way to that of spirits or of God. In the Baroque the soul entertains a complex relation with the body. Forever indissociable from the body, it discovers a vertiginous animality that gets it tangled in the pleats of matter, but also an organic or cerebral humanity (the degree of development) that allows it to rise up, and that will make it ascend over all other folds.

The reasonable soul is free, like a Cartesian diver, to fall back down at death and to climb up again at the last judgment. As Leibniz notes, the tension is between the collapse and the elevation or ascension that in different spots is breaching the organised masses. We move from funerary figures of the Basilica of Saint Laurence to the figures on the ceiling of Saint Ignatius. It might be claimed that physical gravity and religious elevation are quite different and do not pertain to the same world. However, these are two vectors that are allotted as such in the distinction of the two levels or floors of a single and same world, or of the single and same house. It is because the body and the soul have no point in being inseparable, for they are not in the least really distinct (we have already seen it for

the parts of matter). From this moment on any localisation of the soul in an area of the body, no matter how tiny it may be, amounts rather to a *projection* from the top to the bottom, a projection of the soul focalising on a 'point' of the body, in conformity with Gesarnes' geometry, that develops from a Baroque perspective. In short, the primary reason for an upper floor is the following: there are souls on the lower floor, some of whom are chosen to become reasonable, thus to change their levels.

Movement, then, cannot be stopped. The reciprocation of the Leibnizian principle holds not only for reasonable souls but also for animal or sensible souls themselves: if two really distinct things can be inseparable, two inseparable things can be really distinct, and belong to two levels, the localisation of the one in the other amounting to a projection upon a point ('I do not think that we can consider souls as being in points, perhaps we might say . . . that they are in a place through a connection'). As degrees of unity, animal souls are already on the other floor, everything being accomplished mechanically in the animal itself at the lower level. Plastic or machinic forces are part of the 'derivative forces' defined only in respect to the matter that they organise. But souls, on the contrary, are 'primitive forces' or immaterial principles of life that are defined only in respect to the inside, in the self, and 'through analogy with the mind'. We can nonetheless remember that these animal souls, with their subjugated organism, exist everywhere in inorganic matter. Thus in its turn inorganic matter reverts to souls whose site is elsewhere, higher up, and that is only projected upon it. In all probability a body – however small– follows a curvilinear trajectory only under the impulsion of the second species of derivative forces, compressive or elastic forces that determine the curve through the mechanical notion of the surrounding bodies on the outside: isolated, the body would follow the straight tangent. But still, mechanical laws or extrinsic determinations (collisions) explain everything except the *unity* of a concrete movement, no matter how irregular or variable it may be. Unity of movement is an affair of the soul, and almost of a conscience, as Bergson will later discover. Just as the totality of matter arches back to a curving that can no longer be determined from the outside, the curvilinear course followed by a given body under the impetus of the outside goes back to a 'higher', internal and individuating, unity on the other floor, that contains the 'law of curvilinearity', the law of folds or changes of direction. [31] The same movement is always determined from the outside, through collisions, insofar as it is related to derivative force, but unified from the inside, to the degree it is related to primitive force. In the first relation, the curve is accidental and derived from the straight line, but in the second it is primary, such that the motive force sometimes is mechanically explained through the action of a subtle surrounding, and sometimes is understood from the inside as the interior of the body, 'the cause of movement that is already in the body', and that only awaits the suppression of an obstacle from the outside. [32]

Hence the need for a second floor is everywhere affirmed to be strictly metaphysical. The soul itself is what constitutes the other floor or the inside up above, where there are no windows to allow entry of influence from without. Even in a physical sense we are moving across outer material pleats to inner animated, spontaneous folds. These are what we must now examine, in their nature and in their development. Everything moves as if the pleats of matter possessed no reason in themselves. It is because the Fold is always between two folds, and because the between-two folds seems to move about everywhere: is it between inorganic bodies and organisms, between organisms and animal souls, between animal souls and reasonable souls, between bodies and souls in general?

Translation by Tom Conley

Notes

1 *New system of Nature and of the communication of substances*, §7.

2 *Monadologie*, § 61 and *Principles of Nature and of Grace founded in reason*, §13.

3 On Liberty (Foucher de Careil, *New letters and opuscules*).

4 On cryptography as art of inventing a key of something enveloped, fragment *A book on combination . . .* (Couturat, *Opuscules*). And *New Essays on human understanding*, IV, ch17, §8: the folds in Nature and the 'summaries'.

5 *New Essays*, II, ch12, §1. In this book, Leibniz 'remakes' the *Essays* by Locke: the dark room is well invoked by Locke, but not the folds.

6 Cf Wölfflin, *Renaissance and Baroque*, Ed Monfort.

7 *New Essays*, preface.

8 Letter to Des Billettes, December 1696 (Gerhardt, *Philosophy*, VII, p452).

9 *Table of Definitions* (C, p486) and *New Essays*, II, ch 23, §23.

10 Placidus *Philalethi* (C, pp614-615).

11 Letter to Des Billettes, p453.

12 *Protogaea* (Dutens II; and tr . . . fr by Bertrand de Saint-Germain, 1850, Ed English). On the conical veins, ch 8.

13 This theme will be developed by Willard Gibbs. Leibniz supposes that God does not trace 'the first alignments of the tender earth' without producing something 'analogous to the structure of animal or of plants' (*Protogaea*, ch 8).

14 Letter to Des Billettes; and Letter to Bayle, December 1698 (GPh, III, p57) cf Gueroult, *Dynamic and Metaphysical Leibnizians*, The Beautiful Letters, p32: 'How is the spring conserved if one does not suppose that the body is composed, such that it can contract in pursuit of its pores the particles of subtle manner which penetrate it, and in return this more subtle matter can expel from its pores an even more subtle matter etc to infinity?'

15 On elasticity and the detonation, which inspire the concept of reflex in Willis (1621-1675), on the differences of this model with that of Descartes, cf Georges Canguilhem, *The Formation of the Concept of Reflex in the XVII and XVIII Century*, PUF, pp60-67. Malebranche attempts to reconcile the theme of the spring and of relaxation (*loosening*) with Cartesianism, at the same time in the inorganic and in the organism: *Search for Truth*, VI, ch 8 & 9 ('any stiff body which does nothing can spring . . .').

16 Letter to Lady Masham, July 1705 (GPh, III, p368) and *Considerations on the Principles of Life and on Plastic Nature* (GPh, VI, pp544 & p553): the principles of life are immaterial, but not the 'plastic faculty'. On fossils, cf Protogaea, ch 28.

17 New system of nature, §10. *Monadologie*, §64: 'The tooth of a brass wheel has parts or fragments that to us are no more than something artificial, which have no relation to the machine other than to the use of the destined wheel. But the machines of nature, that is to say living bodies, are again machines in their small parts until infinity'. Letter to Lady Masham, p374: '*The plastic force in the machine*'.

18 On the technological conception of Leibniz, his opposition to that of Descartes and his modernity, cf Michael Serres, *The System of Leibniz*, PUF, II, pp491-510, p621.

19 Letter to Arnauld, April 1687 (GPh, II, p99).

20 New Essays, III, chap 6, §23. It is thus by mistake that Bonnet (*Philosophic palingenesie*) reproaches his teacher Leibniz for having refrained from

variations of cutting.

21 *Monadologie*, §67-70.

22 Cf Serres, I, p371.

23 Letter to Arnauld, September 1687 (p118).

24 In the name of the epigenese, Dalcq may say: 'A caudal appendices could have obtained from a system of action and of reaction . . . or nothing is caudal *a priori*' (*The Egg and its Dynamic Organisation*, Ed Albin Michel, p194).

25 Geoffrey Saint-Hillaire, partisan of *epigenese*, is one of the greatest thinkers on organic folds. He considered different folds as modifications of a single animal, one can go from one to the other to fold again (united by a plan of composition). If one folds a vertebrae 'in such a way that the two parts of its spine are brought together, the head near its feet, its pelvis near its nape, and its viscera inside the cephalopodes'. This instigates the opposition by Baër, in the name of the *epigenese,* and already the anger of Cuvier who poses the diversity of axes of development or of plans of organisation (cf Geoffrey, *Principles of Zoological Philosophy*). Despite his monism, however, Geoffrey could call himself leibnizian in other respects: he explains the organism by a material force which does not change the nature of the body, but adds to it in new ways and new relations. It is an impulsive, electric force, or tractive in the manner of Kepler, capable of 're-folding' the elastic fluids and operating at three short distances in the 'world of details' or in the small infinity, no longer by summation of homogeneous parts, but affronted by homologous parts (Synthetic notions and histories of natural philosophy).

26 Letter to Des Bosses, March 1706 (in Christiane Fremont, *The being and the relation*, Ed Vrin) and in a letter to Arnauld, April 1687 (p 100): an insect having been cut into a thousand pieces, its soul stays 'in a certain living part, which will always be smaller than it made to be covered by the action of that which tore him apart. . .'

27 Letter to Lady Masham, June 1704 (p357).

28 *Principles of nature and of Grace*, §4: 'an infinity of degrees' in the souls and *New System of Nature*, §11.

29 *Monadologie*, §74.

30 *God's cause interceded by his justice*, §§81-85 and *Theodicee*, §91, 397.

31 *Clarifications of difficulties that Mr Bayle found in the new system . . .* (GPh, IV, pp544, 558). Gueroult has shown how the external determinism and the internal spontaneity reconcile themselves perfectly, already by account to the physical bodies: pp203-207; and p163 ('the elasticity is now considered as an expression of the first spontaneity, of the primitive active force'.)

Page 16: *Peter Eisenman, Rebstock Park, Frankfurt, view of the model*

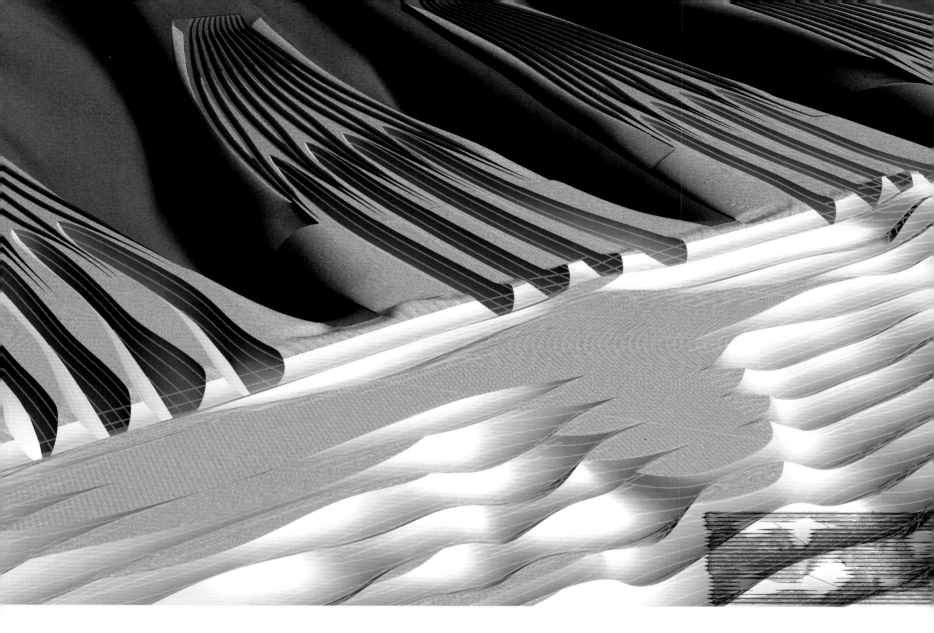

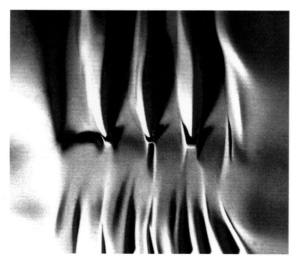

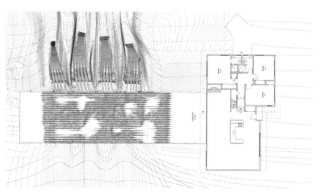

ABOVE: Oblique rendering; CENTRE: Model plan; site plan;
RIGHT: Density map of laminar system

REISER + UMEMOTO
WITH DAVID RUY AND JEFFREY KIPNIS
WATER GARDEN

The architecture of the garden has historically encompassed the full range and implications of Man's engagement with the material environment. A more or less permanent feature of Western architecture has been the almost ineradicable idea that there exists a permanent and unchanging essence behind the world of appearances, that is universalised themselves in fixed, simple geometries and timeless typologies. Time thus makes itself evident within two distinct yet related schemas: first, architecture as a stable and unchanging framework within which, and against which, the temporal unfolds; and second, experimentation with how the mutable character of nature can be made to approach or deviate from a certain ideal.

In the 18th-century French topiary garden for example, the relative crudity or refinement of simple geometrical forms in plant materials served to establish the norms and limits for their speculation and enjoyment. If, however, we shift our focus from such static models of nature and architecture to dynamic (essentially time-based) systems, a new horizon of possibilities emerges. Time, reappears as something real – as a destabilising but creative milieu. That is to say, time is not understood to be prior to, above, or separate from the material world, but is engendered by, and finds its particular incarnations within it.

Nature then, is less a 'creation' on which to speculate than an inventive and modifiable matrix of materials. It might be argued that abandoning the two schemas outlined above leads to forms where nature is in some sense allowed to take its own course (with the assumption that natural development without human intervention will display its own creativity and inherent virtues). However, a fourth possibility exists, which contrary to a passive naturalism, requires intensive artifice towards the production of natural effects. Nature will of its own inertia tend towards developments of increasing stability and banality. A salient and

intensive architecture requires the deliberate production of instability in order to produce novelty. And here it will be necessary to set aside the nature/culture dialectics and focus instead on the processes that establish transverse developments across these regimes.

The French philosopher Gilles Deleuze coined the concept of the 'machinic phylum' to refer to the overall set of self-organising processes in the universe. These include all processes in which a group of previously disconnected elements (organic and inorganic) suddenly reach a critical point at which they begin to 'co-operate' to form a higher-level entity. Recent advances in experimental mathematics have shown that the onset of these processes may be described by the same mathematical model. It is as if the principles that guide the self-assembly of these machines 'are at some deep level essentially similar'. The notion of a 'machinic phylum' thus blurs the distinction between organic and non-organic life.

This material geometry constitutes the 'primitive', through which a hierarchical series of global and local transformations (warps, dimples, folds) is expressed. Extreme and unstable configurations in the topology are essentially built into the concrete substrate, materialising in the vital media (water, soil, plant materials and chemical salts) of the 'flow space' above. The topology of the substrate induces transformational events that introduce real discontinuities in the evolution of the media flowing on it. In such manifold topologies the characteristics of the mapped media are not determined by the quantitative substrate, but by the specific singularities of the 'flow space' of which it is itself part. This means that the 'dead' yet intensive geometry of the grooves excites material and/or biological novelty in the media. In literal and instrumental fashion, multiform gradients in the geometry 'diagram' trigger the gradients of growth inherent in natural systems and yield a prodigious, if only partially manageable, field of blooms.

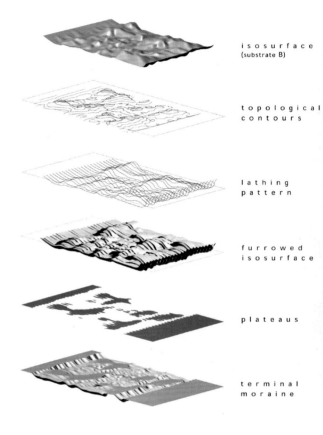

isosurface
(substrate B)

topological
contours

lathing
pattern

furrowed
isosurface

plateaus

terminal
moraine

ABOVE: Isometrics; BELOW: Model

CLAIRE ROBINSON
THE MATERIAL FOLD
Towards a Variable Narrative of Anomalous Topologies

The fold, the fringe, the dovetail, the butterfly, the ombillic hyperbolic, the elliptic ombillic, the parabolic umbillic: René Thom's Catastrophe Theory invites the discontinuous, the topological into architecture. Topology becomes a geometry of reconciliation between building and ground, logos and noise. Inherent in his work of identifying and naming mathematically singular discontinuities is a concern for the phenomenological otherness inherent in the resultant geometries.[1] This otherness has a materiality. To take the fold as solely formal gesture is the same as allowing its materiality to be evacuated.

If one is content to uphold the extrapolated image of Thom's 'remarkable section' as an invitation to create a 'new form'; the fold's spatial potential is suppressed in favour of a reiterated platonism. Although the mathematical impetus of the Catastrophe Theory may have been Platonic in origin, the age-old query of how to explain the relation between a pyramid and a dodecahedron, a tetrahedron and a cube, a cube and an icosahedron . . . seems to give way. Another potential cosmology emerges from Thom's work; one with tremendous ramifications for architects and other proto-workers of space. 'The chosen model is a fluid one, it is no longer a crystal, nor the five regular polyhedrons that are the solids of the Timaeus; it is flow.'[2]

Venus her(e) folds.

Chora, Her, Space: a continually folding, constantly evolving, perpetually holding and loosing ephemeral place. Chora should not receive but allow itself to borrow, or receive only in order to give away, to possess nothing and to be in and of itself nothing other than the process which inscribes itself on it. Chora is neither subject or support; is giving way and not giving place, more situating than situated. Chora is inaccessible, impassable, amorphous? Chora is virginity resistant to anthropomorphism.

Seaweed.

Applying the lessons of the turbulent dance of seaweed (a continually folding entity) to architecture, one is faced with that existing outside the idea of the 'flat', outside of the impetus of perfect horizontal and perfect vertical. Locally, seaweed's ease of movement is rendered possible by a crucial absence of material, a series of perforations along crease lines. The holes throughout the seaweed are not faults but necessary interruptions – perpetual thresholds for water's passage. A chora work, seaweed's global structure allows it to be malleable and permeable to its surroundings. Unharmed by, 'maritime turbulence, turbantibus aequora ventis . . . in th(is) theoretical text the reference to individual bodies is again only related to fluids: imbris utiguttae . . . certainly a question of weight, of gravity, but never of solids.'[3]

René Thom, speaking of the constructive and the destructive aspects of the catastrophe, names the following archetypal morphologies: to finish, to begin, to unify, to separate, to become, to capture, to emit, to fault, to suicide, to agitate, to cross, to give, to take, to send, to link, to cut.[4] With respect to the fold's topological properties, the act of architecture is one of embodying the rupture which is also the link between physically discontinuous realms of space.

Unable to resist, (s)he caught the seaweed, pulled it out of the flow, and set it upon the rock – glistening. The space between the undersurface of the seaweed and the surface of the rock fused to form an admirable, if ephemeral, model for a crenellated building envelope.

The fold – this catastrophe V=x3, the border, the end, the beginning, is not static geometry but one of spatial, temporal, material flux.

From fluid to solid, an architectural interest in 'the fold' is commensurate with an obsession for cyclical processes. One may embrace the fold as a design choreography of discontinuity, a design process in which the 'architecture' is not primarily upheld as an immutable object. One in which the building is not thought of as autonomous, as hermetically sealed without interstices or breaks; not idealised as a perfect uninterrupted connection of parts.

Around the graaf follicle, the swollen

ovarian lining folds to form a pocket. On the verge of rupture and ready to flow across the breach into the uterine oviduct, it is an entity maintained in position by continuity with the uterus. In ordinary conditions, the uterine tube is held between leaves of the large ligament, however, during pregnancy, it becomes very mobile.

Back on the rock, the water shed quickly from the surface of the translucent seaweed; moisture steadily evaporating. In the dazzling sunlight the glistening object did not survive in immutable form but collapsed suddenly onto the surface of the rock. After this point the seaweed's process of desiccation continued quietly, introducing further complicated folds.

Leibniz's law of continuity (germ of catastrophe theory) sustains a fold 'where there is continuity between data such that one case continually approaches and at length loses itself in another, there will be corresponding continuity in results or properties'.

'What noise did the classical age muffle, to which sounds did it close its ears in order to invent our rationalism? It is necessary to have the audacity to uncover ichnography - that which one always carries around with oneself, in the dark and as if secret, in a set back alcove, or under a veil.'[5]

Venus her(e) folds.
Her architecture would be thus a local emergence within a saturated landscape. Questions situated deeply within, yet extending to the exterior surface . . . of the discipline. The folds of mons veneris. The fringe of History. The dove(tail) whispers: 'butterfly goddess, ombillic hyperbolic concavity, elliptic hyperbolic placenta, parabolic ombillic convexity.' The architecture of the fold is one of becoming; one of a specific gestational process. If the task is to define or theorise the fold as a place in architecture, this must certainly be within place(entation). If not . . . 'language will reproduce with you in the folds of skin, this endless version of your body from now on unalterable'.[6]

For some architects, the earth's crust may be understood as placental; for others, the strata of the 'site' are seen as bulk, the architectural intervention as penetration (without possible unfolding): violation, transgression. 'The three membranes of the uterus tie themselves together by means of the cotyledons . . . just as fingers of the hand are interwoven, one in the interval of the other . . . so these fleshy rosettes interlock and are attached as burrs do among each other. The cotyledons have

male and female parts. You will now note whether the male or female remains attached to the uterus or not.'[7]

The place(nta) is formed of a series of folds; within these pliant swells, are gently interfering waves: the Herme-Aphrodite architect. At the place where the foot touches the ground, the movement is downward toward the roots of building. The building becomes porous to chthonic presences, to dreams to oracles, traditionally located beneath the earth's crust.

Within the fold, certain navigational horizons are inscribed. The placental wall – a translucent barrier characterised by the dynamics of the concave and the convex – is a receptacle within a receptacle. What of architecture as a culmination of a cycle within cycles: the incredible presence of the red rooms, the utter sophistication of the uterine wall, villa of the mysteries, delicate translucent veils externalised in paintings of her? In placental logic, the weather/whether of architectural design emerges; within the welcoming, ever changing section of the wall one finds local conditions of heterogeneous spatial varieties. The wall locally becomes an intelligent and responsive membrane with innate capacities to direct the flow of space; the separation and connection between discreet places. The Herme-Aphrodite is working on both sides of the fold: on one side losing the clear edges of plane geometry to find the feminine lurking somewhere in the centre; on the other embracing the 'grid' as overlay of order.

Despite the Jeffersonian effort, the chaotic paths of tumbleweeds, grains of dust, constantly shifting waves of low flying turbulence continue to ripple over the earth's surface. Reverse this fold: 'reason has triumphed over myth. Euclidean space has repressed a barbarous topology . . . Myth is effaced in its original function, the new space is universal. As is reason of the ratio that it sustains, only because within it there are no more encounters.'[8]

Question 1 – Lucretius and the Architecture Firm: If the hermaphrodite architect made a perfect, platonic solid – and threw it into a bog where the ground is unstable, wet, porous, topological in nature – how would these two entities fold together? With respect to the Blue Sea, or the Mer Bleue Bog; if there is an architecture nascent here it does not emerge from solid ground. It is not necessarily hard and dry. This fold of architecture may not be limited to orthogonal projective geometries and building systems.

Question 2 – The Hesiodic Earth: If the hermaphrodite architect seeks a place of projection, how might the folds of the earth's surface be assimilated into the 'deadly flat' of the drafting table?

With every step on to the Blue Sea Bog, the earth bears a compressive collapse which is audible. This noise is associated with the giddy earth and with that which is folded into and hidden within the ground. Churning within the buoyant mass of peat are plants and seed which have blown in from the outskirts of the bog for thousands of years.

The top side, in evidence, in print, written (and built). The other side, of an intimate yet unrealised immediacy, whispers. She offers a new understanding of 'section'. 'Immediately Mrs Ramsay seemed to fold herself together, one petal closed in another, the whole fabric folding in exhaustion upon itself . . . like the pulse of a spring which has expanded to its full width and now gently ceases to beat, the rapture of successful creation.'[9]

You hold the book, the room you read in holds you; one pocket of thick contracting wall. The hermaphrodite architect: on one side '(s)he is the worker of a single space, the space of measure and transport. The Euclidean space of every possible displacement without changes of state. On the other side, (s)he is the worker of proliferating multiplicities, of unlinked morphologies.'[10]

The material fold.

Notes

1 Refer to René Thom, *Morphogenese et l'imaginaire*.
2 Michael Serres, *Hermes: Literature, Science, Philosophy*.
3 Ibid.
4 Refer to René Thom, *Mathematical Models of Morphogenesis*.
5 *Genese*, M Serres: 'Quelle noise l'age classique refoule-t-il, à quel bruit ferme-t-il ses oreilles, pour inventer notre rationalisme? . . . il faut avoir l'audace d'évoiler l'ichnographie, parfois, celle qu'on porte toujours avec soi, dans le noir, et comme au secret, dans une alcôve retiré, sous un voile.
6 Nicola Brossard, *Picture Theory*.
7 Refer to description in Leonardo da Vinci's Notebooks.
8 Michael Serres, *Hermes: Literature, Science, Philosophy*.
9 Virginia Woolf, *To the Lighthouse*.
10 Michael Serres, *Hermes: Literature, Science, Philosophy*.

FREDERIK STJERNFELT
THE POINTS OF SPACE

For Immanuel Kant, space was a pure intuition a *reine Anschauung*. This seems to be underlined by the fact that we can hardly imagine any human activity of thought except in spatial concepts. Classical physics is famous for proceeding to make even time a purely quantitative parameter, a line, and hence nothing but yet another spatial dimension; but also Quantum mechanics is based on spatial representations, even if in a less straightforward manner – the complementarity between wave and particle derives from the fact that each of these two ways of representing a phenomenon are determined by their own set of spatial pictures, of metaphors: the wave in the water and the grain of sand. It is evident that semiotics, the science of signs, must be implementing spatial metaphors as well; in so far as by its very definition it contains the various spatial imaginations as objects: representations of mind and hence conceivable as signs. It is hardly possible to treat meaning and signs outside a structure which is in itself already an architectonic metaphor (structure, from Latin *struere*, to build) that separates an abstract space into partial spaces which can then be invested with signification (content): black against white, culture against nature etc, featuring characteristic zones of mediation between them in the abstract space of imagination: grey, cultivated etc. All kinds of qualities are probably conceived within such spaces. The possibility of change or development is inscribed therein by means of the routes through space; forcing, for instance, the change between red and green to proceed through yellow, blue or brown via a specific voyage of nuances depending on the route chosen. Thus it is no wonder that our imagination, working in its complicated network of abstract spaces of quality imposed on everyday 3-D space, has to make intense use of metaphors fetched from the most concrete space of experience: architecture.

Architecture is so obviously spatial because its very task is to seek a certain control over the space of living and its

design. But all other sciences, too, find their foundations in space – to use a more than central metaphor of architecture: the foundation. Science, fantasy and literature are full of foundations, thresholds, entrances, labyrinths and enlightening views. They articulate themselves immediately 'as if' their subject was an intricate building in which the lover, the scientist, the philosopher is wandering about seeing connections and establishing distinctions. 'As if', we said, and the question is whether what is dealt with here is but a series of metaphors to be seen through, dismantled, deconstructed and so on. Does science have to impose upon itself the task of self liberation from metaphors of architecture? If it is an essential condition of thought to make use of these pictures, then there is no way out (sic!) – one has to merely attempt to control them in relation to the subject that one is seeking to love, to comprehend, to describe. A central 'field' that can hardly be thought without these archi-architectural basic concepts is the subject itself. Already, the body in which it most often finds itself situated is naturally obeying central architectonic relations (up/down, outside/inside, laterality, the body as a building [*Körperbau*]) that seem indispensable when one thinks of the subject as such. The opposition outside/inside can hardly be dispensed with if a soul, a mind, should be thought of as occupant of the building of the body. One only has to cast a glance at the three-storey house of Freud (id/ego/superego) or the Lacanian set of partitions (the 'split subject') to see that these spatial archetypes do not necessarily imply any idealistic metaphysics on behalf of the subject but rather the contrary. The fact that the subject might be a house does not imply that it should mistake itself for a transparent totality, self-controlling, well-arranged. Think of ruins and enormous Piranesian interiors to be convinced that the building does not in this way imply any necessarily organic or metaphysical ideology. On the contrary, if one first conceives oneself exploring, like a building, one is placed at a distance to the

immediate consciousness and its self-reflection.

A structure, a subject, a piece of architecture – in each case it is evident that the various kinds of borders in space are crucial to their definition. Perceived from a topological point of view, these borders, walls, partitions and lines drawn in space are singularities; that is, they are sets of points of less probability than the rest of the space – singularities with lower dimension than the space in which they appear. The plane, the line, the point being singularities in 3-D space with decreasing dimension and hence probability. In this purely spatial conception, a piece of architecture would simply mean a structure of connected singularities in space: a composition of walls parting the space and defining it into segments, rooms, yards and so on; or, in the language of the topologists, a manifold, which does not imply any kind of naive pluralism but merely a complex object in several dimensions. In this respect, the less probable singularities, the line and the point, almost become literally on the edge of space: they do not really exist in space – only in so far as a subject is positioned to see, to construct them: when a subject experiences architecture, its body forms a point moving along a line, a route through architectural space. This leads us to two possible notions of this abstract as well as architectural space. Is the space a given continuum, of which the points, lines etc are mere intersections of no real existence; or, is the space itself made up as a mass of singular points, and hence nothing but a compilation of an infinitude of smaller elements? The second view is the one opted for by traditional geometry, but in fact the two points of view go back to two different views of the fundamentals of mathematics. In contrast to the stance taken by ordinary geometry, the French topologist and inventor of the so-called Catastrophe Theory, René Thom, maintains that the only really 'existing' space is 3-D and henceforth the only phenomenology in a given field comprehensible by man is such a space inhabited by 'balls' – connected beings with closed surface: 'atoms', 'elements', 'bodies' 'objects'; in every case small coherent parts of 3-D space. Thus, he posits continuity as superior to discontinuity. On the other hand, geometry makes discontinuity fundamental; thereby conciliating itself with arithmetic and its base, the act of counting. Space is, in this conception, a set of points emerging by virtue of a generative procedure, proceeding from the singular point to larger sets of points. From the latter point of view, the point is a kind of prerequisite to and renunciation of space. From the former, space is the basic and the point only visible therein as a construction. The romantic philosophy of Hegel saw in this antinomy between point and space a veritable dialectics: on the one hand, the point was a negation of space, having in itself no extension; on the other the empty space was the truth of the points, lines and surfaces. This dialectics then found its *Aufhebung* in concrete space, filled with objects defined by precise lines, points and surfaces. Time was then nothing but this very dialectics, this *Werden* working between space and its elements of less dimensions.

This antinomy between point and space, in turn implies certain consequences for architecture. With regard to deconstruction, a possible approach lies in interposing several systems on each other so that the resulting image does not depend on one single system but consists of entangled fragments of several structures; for instance, structures deriving from points, lines, planes respectively. Within this practice the fight waged in our spatial intuition between several possible systems is sought formalised, thereby opening the question of a play between decidability and indecidability. But this question, in turn, throws light back on the very concept of 'metaphysical' architecture. If architecture, by making houses like bodies and thereby giving them all the presuppositions of teleology, of meaning, of fundamentals and so on, is metaphysical – isn't it then already deconstructing itself by the doublesidedness of the singularities of which it consists? The necessary materiality of the singularities, eg, the bricks of a wall, makes possible a zone which is neither inside nor outside, the prerequisite to the uncanniness of houses and their traditional habitation by ghosts and geists which transcend walls and somehow live within them? The simplest singularity of all is the point, dividing the line into two. The next simplest is what René Thom calls a fold,

which makes possible the articulation of a wall: that which is neither inside nor outside. In this way, the fold is an articulation of the indecision already present in architecture: raised in concrete it becomes a monument of formal strength and indecision at the same time; the room under the fold is neither inside nor outside, or is both, depending on the point of view. Here, the subject becomes either spirit or nothing: a ghost. Thus, it is an articulation as well as a questioning of the inside/outside dichotomy: it marks a field of spatial indecision to the subject making its line through it. The fold folds a grid placed on the ground before folding. Now, thanks to gravity, the same effect as contained in Catastrophe Theory appears: it is possible to walk on the fold as well as beneath it, but never on its underside.

By this architecture of indecision, the line is drawn back to the vicissitude of the old *Anhalter Bahnhof* which, after being bombed during the war, was left like a roofless building, a temple (from *templum*, cut out) cutting a section of the sky and making a *coincidentia oppositorum* between inside and outside, sacred and profane. This inherent sacrality of architecture might seem to derive from its metaphysics, from its pretension of being a structure endowed with sense, an aesthetic, unambiguous or functional body. It is quite the contrary: its holiness depends on the fact that it always transcends these determinations. Hence it is in some sense superfluous to aim at architectural deconstruction by emphasising the insistence of points against space – the points are already working within space. This 'dialectics' without *Aufhebung* is contained within the fold; being an unfolding of one single point, a singularity, the point on top of its curvature, the point where the fold starts folding. This is the point that marks the locality as a place.

Now, how does the architectural subject behave? Not only is he a point himself (viewed from the scale of architecture) and a space (the body as a house) but he mediates between point and space by drawing a line – or, as belonging to a mass, covering a surface – in the construction. Attempting to make one's way by constructing an inner map of the surroundings is probably the primordial architectural 'experience', primary to any Heideggerian metaphysics of *Wohnen* (one dwells in a place only in so far as one has already constructed or been given a map thereof). In this walk, in the mind or in reality, several

specific situations occur. Following a path is the most simple: one is simply forced by architecture to choose the route as between two of the small buildings of the grid. Another situation is the dead-end: this is either the (partial) goal, with all the metaphysics of dwelling, function as well as religion, pouring forth; or on the contrary, the fatal sign of having got lost. The third possibility is the crossroads where several choices are possible and one has to choose. These three archi-situations have a common narrative ratio. On his way through architecture, the subject follows the same eternal structure as the prince seeking his princess. And if it is not the case that the fold forms an architectural body giving ends to the subject (like the mega-body of the church), then the fold is rather an orifice, a mouth – one mighty, obscene staring slit, an enormous version of the door with its sensible lips of door frames around it; but like the door, no longer leading anywhere. The fold is a cavern; a simple marking of a place as being neither inside nor outside, making possible the primitive cult or dwelling – and thence it marks the subject seeking its way within it and between the various small buildings on the grid folded up through it. Creeping inside as far as possible and becoming the ghost in the machine; or wandering onto the top of the fold and becoming a god lifted over the indecision of the fold, the subject is left to itself by being given all the narrative possibilities. Here, no entrance or system of passages is forcing or securing the roads, only the pure and indecisive distinction between inside or outside. Grasped as a totality the fold is easily imagined and controlled. As an object for a diversity of routes or being a mere punctiform orifice on the earth's surface, it depends on the infinitude of points in space – hence its *unheimlich* character.

The narrative that defines the subject by leading it through space can never be totally determined; the points being the ends as well as the beginnings of space. The interplay between point and space never ceases to create effects of sacrality and delusion because they are folded together in our Kantian imagination. The battle between point and space need not be dramatised as a battle between systems. It is waged within every system due to the very character of a system: an ordered set of points in space. Thus the fold might be the most simple and crude expression because any architecture, from a topological point of view, consists of many folds.

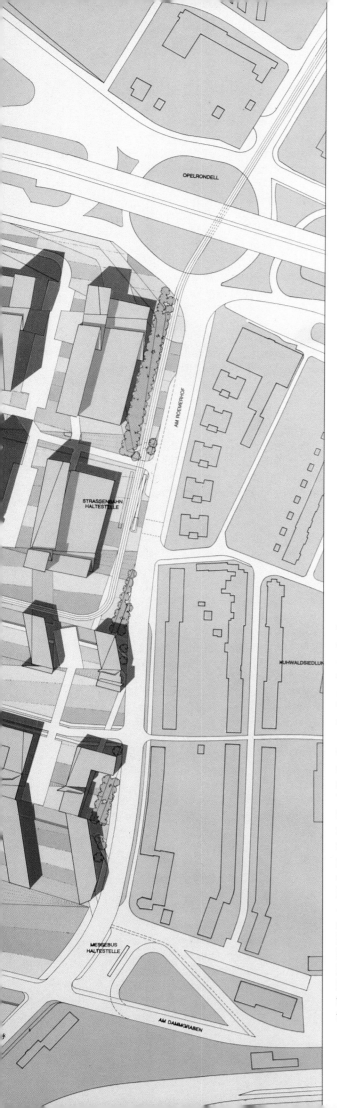

PETER EISENMAN
FOLDING IN TIME
The Singularity of Rebstock

Modern urbanism, which marked a radical change in urban form, was articulated in three different building types: the high-rise or point block; the piloti or the horizontally extruded slab and the *siedlung*. While all three played a dominant role in the development of the city in the 20th century it was the *siedlung* form which dominated German urbanism in the first half of the century. Nowhere was this evocation more prominent than in the area in and around the city of Frankfurt.

With the advent of the idea of mass production, multiplicity and repetition on the one hand and the need for health and hygiene on the other coupled with the emerging need for mass housing – a new housing industry and with it a new technology of standardisation was born. These new ideas of repetition and standardisation brought about a need to re-think urban form typology and in particular the perimeter block which had been the staple of German housing in the previous centuries. The problem with the perimeter block was twofold: on the one hand it conformed to an outdated urban pattern of streets which made each repetition unique rather than standard; and on the other hand the perimeter block was enclosing and therefore not metaphorically open to the new concerns for health and hygiene.

The *siedlung* form brought a new attitude to urban structure. In the 18th century, urban building was considered traditionally as ground with the void spaces as figure. This changed in the late 19th century when the grand boulevards and avenues cut through not only the existing fabric, but into the open land surrounding the cities where no urban pattern existed. Now the thoroughfares became the ground to figural building which defined its edges. The *siedlung* changed this again and the ground became a neutral datum, while the buildings which were still seen as figural had no relationship to any existing pattern. However, the *siedlung* was not a true figure in the sense of a perimeter block or a freestanding villa. It was a new linear type form that could be extended infinitely in one

direction. However, unlike the horizontal extrusions of Le Corbusier at Algiers and Nemours, it eschewed pattern for its autonomous condition of form. This autonomy brought a new principle to building typology. The *siedlung*, unlike any other previous building type had no back or front. In a sense it was all front since the apartments were entered on both sides of what was a conceptual line; a line which had no hierarchy and no regard for the traditional ideas of place and the public and private realm. In one sense the *siedlung* form with its denial of former patterns of land ownership and privilege was an ideal incarnation for the social ideas of the time. In the world of the *siedlung*, everyone and everywhere was equal. Whether of spatial modulation or individual identity, difference was homogenised in favour of an implacable idea.

Quite naturally such a totalising idealisation would be eventually problematised. This was the case in the immediate post-war years when the devastation of the European city required an urgent solution. Now, while the problem of the mass remained the same, the solution was of necessity to be different. No longer was the cool rationality and autonomy of the *siedlung* form thought to be sufficient to provide for the possibility of a restored urban fabric. In fact, the desolation of the *siedlung* was seen to be as much of a problem to the urban context as was the bombing. In the flight from the grim reality of post-war Germany, the *siedlung* was abandoned and the picturesque nostalgia of the perimeter block returned as an evocation of the past, now projected into the future present.

The argument proposed here is that the idea inherent in the *siedlung* type was not wrong but was rather poorly or inadequately conceptualised, particularly in relationship to the changing ideas of the individual and mechanical repetition. Therefore, it will be argued that it is not a return to the structures of the past that is the solution to urban form today, but is perhaps a reconsideration of the *siedlung* type with respect to ideas of the individual and repetition which may provide a possible context for a solution. This reconsideration of the *siedlung* is the basis for the urban strategy deployed in the Rebstock project.

Basically, this reconsideration deals with two aspects of 20th-century urbanism: space and time on the one hand and repetition and the individual on the other. What the *siedlung* did was to treat the idea of the individual unit within a new idea of the multiple; that is the repetitive unit was treated as if it were the same as the individual unit in the figuration of the perimeter block. In doing so it caused the individual unit to lose its specific identity. Whereas the unit in the perimeter block retained its individuality because of the overall specific character and figuration of the block, in the *siedlung* the block lost its identity and so did the individual unit.

This change in the idea of the individual unit in the *siedlung* can also be seen in the change in the role of individual expression. With the individual unit this change lies partly in the nature of the conception of its repetition. In this context, repetition not only involves space but also time. It will be argued here that the idea of repetition has been greatly altered by the shift from what can be called the mechanical paradigm to the present era of the electronic paradigm. The idea of repetition has changed because the idea of time has changed. Formerly, time in the mechanical paradigm was narrative, linear and sequential.

Now, because of media, time has lost its immediacy. Time can be speeded up or slowed down, replayed or fast-forwarded. The consequence of this change of the condition of time in the electronic media also clearly faces us with the loss of individual expression and response to an *immediate* or present action. This loss cannot be replaced by merely reinstating the old forms of individual expression, because media has brought about a permanent change in the nature of multiplicity and repetition. This difference became important as early as the late 19th century. The change is addressed by Walter Benjamin in his essay *Art in the Age of Mechanical Reproduction* in which he states that a photograph is clearly an original, although a different kind of original from that which, let us say, is crafted by hand. In one sense the art or the craft product, such as a handmade piece of furniture or a handmade book, is different from a book that is made on a mechanical press or a piece of bentwood furniture which is reproduced many times. In another

sense they are both original; the craft product being individual and the bentwood furniture multiple. Now there is a difference between the multiple or repetition in mechanical reproduction and repetition in electronic reproduction: this is the difference between a photograph and a telefax.

The photograph is produced mechanically. It is a product of repetition not a unique handmade artifact – that is, it is not an object of art as craft. The mechanical paradigm dealt with the shift in value from the individual hand (the hand of a painter as an original maker) to the value of the hand as intermediary (as in the developer of raw film); from the creation of an individual to the mediation of the multiple. The photograph can be manipulated by an individual to have more contrast, more texture, more tone. Thus, within the mechanical repetition of a photograph there remains a unique, individual quality; it remains a particular object, even within the idea of the multiple.

In electronic repetition, that is, the telefax, there is less human intervention, a less value-added dimension by the individual. Furthermore, the condition of the original is thrown into question. Whereas one can agree that there is an original negative plate for a photograph and that this plate can be reproduced, there is no negative plate in a telefax. The original that may be on a disk in a computer is no longer an object but rather a series of electronic impulses stored in a matrix. Even the disk original is often modified by corrections and thus a unique original is rarely kept. And in fact now, with telefax, the original may not even ever be sent so as to not confuse its reception with the reception of the telefax.

The question remains how does one make an urbanism in this new media time, a simultaneous time of narration and repetition? For this answer it is possible to introduce two interconnected concepts: the idea of the fold and the idea of singularity – concepts which are both active in the Rebstock project.

For Gilles Deleuze, the fold opens up a new conception of space and time. He argues in *Le Pli* that, 'Leibniz turned his back on Cartesian rationalism, on the notion of effective space and argued that in the labyrinth of the continuous the smallest element is not the point but the fold.' If this idea is taken into architecture it produces the following argument. Traditionally, architecture is conceptualised as Cartesian space, as a series of point grids. Planning envelopes are volumes of Cartesian space which seem to be neutral. Of course these

volumes of Cartesian space, these platonic solids that contain the stylisms and images of not only classical but also modern and post-modern space, are really nothing more than a condition of ideology taken for neutral or natural. Thus, it may be possible to take the notion of the fold – the crossing or an extension from a point – as an *other* kind of neutrality. Deleuze goes on to argue that Leibniz's notion of this extension is the notion of the event: 'Extension is the philosophical movement outward along a plane rather than downward in depth.' He argues that in mathematical studies of variation, the notion of object is change. This new object for Deleuze is no longer concerned with the framing of space, but rather a temporal modulation that implies a continual variation of matter. The continual variation is characterised through the agency of the fold: 'No longer is an object defined by an essential form.' He calls this idea of an object, an 'object event.'

The idea of event is critical to the discussion of singularity. Event proposes a different kind of time which is outside of narrative time or dialectical time. This other time, this outside of time begins to condition the idea of event as well as the idea of singularity. The latter attempts to restore that quality of individuality lost in the *siedlung*, without resorting to the static 19th century idea of individuality. Singularity can be defined as different from either the individual, the specific or the particular. Whereas the particular can always be defined in relation to the general, singularity can not. Singularity is always other, always different. Singularity is an individuality no longer able to belong to the realm of multiple as formerly defined. For singularity does not mean that a thing is simply unique. Singularity refers to the possibility in a repetition or a multiple for one copy to be different from another copy. The difference lies not so much in form, in size or in shape as in the distinction of a *this* thing from any other like thing. Singularity resides in this 'otherness' of the *time* of such a *this* thing; not so much in its form or space.

Place and time when no longer defined by the grid but rather by the fold, will still exist, but not as place and time in its former context, that is, as static, figural space. This other definition of time and place will involve both the simulacrum of time and place as well as the former reality of time and place. Narrative time is consequently altered. From here to there in space involves real time; only in mediated time, that is, the time of film or video, can time be speeded up or collapsed. Today the architecture of the event must deal with both times: its former time and future time of before and after and the media time, the time of the present which must contain the before and the after.

Events correspond to what Deleuze calls a heterogeneous series, which is organised into a system which is neither stable nor unstable; in other words, not in a dialectical either/or relationship but rather endowed with what can be called a potential energy. Potential energy is the energy of the event. Potential energy lies in the pre-present. An event is that which is previous to the present and which also lingers after. It includes the time of nothingness which is prior to and after the present of the event.

These events can never realise the old linear time of a stasis that inhabited those places, because today these very places are overwhelmed with a new mediated time of repetition – with speeding up and slowing down; with 'instant replays' that do not replicate narrative time. Therefore, any condition of place has to be more concerned with this 'other' notion of the particular and the specific which acknowledges this time of repetition. Image must be replaced by mapping, and individuality reconceptualised in the idea of singularity. This raises the possibility of reading the *siedlung* in another frame of reference, one different from the traditional figure-ground.

The *siedlung* form assumed a ground datum as both neutral and ideal. It was a ground that was infinitely extendable and repeatable – there was no specificity of context and thus no realisable edge or boundary, because the ground was neutral. Singularity is not something that emerges from a ground or from a figure form. It is the quality of unfolding in time that allows the possibility of singularity. Thus the fold can never be a neutral datum; it will always be a moment if not a specific object or place in time. As such, it can be an unstable or non-static being in time as well as place. The fold in this sense is neither a frame nor a figure as ground, but contains elements of both. Thus the ground of the Rebstock project must be distinguished from a ground as origin, or a ground as in figure-ground. The ground of Rebstock is no longer a datum or a base condition but rather is, in fact, something which already contains a condition of singularity; that is a groundlessness which can be said to be inherent in the notion of ground. It is a groundless ground. This groundless ground as realised at Rebstock is in the

possibility of the fold.

The folded ground of Rebstock inhabits a nether world of a time between the organic and the crystal; between surface and depth. The mediating device between the organism and the crystal is the idea of the membrane, and in the case of Rebstock it is the folded surface. The fold is an aspect of singularity. The fold is never the same, either in space or time. It is a physical condition of difference, of a 'thisness' rather than an 'objectness'. A folded surface maps relationships without recourse to size or distance; it is conceptualised in the difference between a topological and a Euclidean surface. A topological surface is a condition of mapping without the necessary definition of distance. And without the definition of distance there is another kind of time, one of a nomadic relationship of points. These points are no longer fixed by X, Y and Z co-ordinates; they may be called X, Y and Z but they no longer have a fixed, spatial place. In this sense they are without place, they are placeless on the topological ground. Thus, Rebstock uses the fold as an attempt to produce conditions of a singularity of place and time using the *siedlung*. Here the topological event, the dissolution of figure and ground into a continuum, reside physically in the fold; no longer in the point or the grid. The ground surface as a membrane which becomes a topological event/structure is also simultaneously the building form. This topological event/ structure which has a before and after as well as its own present is distinguished from pure media which has only a present. It is the time of art beyond media. If media time is concerned with time in the present – the time of the simulated event – then the time of singularity contains the time before and after within the present of the event itself.

The thought-to-be neutrality of the Cartesian grid or the Platonic solid was seen as a value – a place where order and rationality could begin to create specificity. The Cardos and Decumanus, the earliest articulation of gridded urban space, was if nothing else a specific symbolic point. The fold is a different kind of symbol, it is no longer about image or iconic representation, but rather about index and mapping its own being; a mapping of its thisness in time as an event or a spectacle. As the sublime was to the time of the classical, so too is the spectacle to the time of the fold. Thus, where the specificity of the grid referred to place, the singularity of the fold refers to time. In the movement from grid to fold place no longer remains the dominant

spatial condition. In the fold there is a specificity of location but now as a singularity not bound by traditional co-ordinates of space and time.

The use of the fold in Rebstock might reveal other conditions which may always have been immanent or repressed in the urban fabric of Frankfurt: conditions of singularity seen in terms of the ebb and flow of time which could reframe existing structures. The idea of the fold as a time event is neither a call for a radical intervention into the Rebstock area nor a return to the nostalgia of context as a tabula rasa. Rather, it is to see something which extends an existing context into time, producing in this extension the possibility of singularity. Due to the omnipresent simulacra of the electronic paradigm, a time-bound place has lost its placeness. It has moved to a kind of placeless, timeless condition. The fold attempts not to return place and time as they were formerly, but to bring them into the fold.

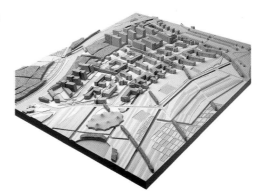

Previous Page: *Competition site plan;* Above: *Views of site*

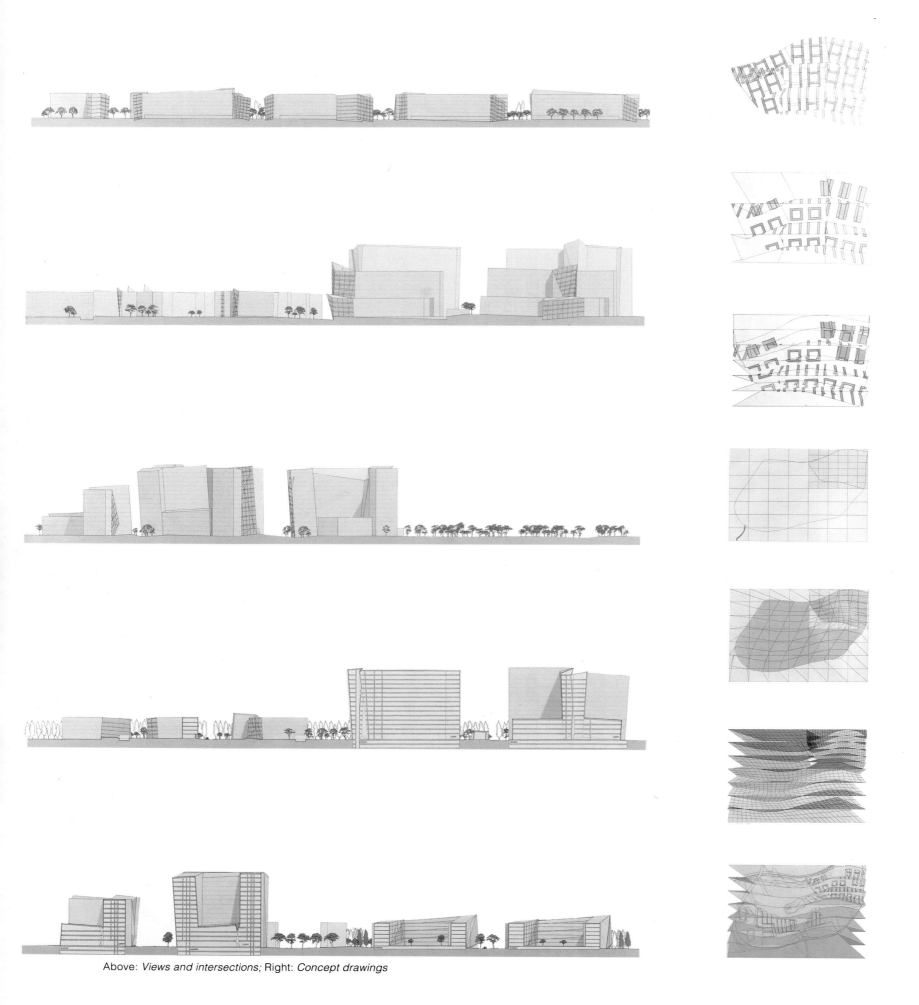

Above: *Views and intersections*; Right: *Concept drawings*

PETER EISENMAN
REBSTOCK PARK MASTERPLAN
Frankfurt, Germany

In the late 18th and early 19th century the typical perimeter housing and commercial block of German cities defined both the street space and the interior court space as positive. These spaces seemed literally to have been carved out of a solid block of the urban condition. In the mid-19th century with the development of the grand boulevards and allées a new kind of spatial structure appeared. The streets were still positive spaces but were lined with ribbon buildings, so that the rear yards became left over space. This idea led to the development of the German *siedlung* where, since there were no streets adjacent to the buildings, the backs and fronts were now the same. Now all of the open space was in a sense left over; the 'ground' became a wasteland. The object buildings seemed detached, floating on a ground that was no longer active.

Nowhere was this siedlung urbanism more prevalent than in the developing ring around the urban centre of Frankfurt. In the post war era, with the expansion of the autobahn and air travel, a new, more complex task faced urban development. The Rebstock Park masterplan endeavours to reassess the entire idea of a static urbanism, one which deals only with objects rather then events, by taking into account the evolving reality of a media age where dimension of the present becomes an important aspect of the past and the future. This new reading might reveal other conditions which may have always been immanent in the urban fabric allowing for the possibility of new urban structures and for existing structures to be seen in such a way that they too become displaced.

One such displacement possibility can be found in the very history of German thought. Leibniz conceived of matter as explosive and continuous; the smallest element is not the point, but the fold. Framed by a segment of the Mercator Grid, the Rebstock Park masterplan floats within a rectilinear container to obscure the residual position it occupies along Frankfurt's third green belt. By compressing the large grid segment onto the site perimeter and similarly compressing the small scale grid onto the close site, contingent readings emerge as the two site figures fold and unfold, each relative to its expanded position. The idea of the fold gives the traditional idea of edge a dimension. Rather than being seen as an abrupt line, this dimension provides both mediation and a reframing of conditions such as old and new, transport and arrival, commerce and housing. Thus the idea of folding was used on the site to initiate new social organisations of urban space and to reframe existing organisations.

Rebstock Park is a five million square foot housing and commercial development located on the perimeter ring of Frankfurt between the international airport and historic city centre. The project is the winning entry in an international competition. Work on the masterplan guidelines is scheduled for completion in early 1992 with building design slated to begin shortly thereafter.

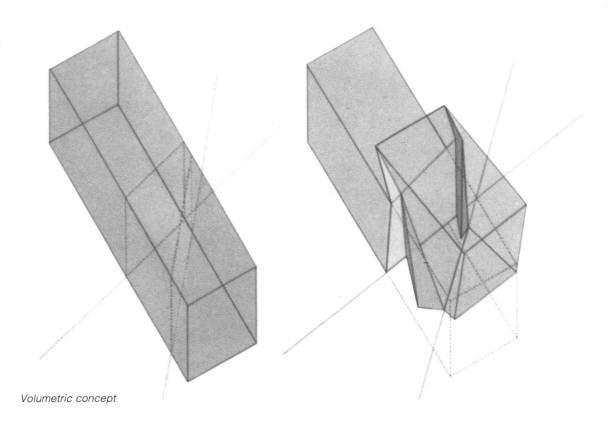

Volumetric concept

PETER EISENMAN
ALTEKA OFFICE BUILDING
Tokyo, Japan

Typological elevation

Tokyo, a paradigmatic city of accumulation, juxtaposition and compression is an index of contingent, tentative relations and new, complex urban realities. A city enfolded within the evolving reality of a mediated age, each site is a nexus of activity that each building tries to stabilise and repress; a series of discontinuous and 'monumental' episodes they are assumed to be essential and unchangeable .

Our project suggests an-other relationship to the city. For, situated within a condition caught between the traditional city fabric and the *Jigamae* – a new, large avenue (its angular shape the residue of the superposition of many consequent decision frames) – it suggests the notion that an object is no longer defined by an essential form where the idea of standard was one of maintaining an appearance of essence and of imposing a law of constancy, but of our actual situation where the fluctuation of the norm replaces the permanence of law when the object takes place in a continuum by variation. Thus with this other status the object doesn't correspond any more to a spatial mould but to a temporal modulation that implies a continual variation of the matter as much as a perpetual development of the form. This conception is not only temporal but quantitative of the object. The object becomes an event: it is 'eventalised', opening-up, un-folding. It is becoming.

The building's concept is related to this perpetual state of becoming: this evolution/involution. The typological 'el' frees its own folds from their usual subordination to the finite body, emerging from the context to fold/unfold, contract/dilate, envelope/develop, envolve/involve, compress/explode in a matter-fold participation that is a matter-time in which phenomena are like a continuous discharge. In the labyrinth of the continuous, the smallest element is not the point but the fold. The building evades its cartesian definition: not representing an essential form, but a form 'becoming'.

The Alteka project, a mixed use commercial venture in the Shibuya district, combines 30,000 ft ^{2} of retail and office space.

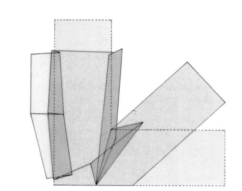

Infolding

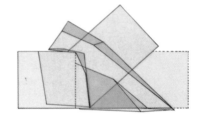

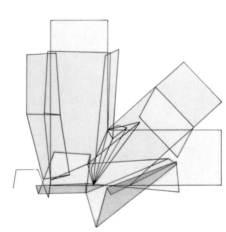

Unfolding

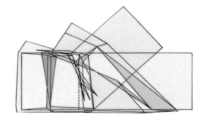

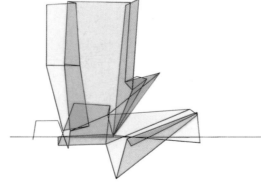

Envelop(e)

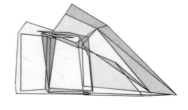

Above: *Schematic drawings*

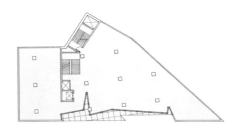 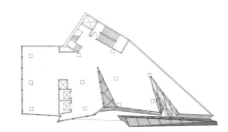 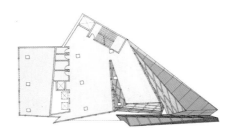

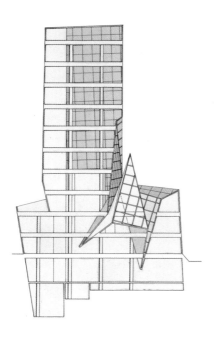 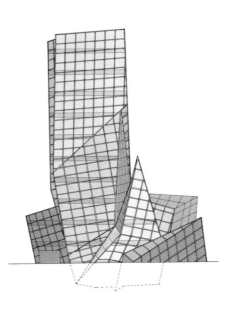 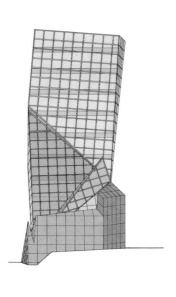

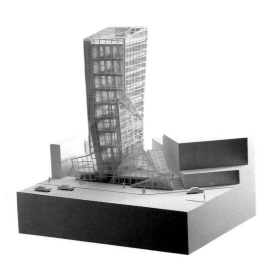 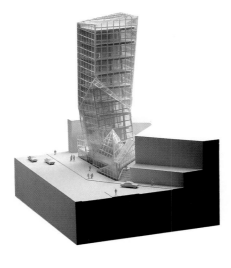 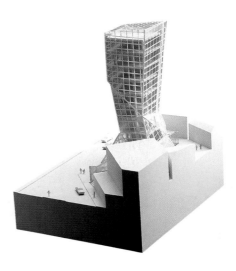

Above: *Basement level plan; second level plan; third level plan;* Centre: *Section to North; south elevation; east elevation;* Below: *Model views*

57

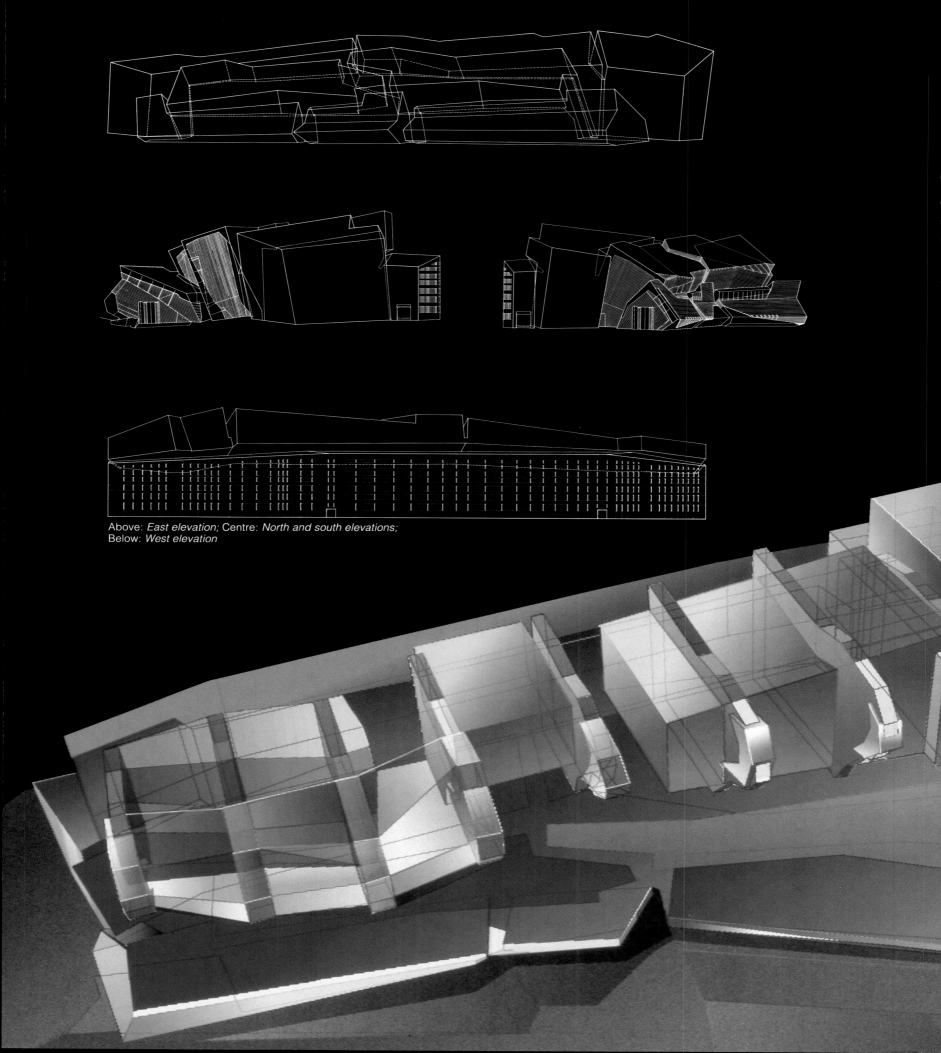

Above: *East elevation;* Centre: *North and south elevations;*
Below: *West elevation*

BAHRAM SHIRDEL
NARA CONVENTION HALL

Our goal for the Nara Convention Centre is to weave the three principle functions of a major civic building – the aesthetic/symbolic relationship to cultural context, the relationship to the immediate site, and the programmatic experience – into a complex spatial unity guided by the theme of the symbiosis of history and the future. To accomplish this, we have employed the space and the geometry of the FOLD. The spatial structure of the Fold establishes the architectural space of symbiosis; that is, a collaborative relationship between two distinct spaces. The geometry of the Fold lies between the pure abstract geometry of Modernism and the representational figure of Historicism. However, the Fold is not the simple synthesis of geometry and figure; rather, it is the situation in which the geo-

metric and the figurative collaborate without dominating. Using the Fold enabled us to attempt to realise the difficult goal of a symbiosis of history and the future.

The City of Nara is a distinct, anomalous entity participating in a symbiotic relationship with the dominant cultural tradition of Japan. To capture the feeling in the Convention Centre of one space operating collaboratively within another, explicit representational reference has been avoided. A more abstract language is employed to realise the spatial aspirations of the project. While the form of the building suggests both the traditional and modern aesthetics of context it is, on the other hand, entirely unique and mimics neither. The form relates to Nara as Nara relates to Japan.

In order to capture and experience the space of the Fold in the interior of the Convention Centre, the spatial structure echoes that of the Todai-ji Daibutsu-den which is entered on a frontal axis with the great Buddha. The Daibutsu and the two accompanying figures hover in the space of the Temple enclosure, which is thus confiscated by scale, mass and spiritual presence, creating a memorable spatial experience for resident and visitor alike.

The Convention Centre reveals how we

have adapted the transverse section of the Temple and floated the three great masses of the theatres within a single envelope. The relationship of the theatres to the figures of the Todai-ji Temple is echoed further in the choice of material. While the Temple figures are alive in the spiritual sense, the theatres of the Convention Centre are alive in the programmatic sense. However, in a distinct way from the frontal axis of the Daibutsu-den, we have oriented tangentially the relationship of the floating theatre forms to the visitor, to create a modern, secular axis and a striking vista. The visitor is compressed between the folded skin of the envelope and the presence of the theatres. Hence, he at once feels both the historical/spiritual memory of the space of the Daibutsu-den as well as the contemporary space of modernity. From the Space of the Fold, the visitor proceeds to the Geometry of the Fold. Having assembled in the main space, he moves to the theatres by way of escalators located within the piers. The organisation and form of the piers articulate the structural geometry of the Fold. The visitor lands on a mezzanine/lobby from where the entire space and form of the Centre can be viewed dramatically.

The massing of the building symbolises the transition from the permanence of ideal form to unpredictable changes of the earth. Offices and auxiliary services are located in a modern bar on the west side of the site. The movement from ideal form to the articulated form of the Fold can be discerned as the building proceeds from west to east. This bi-directional movement is symbolic of the movements of History and Culture; alternating between the Ideal and the Real, the East and the West. The Fold continues from the building into the Urban Park and landscape, creating a unity of form and site.

In order to unify the spatial effects further, the Y-diagram of the building is to be found in both section (as the Fold) and in plan. In the latter, the diagram frames the relationship between the Centre and Rail Station; capturing and unifying space of the main processional.

Opposite, From Above: *Transverse section; ground floor plan; second floor plan; first floor plan;* Left: *Axonometric massing;* Centre: *Folded space grid;* Below: *Folded axonometric massing*

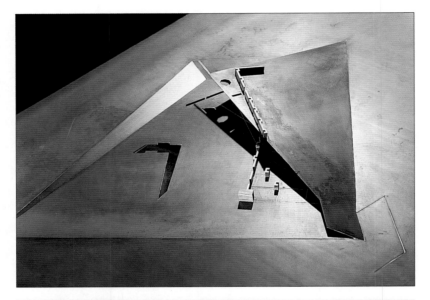

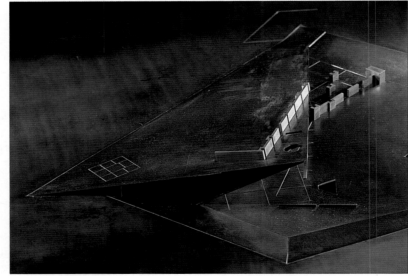

CARSTEN JUEL- CHRISTIANSEN
THE ANHALTER FOLDING

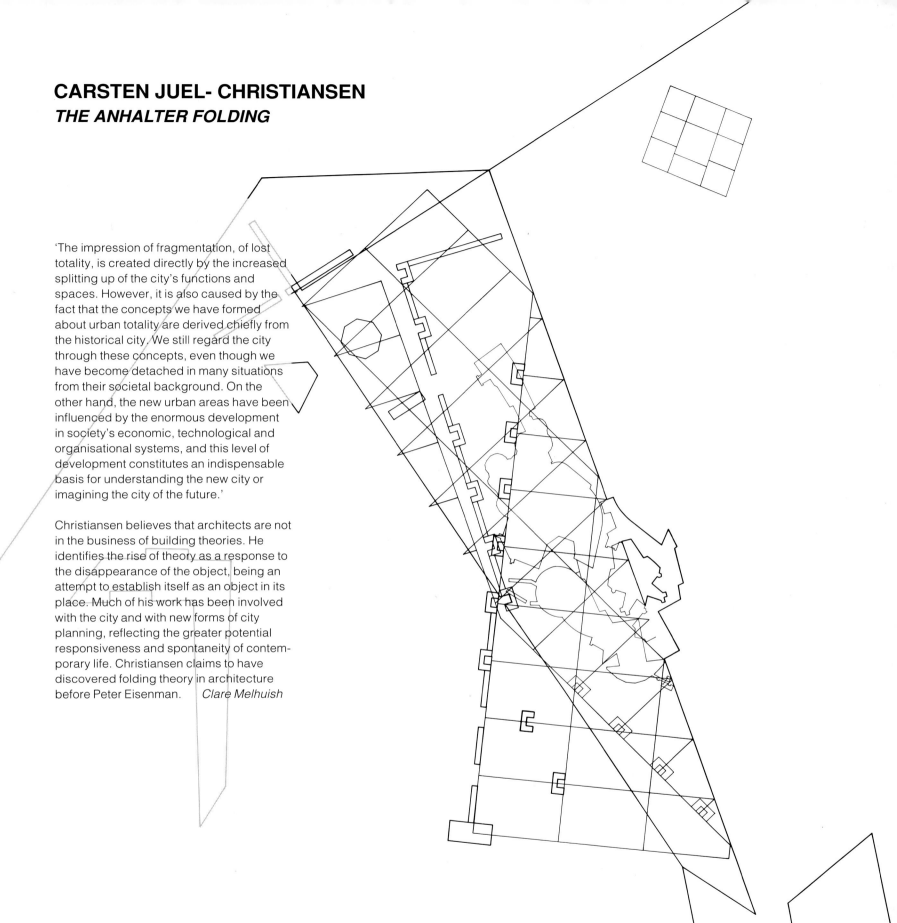

'The impression of fragmentation, of lost totality, is created directly by the increased splitting up of the city's functions and spaces. However, it is also caused by the fact that the concepts we have formed about urban totality are derived chiefly from the historical city. We still regard the city through these concepts, even though we have become detached in many situations from their societal background. On the other hand, the new urban areas have been influenced by the enormous development in society's economic, technological and organisational systems, and this level of development constitutes an indispensable basis for understanding the new city or imagining the city of the future.'

Christiansen believes that architects are not in the business of building theories. He identifies the rise of theory as a response to the disappearance of the object, being an attempt to establish itself as an object in its place. Much of his work has been involved with the city and with new forms of city planning, reflecting the greater potential responsiveness and spontaneity of contemporary life. Christiansen claims to have discovered folding theory in architecture before Peter Eisenman.   *Clare Melhuish*

GREG LYNN
STRANDED SEARS TOWER

This project is a response to an ideas competition held for the city of Chicago: the American city which has the richest tradition of competitions for architectural monumentality. Along with the airport, the corporate office tower has been the primary vehicle for innovations in urban monumentality in Chicago and the United States in general. This project attempts to reformulate the image of the American monument by reconfiguring the existing dominant icon on the Chicago skyline and the tallest freestanding building in the world: the Sears Tower. The existing Sears Tower is disassociated from its context in order that it can stand as an icon. It establishes itself as a discrete and unified object within a continuous and homogeneous urban fabric. This project attempts to affiliate the structure of the tower with the heterogeneous particularities of its site while maintaining monumental status. The monument must maintain its presence while remaining flexible enough to exploit possible involvements with the particularities of context. By laying the structure into its context and entangling monolithic mass with local contextual conditions, a new monumentality emerges from the old forms.

'Buildings are no longer obelisks, but lean one upon the other, no longer suspicious of the other, like a statistical graph. This new architecture incarnates a system that has ceased to be competitive, but is compatible; where competition has disappeared for the benefit of correlations.'

In *The Order of Simulacra* Jean Baudrillard describes a new paradigm for the contemporary office tower in the United States. The previous paradigm of competitive verticality was supplemented with a desire not only for excessive size but for excessive numbers. The Twin Towers, New York inaugurated this tendency toward multiplicity through double identity. Duplication reinforces self-identity of the identical twins as they merge into a singular monumental structure. The response of the Sears Tower to this new (York) paradigm, lay not only in exceeding the height of the Twin Towers but in exceeding its duplicity.

The Sears Tower internalised its multiplication by dividing differentially into the record nine towers which Fazlur Kahn termed the 'bundled tube'. Where the identical Twin Towers duplicate, the differentiated Sears Tower proliferates. 'The basis of the Sears Tower is the bundled tube. In the Tower, nine contiguous tubes, in essence nine towers 75 feet square, make up the 50 storey base of the building. Their tubes are interlocked; thus each tube helps to support its neighbour.'

The 225 foot square footprint is made up of nine 75 foot square tubes; two of which are 650 feet in length; two are 860 feet in length; three are 1,170 feet in length; and the last two of a record 1,450 feet in length. Each tube is striated into five structural bays yielding another 25 tubes per tower. Each of these 225 independent structural bays is subdivided into three five-foot window bays yielding another nine-square tube within each structural bay for a total of 2,025 tubes. The bundled tubes are a multiplicity; as a construction that is simultaneously one and many. The Sears Tower is at once single and multiple as if it were a strand: a collection of 'fibres or filaments twisted, plaited or laid parallel to form a unit.' This strand is both a system of interwoven filaments and a singularity capable of further twisting or plaiting into a larger or more complex yarn, thread, rope or cordage.

This project reformulates the vertical bundle of tubes horizontally along a strand of land between Wacker Drive and the Chicago River's edge adjacent to the existing Sears Tower. To engender affiliations with particular local events, the rigid geometry that dictated the exact parallel relations between tubes was rejected for a more supple description. Through a geometry that is more supple, the nine contiguous tubes accommodate themselves fluidly and flexibly to the multiple and often discontinuous borders of the site. The relations between tubes are not exactly parallel. These supple deflections allow connection to take place which would have been repressed by a more rigid and reductive geometric system of description. Although the increments of the floor plates are oriented perpendicularly to the surface of the drawings in general, the particularities to the river's edge, roads and sidewalks often deflect any single ideal orientation in favour of multiple oblique orientations. The deformations of twisting result from the external forces within the context. These more supple systems are the techniques employed in the surveying of land forms, in fluid dynamics and other empirical sciences which cannot reduce matter to purely geometric or ideal quantities. The nine initial strands untangle themselves further to align to finer grain local conditions by bifurcating along the lines of their structure and fenestration. The context provides these lines of bifurcation to the tubes and these become potential lines for the projects proliferation into the site. A single body begins to become multiplicitous because of these lines of development imposed from the outside. The bundled tube is a potential paradigm for a multiplicitous monument. It is an assembly of micro-systems which constructs an icon which is provisional. Upon close examination the unified image of the monument unravels into heterogeneous local events. Irreducibility to any single type and the potential to participate with external systems are the characteristics of a stranded and supple urbanism. The Stranded Sears Tower is neither discrete nor dispersed but rather defers any single organisational idea for a system of local affiliations outside itself. The strands exploit possible connections with and between adjacent buildings, sidewalks, bridges, tunnels and landforms. These connections are not accidental but unpredicted as they result from the combination of the disparate systems of the 2,025 bundled tubes with the existing site. The resultant image is neither monolithic nor pluralistic but is of the now supple and flexible internal order of the 'bundled tube' that is differentiated by the external forces of the river's edge, the Chicago grid and the vectors of pedestrian and transportation movement.

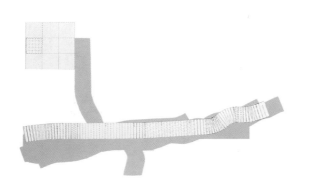

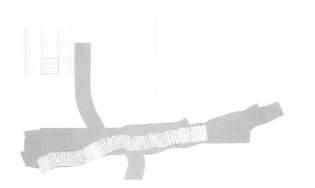

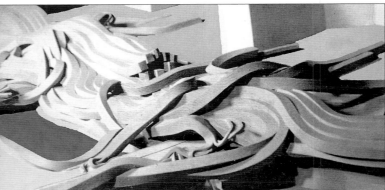

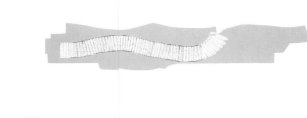

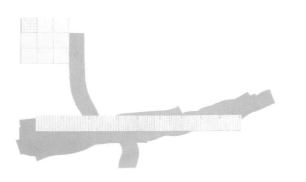
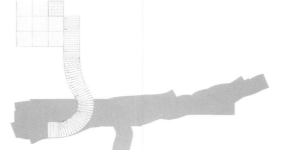

Previous page: *View of model*; Above: *Plans, sections and views of model*

66

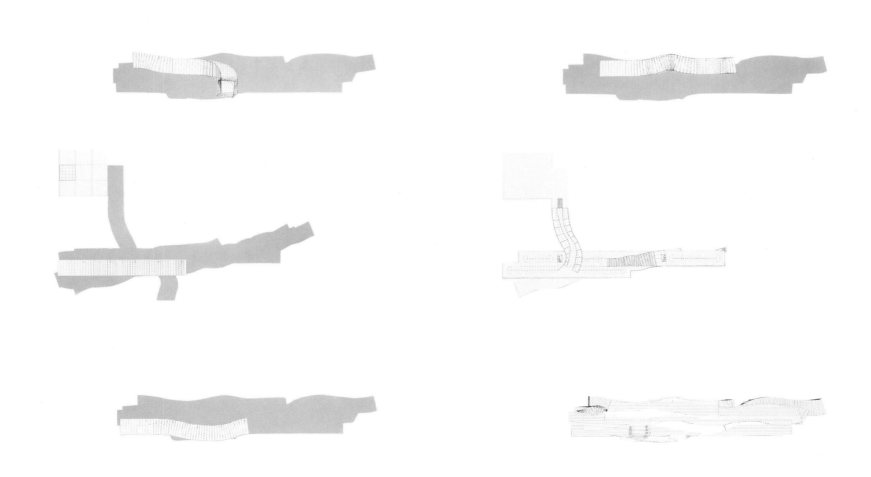

FRANK GEHRY AND PHILIP JOHNSON
LEWIS RESIDENCE
Cleveland, Ohio

The Lewis Residence to be built on a hilltop in Lyndhurst, a suburb of Cleveland is a 22,000 square foot house for Peter Lewis, an insurance executive. Functioning as a mix of semi-public areas for entertaining and private areas for residents, the complex includes a main house with living room, dining room, two master bedroom suites, hall/gallery, library, exercise area and an enclosed lap pool. There are also three guest houses and a six car garage.

The house is a collaborative effort between Frank Gehry and Philip Johnson. Gehry's sweeping sail-like forms of the main house are in contrast to the euclidean geometries of the guest suites by Johnson.

The design of the house is conceived of as a composition of complex curved elements that will be constructed from a variety of materials including stone, metal and glass. The participation of trades and artisans in the process is integral to the form-making envisioned. 3-D computer modelling can provide the means on this project for reintegrating the architects with the trades.

The residence is organised around a main court that is cut into the hilltop. The court can be tented for lavish affairs and compliments the main hall and gallery.

Opposite: *Detail of model;* Left: *Site plan;* Above: *Model;* Below: *Site model*

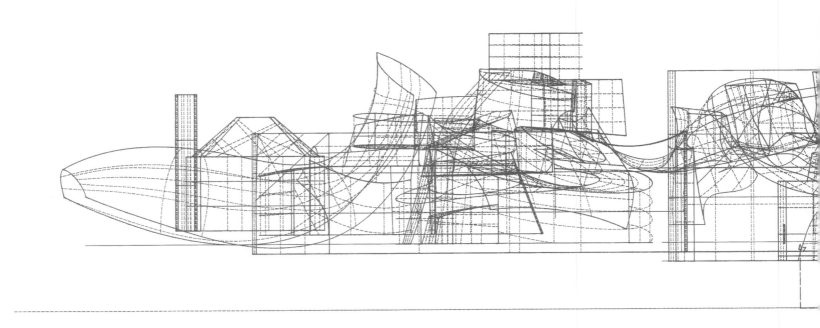

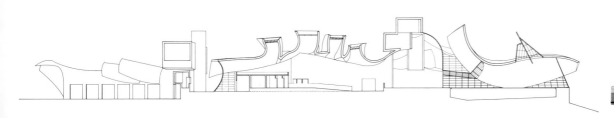

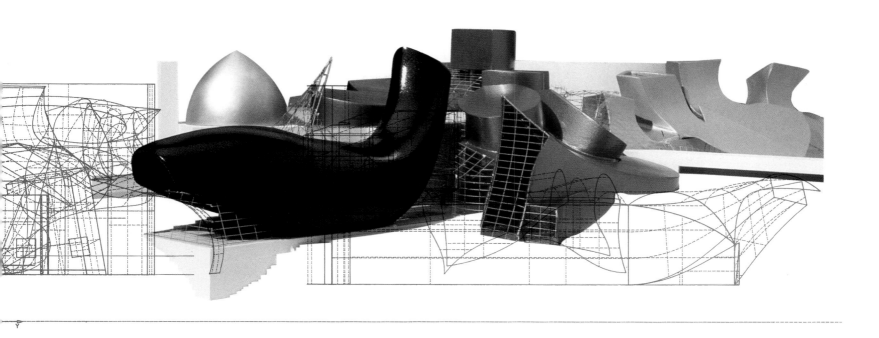

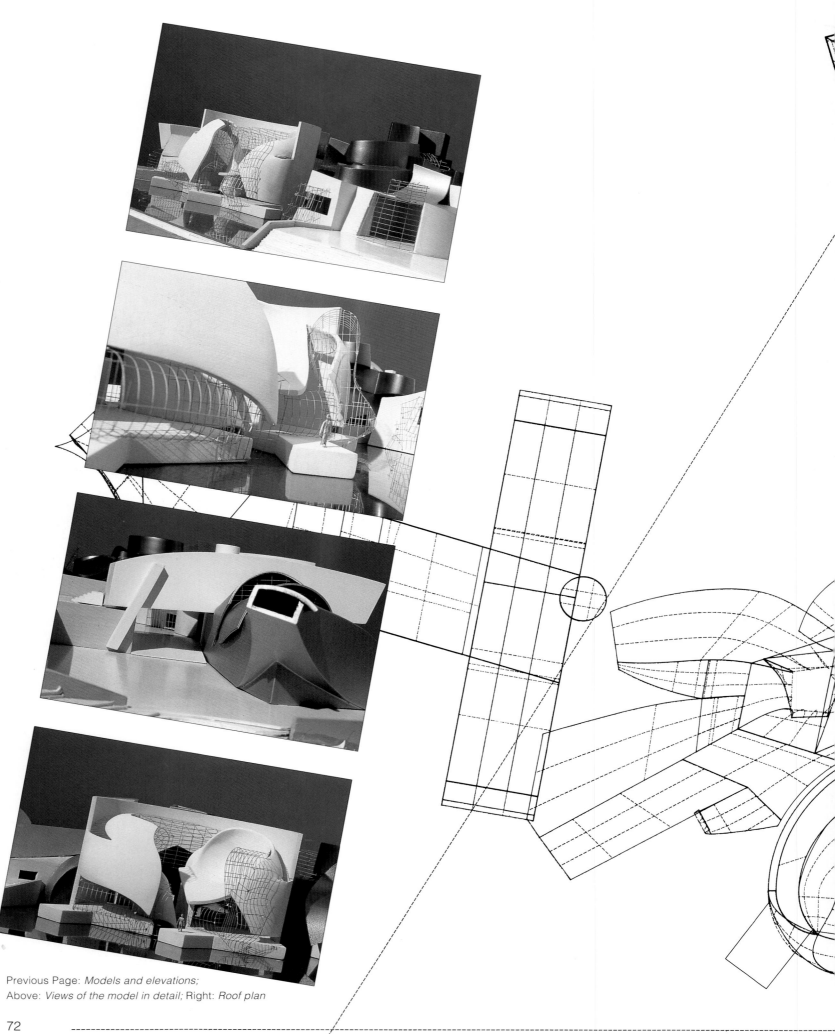

Previous Page: *Models and elevations;*
Above: *Views of the model in detail*; Right: *Roof plan*

FRANK O GEHRY

THE GUGGENHEIM MUSEUM

Bilbao, Spain

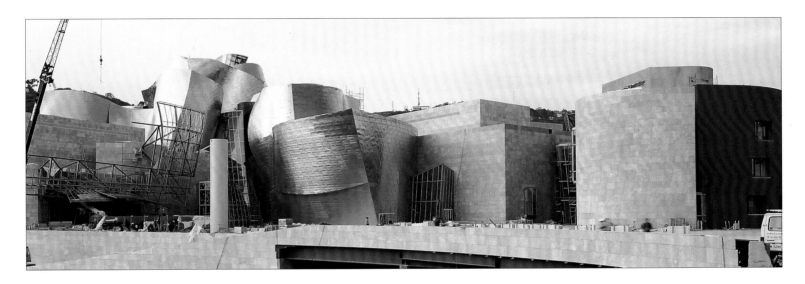

The site for the museum is in a prominent location at the edge of the river bank where the main vehicular bridge crosses it, between the Museo de Bellas Artes and the City Hall. It is very close to the major business district of the city which was created on a 19th-century street grid. Connections to the city via tree-lined walkways and public spaces, plazas and the river front promenade are emphasised in the scheme. Vistas from the city have been created so that the river is visible through the buildings.

The scale of the expressed building parts relates to the existing buildings across the road and river, while the height of the atrium roof relates to the adjacent roof tops. The tall tower at the east end of the scheme 'captures' the bridge and makes it part of the building composition. Bilbao's river has been very important in its history and this is reflected in the introduction of the large areas of water in the project.

The programme for this design requested a 30,000 square-metre world class, modern and contemporary art museum including three different types of exhibition space: permanent site and specific installations; and temporary exhibition galleries. Additionally, the design includes other public facilities such as a 400-seat auditorium, a restaurant, a café, retail space, and a large central atrium/orientation space which was envisioned to function almost as a public town square. Loading, parking, support, storage and administrative office space is also included but because of the unique nature of the collection, the proportion of front-of-house to back-of-house space is about 2:1, as opposed to a more normal ration of 1:2.

The programme of the museum is distributed on the site in several interconnected buildings, with a large central atrium space with its figural roof unifying the composition. Parking and back-of-house support facilities are located on the lowest levels adjacent to the truck dock and freight elevators.

The entry plaza leads into the central space which is surrounded on all four levels by galleries and has a large glass wall facing on to the river. Ramps and stairs provide access to the roof terraces where there are views out over the river and city. The external circulation also provides opportunities for routing large crowds during 'blockbuster' shows outside the flow of normal circulation.

Gallery spaces are articulated as large rectangular volumes stacked upon one another, some of up to 30 metres width at the east end under the tall tower and column free space. Skylights are provided via the sculptural roof forms above the temporary exhibition gallery building and a shaft through the west gallery. Gallery ceiling heights are generally maintained at six metres or more.

The auditorium is located on the entry plaza so that it can be used independently or as part of the museum. A restaurant is located at the north-west corner of the site overlooking the river and a café is located by the river walk.

The major materials for the gallery buildings are limestone and sandblasted stainless steel, both of which are available locally. The structure is a composite of concrete and steel frame with a tense ring created to hold the atrium roof together. Mechanical systems are designed to maintain appropriate levels of control for the various uses. An access floor is used throughout the gallery space to allow flexibility for the infrastructure.

Lighting will be a combination of indirect ambient light; direct exhibition light from a flush flat monopoint system; and filtered daylight from skylights and windows.

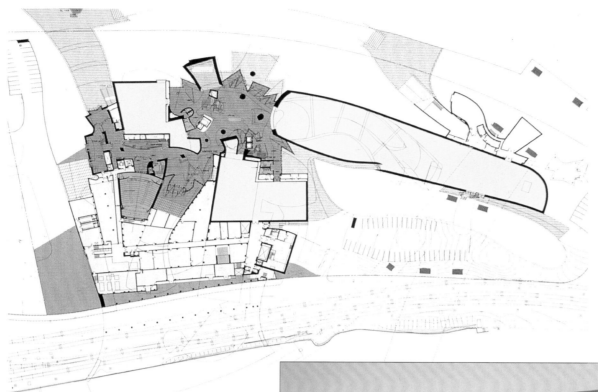

ABOVE: First floor plan; BELOW: Computer-generated perspectives

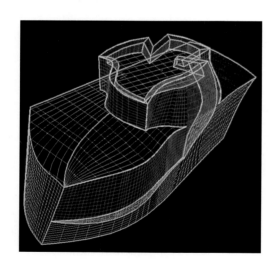

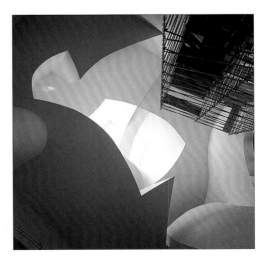

DANIEL LIBESKIND
BETWEEN THE LINES
Berlin

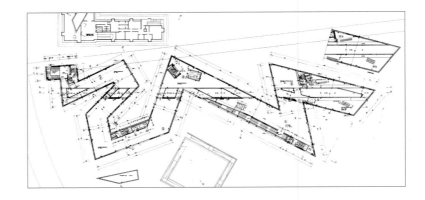

The official name of the project is the 'Extension of the Berlin Museum with the Jewish Museum Department' but I have called it 'Between the Lines'. I call it this because it is a project about two lines of thinking, organisation and relationship. One is a straight line, but broken into many fragments; the other is a tortuous line, but continuing infinitely. These two lines develop architecturally and programmatically through a limited but definite dialogue. They also fall apart, become disengaged, and are seen as separated. In this way, they expose a void that runs through this museum and through Architecture – a discontinuous void.

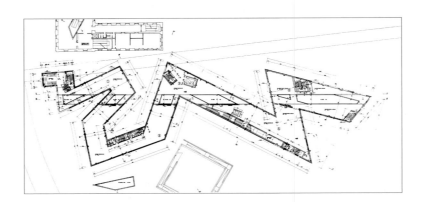

The site is the centre of the old city of Berlin on Lindenstrasse, near the famous Baroque intersection of Wilhelmstrasse, Friedrichstrasse and Lindenstrasse. At the same time, I felt that the *physical* trace of Berlin was not the only trace but rather that there was an invisible matrix or anamnesis of connections in relationship. I found this connection between figures of Germans and Jews; between the particular history of Berlin, and between the Jewish history of Germany and of Berlin.

I felt that certain people and particularly certain writers, scientists, composers, artists and poets formed the link between Jewish tradition and German culture. So I found this connection and I plotted an irrational matrix which was in the form of a system of squared triangles which would yield some reference to the emblematics of a compressed and distorted star: the yellow star that was so frequently worn on this very site.

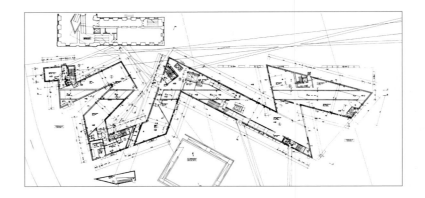

I looked for addresses of where these people lived or where they worked. For example, someone like Rachel Varnhagen I connected to Friedrich Schleiermacher, and Paul Celan to someone like Mies van der Rohe and so on, and I was quite surprised that it was not so difficult to sense and plot the addresses of these people; that they formed a particular urban and cultural constellation of Universal History. This is one aspect of the project.

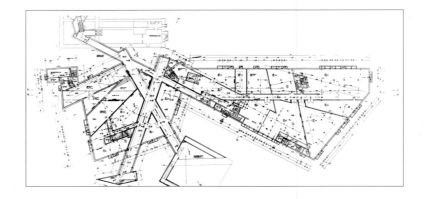

FROM ABOVE: Second floor plan; first floor plan; ground floor plan; basement plan; OPPOSITE: View of Holocaust void

OPPOSITE: View up main stair;
ABOVE: Finished facade
RIGHT: Aerial view

Another aspect was Arnold Schoenberg. I was always interested in the music of Schoenberg and in particular his period in Berlin. His greatest work is an opera called *Moses and Aaron*. For some reason the logic of the text, which was the relationship between Moses and Aaron – between, one can say, the revealed and unimaginable truth and the spoken and mass-produced people's truth – led to an impasse in which the music, the text written by Schoenberg, could not be completed. In the end, Moses doesn't sing, he just speaks, 'oh word, thou word': a form of communication which is opposed to the norm of opera wherein performance usually obliterates the text. When there is singing the words can not be understood but when it has ceased one understands very well the missing word uttered by Moses, which is the call for the deed. This was the second aspect of the project.

The third aspect was my interest in the names of those people who were deported from Berlin during the fatal years of the Holocaust, that one knows only historically. I received from Bonn two very large volumes called *Gedenkbuch*, which make a strong impression because all they contain are names; just names, dates of birth, dates of deportation and presumed places where these people were murdered. So I looked for the names of all the Berliners and where they had died – in Riga, in Lodz, in all the concentration camps.

The fourth aspect of the project, which is formed by Walter Benjamin's *One Way Street*, is incorporated into the continuous sequence of 60 sections along the zig-zag, each of which represents one of the 'Stations of the Star' described in his text.

To summarise this four-fold structure: the first aspect is the invisible and irrationally connected star which shines with absent light of individual address; the second one is the cut of Act II of *Moses and Aaron* which has to do with the non-musical fulfilment of the word; the third aspect is that of the deported or missing Berliners, and the fourth aspect is Walter Benjamin's urban apocalypse along the One Way Street.

In specific terms it is a very large building: more than 10,000 square metres. Its budget is something like 120 million Deutschmarks. The building goes under the existing building, crisscrosses underground and materialises itself independently on the outside. The existing building is tied to the extension underground, preserving the contradictory autonomy of both the old building and the new building on the surface, while binding the two together in depth, underground.

Out of the terminus of history, which is nothing other than the Holocaust with its concentrated space of annihilation and complete burn-out of meaningful development of the city, and of humanity – out of this event which shatters this place comes that which cannot really be related by architecture. The past fatality of the German-Jewish cultural relation in Berlin is enacted now in the realm of the invisible. (It is this remoteness which I have tried to bring to consciousness.)

The work is conceived as a museum for all Berliners, for all citizens. Not only those of the present, but those of the future and the past who should find their heritage and hope in this particular place, which is to transcend involvement and become participation. With its special emphasis on housing the Jewish Museum, it is an attempt to give a voice to a common fate – to the contradictions of the ordered and disordered, the chosen and not chosen, the vocal and silent.

Thus the new extension is conceived as an emblem, where the invisible – the void – makes itself apparent as such. The void and the invisible are the structural features that have been gathered in the space of Berlin and exposed in an architecture in which the unnamed remains in the names which keep still.

In terms of the city, the idea is to give a new value to the existing context, the historical context, by transforming the urban field into an open and what I would call a hope-oriented matrix. The proposed expansion, therefore, is characterised by a series of real and implied transformations of the site. The compactness of traditional street patterns is gradually

dissolved from Baroque origins and then related diagonally across to the 1960s housing development and the new IBA projects.

In other words, to put it simply, the museum is a zig-zag with a structural rib which is the void of the Jewish Museum running across it. And this void is something which every participant in the museum will experience as his or her absent presence.

That is basically a summary of how the building works. It is not a collage or a collision or simply a dialectic, but a new type of organisation which is organised around a centre which is not: the void around what is not visible. And what is not visible is the collection of this Jewish Museum, which is reducible to archival and archeological material since its physicality has disappeared.

The problem of the Jewish Museum in Berlin is taken as the problem of culture itself. Let us put it this way as the problem of an avant-garde humanity; an avant-garde that has been incinerated in its own history, in the Holocaust. In this sense, I believe this scheme joins architecture to questions that are now relevant to all humanity. What I have tried to convey is that the Jewish history of Berlin is not separable from the history of Modernity, from the destiny of this incineration of history: they are bound together. However, they are bound not through any obvious forms but rather through a negativity; through an absence of meaning of history and an absence of artefacts.

Absence, therefore serves as a way of binding in depth, and in a totally different manner, the shared hopes of people. It is a conception which is absolutely opposed to reducing the museum or architecture to a detached memorial or to a memorable detachment. A conception, rather, which reintegrates Jewish Berlin History through the unhealable wound of faith, which in the words of Thomas Aquinas is the 'substance of things hoped for; proof of things invisible'.

Transcript of a talk given at Hannover University, 5th December, 1989

OPPOSITE: Detail of facade

DANIEL LIBESKIND

THE VICTORIA & ALBERT MUSEUM BOILERHOUSE EXTENSION
London

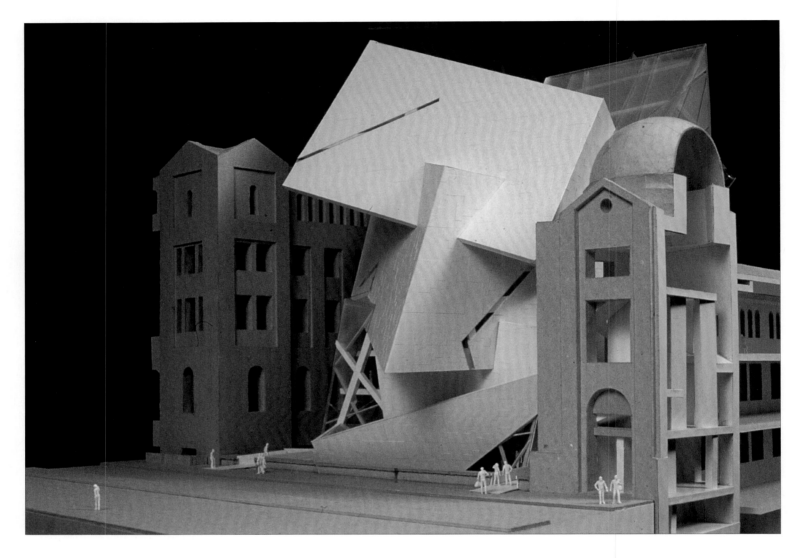

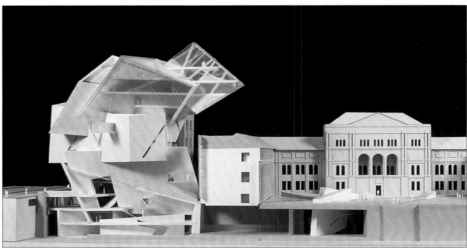

Model perspectives

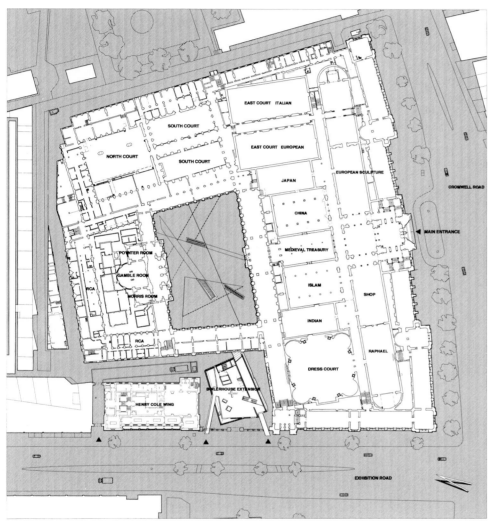

Location plan

When facing the old entrance of the Victoria & Albert Museum, one is confronted by two words to the left and right of the main gate: *Imagination* and *Knowledge*. This twin inscription describes the inspirational force, or muse, steering the idea of the museum. In the next century, this profound dialectic must continue to engage the wide public and open the experience of the visitor to new ways of viewing and using the museum. The museum of the 21st century must itself be open to the future of still unknown possibilities lodged between these guideposts.

The Victoria & Albert Museum has taken up this challenge with a proposal to build an extension including an integrated mixture of exhibition spaces, educational facilities and accommodation for new methods of interactive orientation. The V&A's mission to provide a gateway to the 21st century via its own rich and diverse collection requires a vision that gives new significance to its great traditions and goes beyond the purely passive relation between the arts and the public. This proposal offers new kinds of experience eluding the closure that would categorise the museum as 'ready-made', rigidly defined, or passively neutral.

The design (1996-99) is structured around three dimensions: the spiral movement of art and history; the interlocking of inside and outside, and the labyrinth of discovery. It takes these dimensions and translates them into a coherent ensemble of functionally related spaces.

The spiral of art and history manifests itself in the overall form of the extension building and its circulation system. The enclosure is created out of a continuous wall, whose extent mirrors that of the perimeter walls of the entire V&A block, spiralling around a virtual and ever shifting vertical axis. Visitors are implicated in a spiral movement as they circulate through the various functions of the museum. This movement distributes the public in a dynamic way to the rest of the museum through strategic connections

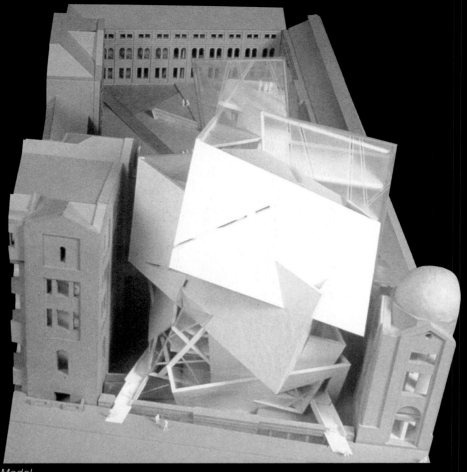

Model

and is a counterpoint to the lateral, horizontal movement in the existing buildings.

Interlocking of the inside and the outside of the new building is created by the winding and the unwinding spiral which brings the visitor into close relation with history and the present, the city and the museum, through a direct experience of interpenetrating views and histories. From the extension one sees ever-changing views of the existing facades and the skyline of London, while from within the old museum block, one is reoriented by the shifting movement of the new building.

The relationship between form and function generates a variety of sequential and dramatic narratives of space and light. The whole is a composition of layered sequences in which the new building becomes a veritable beacon of energy towards the inside and outside world.

The labyrinth of discovery is the organisational leitmotiv mediating between the existing galleries and the museum's new programme requirements. The image of the labyrinth is not only a symbolic device but a reinforcement and intensification of the unique qualities of the V&A. This emblem of a heterogeneous and open system of organisation for the artefacts and exhibitions provides a diversity of experiences woven into a net of similarities and differences – an aggregate of traces about unexpected topoi still to be explored. The seamless transition from place to place, and floor to floor envelops the visitor in a unique continuity throughout the many dimensions of the Museum as a whole.

The spiral form fuses the archaic and the new in its organisation and urban image. It provides an emblem articulating the cross-cultural collections of the V&A, the multi-cultural profile of its visitors and the fusion of the arts, technology and

history. The structure of discovery in the new extension is a microcosm of the multi-faceted order of the museum and a gateway to the history of the decorative arts. The visitors are celebrated as participants in the sensory and intellectual experience, an ongoing discovery of the drama of art and its history.

The structure and cladding of the new extension are formed by the 'fractile', a new kind of tile pattern whose economy allows a multiform language to emerge out of an elementary geometric piece, interpreted in a variety of different ways. As a strategy towards the surface, the 'fractile' bridges the gap between the wondrous tiles of Granada and Isfahan and the tile technology used on the space shuttle, bringing the decorative arts onto the surface of the building. This pattern offers endless variation in formal articulation and the relationship between surface and structure within the economy of building construction. The design of motifs and patterns could be developed through the educational activities of the museum via an interactive participation programme, so that the building surface becomes an ongoing expression of unpredictable yet controlled interactions between Arts and Crafts, around the theme of the contemporary museum.

The new extension is divided into two parts:

• In the upper levels, an interactive field continuum of traditional and non-Cartesian spaces is enclosed within the folds of the spiral. These floors house the new galleries for the permanent collections, the orientation centre and the museum administration on several upper floors. The exhibition galleries are lifted out of the anonymity with which such spaces are often associated, and instead articulate a new configuration responding to the creative tension between spatial relation and programmatic field. Out of these special qualities, spaces are created which can accommodate a wide variety of exhibitions, from traditional installations to new events emerging out of technological media forms. In this way, the kinetic and sensory experience offers multiple ways of discovering the familiar.

• In the levels below the street, one finds a highly modern gallery for temporary exhibitions, educational facilities and an auditorium for performances, theatre, lectures and film. These diverse activities are organised within a rigorous functional system designed for maximum flexibility. These spaces extend under the existing buildings into the Pirelli gardens, tying the extension in depth to the heart of the museum complex and functioning as the foundation for the galleries above – the infrastructure supporting the lantern of history.

These two parts are separated by the entrance lobby spaces, which the visitor enters across a bridge overlooking a new sunken garden out of which the building grows. In this way an open and inviting new entrance is created as an exhilarating symbol of the dynamics of the museum's diverse exhibitions. Fronting and visible from the street is a gift shop and bookstore, welcoming the visitor into the museum lobby. Once inside, one sees the central position of the information and ticket desk and the core of elevators.

The lobby space extends vertically down to the restaurant and children's play area directly below which look out over the new garden. These two levels form a unit constituting the lobby space as a whole, connected at ground level to the existing buildings.

From the lobby, visitors to the museum's collections take the glazed express elevator directly to the observatory of the orientation centre on the top floor; glimpsing along the way the offerings in the new permanent collection galleries. From here, overlooking the Pirelli Garden and the roofscape of the entire museum, a route around the galleries can be planned using the materials and technologies of the centre. Next to this is a café/bar looking over the museum and the city. The route from here to the museum proper takes the visitor on a spiral descent via escalators to the new galleries housing the permanent collection and back towards the lobby. Linkages to the rest of the museum's collections are located on various levels along this route, allowing direct connection from multiple points.

Visitors to the museum who wish to see the temporary exhibition, or use the educational facilities, access these spaces by descending directly from the lobby; passing on their way the restaurant and children's play area. The auditorium is directly underneath this, on the same level as the temporary exhibition galleries which extend under the Pirelli Garden. From this point, a staircase leads straight to the educational facilities and workshops beneath and a ramp rises into the garden creating a connection between the changing exhibitions, the learning facilities and the rest of the museum. The garden itself is restructured as a dynamic landscape punctuated by skylights which provide the temporary exhibition galleries and educational spaces with natural light.

From Exhibition Road a second bridge offers alternative access to the lobby and direct entrance for groups to the temporary exhibitions, auditorium and educational facilities. By lowering the Webb Screen to face the garden, it becomes the frame for an outdoor exhibition space, visible from the lower levels of the new extension. In this way Aston Webb's architecture is given new significance; no longer a screen but a frame for activity and a stage for events.

The administration spaces of the programme are located on several floors at the top of the spiral near the orientation centre, with separate access via a bridge link to the Henry Cole Wing. The offices are provided with views of the existing museum buildings and are connected to the new exhibition spaces by an atrium. Although embedded within the exhibition galleries they can thus function completely independently of the public parts of the extension.

The new museum for the V&A, constructed on its last available site (1998-2001), is perhaps best likened to the last chord of a symphony. Only when this chord is played do the first notes acquire the form of their fulfilment. This proposal extends the zone of boundaries and connections (between old/new; inside/outside; structure/form; architecture/decoration; technology/craft) by shifting them to ever new and open perspectives, intersections and relations through its fugal construction. By opening instead of closing the block of the V&A, this last chord does not end the music of the museum, but extends it towards unknown and future horizons of the mind and of space.

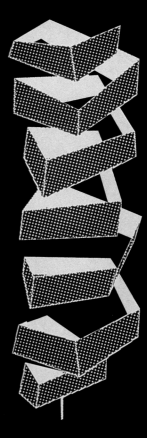

Engineering design diagram of wall

87

FOREIGN OFFICE ARCHITECTS
YOKOHAMA INTERNATIONAL PORT TERMINAL
Yokohama, Japan

The concept of *ni-wa-minato*, proposed by the client as the starting point of the project, suggests a mediation between garden and harbour, but also between the citizens of Yokohama and those from the outside world. This proposal for the new Yokohama terminal aims for an artefactual rather than a representational mediation between the two elements of this concept.

The artefact will operate as a mediating device between the two large social machines that make up the new institution: the system of public spaces of Yokohama and the management of cruise passenger flow. The components are used as a device for reciprocal *de-territorialisation*: a public space that wraps around the terminal, neglecting its symbolic presence as a gate, decodifying the rituals of travel, and a functional structure which becomes the mould of an a-typological public space, a landscape with no instructions for occupation. The aim is to achieve a mediation of a differential nature: a machine of integration that allows us to move imperceptibly through different states, turning states into degrees of intensity, countering the effects of rigid segmentation usually produced by social mechanisms, especially those dedicated to maintaining borders. The proposed artefact will reduce the amount of energy required to pass between the states, articulating in a differential mode the various segments of the programme throughout a continuously varied form: from local citizens to foreign visitor, from *flâneur* to business traveller, from voyeur to exhibitionist, from performer to spectator.

Using the ground surface to create a complementary public space to Yamashita Park, the proposal will result in the first perpendicular penetration of the urban space within the Yokohama Bay. The ground of the city will be seamlessly connected to the boarding level and from there it will bifurcate to produce a multiplicity of urban events. As a consequence, the building will become an extension of the city.

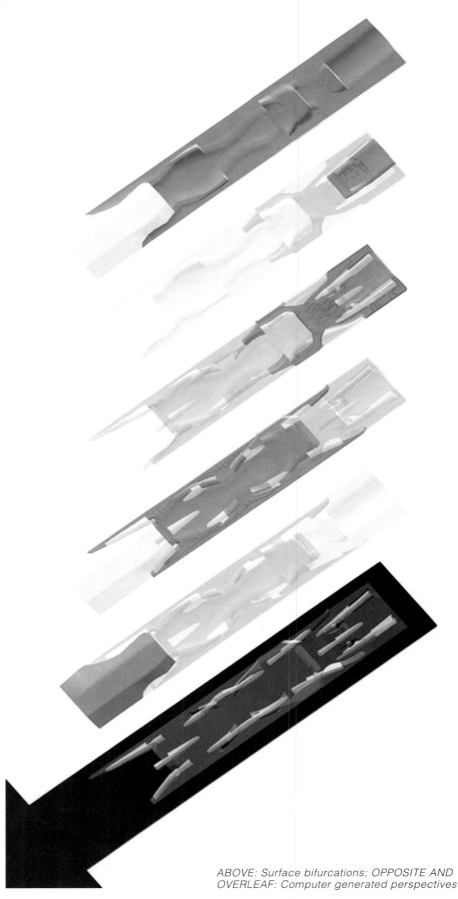

ABOVE: Surface bifurcations; OPPOSITE AND OVERLEAF: Computer generated perspectives

88

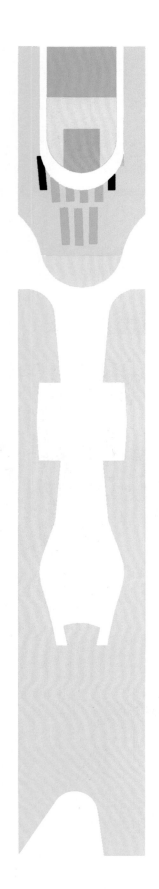

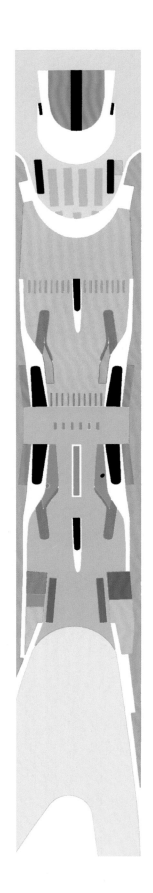

Solenoid
The plaza/terminal's function will not be simply to organise flows, but also to construct a field of urban intensity through enhancement of multiple paths and directions. In the Osanbashi plaza, the aim is to produce a *solenoid* – an inductive organisation of flows – to project urban intensity within the bay.

Battlefield
Owing to the varying size and schedules of the carriers, there will be constant fluctuations in the volume of space required by the domestic and international facilities. This calls for a structure in which the boundaries between domestic and international could be shifted to allow for such fluctuations. However, the demand for flexibility did not lead us to create a space of the utmost neutrality, but led to a highly differentiated structure, a seamless milieu which allows for the broadest variety of scenarios: an ideal battlefield where the strategic position of a small number of elements will substantially affect the definition of the frontier. Mobile or collapsible physical barriers and surveillance points will enable the reconfiguration of the borders between territories, allowing the terminal to be occupied by locals or invaded by foreigners.

Origami
The surface of the ground folds on to itself, forming creases that not only produce and contain paths through the building, creating the differential conditions for the programme, but also provide

structural strength. Thus the traditional separation between building-envelope and load-bearing structure disappears.

The use of segmented elements such as columns, walls or floors has been avoided in favour of a move towards a materiality where the differentiation of structural stresses is not determined by coded elements but by singularities within a material continuum.

Mille-Feuille

An entirely steel construction is proposed in order to provide the flexibility and lightness which are needed to resist earthquake damage. The construction system extends the concept of accumulating layers – structural layers, programmatic layers, finishes, etc.

No return

The building's circulation system has been organised as a series of loops in which the borders between the dynamic and the static have been removed. A variety of alternative paths will intensify the experience of passing through the building by duplicating the number of events which are encountered.

Weaving

The circulation system used by the citizens of Yokohama and the boat passengers is interwoven by reinforcing the connections between them. Interaction between the two systems is further increased by the inversion of the conventional position of the terminal facilities and the leisure facilities.

OPPOSITE: Plans; ABOVE: Model sections; BELOW: Longitudinal section

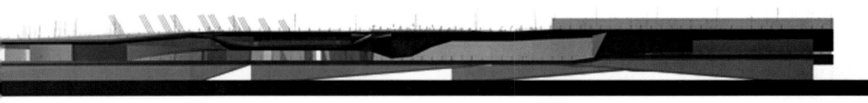

VAN BERKEL & BOS

THE ERASMUS BRIDGE

Rotterdam

The Erasmus Bridge is generated by an intricate system of references to and deviations from surrounding typologies – a system which calls to mind Derrida's term *differance*. While dockside cranes may be recognised in the main shape of the pylon, such meanings are simultaneously subject to undermining by transformations and deviations. The bridge, however, is also a project permeated with the political aspects of the mobile forces. Even more important in this context than the insidious power of its geographical surroundings is the project's large-scale double identity with all its interlocking public and engineering implications.

Although most observers choose to reconstruct the bridge as an intuitive gesture stemming directly from the personality of the architect, this would be simplistic. The mobile forces guiding this project were many and varied; the political aspects involved pertained to those forces most subject to mutability. It says much about the public significance attached to the bridge, long a controversial issue in the city, that when it was the subject of a prize last year, this was awarded to the Rotterdam councillors who had voted in favour of the bridge. The public dimensions of a project with such consequences for a city cannot be denied; yet they go beyond the tactical manoeuvres of the moment.

The primary issue is the deeper, almost hidden political significance of the bridge in the context of the self-image of the city, its history and projected future. It is the energy of the docks, the abrupt 20th-century modernity of architecture and infrastructure, the pragmatism and drive that form the principal constituents of what Rotterdam classifies as its authentic self. These qualities differentiate it from Amsterdam (17th-century classical/atmospheric) and The Hague (administrative/19th-century respectable). And the expectations are that the bridge – the last connection between north and south before the North Sea, and the object of speculation as the presumed attractor of new developments in the Kop van Zuid area – will comply with these images of authenticity.

When these public expectations are related to the rather inaccessible discourse of civil engineering, the contours present themselves as a bridge which, as a synopsis of the desires of the city, distributes its forces resolutely, rationally and in hierarchic poise over the river. That the Erasmus Bridge, on the contrary, displays an asymmetrical balance more fragile than robust, can be ascribed to a rereading of the city in all its undiagnosed complexity, together with an interest in the anti-tradition of civil engineering.

Informing the process of making the Erasmus Bridge is a constantly modulating conflict between the two traditions of bridge building; the rational and the experimental. The existence of these two traditions in civil engineering has been suppressed by the moral rhetoric of the rationalists. They persistently deny the existence of interests other than structural and economic ones, whereby Early Modern design principles are still accorded unconditional validity. It is becoming increasingly clear, however, that in practice the two contrasting traditions modify each other and that the stasis of the rationalist discourse bases its legitimacy on an impossible condition of immutability.

Architecture's contribution consists of blurring further the distinction between the two engineering traditions; for large-scale civil engineering projects, particularly those in urban contexts, are not impervious to architecture. That this civil engineering dispute has 'political' implications which influence the course of the project (taking sides involves being attacked, as the project contested) is a consequence as inexplicit and unacknowledged as it is inevitable. Studying the history of the project clearly shows that one manifestation of this conflict emerged in the preliminary design phase and concerned the placement of the back stays. These were present in the first sketches, but set fairly low; they subsequently disappeared and became the issue at stake in a public sparring match. After further structural studies they returned, though now placed high and close to the pylon so that they rose steeply, while the pylon itself became shorter and more slender.

Only one element remained the same through all these changes, and though permanently visible was hardly remarked upon: this was the horizontal foot of the pylon hugging the slender road deck. The fact that the back stays also connect to this horizontal component meant that the support structure now took the form of a bracket. The high placement of the back stays resulted in a bending moment in the diagonal pylon; this moment was exploited so that the bend could be permanently fixed, which in fact precipitated a new bridge type. Ensuing from this, the construction of the pylon was worked out in greater detail; the ratio between the height of the pylon and the width of the span across the river was reduced from 1:1.5 to 1:2; the width of the pylon was reduced to a mere 3 metres at its narrowest point.

These continual permutations are themselves an important component of the potential countermovement of the bridge. For if we analyse the shifting areas of tension, interplay of forces and events leading up to the Erasmus Bridge project, public response mechanisms and civil engineering defiance are almost impossible to tell apart.

Although it is impossible to isolate one factor that has guided these processes, the surprising importance of the computer drawing in these subordinate activities needs to be acknowledged. The computer offers the architect so much insight into a field once largely beyond his grasp, that he now has a much greater say in engineering projects. At the same time this argument cannot be seen as distinct from other interests; the shared, public space of the computer simulates

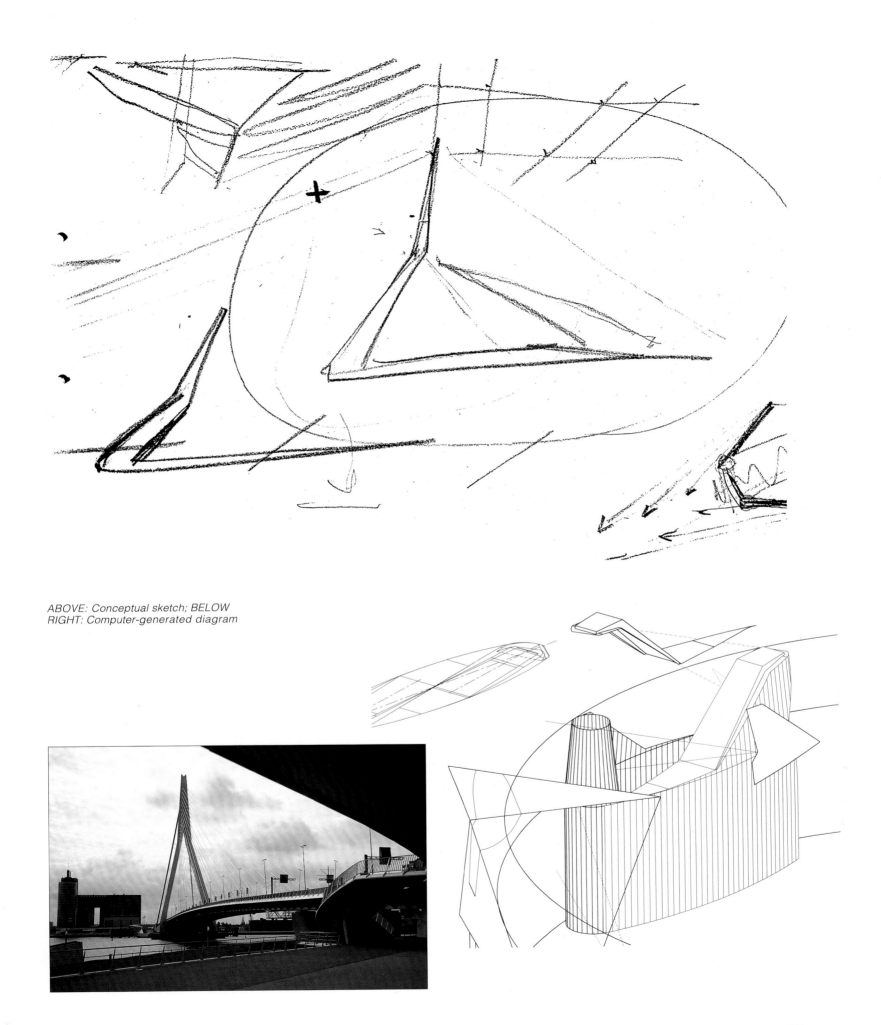

ABOVE: Conceptual sketch; BELOW
RIGHT: Computer-generated diagram

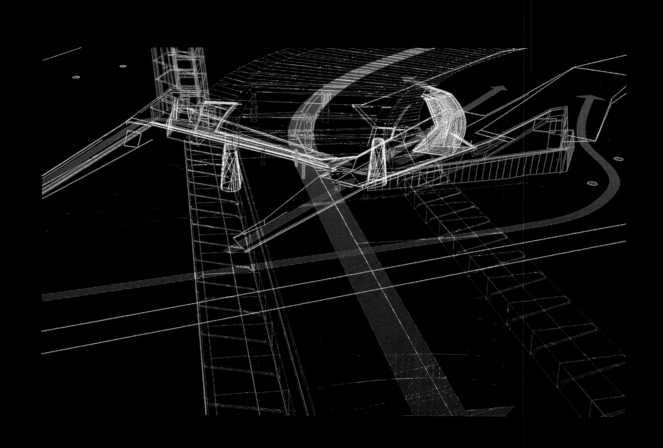

ABOVE: Computer generated perspective;
BELOW: Model

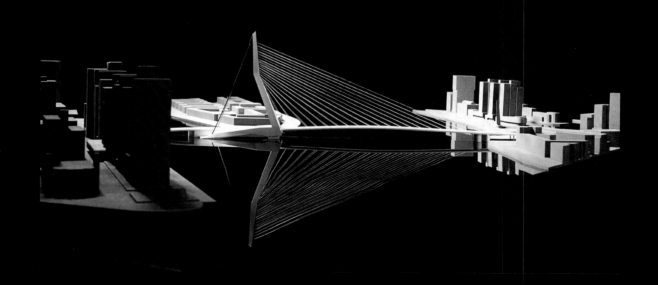

hat of the city, supplementing it with a
new calculated image of urban phenomena. For instance, it provides intensity
graphs in which the bridge emerges as
an urban artefact in a way quite separate
from every traditional planning discourse.

What these and other studies demonstrate is a sharpening of the double life of
each extensive urban and infrastructure
object; despite its ineluctable solitary
permanence, in the individual, subjective
experience it is short-lived, intensive and

massive. The two realities exist concur-
rently, the bridge being there as a fixed
point in the city and also as a fragmented
series of images of stays, lights, traffic
lanes. Its multiple identity is insurmount-
able at every level. However one approaches the project, ambiguities,
transformations and combinations of
forces keep clamouring to the fore. The
combining of forces at this scale is
continued down to the level of detail by
the bridge's involvement in infrastructural

and urbanist considerations.

To attribute such manifest asymmetry
to an urban project is probably the
bridge's most provocative aspect. It is
impossible to simply reduce the urban
effect of the bridge to that of a andmark,
for it stems from an extensive programme
at various levels of planning to which no
single architectural gesture is applicable.

Ben van Berkel and Caroline Bos

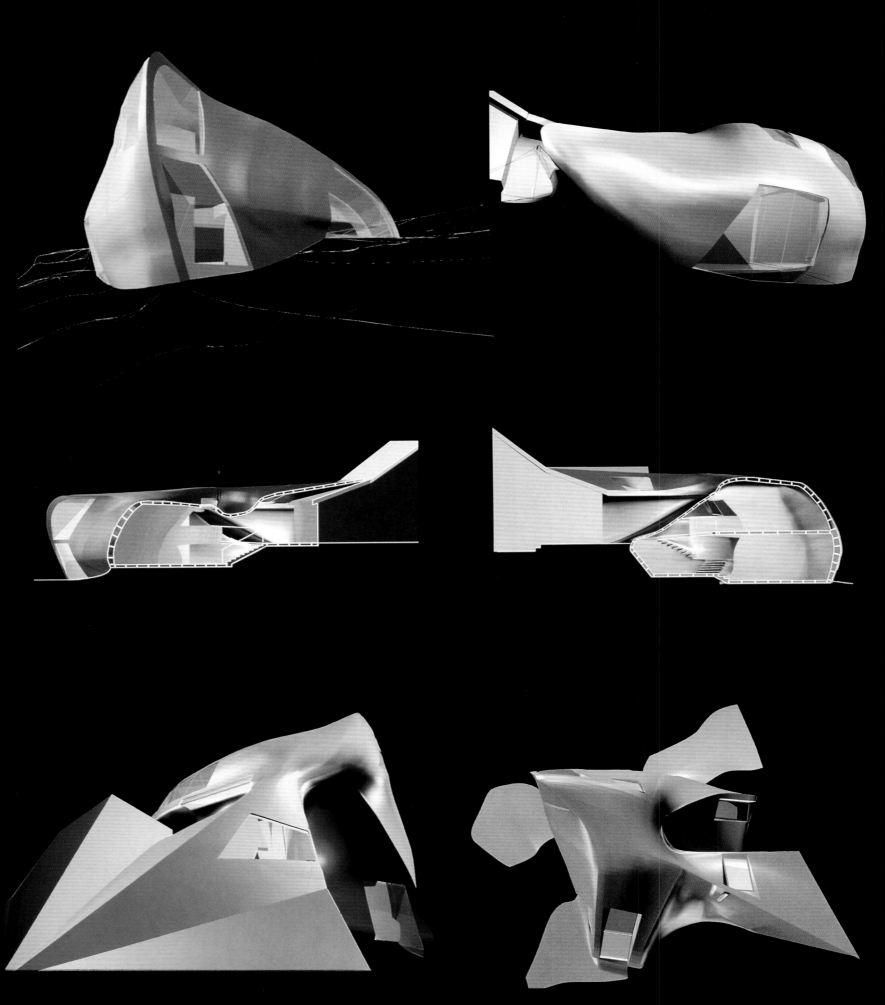

KOLATAN/MACDONALD STUDIO
RAYBOULD HOUSE ADDITION
Sherman, Connecticut

This project explores the potential of a hybrid architecture. The computer's specific capacity to map similarities across different categories while performing transformative operations is crucial to its conceptual and physical production.

For the design of this 'weekend home' addition, completed in 1998, information has been culled from the existing house, the landscape and the car. Their respective protocols and structural and spatial identities were electronically cross-referenced and systemically transformed into the new house.

The brief was to provide a 150-square-metre addition to the existing house, primarily used by the New York-based client to entertain guests. The new extension consists of two adjoining living areas, two bathrooms, and two bedrooms.

The 5.5 acre site is a gently sloping, 'pie-shaped', wooded parcel of land adjacent to an intersection on the south, a roadway on the east and farmlands to the west and north. The area of the compound includes a stream (with dam), which splits the site nearly in half along its longitudinal axis; two existing 17th-century structures (a 150-square-metre house and a 370-square-metre barn); a kidney-shaped, 1950s swimming pool and a small entry bridge.

The entry drive is on the eastern-most boundary of the site, running perpendicular to the stream. The immediate site of the addition is on the north-eastern side of the existing house. In this area, the landscape slopes some 30 per cent from west to east. The site drops sharply at the rear of the existing house, creating a 2.5-metre differential between the plateau on which the existing house rests and the lowest ground level of the new addition on its most eastern facade.

As a result of the project's proximity to a wetlands area, the addition had to be located no less than 23 metres from the top of the stream's bank. The structure's entire height could not exceed 10.5 metres.

The three-dimensional geometry of the building has been developed as an 'open-net shell'. This faceted structure is comprised of varying lengths and thicknesses of wood, which were calculated and designed by consulting engineers through structural analysis on a computer. The joinery of the wood members utilises a metal box that typically receives four struts in each of the intersection points of the faceted structure (not unlike a geodetic system). The double membrane panels are sheathed by rubber-cored plywood, which allows for the double-curving surface.

Most of the interior of the shell is finished in Philippine mahogany-veneered, rubber-cored plywood. The bathroom walls and floors are mainly tiled. The exterior, waterproof membrane is covered in a custom-tailored, reinforced-thermoplastic membrane with hot-air welded seams. The window mullions continue the faceted structure.

For drainage purposes the window and door openings (along with their deflector and gutter systems) are strategically placed in the flattest surfaces of the structure. The mechanical systems are central air-conditioning and radiant-slab heating. All other flooring is carpeted.

OPPOSITE: Computer-generated images of exterior and sections; BELOW: Site plan

EISENMAN ARCHITECTS

ARONOFF CENTER FOR DESIGN AND ART
UNIVERSITY OF CINCINNATI
David Gosling

This is a brilliant design in many ways. Like all iconoclastic architecture, it is not without its contradictions and aberrations, although most of these were beyond the control of the designer. The University of Cincinnati is a large, midwestern university with some 35,000 students. Founded in 1815, it is an urban university on a 212-acre campus, three miles from the city centre. Its explosive growth during the 1960s led to the building of some of the unsightly architecture of that decade.

In the mid-1980s, the University embarked on a brave, visionary (though highly controversial) further development of the campus. Although journalistic terms like 'signature architects' or 'windows of opportunity' are repugnant to this writer, the new policy of the University administration engaged the services of the best of American architects. It may be argued that an essentially 60s campus (although the 19th-century buildings are elegant) could not be welded together to form a coherent whole. Such is the problem of many British universities, yet the European idea of the American university campus is of manicured lawns, mature trees and a feeling of arcadia epitomised in the campuses of Harvard or Yale. It could be argued that the architecture of Eisenman or Gehry would do little to bring together such a disparate urban sprawl but the opposite was, in fact, the case.

Perhaps one great architect should have been invited to design the whole of the university campus, like Maki at Keio University in Japan or Isozaki at Bond University in Australia, or even Thomas Jefferson at the University of Virginia. However, these were built on virgin sites. Instead, in 1991, George Hargreaves, the San Francisco landscape architect, was invited to prepare a campus 'masterplan' – something of a misnomer since it is really a comprehensive landscape design. Michael Graves' design of the College of Engineering Research Centre is one of powerful architectural imagery and is a surprisingly contextual success. The campus power plant was designed by the Cambridge Seven; the Sigma Sigma tower by Machado and Silvetti, who are also designing the new student halls of residence; the Swing building (constructed as overflow accommodation whilst other structures were being built) by David Childs of Skidmore, Owings and Merrill; the outdoor spectator terrace and plaza by Wes Jones; the Molecular Sciences Institute by Frank Gehry, and Pei, Cobb, Freed have designed extensions to the nationally renowned College Conservatory of Music. All bring together spectacular aspects of late 20th-century architecture.

Peter Eisenman's design was for the addition to the College of Design, Architecture, Art and Planning (henceforth referred to as DAAP). The College had three linked, existing buildings of some 16,000 square metres, and Eisenman's brief was to double the size. The DAAP has approximately 1,750 undergraduates and graduate students and approximately 120 full-time and part-time members of the teaching faculty. Eisenman began his design in August 1987 and the building opened in October 1996. The delays and cost overruns were not overlooked by the press but one has to realise that the teaching staff represent not only architecture, interior design, urban planning and fine art departments but also industrial design, graphic design, fashion design and art history. The DAAP could and should have been the Bauhaus of the late 20th century but like universities throughout the world, there were always internecine rivalries between the factions who argued at length about the internal planning. The object of the university administration was to bring these factions and their students together within the new building and in the first months of its use, this seems to be succeeding.

Eisenman himself performed in an exemplary way. From the very beginning, he visited the campus at monthly intervals to present his designs not only to the entire college (always to a packed house) but to the University Building Design Review Committee and the University Board of Trustees.

Attention was first drawn to his design when he won the *Progressive Architecture* Award in January 1991.[1] Eisenman describes his design thus:

> [Located] on the north side of the existing college, three structures end to end in chevron pattern stand at the top of a knoll sloping east. Library, administration offices, auditorium, photo lab, café and additional studios, laboratories and others together with multi-purposes spaces for juries and exhibits.' The solution: 'the building was conceived as a symbol of the new cosmology of man and information. Just as information comes to us in the media in a fragmented, ambiguous manner, so does this building arise out of a series of formal transformations that fracture and blur traditional architectural dichotomies such as old and new, inside and outside, structure and infill. The form of this architecture school addition takes its cue from the chevron shape of the re-existing building. [We] torqued, tilted and shifted this shape out of phase, resulting in an architecture that carries within its plans and elevations the trace of these formal moves like the after-image on a television screen or the interpenetration of radio frequencies. The chevron shape finally becomes so fuzzy that it takes on the undulating quality of the site. Captured between the space between the new building and the old is a complex skylighted atrium. Walkways and bridges overlook this public space.

It is interesting to note the jury's response. Adele Santos commented:

> Its response to the sloping site is really quite nice. It also has some very fine sections. I think the way the light will come filtering down into the walkways will be very beautiful. What astounds me is that a school of architecture would pick an architect whose work is going to be so clearly defined at a point in time, knowing that would be the image of the school forevermore. This is precisely one of the building types that requires a certain type of neutrality,

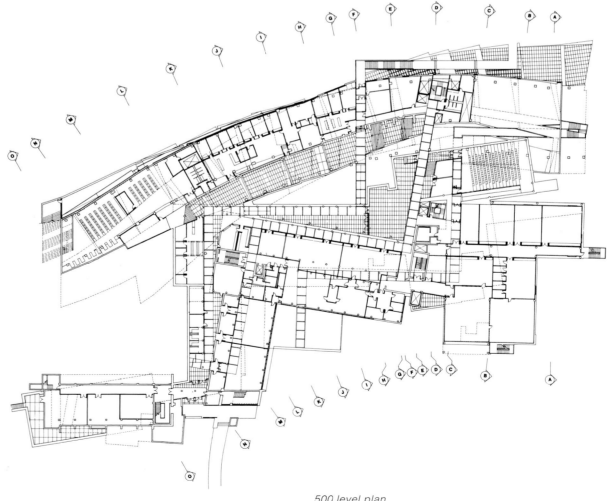

500 level plan

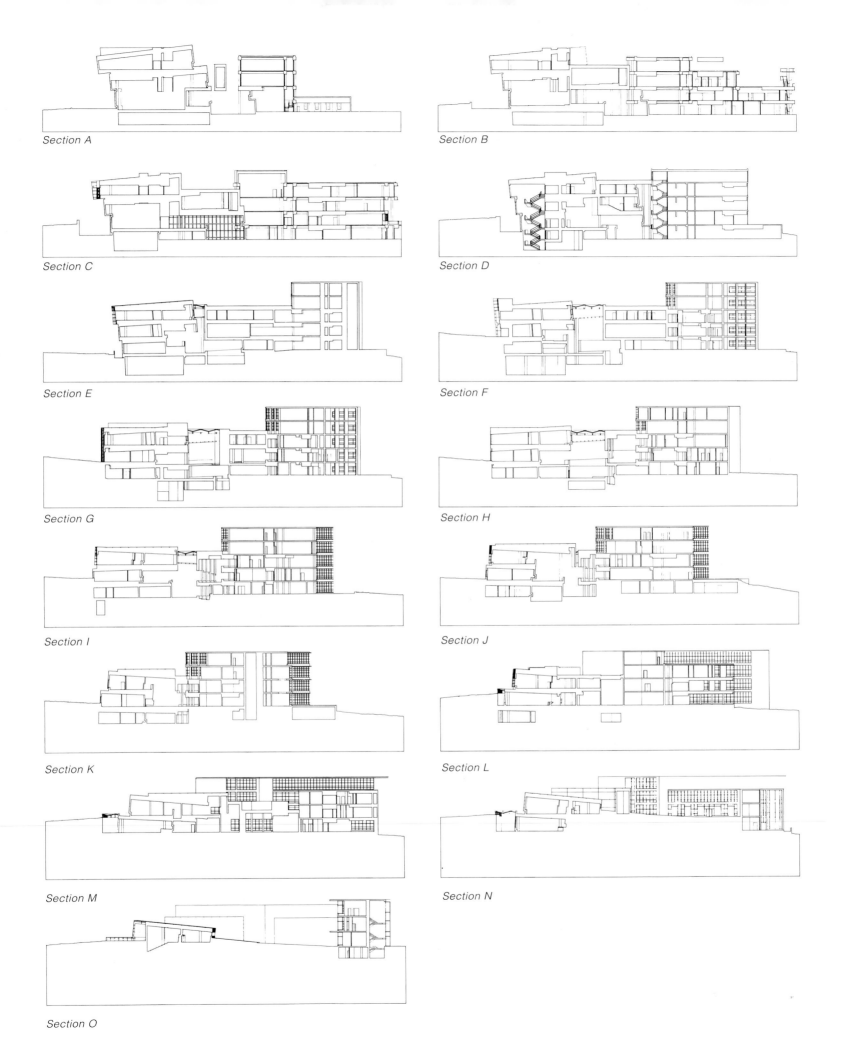

Section A

Section B

Section C

Section D

Section E

Section F

Section G

Section H

Section I

Section J

Section K

Section L

Section M

Section N

Section O

flexibility and open-endedness. This is an enormously particular and highly personal statement.

Ralph Johnson agreed, stating: 'That is true. Architecture schools do tend towards more neutral types of spaces.' (This comment is hardly true in the context of Louis Kahn's Art Gallery and School of Fine Art or Paul Rudolph's School of Architecture, both built at Yale University in the middle of this century.)

Rem Koolhaas continued: 'Yes, but this building is quite clever in terms of organising the utilitarian parts in a utilitarian way. Only with the public spaces does it become expressive', a comment concurred by Dana Cuff: 'The existing buildings are pretty awful.' Ralph Johnson asserted: 'It has an extremely skilful definition of the public spaces and a beautiful treatment of the public corridor.'

What is most remarkable about the design drawings shown in the issue of *Progressive Architecture* in September, 1991 is that the final built form, externally and especially internally, is astonishingly faithful. Rarely has any radical architect achieved this and one can only think of the extreme tenacity of Frank Lloyd Wright on a comparative basis.

When Peter Eisenman first began the design of this building, there was commentary on his work in general in a special edition on Deconstruction Theory in *Architectural Design*.[2] Andrew Benjamin suggests that in examining the architectural metaphor in Descartes,[3] a series of oppositions has emerged in creating a structural role within this philosophical position – he further suggests that it is in relation to these oppositions that the force of Deconstruction can be located. Jacques Derrida suggests that in Deconstruction, analyses and comparative conceptual pairs which are currently accepted as self-evident and natural, appear as if they had not been institutionalised at some precise point, as if they had no history. Derrida considers the work of Tschumi in his plan of the Parc de la Villette in Paris,[4] especially the series of constructs known as 'Les Folies', an architectural expression commonly mis-used in the 19th century. Derrida makes the point that they are not 'madness' (*la folie*). He suggests that despite appearance, Deconstruction is not in itself an architectural metaphor. Benjamin further suggests that 'the challenge presented by Deconstruction is the same challenge it presents to all the arts, as well as philosophy, literary criticism (linguistic theory?) and so forth. It is a challenge that initially takes place on the level of thinking – here in the example of architecture. Thinking becomes enacted in the architectural work of both Eisenman and Tschumi.'

Charles Jencks refers to Eisenman as the 'positive nihilist',[5] suggesting that the latter became a disciple of Deconstruction at the same time as he was undergoing personal trauma and psychoanalysis. He was a member of the New York Five (Eisenman, Gehry, Graves, Gwathmey, Hejduk) in the 1970s and the founder of the Institute for Architecture and Urban Studies in New York City which reached its zenith in 1976-78, closing in 1984. These facts are pertinent in a special way. The jewel-like villas built by the New York Five owed much to neo-Corbusian philosophy and, to a lesser extent, to Terragni. Eisenman's earlier house designs such as House I (Princeton, New Jersey, 1967), House II (Hardwick, Vermont, 1970), House III (Lakeville, Connecticut, 1971) and House IV (Cornwall, Connecticut, 1975) were not really precursors of his later exuberance displayed in the much larger Deconstructionist buildings in Ohio (the Wexner Center for the Visual Arts 1983-89), the Greater Columbus Convention Center (1989-93) and the University of Cincinnati DAAP building (1988-96). The villas explored rectilinear spatial sequences and

interpenetrating volumes and planes with consummate skill. Although House III showed a distinct shift in complexity and contradiction, deliberately lacking the apparent serenity of the other houses, it, perhaps, in 1971, foreshadowed Eisenman's major change in direction. Later, theoretical house studies such as the Fin d'ou T Hous S in 1984 for the Venice Cannaregio Project, or House X, displayed, albeit through orthogonal grids, a different form of complexity.[6]

Philip Johnson selected two American architects for the Fifth International Exhibition of Architecture at the Venice Biennale in 1991, organised by Francesco Dal Co.[7] The two were chosen as architects who were challenging their discipline in an aggressive way and challenging dogma above all else. Johnson suggested that there were, however, great differences in their personalities: Eisenman as the East Coast intellectual and Gehry as an intuitive, anti-intellectual West Coast savant. Eisenman's key display at the Biennale was the design drawings for DAAP.

And yet, for all the praise showered upon Eisenman as the leader of Deconstruction Theory and its architectural application, far less is known about his formidable talents as urban designer. Charles Jencks says in his book, *The Architecture of the Jumping Universe* [8] that no one has looked at the lessons of emerging sciences more strenuously than Eisenman.

Jencks suggests that Peter Eisenman's shift to the non-linear sciences and the new urbanism began in 1987, as with his Rebstock Housing Project in Frankfurt, making extensive use of the 'fold'. In Cincinnati, he introduced the wave form as a transformation of the 'zig-zag' rectangles of the three existing buildings. The Frankfurt Rebstock park has been referred to by Jencks as a shift to the non-linear sciences and a 'new urbanism'. Yet this terminology is confusing because 'The New Urbanism' eloquently explained in a book by Peter Katz[9] and currently sweeping the United States, is generated in part by the forces of conservatism and reaction. 'Seaside' by Andres Duany and Elizabeth Plater-Zyberk, for all its romanticism and elegance, has little to do with urban exploration or 'real' communities for that matter. Eisenman, on the other hand, explored ways of developing new communities of social housing on a major scale, carried out in collaboration with Albert Speer & Partner (Germany) and landscape architects Hanna/Olin in Philadelphia, PA. The findings were published in 1992.[10] The site is a vast tract of land to the north of major railroad marshalling yards. The plan, starting with orthogonal grids, transformed subsequently into warped folds and twisted grids or torques, the initial studies showing a mixture of low-rise and medium-rise housing.

These observations on the Frankfurt project are relevant in view of this critic since the DAAP is essentially more about urban design, both within (with great success) and without (with somewhat lesser success) than it is about a single building or even a group of buildings).

The professional press was generally euphoric about the new building; the local press less so. The *Cincinnati Enquirer*, in an editorial of 2 February, 1997, stated:

The University President said that $71.4 million had been cut from UC's budget in the last decade . . . But rather than see that as falling bad sky news, we think his fiscal responsibility is good news. And so is UC's campus where new buildings . . . seem to grow faster than Magic Rocks. The aim of today's comparison photos is not to disparage UC or suggest that University classrooms should be as shabby and dilapidated as many of our elementary schools.

104

Benjamin Forey, writing in the *Washington Post*, said that although Eisenman is not great in the way that Frank Lloyd Wright and Le Corbusier were, who changed architectural direction fundamentally, Eisenman's design emphasises the importance of 'route' which neither of the two great 20th-century masters confronted. Forey believed that the design was intended to be a polemical statement – sometimes to invigorate, sometimes to annoy. An open-closed-open spatial sequence clothed in unconventional forms, intended to heighten surprise and pleasure, snakes up the hill; the more conventional spaces, such as the classrooms, library and offices, tended to be left over spaces – little nooks and crannies. He thought that 'Eisenman identified himself as a radical avant-gardist, critical of mainstream architecture'. Yet Eisenman's Convention Center in Ohio's state capital, Columbus, is a totally mainstream building as he suggested; however, the Wexner Center at Ohio State University in Columbus is not. Forey commented on Eisenman's sources – archaeological excavations, a fascination shared with Hargreaves (the triangulated 'Indian Burial Mounds' are an integral part of the DAAP design), mathematical models, the Boolian cube used in computer modelling, chemical compounds such as DNA, geometrical conundrums and philosophies as diverse as Noam Chomsky and Jacques Derrida.

Each of the three Ohio buildings are quite different. DAAP is his first truly curvilinear building of brick, glass and steel with dramatic grids, diagonal lines and towers – together with lay-lines or lines of force of the Druids (which Hargreaves in his landscape design for the University of Cincinnati refers to as the 'braids'). The Columbus Convention Center is a big box deliberately fragmented with a startling array of abstract forms. The DAAP building, Forey commented, was externally curiously modest and reticent.

Due to the wishes of the University administration the knoll upon which the DAAP is sited was not reduced in height, as Eisenman originally wished. This is quite tragic since half the height of Eisenman's building is hidden behind berms and grass mounds. Pastel pinks, greens and blues are used. Again, as in earlier designs, Eisenman wanted to use much bolder colours; again, he demurred to the University's wishes but a look at the *Casabella* appraisal by Kurt Forster[11] reveals how it could have been, through the use of skilful printing techniques. The juxtaposition of the harsh 1960s concrete and mechanical stacks of the Wolfson building at the eastern end of the campus is unfortunate and should have been screened. Their existence was referred to as 'value engineering' – better known as cost cutting. The ridiculous bright yellow parking kiosk was obviously erected without consultation with Eisenman. The internal signage throughout the building is a debased form of Roman typography on brown plates, and raises the question, 'who selected it?' (certainly not Eisenman). These petulant thoughts are raised here only because, given a radical design of such quality, why spoil it with badly considered extras? Other questions arise about the use of external materials such as Dryvit which is a 2.5cm-7cm styrofoam panel with (in European terms) painted cement render.

Forster suggests the total design is like 'a gently orchestrated earthquake'. The building, Eisenman suggests, is like 'the plates of an armadillo or the segments of an airport baggage carousel'.

Paul Goldberger, writing in the *New York Times*, suggests that Eisenman treats this as the most important event in American architecture since Frank Lloyd Wright was able to convince Solomon Guggenheim that pictures look good in round spaces.

Philip Johnson announced that it has 'no equal in American architecture'. Goldberger describes it thus: 'Few walls are perpendicular; three bland institutional buildings are joined together, frozen after the first shocks of an earthquake. (There is a sense of vertigo and seasickness in some of the spaces.)'[12] Is this, Goldberger asks, the final gasp of modernism and the beginning of something else? Was it just intended to grab attention? The breaking of barriers between inside and outside, the blurring of form and function? These questions can only be answered by studying Peter Eisenman's design process.

In an elegant, limited edition book edited by Cynthia Davidson, *Eleven Authors in Search of a Building*, one of the essays by Donna Barry (a key project architect) explains this succinctly. Barry and Michael McInturf, the project site architect, offer a great insight into this process: Eisenman is not the director of a huge practice which delegates design. Like Frank Lloyd Wright, he *is* the designer. Nevertheless, as Wright influenced the impressive architecture of Fay Jones, his former apprentice, McInturf, who is now on the teaching faculty of the School of Architecture, won a 1997 *Progressive Architecture* Award in his own right, and is a member of the Senior Year Thesis studio team under the leadership of David Niland. Donna Barry summarises the design process as follows:

The strategy was to react to the fundamental rules of construction while creating a space that appears to contradict or ignore them. For example, in science the process of symmetry breaking explains observed complexity within a non-linear system. Space can be curved, mass is not constant and the relative position of the body affects the measurement of the space between the object and the body.

The building represents a process of symmetry breaking in the design process of the building, providing a new awareness of the human experience in space by disrupting the conventional relationships between form, function and meaning. The idea of self-similarity is an example of a process analogous to symmetry breaking. Self-similarity is a process of repetition that produces an asymmetry. Self-similarity sets up a duality between the original form and the copy or trace of that form. The original and the trace are then superimposed to create a third form that incorporates them both.

The resulting design is based on a dynamic mathematically non-linear design process. The series of displacements attempt to redefine the human experience of space.

Step 1: A series of three-dimensional rectangles creating the juxtaposition of studio, corridor and office (each rectangle approximately 13 metres x 21 metres). The height of the box is the floor-to-floor height of approximately 4.8 metres.

Step 2: The line was transformed into a curve to contrast with the hard rectilinear edge of the three existing buildings. The curved line was made complex in both plan and section. Graphically, such a curved line describes a non-linear, mathematical relationship. The line was transformed into the construction of a curve without a centre.

Step 3: The transformation of the segmented line into a curve and the box geometry was overlapped horizontally, based on a logarithmic function. In the non-linear nature of the relationship between the boxes, the algorithm that produced this logarithmic function was developed so that no overlap would be sequentially repeated.

Step 4: Another algorithm was derived simultaneously with the overlap to introduce a tilt or twist to each box in the *x-y* axis. The algorithm produced the twist applied to a particular box. The asymptotic curve is generated out of the two systems such that this lack of relationship between the two systems reinforces the idea that nothing in the lines is constant or predictable. The resulting conditions are neither regular nor random; nor are they an example of individual expressionism or related to any historical iconography.

Step 5: In order to locate the diagram in section, a relationship between the box and the floor slab had to be determined, certainly as a practical response to the reality of construction. The dimension of this relationship was required to be approximately one metre, measured from the north bottom of the box along the axis. Each box was torqued independently along the *z* axis while changing direction along the *x-y* axis. There was a resulting relationship between the horizontal datum and the torqued box, allowing a consistent reading between the two elements. This set of overlapped, twisted and torqued boxes is referred to as a phase. In physics, phase transitions refer to the behaviour of matter near the point where it changes from one state into another, from a liquid to a gas, or from magnetised to unmagnetised.

Step 6: The original geometric phase is shifted twice along the *x* axis in order to produce a series of three phases for each functional level (levels 400, 500 and 600). Each phase maintains the form of the original *x-y* twist. The applied torque to each box of each phase varies at each level, so there is no one-to-one relationship possible in section. The uppermost 600 level has the most extreme torque, while the lower 400 level has the least torque. This series of torques is descriptively referred to as the torqued solid series.

Step 7: The torqued solid series is shifted and copied along the *x-y* axis and dropped in elevation as a complete series. This lowering in the *x* plane purposely blurs the section while the shift in the *y* plane blurs the plan. This series of phases traced over the torqued solid series is referred to as the torqued trace series. The original phase is copied to form a self-similar series. This series is then copied to form a self-similar trace. These two series create an overlapped figure that became programmatically the atrium space of the building.

Step 8: The diagrams could not merely be placed level on the site. The east edge of the site became the 200 or mechanical level of the building while the west edge climbs to an elevation referred to as the 600 level. This creates the need to walk not only through but up the building. The stepping phase takes the same form as the initial phase but with three distinct differences. The height of each box totals the three levels – approximately 14 metres and each box steps consecutively in elevation. Each box is vertical without a torque along the *z* axis. This distinguishes the stepping boxes from the torquing boxes so that one can be read against the other. Finally, these two series are shifted in plan, necessary to provide the notation for stepping 'on and up' the slope. The stepping series that takes the form of the original phase is referred to as the stepping solid series, while the shifted image of this phase is referred to as its trace.

Step 9: The figure created by the overlapping torqued solid

Jeff Goldberg/Esto

Jeff Goldberg/Esto

Jeff Goldberg/Esto

series and torqued trace series of boxes defines the space of what is called the atrium or 'College Hall'. This third element is created by the superimposition of the solid form and trace form. It is a negative space produced from the overlapped condition. It becomes a path that traverses the sectional contours of the site notated by the stepping series. Beginning at ground level as an exterior element of the east 200 level garage, the atrium space ascends through a series of platforms to the 400 level entry and forms the main interior, the central space. This negative space continues to rise through yet another series of platforms used as critique areas for all the four schools to the 500 level. At the entry to the library in the west segment, the negative space rises again to the 600 level and exists to the west at the top of the hill with a cascade of stairs down to Clifton Avenue. In the case of the existing three buildings, each is separated by a stair tower. The addition has independent floor levels and the 500 level of the new building is the only common level for all four buildings.

The three-metre wide corridor in the original DAAP is described as a chevron, used to extend a similar figure across the site. The northern chevron refers to the Alms trace. The southern chevron is referred to as the Wolfson Building trace. The composite in these traces creates a blur between the original and the trace. The chevron zone is defined as the space between two chevron figures. The portion of a box edge that passes through any chevron remains in its original location. Just as the existing building traces blur, in plan, the edges of the existing building, the chevron figures blur the edges of the box geometry. The combination of interlocking boxes and traces is reminiscent of the moving facets of an airport baggage carousel.

Step 10: The structural 'grid' is organised by the 500 level torqued solid phase of boxes. As a result, the rectilinear column grid moves through the space, independent of the form of that space. Columns pass in, out and through the walls. Vertical on one side and sloped with the building's geometry on the other, these columns read against the round columns that are part of the trace of existing buildings. Some columns are not structural – in some cases, they are part of a figure traced from the existing buildings, contradicting the notion of the structural column.

Step 11: The examination of space in the third dimension afforded by the computer creates a problem for construction that is based on the convention of planar extrusion. The programming and planning of functions were organised, and a form evolved from *within* the three-dimensional wire frame provided by the computer. The space of the building was not conceived a priority but rather emerged from the process of design. The conventional building section is incapable of providing the information required to build this form, in part because it is not possible to draw a meaningful section of the building since it would be orthogonal to only one box in the wire frame.

The co-ordinate system typically used in surveying was introduced as a method for dimensioning this project. Conventional string dimensions on the floor plans were not useful to locate each box edge in reference to the column grid and Euclidean measurements of length depth and thickness. Ideas of longitude, latitude and altitude were better suited to the twisted and the torqued geometry of this project. A benchmark was located at the northwest corner of the old Alms building. The edge of each box was located in relation to this control mark in x-y-z co-ordinates. Co-ordinate points were assigned at the intersection of the floor slab and the interlocked edges of the torqued walls. The contractors used a laser transit method of triangulation to locate points on lines and to calculate distances between co-ordinate points. The staked points were connected by lasers to lay out the track for studwalls and ceilings. The co-ordinate plans are like 'join-the-dot drawings' but without numbers. The contractor was able to 'join these dots' without prior knowledge of the object to be drawn.

Step 12: Conceptual transformations and the construction drawings do not describe the space of the building. Drawings can only depict the form, of which the oneric space is the result . . . the logic remains elusive. This intrinsic logic is not intended to be read easily by the building's viewer or user.'
Donna Barry concludes her analysis thus: 'The space of this project has a labyrinthine quality. It is experienced as a logical but not easily read path: a discovered path'.[13]

Cynthia Davidson refers to Colin Rowe's *Promenade Architecturale*,[14] suggesting that as the building climbs a hill, a route, giving continuously unfolding views, talks of chevrons, x-y-z co-ordinates, asymptotic tilts and torquing. No facade. The entry at 300 level reveals no promenade architecturale and there is re-entry at the 400 level.

However, this is what the design is all about and analogies with the theories of Gordon Cullen's 'serial vision' and Frank Lloyd Wright's 'organic architecture' and the Usonian House seem to be pertinent. It is unlikely that all three, Wright, Cullen and Eisenman, would agree with this!

Gordon Cullen suggested that the perception of the town as a piece of moving scenery hardly enters the head of the person in the street, yet, this is usually what the town is – a moving set. Cullen showed this in a remarkably evocative way, illustrating an uninterrupted sequence of views which would unfold themselves like 'stills' from a movie.[15]

Many theorists of the Modern Movement[16] included two important concepts which came together in the 1920s and which are relevant to urban designers. The first of these, with origins in De Stijl painting and the architecture of Frank Lloyd Wright, was the concept of space as a natural continuum, with no distinction between external and internal spaces. Both Sigfried Giedion's 'space time' and Moholy Nagy's 'Vision in Motion' drew attention to a more dynamic approach to visual understanding which seemed to offer new insights into the processes of describing and analysing urban environments. The distinction between this appreciation based upon a mobile observer and the former perception from static, frontal viewpoints was similarly developed by other commentators such as those of Roger Hinks.[17] Similarly, Arata Isozaki has maintained that the Japanese do not recognise the Western concept of space and time.[18] Both are, rather, conceived in Japanese terms of intervals, as reflected in the use of the term 'Ma' in architecture, landscape design, music and drama, a concept which can signify the 'natural distance' between two or more objects existing in a continuity.

Peter Eisenman's DAAP building is a lesson in space-time. It is an enigma. Modest on the exterior, half-buried in the hillside landscape, it reveals little of its dazzling interior. In seeding analogies with Frank Lloyd Wright, America's greatest organic architect says:

Plasticity was a familiar term, but something I had seen in no buildings whatsoever . . . You may see the appearance of the thing in the surface of your hand as contrasted with the articulation of the bony skeleton itself. This ideal, profound in its architectural implications, soon took on another conscious stride forward in a new aesthetic. I called it continuity (it is easy to see it as a *folded plane*). Continuity in this aesthetic sense appeared to me as the natural means to achieve truly organic architecture . . . [19]

Externally, Eisenman's design, in its sinuous curvilinear way, exemplifies in its relationship to the hillside everything that was true about Wright's organic architecture. It grows out of, and is part of the landscape. It is surprisingly reticent. And yet, the only point of the building which is separated from its predecessor, is the northwest corner (ignored by architectural photographers). It is the one point where 'serial vision', 'space time' and sequential spaces between inside and outside come into play. It is separated at this point from the chevron of the three existing buildings. It is almost perfect in itself. Yet, all of the external building is mostly north-facing where sunlight can play little part in enhancing the articulation of the elements. Some of the beautiful black leather and white steel furniture by Knoll in public spaces could well have been sacrificed for floodlighting this building at night. Even without this, the illuminated interior of the 500 level library with its great beams and its uplighting at night is magical to behold.

However, the real magic of this building is its interior public space. It is one of the rare occasions in contemporary design where 'serial vision' as urban design concept comes into play. The continuous cascade of stairs and platforms from the 300 level at the eastern end to the 600 level at the western end is breathtaking. It does not end at street level as other critics have suggested but 12 metres above it. The contrast between the Wexner Center and DAAP is interesting. The Wexner Center has been criticised elsewhere for its exuberant architecture internally. As an art gallery, one should expect it to be reticent like the admirable Van Gogh Museum in Amsterdam but as a piece of urban design with its delicate white pergolas-cum-arcade-cum-colonnade welding together disparate pieces of academic architecture spanning a century, it is a stroke of genius. Externally, DAAP has no such pyrotechnics. It is certainly not contextual, although the urban context is mediocre.

Internally, the spatial experience of ascending (or descending) from level 300 to 600 is breathtaking. At the 400 level, the atrium breaks into a public space, gathering ground, social meeting place, café and party space, fulfilling the requirement of bringing the schools of the College together. It is interesting that most of the architectural photographers, following the example of their Japanese peers, show no people in their photographs. Yet the DAAP atrium is a rare contradiction – at one of the opening celebrations, the atrium was packed with people and it looked marvellous; it needed to be populated, as I am sure Peter Eisenman intended. Its Piranesi-like qualities, with its soaring criss-cross bridges and overlook galleries make it a procession, a 'promenade architecturale', a 'serial vision', a 'space time' experience to be treasured. It is an internal masterpiece.

David Gosling is the State of Ohio Eminent Scholar in Urban Design and Professor of Urban Design at the University of Cincinnati, USA. He is also the author of Gordon Cullen: Visions of Urban Design, *Academy Editions, 1996, which received an American Institute of Architects Award for Architectural Advancement in November 1996.*

The author wishes to acknowledge the assistance of Erica Stoller (Esto photography), Juliette Cezzar of Eisenman Architects and Cynthia Davidson, editor of *Eleven Authors in Search of a Building*.

Notes

1 *Progressive Architecture* 01-09, Progressive Architecture Awards, 1991, pp82-83.
2 Editorial, p7 and pp8-11, Andrew Benjamin, *Architectural Design*, Vol 158, No 314, 1988.
3 Descartes, R, 'Discourse on Method', *The Philosophical Writings of Descartes*, Vol 1, Cambridge University Press (Cambridge),1985.
4 Derrida, J, 'Architetture ove i' desiderio può arbitare', *Domus*, No 671, April 1986.
5 Jencks, C, *Architectural Design*, Vol 158, No 314, 1988, pp26-31 and 49-61.
6 Eisenman, P, *House of Cards*, Oxford University Press (Oxford and New York), 1987.
7 *Architectural Design*, Vol 162, No 1/2, 1992.
8 Jencks, C, *The Architecture of the Jumping Universe*, Academy Editions (London), 1995.
9 Katz, P, *The New Urbanism*, McGraw Hill (New York), 1994.
10 Eisenman et al, *Frankfurt Rebstockpark: Folding in Time*, Prestel-Verlag (Munich) and Deutches Architektur Museum (Frankfurt), 1992.
11 Forster, K, *Casabella*, No 638, October 1996, pp12-16.
12 Goldberger, P, *New York Times*, Monday 14 October 1996, ppB-1 and B-5.
13 Davidson, C (ed), *Eleven Authors in Search of a Building*, Monacelli Press, Inc. (New York), 1996, pp48-95 (Donna Barry).
14 *Ibid*, p14.
15 Gosling, D, *Gordon Cullen: Visions of Urban Design*, Academy Editions (London), 1996, p24.
16 Gosling, D, and B Maitland, *Concepts of Urban Design*, Academy Editions (London), 1984, pp42-43.
17 Hinks, R, 'Peepshow and the Roving Eye', *Architectural Review*, August 1995.
18 *Japan Architect*, February 1979.
19 Frank Lloyd Wright, *The National House*, Horizon Press, 1954, 1982, p18.

NONLINEARITY
WHAT IT IS AND WHY IT MATTERS
PETER T SAUNDERS

Modern science was founded on the assumption that the universe runs according to a small number of simple laws which humans can discover and understand. The task of the scientist is to find these laws and to work out how they combine to produce all the different phenomena that we observe. Explanations of highly complicated phenomena may fall short of this ideal, but they are generally considered to be inferior, which is why physics and chemistry are 'hard' sciences, while biology is a 'soft' science.

The 18th-century French mathematician, Laplace, once claimed that if he were told the position and momentum of every particle in the universe at a single instant in time, he could predict the entire future and reconstruct the whole of the past. I doubt that anyone has ever believed this could really be done, but it has defined the project: everything should be explained in terms of the lowest possible level and ultimately in terms of the motions of individual particles obeying Newton's laws.

Of course this world view did not begin with Newtonian mechanics. It is a part of European culture that goes back to the mathematics of the Greeks and to the Old Testament tradition of a single deity who dictated a book of laws for his chosen people to interpret and obey. A Talmudic scholar and a theoretical physicist have a lot in common. But it was given a tremendous boost by Newton and his successors, who created an enormously successful science based on it.

The influence of the Newtonian paradigm has been felt outside physics as well. The theory of evolution by natural selection is not based on Newton's laws, but its claim to account for the whole of the living world in terms of a single mechanism places it firmly within the paradigm; Darwin is indeed the Newton of the grass blade. Karl Marx claimed to have discovered the laws of motion of society. Modern scientists have similar ambitions: the goal of sociobiology is to base the social sciences on the principles of population genetics.[1]

Ironically, physicists themselves no longer believe in the solid, deterministic, clockwork universe that gave such support to the paradigm. In its place they have created a world in which space and time depend on the observer, in which certain properties exist only when we measure them, in which one part of the theory insists that particles that are far apart cannot communicate instantaneously and another part contains results that cannot be explained unless they do, and so on.

Despite all this, the Newtonian paradigm has survived almost unscathed. This is partly because few people outside nuclear physics really understand exactly how deep the problems are, and partly because however strange the quantum universe may be, it could be that the everyday world is largely unaffected, that the problems are all smoothed out by the law of large numbers. We may draw on the new physics occasionally, for example if we believe that quantum uncertainty in the brain is the source of free will, but that need not affect the general thrust of our research.

How far such a view is justifiable remains to be seen.[2] Besides, while we may well be able to study, say, economics without explicit reference to quantum mechanics, it must be unsatisfactory to restrict ourselves to a world view which is no longer accepted within the subject that is most responsible for its present dominance. If physics is to be the model for all science, it should be the physics of today, not of the 19th century.

In any case, the Newtonian paradigm is now faced with a challenge from a totally different direction. The problems arise because the universe is nonlinear, which we have always known, and that this matters, which is only now becoming clear.

Some of the properties of nonlinear systems have been understood for a long time; the mathematical analysis of the straw that broke the camel's back goes back to Euler in 1744. The modern subject began with a paper published by the great French mathematician Henri Poincaré in 1890, just before the appearance of relativity and quantum mechanics. The full impact has only recently been recognised, however, because it required new mathematical tools and, above all, powerful computers that allow us to explore nonlinearity in a way that was previously impossible.

Briefly, the message of nonlinear dynamics is this. Even if we restrict ourselves to Newtonian mechanics, we find that the world is not as the Newtonian paradigm would lead us to believe. In the first place, we could predict the future course of the universe from its present state only if we were given the data with infinite accuracy. Anything less than that, and the Laplacian project fails utterly. Second, nonlinearity endows systems with many properties which previously we thought had to be imposed on them by external forces. Phenomena that appeared to require special explanations can now be seen as no more than what we might expect. The universe is just like that. Why it should be like that is another question, but it is.

Nonlinear dynamical systems

Dynamical systems theory is the study of processes in motion, and since most processes are nonlinear, it is in effect the study of how most things behave. More precisely, and this is why it is a nontrivial subject, it's the study of the difference between how most things behave and how we suppose they behave if we don't think carefully enough.

The obvious meaning of linearity is having to do with straight lines, and since the equation of a straight line is $y = a + bx$, which has no powers of x or y higher than the first, linearity also implies that a system is describable by very simple equations, with no squares, products of variables, or anything else at all complicated. Mathematicians do use the word in that sense, but for them the most important meaning is additivity. A system is said to be linear if the sum of two solutions is a solution; in other words, if the total is precisely the sum of the parts.

To see why linearity in the usual sense is related to being able to add solutions, think of the simplest nonlinear operation: squaring. As you learned at school, you can't get the square of a sum by doing the squarings separately and adding the results: if $z = x + y$ then it is not true that $z^2 = x^2 + y^2$. There is a bit more to come, $2xy$ in case you've forgotten. And squaring is a particularly simple example: there's no sensible way of writing $\log (x + y)$ as $\log x + \log y$ plus a simple term in x and y.

The great advantage of linear systems is that they are relatively easy to analyse. Because we can add solutions, we can break a problem down into manageable bits, solve each of them separately, and then add everything up at the end. Even if the system isn't actually linear, the method may give the answer as accurately as we need or, if it doesn't, it may at least provide a first approximation which can be improved. This is a very powerful technique, and it has produced a lot of good science, but it doesn't always work. Above all, it is not appropriate for dealing with phenomena that arise directly out of nonlinearity.

Everyone knows the Earth is round, but you don't have to bother about this if you are planning a garden or even a city. With a much larger region, like the Canadian province of Saskatchewan, you have to be a bit more careful. When the pioneers were moving in, the government had the southern part of the province divided into square counties. Because the lines of longitude on a sphere are not parallel, the squares don't fit exactly, and you can see on a map of Saskatchewan that the counties on the borders with Alberta and Manitoba have had to be made a slightly different shape. With this minor adjustment, the basic linear plan still works.

If, however, Christopher Columbus had thought the Earth was flat, no minor adjustments to his charts would ever have suggested to him that he could get to the East by sailing west. The fact that you can travel around a sphere is an essentially nonlinear property, and we will not discover it by a process of successive approximations starting from a linear model.

This can be a serious problem for mathematical modelling, because it is not always easy to tell whether a system has important nonlinear properties. The classic example of the power of Newtonian mechanics is the calculation of planetary orbits. The theory predicts these should be very nearly elliptical, which is indeed what is usually observed. The point of Poincaré's famous paper was to show that this need not always be the case, and it has recently been verified by computer that very complicated orbits can exist within our own solar system. This is probably the reason there are gaps in the asteroid belt: the orbits of small bodies at that distance from the sun eventually move out of the region.

The assumption of linearity is at its most insidious when we aren't using mathematics at all, however. It creeps in because so much of our intuition is based on our own and other people's experience of the most intensively studied systems, which are linear. Most of the time, we tacitly assume that the whole is

essentially the sum of the parts, that large effects must have large causes, and so on.

Of course we have all heard about the straw that broke the camel's back, and we all know that a stitch in time saves nine, but we see these as occasional exceptions to the general linear rule. They do not occur in the most commonly used mathematical models, which makes them seem less plausible – less respectable one might say. Besides, it is one thing to write down a nonlinear mathematical model and analyse it carefully; to introduce sudden jumps and thresholds on a purely *ad hoc* basis is generally unconvincing, to say the least.

As nonlinear dynamics becomes better understood, we will become more accustomed to the idea that the characteristic features of nonlinear systems can and do occur, so they will become part of our intuition. We will also learn where they fit in and where they do not. Without a detailed mathematical model, we may not be able to prove that a sudden jump must occur at a certain stage, or that a certain shape will appear, but we often can explain why we would expect it, why it is consistent with the rest of what is going on at the time.

Paradoxically, the two most characteristic features of nonlinear systems are chaos and order, each occurring where we might not have expected it.

Chaos

For mathematicians, the term 'chaos' does not imply total disorder. Instead, they mean what they call 'deterministic chaos', which sounds like a contradiction in terms, but is not. The behaviour is deterministic in that it has no inherently random element: in principle (and sometimes in practice too) we can write down the equations of motion and solve them. The chaos arises because the system is so sensitive to perturbations that even the slightest disturbance can rapidly build up into a major effect.

Now just about everything in real life is subject to perturbations. We can never specify the conditions precisely at the beginning, and there will always be disturbances along the way. So while we may be able to predict the behaviour of a chaotic system for a while, the small errors and perturbations rapidly build up to the point where the process may appear totally random. This is the hallmark of deterministic chaos: short-term predictability (because it is deterministic) together with long-term unpredictability (because it is so sensitive).

A familiar example is the weather. The Meterological Office has a very complex and detailed mathematical model of the Earth's atmosphere. They get reports from weather stations all over the world, and with these as starting values they solve the differential equations on a very powerful computer. This enables them to forecast the weather quite accurately for about a week in advance.

Now you might think that if they could keep increasing the number of weather stations and the power of their computer, they could extend the forecasts as far as they want. In fact, this isn't so. The system is chaotic, and even the smallest errors build up so rapidly that it is generally accepted that the practical limit is at most three weeks.

This is not because the atmosphere of the whole Earth is a large and complicated system. If that were the reason, then this would be nothing more than an extension of the obvious idea that it's not easy to make predictions about large, complicated systems.

In fact, the study of deterministic chaos began with the work of a meteorologist, Edward Lorenz.[3] He was working before powerful computers were available, and so he was studying just one small part of the system. Even that was beyond the capability of his computer, so he had simplified the model down to three very simple equations which he believed – rightly, as it turned out – captured the essence of what was going on:

$$dx/dt = -10x+10y \quad dy/dt=28x-y-xz \quad dz/dt=-(8/3)x+xy$$

Whether you understand differential equations or not, you can see that there are only two nonlinear terms, the two products xz and xy. So systems don't have to be very large to be chaotic, they also don't need to be very nonlinear. If large systems are more likely to exhibit chaos, it is mostly because the more subsystems there are, the more likely it is that at least one of them is chaotic.

But while weather forecasting beyond a couple of weeks or so may not be possible, we can still say something about what will happen. We can, for example, be quite confident that on the first day of the new millennium the temperature at noon in London will not be over 30°C. We don't need the Met Office's computer to know that; it comes from our experience of the climate in England.

If we did solve the equations on a computer, we would almost certainly end up with a prediction of a temperature between, say, 0 and 30, but it wouldn't be reliable, on account of the chaos. So

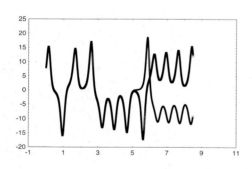

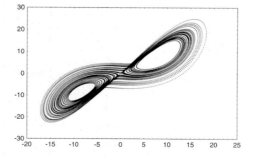

Figure 1. Computer graph of Lorenz's equations: x against t (above); y against x (below)

one result wouldn't be of any use. The best thing to do would be to run the program many times, using slightly different starting values each time. If we did this often enough we would build up a picture of the probability distribution of the temperature. But this would be no better than what we could have obtained far more easily from looking at past records.

You can see the effect in Figure 1, in which Lorenz's equations have been solved on a computer. The upper graph is a plot of x against t. The integration has been done twice, using different starting values of x that differed by less than 0.1 per cent. As you can see, the solutions are quite complicated, and while they stay together for a while, by the end there is no obvious correlation between them.

The lower graph is a plot of y against x. In contrast to the other one, this has a reasonable degree of order, even if the trajectory is a bit complicated. What is more, if you let the system run long enough, then no matter what starting values you choose, to within the resolution of the graph plotter you get the same figure, although it will be built up in a different order. This is why you've almost certainly seen this picture before, though not the one above it. There is order within the chaos.

Thus in addition to short range predictability and long range unpredictability, we also have a very stable long range predictability but only of some general features, not of the whole process. Thus in the midst of the first of one of the typical signs of nonlinearity, chaos, we see the other one, order.

Some properties of nonlinear systems

We can see the difference that nonlinearity can make by thinking of the familiar example of simple algebraic equations. The linear equation $ax+b=0$ has exactly one root (unless $a=0$) and it is real. The quadratic equation, $ax^2+bx+c=0$, has two roots, which may be real or complex. Thus when we move from linear to quadratic two things change. First, we no longer have a unique solution. Second, the solution can be an entirely new sort of object, a complex number.

If we get such significant changes with just a little bit of nonlinearity, you might ask what a lot more will do. The answer is, not much: there may be more than two roots, but that's about it. The roots are still either real or complex; there's nothing more exotic to come. Much the same is true of nonlinear dynamical systems. There doesn't have to be much nonlinearity before the important new features appear. This is why it is possible to study some carefully chosen simple nonlinear systems and have some confidence that we know what they are like in general.

While linear systems have at most a single equilibrium point, nonlinear systems typically have more than one equilibrium state and these can include trajectories as well as points. There are often bifurcation points, and also transitions from one stable trajectory to another, i.e. large changes on a very short time scale. Indeed, large changes usually happen in this way; the stability of the trajectories prevents small perturbations from accumulating.

To see what this amounts to in non-technical language, you can think of a system at a stable equilibrium like a ball at the bottom of a cup. If you disturb it, it goes back to its original position, but apart from that, it doesn't actually do anything. And indeed, linear systems in general are pretty limited, unless someone pushes them.

A system on a stable trajectory is more like a bobsleigh travelling down a run. Far from just sitting still, it is in motion all the time. It, too, can recover from being disturbed, but it doesn't go back to where it was; it picks up the track further down. To complete the picture, you have to imagine that there are typically several runs close together, so that if the bob hurtles out of one it may well land in another and finish its descent at a different end point. You have also to imagine that there are also forks, where one run splits into two and the driver can choose which branch to take. Even this doesn't fully describe what can happen, but at least you can see that nonlinear systems are much richer than linear ones. What is more, much of what happens depends on properties of the system itself (the layout of the runs, in the metaphor) and not on the external forces.

1. Biological development

Over half a century ago, the biologist CH Waddington was struck by some properties that seemed common to all developing organisms.[4] The process is stable: embryos do not need an absolutely perfect environment in which to develop and they can survive many small disturbances and even some large ones. If they are disturbed, development does not stop until they recover. Instead, they gradually return to the normal developmental pathway. Embryos do not have to be genetically identical to develop into very similar organisms. Apart from minor details, however, organisms tend to come in separate kinds; there are discrete species and varieties, not a continuous spectrum of types.

We can now see why developing organisms have these properties: it is simply because they are complex nonlinear systems. That is not to say that we should take organisms and their properties for granted, of course not. It is certainly wonderful that there are such things as organisms. On the other hand, once we know that there are such things as organisms, we should not be surprised that they have these properties. It is hard to imagine how they could be otherwise.[5]

2. Punctuated equilibria

The majority of evolutionists has always insisted that evolutionary change is gradual – in Darwin's words, *Natura non facit saltum*. If the fossil record shows discrete types with no intermediate forms, that is only because the record is incomplete.

About 20 years ago, however, Eldredge and Gould[6] put forward the theory known as punctuated equilibria. They claimed that the gaps in the fossil record are real, and that on the whole evolution proceeds not steadily but in rapid bursts, with long periods in between in which very little happens. This provoked a considerable controversy, with people writing about 'Evolution by Jerks' on the one hand and 'Evolution by Creeps' on the other.

It is not hard to see why. Neo-Darwinists (i.e. modern Darwinists) hold that evolutionary change occurs in the following way: random genetic mutations occur, some of these lead to changes in the phenotype (i.e. in the organism itself), and if these happen to be advantageous they are selected.

The theory locates the origin of the change in the genes, whereas selection acts on the phenotype. Neo-Darwinists seldom say anything about the connection between the two, but they implicitly assume that it is linear. A large change in the organism must have been caused by a large change in the genome. What is more, if the change in the genome is random, that in the organism must be random as well. Since it is totally implausible that the large genetic change required to bring about a significantly different but viable organism could occur by chance, evolutionary change *must* be gradual.

When we take nonlinearity into account, the whole picture changes. Because nonlinear systems typically have multiple equilibria and stable trajectories, we would not expect that major changes will occur as long sequences of minor ones. Instead, we would expect organisms to remain more or less unchanged for a long time and for large changes to occur rapidly as the developmental system moves to an alternative trajectory. Thus punctuated equilibria, far from being an awkward observation to be explained away, is precisely what we would expect to observe.

Self organisation

Nonlinear systems are capable of self-organisation, they can spontaneously generate order. For example, if water in a shallow tray is gently heated from below, the warmer water at the bottom will soon start to rise, while the cooler water at the surface will descend. Initially, the motion will be irregular, but after some time a pattern will appear. It usually resembles a honeycomb, though it can also be a series of parallel rolls. The same effect, called Bénard convection after the person who first described it, can also be seen in 'stone nests', regular arrays of stones which have been put in position by Bénard convection in the air, and in the motion of large numbers of a microorganism, *Euglena viridis*. The famous red spot on Jupiter is not a fixed coloured region on the surface of the planet, but another example of self-organisation. So is the complicated shape that can be formed by a simple drop of milk (Figure 2).

In most cases, it is not easy to see how self-organisation arises without working through a nonlinear mathematical model, which is largely why so few have been analysed until recently. One that can be seen intuitively, and which is also very important, is Jim Lovelock's model for the regulation of the Earth's temperature.[7]

Figure 2. Drop hitting the surface of milk

The Gaia hypothesis

When Lovelock put forward his 'Gaia hypothesis' that the Earth is self-regulating, he was immediately criticised by biologists. Applying the linear intuition I referred to before, they argued that since regulation is a coordinated phenomenon which serves a useful purpose, its cause must also be coordinated and purposeful. In other words, a regulated system must have been designed as such, either by an engineer or natural selection, or, if you prefer, the Creator.

Lovelock responded by showing how regulation could arise without design in a system which is a simplified model of the Earth.[8] He imagined a hypothetical planet called Daisyworld, in orbit around a star which, like our own sun, is very slowly becoming brighter. In the simplest version, the only form of life are daisies with black flowers. They grow best at 22.5C, less well above or below it, and not at all below 5 or above 40, though the seeds can survive.

If the sun is not bright enough, no daisies can grow, but when the planet reaches 5C, a few daisies appear. Since they are black, they make the planet darker, so it absorbs more light, which makes it warmer. This makes the daisies grow faster, which makes the planet darker, and so on. This positive feedback doesn't go on forever, partly because the daisies run out of space, and partly because if they raise the temperature to over 22.5C any more growth makes things worse for themselves, not better. On the other hand, if the solar luminosity continues to increase (or even if it decreases) the temperature remains almost unchanged.

The regulation is even more effective if there are white daisies as well, though this is harder to see without the equations. When both kinds are present, each species generally does better than it would if it were alone. If we want to interpret a dynamic in anthropomorphic terms, in this system cooperation is more important than competition.

This model shows how regulation can arise without design. What is more, a more complicated version of the principle almost certainly applies to the real Earth, which has in fact maintained a remarkably constant temperature through geological time, even though the Sun is now about a third brighter than it used to be. The same principle may also explain how regulation has arisen in organisms as well, for example in the maintenance of constant level of blood glucose in humans and other mammals by a combination of simple positive and negative feedbacks.[9]

Generic properties

A characteristic feature of nonlinear systems is that they often have generic properties, i.e. properties which occur time and time again in different systems and in different contexts. We do not fully understand why this is so, though some progress has been made, but at least we can see why it should be a consequence of nonlinearity. Linear systems are shaped by the forces that act on them, and so they will have the same form only if the forces were similar. Nonlinear systems are more autonomous, which makes it possible that they will have generic properties, though it does not explain how they arise.

1. Catastrophe theory

The best understood example is catastrophe theory, developed by the French mathematician René Thom about 40 years ago.[10] He showed that if boundaries between regions are formed by processes that can be described by any one of a very large class of differential equations, then they must have one of a very small number of shapes. The cusped shape of a supersonic shock wave is not an artefact of the way it is formed: it is about the only shape it could have.

This does not, however, mean that the problem is solved. The major limitation is that catastrophe theory is only local, i.e. it tells us what can happen around one focus of activity. That is sufficient to explain a sonic boom, because while it extends over a large region it is all centred on one point, the position of the aircraft. But it is too limited for biology, which was the subject Thom was most interested in and in which the problem of form is the most important, and no one has so far managed to extend the theory in the way that would be needed.

Some progress has, however, been made. For example, Alan Turing[11] showed how a simple nonlinear process, involving an interaction between reaction and diffusion, could produce patterns in an originally uniform region of tissue. This was a very important result, because by demonstrating that patterns can arise *de novo*, i.e. without prepatterns, it enables us to avoid the danger of an infinite regress.

Unfortunately, few examples are known of patterns that actually are produced in this way, and it now seems clear that it is not a major mechanism of pattern formation in nature. Later workers, however, have been finding other, more plausible mechanisms, which operate on the same mathematical principle, even though the equations that describe them can be quite different. They have also found that the patterns that are produced have many features in common with those predicted by the Turing mechanism, for example that the number of 'repeats' depends on the length of the region and that two dimensional patterns tend to be very irregular unless they are built up one dimension at a time.

2. Phyllotaxis

On many plants, the leaves are arranged along a spiral up the stem, with each leaf at an angle of (on average) 137.5° from the one before. This has been known for a long time, and has fascinated scientists because 137.5 is a golden section of 360. If you choose a leaf at random and then start numbering the leaves above it on the spiral, its two nearest neighbours will have numbers that are members of the Fibonacci sequence 1,1,2,3,5,8,13, . . . (each number is the sum of the two before it). The same is true for the florets on many flowers: in the case of

114

sunflowers the numbers are often 55 and 89. It is easy to show that these two properties are related, but no one has found a convincing explanation of why they occur.

Recently, two French physicists, Douady and Couder,[12] carried out an experiment in which they allowed drops of a magnetised fluid to fall on to a plate at regular intervals. They found that as they made the interval shorter and shorter, the angle between successive drops became almost exactly 137.5°.

Because physics is simpler than biology, Douady and Couder were able to write down the equations of motion and solve them. This allowed them to explain their own results, but not why the same angle occurs in plants, since that has nothing to do with magnetic dipoles.

They realised, however, that while the real mechanism – whatever it is – is different, it might lead to the same equations. To test this idea, they repeated the calculations, but using a different formula for the mutual repulsion between the drops. This naturally changed the equations of motion, but while the solutions were different for drops at longer intervals, as the intervals because shorter, the angle between successive drops still tended to the value 137.5°. This angle, and the golden section and the Fibonacci numbers that go with it, are thus generic properties.

Genericity gives certain features a special status, like the archetypes of the pre-Darwinian biologists like Goethe and Geoffroy Saint Hilaire. They are the natural building blocks of a wide variety of phenomena. We can therefore use them without having to justify in detail why they should appear in a particular context.

In science we are used to arguments that begin like this: 'we know, or at least suppose, that the mechanism for this process is such and such, and from that we can compute that there will be a cusp. Knowing that there is a cusp, we can now predict . . .'

Naturally, we would still prefer to do that if we can. But if we cannot, which is likely to be case when we are studying complex phenomena, we can begin instead: 'we do not know the mecha-nism, but whatever it is, in these circumstances it is likely to produce a cusp. Assuming that there is a cusp, we can now predict . . .' This is not as certain as before, to be sure, but it is a way of making progress when the traditional method fails because of the complexity – which in some subjects is likely to be almost all the time.

Conclusions

In recent years, mathematicians have derived many interesting and important results concerning nonlinear systems. They have also become adept at applying the techniques of nonlinearity to conventional problems. Less has been accomplished towards exploring new ways of applying mathematics, especially those to do with genericity. The controversy that surrounded catastrophe theory in the late 1970s (the effects of which can be felt even today) arose because neither the proponents nor the critics were accustomed to the new sort of modelling. The arguments were similar to the debates about structuralism in some other fields, and of course this is not a coincidence: there are elements of structuralism in the new approach.

The Newtonian paradigm places the emphasis on external forces: gravity, natural selection, the market, and so on. Taking nonlinearity into effect means we concentrate more on the system: in evolution the developmental system of the organism, in economics the nature of society and the people who make it up. It does not, as do relativity and quantum mechanics, introduce entirely new scientific principles, but it can completely alter the direction of our research all the same.

Nonlinearity puts more responsibility on the individual. Chaos ensures that the future is not predetermined, and nonlinearity tells us that we cannot put all the blame for what happens on the outside world. The fault, dear Brutus, lies not in our stars but in ourselves . . .

Department of Mathematics, King's College, Strand, London WC2R 2LS.

Notes

1 See for example, E O Wilson, *Sociobiology, the New Synthesis*, Harvard University Press (Cambridge) 1975.

2 See Mae-Wan Ho's article in this issue; also her book *The Rainbow and the Worm*, World Scientific (Singapore), 1993.

3 E N Lorenz, 'Deterministic nonperiodic flow', *Journal of Atmospheric Science* 20, 1963, pp130-141.

4 C H Waddington, *The Strategy of the Genes*. George Allen and Unwin (London), 1957.

5 P T Saunders, 'The organism as a dynamical system', in *Thinking About Biology* (Santa Fe Institute Studies in the Sciences of Complexity, Vol III) W Stein and F J Varela (eds), Addison Wesley (Reading), 1993.

6 N Eldredge and S J Gould, 'Punctuated Equilibria: an Alternative to Phyletic Gradualism', in T J M Schopf (ed), *Models in Paleobiology*, Freeman Cooper (San Francisco), 1972, pp82-115.

7 J E Lovelock, *Gaia, a New Look at Life on Earth*, Oxford University Press (Oxford), 1979; *The Ages of Gaia*, Oxford University Press (Oxford), 1988.

8 A J Watson and J E Lovelock, 'Biological homeostasis of the global environ-ment: the parable of Daisyworld', *Tellus* 35B, pp284-89. See also P T Saunders, 'Evolution without natural selection: further implications of the Daisyworld parable', *Journal of Theoretical Biology* 166 , 1994, pp365-73.

9 J H Koeslag, P T Saunders and J A Wessels, 'Glucose homeostasis with infinite gain: An application of the Daisyworld parable?' *Journal of Endocrinology*, 1997 (in press).

10 R Thom, *Stabilité Struturelle et Morphogénèse*, W A Benjamin, Reading, 1972. (English translation by D H Fowler, *Structural Stability and Morphogenesis*, W A Benjamin, Reading, 1975.) For a much simpler introduction, see P T Saunders, *An Introduction to Catastrophe Theory*, Cambridge University Press (Cambridge), 1980.

11 A Turing, 'The chemical basis of morphogenesis', *Transactions of the Royal Society of London* B641, 1952, pp37-72.

12 S Douady and Y Couder, 'Phyllotaxis as a physical self-organized growth process', *Physical Review Letters* 68, 1992, pp2098-2101.

THE NEW AGE OF THE ORGANISM
MAE-WAN HO

Organic space-time *versus* mechanical space-time

Organic space-time *versus* mechanical space-time I am told that the comet in our sky visited us 4,000 years ago. As it revolves once around the heavens, earth has revolved 4,000 times around our sun, and human beings have gone from stone age to space age in 160 life cycles. The comet looks like a giant eye in the sky, now within our orbit and looking down on us, having seen, perhaps, many other worlds in far-flung reaches of the universe during its space odyssey. Do any of those other worlds contain beings that gaze back at it as we do? One begins to get a sense of a multitude of space-times entangled with our here and now. The here and now contains in its essence a myriad of there and thens. That is the real sense in which the 'fullness of time' is to be understood. It is the reality of organic space-time that the mechanistic world-view has flattened out of existence.

Mechanical space and time are both linear, homogeneous, separate and local. In other words, both are infinitely divisible, and every bit of space or of time is the same as every other bit. A billiard ball *here* cannot affect another one *there*, unless someone pushes the one here to collide with the one there. Mechanical space-time also happens to be the space and time of the commonest 'common-sensible' world in our mundane, everyday existence. It is the space-time of frozen instantaneity abstracted from the fullness of real process, rather like a still frame taken from a bad movie-film, which is itself a flat simulation of life. The passage of time is an accident, having no connection with the change in the configuration of solid matter located in space. Thus, space and time are merely coordinates for locating objects. One can go forwards or backwards in time to locate the precise objects at those particular points. In reality, we know that we can as much retrace our space-time to locate the person that was 30 or 50 years younger as we can undo the wrongs we have committed then. There is no simple location in space and time.[1]

Psychoanalyst-artist Marian Milner[2] describes her experience of 'not being able to paint' as the fear of losing control, of no longer seeing the mechanical common-sensible separateness of things. It is really a fear of being alive, of entanglement and process in the organic reality that ever eludes mechanistic description. And yet, it is in overcoming the imposed illusion of the separateness of things that the artist/scientist enters into the realm of creativity and real understanding – which is the realm of organic space-time. Mechanical physics has banished organic space-time from our collective public consciousness, though it never ceases to flourish in the subterranean orphic universe of our collective unconscious and our subjective aesthetic experience. In a way, all developments in Western science since Descartes and Newton may be seen as a struggle to reclaim our intuitive, indigenous notions of organic space-time, which, deep within our soul, we feel to be more consonant with authentic experience.

Organism versus mechanism

The mechanistic world-view indeed officially ended at the beginning of this century. Einstein's relativity theory broke up Newton's universe of absolute space and time into a multitude of space-time frames each tied to a particular observer, who therefore, not only has a different clock, but also a different map. Stranger still – for Western science, that is, as it comes as little surprise to other knowledge systems, or to the artists in all cultures – quantum theory demanded that we stop seeing things as separate solid objects with definite (simple) locations in space and time. Instead, they are delocalised, indefinite, mutually entangled entities that evolve like organisms.

The profound implications of this decisive break with the intellectual tradition of previous centuries were recognised by a mere handful of visionaries. Among them, the French philosopher Henri Bergson,[3] and the English mathematician-philosopher Alfred North Whitehead.[4] Between them, they articulated an organicist philosophy in place of the mechanistic. Let me summarise some of what I see to be the major contrasts between the mechanical universe and the universe of organisms.

Mechanical Universe	Organic Universe
Static, deterministic	Dynamic, evolving
Separate, absolute space and absolute time, universal for all observers space-time frames	Space-time inseparable, contingent observer (process)-dependent
Inert objects with simple locations in space and time	Delocalised organisms with mutually entangled space-times
Linear, homogeneous space and time	Nonlinear, heterogeneous, multi-dimensional space-times
Local causation	Non-local causation
Given, nonparticipatory and hence, impotent observer	Creative, participatory; entanglement of observer and observed

The contrasts are brought into sharper relief by considering the differences between mechanism and organism, or, more accurately, the opposition between a mechanical system and an organic system. First of all, a mechanical system is an object *in* space and time, whereas an organism is, in essence, *of* space-time. An organism creates its own space-times by its activities, so it has control over its space-time, which is not the same as external clock time. Secondly, a mechanical system has a stability that belongs to a *closed* equilibrium, depending on controllers, buffers and buttresses to return the system to set, or fixed points. It works like a non-democratic institution, by a hierarchy of control: a boss who sits in his office doing nothing (bosses are still predominantly male) except giving out orders to line managers, who in turn coerce the workers to do whatever needs to be done. An organism, by contrast, has a dynamic stability, which is attained in open systems far away from equilibrium. It has no bosses, no controllers and no set points. It is radically democratic, everyone participates in making decisions and in working by intercommunication and mutual responsiveness. Finally, a mechanical system is built of isolatable parts, each external and independent of all the others. An organism, however, is an irreducible whole, where part and whole, global and local are mutually implicated.

I hope you are sufficiently persuaded that we need a radically new way of understanding the organism, if not the whole of nature, as Whitehead intimates. In this project, we – each and everyone of us – are especially privileged, because we are ourselves organisms and know in intimate, exquisite detail, what it is to be alive.

The vast majority of scientists as well as the general public have remained untouched by this conceptual revolution. Quantum theory itself sits uneasily and paradoxically between the necessary limits of a mechanical description (in quantum *mechanics*) and the elusive, organic reality that remains ever out of reach. Mathematics and physics have recently broken out of the strict mechanistic mould to explore the 'organic' realm (see Ho[5, 6] and Saunders, this volume pp48-53). In mathematics, computations have made accessible previously intractable problems in nonlinear dynamics, fractal geometry and chaos. In the meantime, physics has witnessed an astonishing inventory of empirical successes – high temperature superconductivity, quantum coherence and nonlocal quantum superposition of states – even as theoretical descriptions have lagged far behind. It is precisely at the point where theoretical description fails to capture the organic freedom of reality that contemporary science is at its most captivating. It is the realm of imagery where scientist and artist meet, and where no one who is not both can enter.

The end of mechanistic biology
Mainstream biology is left far behind. It is clinging fast to the mechanistic era. The discovery of the DNA double-helix in the late 1950s, which has made its permanent mark on the public consciousness, was the climax to a century of mechanistic, reductionist biology – the idea that the whole is the sum of its parts, that cause and effect are simply related, and can be neatly isolated. The discovery ended the quest for the material basis of the units of heredity – the genes – that are supposed to determine the characters of organisms and their offspring, thus firmly establishing the predominance of the genetic determinist paradigm. The subsequent flowering of molecular biology gave rise to the present era of recombinant DNA research and commercial genetic engineering biotechnology.

What few people realise is that the very successes of recombinant DNA research have completely undermined the foundations of the genetic determinist paradigm, at least ten years ago. There has indeed been a revolution in genetics which exactly parallels the transition between mechanical and quantum physics. The new genetics signals the final demise of mechanistic biology, and is consonant with the diametrically opposite, organicist perspective which has been emerging in the rest of science. The contrast between the old, pre-recombinant DNA genetics and the new genetics is presented below.

The Old Genetics	The New Genetics
Genes determine characters in a linear, additive way	Genes function in a complex, nonlinear, multidimensional network – the action of each gene ultimately linked to that of every other.
Genes and genomes are stable and except for rare random mutations, are passed on unchanged to the next generation	Genes and genomes are dynamic and fluid, they can change in the course of development, and as the result of feedback metabolic regulation
Genes and genomes cannot be changed directly in response to the environment	Genes and genomes can change directly in response to the environment, these changes being inherited in subsequent generations
Genes are passed on vertically, i.e. as the result of interbreeding within the species, each species constituting an isolated 'gene pool'	Genes can also be exchanged horizontally between individuals from the same or different species

The parallel to the transition from classical to quantum physics is best illustrated by focusing on the concept of the 'gene'.[7] In the old genetics, the 'gene' is a continuous stretch of DNA, with a particular base sequence, and a constant, simple location in the

Energy Flow

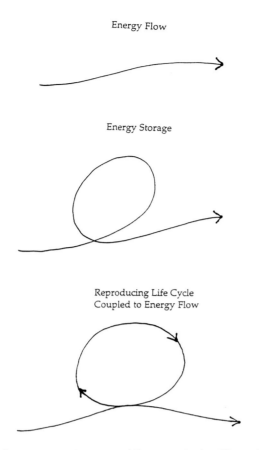

Energy Storage

Reproducing Life Cycle
Coupled to Energy Flow

Figure 1. Energy flow, energy storage and the reproducing life cycle

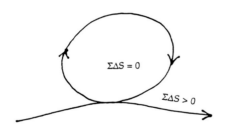

$$\Sigma\Delta S = 0$$

$$\Sigma\Delta S > 0$$

Figure 2. The many-fold cycles of life coupled to energy flow

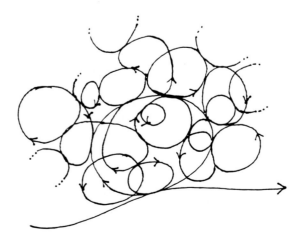

Figure 3. The organism frees itself from the immediate constraints of thermodynamics

genome, that specifies, via a non-overlapping triplet code, the amino-acid sequence of a single protein. The amino-acid sequence of the protein, in turn, determines its function in the organism. The genetic code is universal, and there is a 'one-way information flow' from DNA to an intermediary 'messenger' RNA to the protein, and no reverse information flow is possible. This was the notion of a definite, isolatable gene, specifying a function independently of the cellular and environmental context.

The cracks in the old edifice first appeared when *reverse* information flow was found to occur from RNA back to DNA. Then, the genetic code was discovered to be overlapping and non-universal. Next came a succession of revelations showing that the gene itself has no well-defined continuity nor boundaries, the expression of each gene being ultimately dependent on, and entangled with every other gene in the genome. Far from the one-way information flow that is supposed to proceed from DNA to RNA to protein and on to the rest of the organism, gene expression is subject to influences and instructions from the cellular and environmental contexts. The gene can be recoded, or edited by the cell, it can get silenced, or converted to a different sequence. Genome organisation is infinitely variable, dynamic and fluid. Genes mutate frequently, small and large rearrangements take place, genes jump around, sequences are added or deleted, they get amplified thousands and hundreds of thousands of times or they get contracted. These changes may take place as part of normal development or they occur repeatedly in response to environmental challenges. Some of the genetic changes are so specific that they are referred to as 'directed mutations' or 'adaptive mutations'. Genes can even jump horizontally, by infection, between species that do not interbreed. Genes and genomes are in reality, dynamic, delocalised, mutually entangled and part of larger wholes. In short, biology has been catapulted, over the heads of the old guard, into the new age of the organism.

I have given a good indication of what the new 'physics of the organism' might look like in an earlier book[8] and in other recent publications.[9] In the rest of this paper, I shall outline a theory of the organism, ending with a few remarks on certain key aspects that are most relevant to organic, as opposed to mechanistic forms: organic stability, organic space-time and the integral delocalisation of organic forms.

A theory of the organism

There are 75 trillion cells in our body, made up of astronomical numbers of molecules of many different kinds. How can this huge conglomerate of disparate cells and molecules function so perfectly as a coherent whole? How can we summon energy at will to do whatever we want? And most of all, how is it possible for there to be a singular 'I' that we all feel ourselves to be amid this diverse multiplicity and plurality?

To give you an idea of the coordination of activities involved, imagine an immensely huge superorchestra playing with instruments spanning an incredible spectrum of sizes from a piccolo of 10^{-9} metres up to a bassoon or a bass viol of 1 metre or more, and a musical range of *72 octaves*. The amazing thing about this superorchestra is that it never ceases to play out our individual songlines, with a certain recurring rhythm and beat, but in endless variations that never repeat exactly. Always, there is something new, something made up as it goes along. It can change key, change tempo, change tune perfectly, as it feels like it, or as the situation demands, spontaneously and without hesitation. Furthermore, each and every player, however small, can enjoy maximum freedom of expression, improvising from moment to moment, while maintaining in step and in tune with the whole.

I have just given you a theory of the quantum *coherence* that underlies the radical wholeness of the organism. It is a special wholeness that involves total participation, and maximises *both* local freedom and global cohesion. It involves the mutual implication of global and local, of part and whole, from moment to moment. It is on that basis that we can have a sense of ourselves as a singular being, despite the diverse multiplicity of parts. That is also how we can perceive the unity of the here and now, in an act of 'prehensive unification'.[10] Artists like scientists, depend on the same exquisite sense of prehensive unification, to see patterns that connect apparently disparate phenomena.

In order to add corroborative details to my story, however, I shall give a more scientific narrative involving some easy lessons in thermodynamics and quantum theory. It begins with energy relationships.

The thermodynamics of organised complexity

Textbooks tell us that living systems are open systems dependent on energy flow. Energy flows in together with materials, and waste products are exported as well as the *spent* energy that goes to make up *entropy*. And that is how living systems can, in principle, escape from the second law of thermodynamics. The second law, as you may know, encapsulates the fact that all physical systems run down, ultimately decaying to homogeneous disorganisation when all useful energy is spent, or converted into entropy. But how do living systems manage their anti-entropic existence?

I have suggested[11] that the key to understanding how the organism overcomes the immediate constraints of thermodynamics is in its capacity to store the incoming energy, and in somehow closing the energy loop within to give a reproducing, regenerating life cycle (see Figure 1). The energy, in effect, goes into complex cascades of coupled cyclic processes within the system before it is allowed to dissipate to the outside. These cascades of cycles span the entire gamut of space-times from slow to fast, from local to global, that all together, constitutes the life-cycle (see Figure 2 for an intuitive picture). Each cycle is a domain of *coherent* energy storage – coherent energy is simply energy that can do work because it is all coming and going together, as opposed to incoherent energy which goes in all directions at once and cancel out, and is therefore, quite unable to do work.

Coupling between the cycles ensures that the energy is transferred directly from where it is captured or produced, to where it is used. In thermodynamic language, those activities going thermodynamically *down*-hill, and therefore yielding energy, are coupled to those that require energy and go thermodynamically *up*hill. This coupling also ensures that *positive* entropy generated in some space-time elements is compensated by *negative* entropy in other space-time elements. There is, in effect, an internal energy conservation as well as an internal entropy compensation. The whole system works by reciprocity, a cooperative give and take which balances out over the system as a whole, and within a sufficiently long time. The result is that there is always coherent energy available in the system. Energy can be readily shared throughout the system, from local to global and *vice versa*, from global to local, which is why, in principle, we can have energy at will, whenever and wherever it is needed. The

organism has succeeded in gathering all the necessary vital processes into a unity of coupled non-dissipative cycles spanning the entire gamut of space-times up to and including the life-cycle itself, which effectively feeds off the dissipative irreversible energy flow (see Figure 3).

But how can energy mobilisation be so perfectly coordinated? That is a direct consequence of the energy stored, which makes the whole system *excitable*, or highly sensitive to specific weak signals. It does not have to be pushed and dragged into action like a mechanical system. Weak signals originating anywhere within or outside the system will propagate throughout the system and become automatically amplified by the local energy stored, often into macroscopic action. Intercommunication can proceed very rapidly, especially because organisms are completely *liquid crystalline*.

The liquid crystalline organism

Several years ago, we discovered an optical technique that enables us to see living organisms in brilliant interference colours generated by the liquid crystallinity of their internal anatomy. We found that all live organisms are completely liquid crystalline – in their cells as well as the extracellular matrix, or connective tissues.[12] Liquid crystals are states of matter between solid crystals and liquids. Like solid crystals, they possess long-range orientation order, and often, also varying degrees of translational order (or order of motion). In contrast to solid crystals, however, they are mobile and flexible and highly responsive. They undergo rapid changes in orientation or phase transitions when exposed to weak electric (or magnetic) fields, to subtle changes in pressure, temperature, hydration, acidity or pH, concentrations of inorganic molecules or other small molecules. These properties happen to be ideal for making organisms, as they provide for the rapid intercommunication required for the organism to function as a coherent whole. Some images of live organisms taken from video-recordings are shown in figure 4.

What you are seeing is the whole of the organism at once, from its macroscopic activities down to the long-range order of the molecules that make up its tissues. The interference colours generated depend on the structure of the particular molecules, which differ for each tissue, and their degree of coherent order. The principle is exactly the same as that used in detecting mineral crystals in geology. But, with the important difference that the living liquid crystals are *dynamic* through and through, as the molecules are all moving about busily transforming energy and material in the meantime. So, how can they still appear crystalline?

Because visible light vibrates much faster than the molecules can move, the tissues will appear indistinguishable from static crystals to the light transmitted, *so long as the movements of the constituent molecules are sufficiently coherent*. Actually, the most actively moving parts of the organism are always the brightest, implying that their molecules are moving all the more coherently. With our optical technique, therefore, one can see that the organism is thick with coherent activities at all levels, which are coordinated in a continuum from the macroscopic to the molecular. That is the essence of the organic whole, where local and global, part and whole are mutually implicated at any time and for all times. These images draw attention to the wholeness of the organism in another respect. All organisms – from protozoa to vertebrates without exception – are polarised along the anterior-posterior axis, or the oral-adoral axis, such

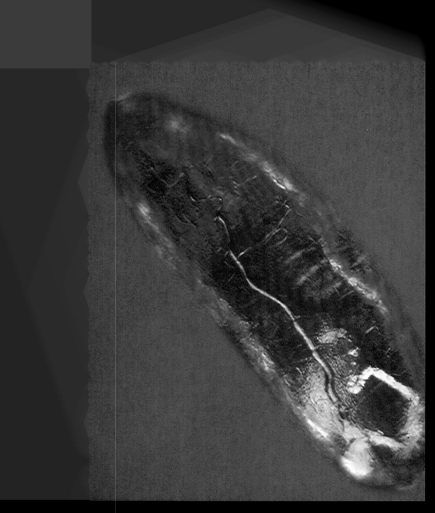

Figures 4a, 4b

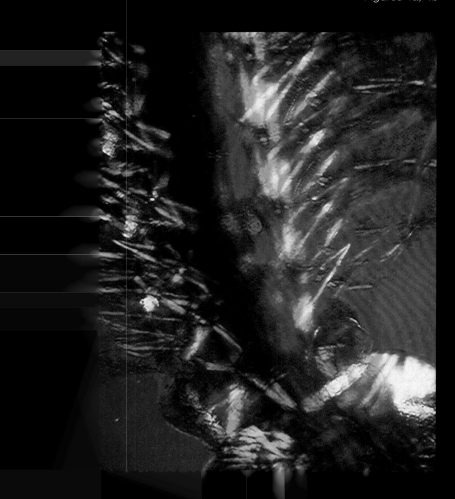

that all the colours in the different tissues of the body are at a maximum when the axis is appropriately aligned in the optical system, and they change in concert as the axis is rotated from that position. The fruitfly larva has cleverly demonstrated that for us by curling its body around in a circle (figure 4 c,d).

The coherence of organisms and nonlocal intercommunication
As I said before, intercommunication can proceed very rapidly through the liquid crystalline continuum of cells and connective tissues that make up the organism. In the limit of the *coherence time* and *coherence volume* of energy storage – the time and volume respectively over which the energy remains coherent – intercommunication is instantaneous or nonlocal. There is no time-separation within the coherence volume, just as there is no space-separation within the coherence time. Because the organism stores coherent energy over all space-times, it has a full range of coherent space-times, which are furthermore, all coupled together. Thus, there is a possibility for nonlocal intercommunication throughout the system. In the ideal, the system is a quantum superposition of coherent activities, constituting a 'pure coherent state' that maximises both local freedom and global cohesion, in accordance with the *factorisability* of the quantum coherent state.[13] Factorisability means that the different parts are so perfectly intercorrelated that the intercorrelations resolve neatly into products of the self-correlations. So the parts behave as though they are independent of one another. This is the radical nature of the organic whole (as opposed to the mechanical whole), where global cohesion and local freedom are both maximised, and each part is as much in control as it is sensitive and responsive.

The 'whole' is thus a domain of coherent activities, constituting an autonomous, free entity,[14] *not* because it is separate and isolated from its environment, but precisely *by virtue of its unique entanglement of other organic space-times* in its environment. In this way, one can see that organic wholes are nested as well as entangled individualities. Each can be part of a larger whole depending on the extent over which coherence can be established. So, when many individuals in a society have a certain rapport with one another, they may constitute a coherent whole and ideas and feelings can indeed spread like wildfire within that community. In the same way, an ecological community, and by extension, the global ecology may also be envisaged as a super organism within which coherence can be established in ecological relationships over global, geological space-times.[15]

The ideal quantum coherent state involving the whole system is a global *attractor* to which the system tends to return when it is perturbed, but as the system is always open, it will invariably be taken away from the totally coherent state. So here is how space-time, as well as entropy or time's 'arrow', is generated.[16] It is generated in proportion to the *in*coherence of actions taken. The more the actions taken are at odds with the coherence of the system, the more time, and entropy, is generated, and the more the system ages. Thus, the biological age of an organism may literally be quite different from the age as measured by external clock-time. In the same way, the earth itself can be ageing much faster on account of our incoherent actions within it. On the other

The liquid crystalline organism: still frames from a video-recording of live organisms viewed with a special polarised light microscopy technique which detects liquid crystalline regimes – figures 4a, 4b, successive frames of a first instar fruitfly larva about to hatch; figures 4c, 4d successive frames of the first instar fruitfly larva shortly before hatching

land, we may indeed enter a state of delocalised timelessness when we achieve a high degree of coherence. Some of us get an inkling of that during an aesthetic experience, or alternatively, a religious experience.

Several people have asked me whether it is possible to get younger. My first reaction was no, because for all real processes, according to the textbook, entropy is greater than or equal to zero. On further reflection, however, I think the answer has to be yes. It follows from the principle of internal entropy compensation in an organic system, where negative as well as positive entropy can be generated, and also because past and present, as well as present and future, can be *nonlocally* interconnected. The challenge is indeed to set ourselves and the earth back on a possibly rejuvenating, or at any rate, anti-entropic and self-sustaining course.[17]

Organic space-time and fractal space-time

Organic space-time is tied to activity, and as elaborated above, these activities are fundamentally anti-entropic on account of their tendencies towards coherence. The organism is thus a coherent space-time structure engendering nonlocal interconnectedness. What is the nature of this structure?

There are several lines of recent evidence converging to a new picture of the 'texture of reality'[18] suggesting that organic space-time does have a structure, and that this structure is fractal. One of the most exciting discoveries in recent years, which has given rise to the science of complexity is that natural processes and natural structures have *fractal* dimensions. That means they have dimensions in between the one, two or three to which we are accustomed. Fractals capture a new kind of order characterised by self-similarity – the similarity of part to whole over many different scales. Snowflakes, clouds, ferns, coastlines, branching patterns of blood vessels, and the 'cytoskeleton' inside each cell are all examples of fractal structures. Natural processes, from weather patterns to the healthy heart-beat and electrical activities of the brain, similarly, exhibit 'chaotic dynamics' that when spatialised as a 'Poincaré section'[19], gives rise to strange attractors' that again have fractal dimensions. If space-time is indeed generated by processes as I have proposed here, then it should also exhibit fractal dimensions, or more accurately, multi-fractal dimensions. This is the basis of the 'space-time differentiation' of organisms.[20]

According to Nottale[21] and others, the whole of present day physics relies on the unjustified assumption of the differentiability of the space-time continuum, which stems from the classical domain, whereas Feynman and Hibbs[22] have already shown that the typical path of a quantum particle is continuous, but *non*differentiable. This is the failure of present-day physical description to capture the organic quantum reality that I have alluded to earlier; for the description is still based on a mathematical representation of space-time as continuous and homogeneous, i.e. as infinitely divisible or 'differentiable'. It so happens that a structure that satisfies the requirement for continuity and non-differentiability is also fractal. Nottale writes:

Giving up the hypothesis of differentiability has an important physical consequence: one can show that curves, surfaces, volumes and, more generally, spaces of topological dimension D_T, which are continuous but non-differentiable, are characterized by a length, an area and, more generally a D_T measure which becomes explicitly dependent on the resolution at which they are considered . . . and tends to infinity when the resolution

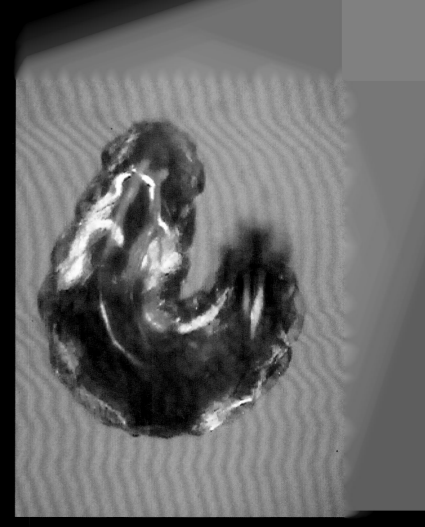

Figures 4c, 4c

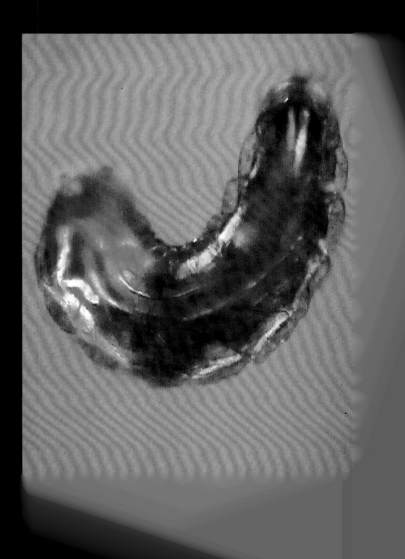

interval e tends to zero. In other words, a non-differentiable space-time continuum is necessarily fractal ... This result naturally leads to the proposal of a geometric tool adapted to construct a theory based on such premises, namely, fractal space-time.[23]

The author then proceeds to describe a new approach that generalises Einstein's principle of relativity to scale transformations. Specifically, the equations of physics are required to keep their form under scale transformation, i.e. to be scale covariant. It allows physicists to recover quantum mechanics as mechanics on a fractal space-time, in which Schrödinger's wave equation is a geodesic equation.

I wonder if that is not the beginning of an approach towards the quantisation of space-time which, I believe, is a necessary consequence of the quantisation of action that Planck's constant already involves. This quantised space-time is also Bergson's 'duration', which expresses the indivisible multiplicity of our subjective experience of organic process.[24] It is the experience of processes cascading through the continuous scales of fractal space-times that are all coupled together or entangled through the coherence of the 'ground' or asymptotic state, over which the scale covariance is defined.

What would an organic architecture be like?

Organic architecture is nothing new. As Jencks points out, '"Organic unity, where not a part can be added or subtracted except for the worse" are injunctions that have rebounded through the halls of building sites for 2,000 years.'[25] The artists have been well ahead of scientists after all. Jencks touches on some of the themes developed in this chapter in his grand panoramic sweep of how the new 'science of complexity' is changing architecture and culture. However, as with quantum theory itself, much of the science of complexity is still mechanism aspiring towards organism. So, perhaps there is an excuse for me to give in to the temptation of trying to imagine what organic architecture would be like, based on the new view of the organism just presented, and to make connections with some well-known and lesser known concepts in established organic architecture.

Organic stability versus mechanical stability

One question which arose (for some of us) in the wake of the discoveries of the new genetics is, how do organisms and species maintain their stability when genes and genomes are so mutable and fluid? That is a question on the nature of organic stability in general.

The conventional, neo-Darwinian explanation is that natural selection is always at work to select out those that are unstable, and hence 'unfit', so only those that are sufficiently stable remain to propagate offspring like themselves. A neo-Darwinian account of architecture, might similarly explain that buildings are selected for stability – those that were not stable simply fell down and eliminated themselves, leaving the stable ones for us to admire and to imitate.

I do not know how that explanation fares in architecture, but it certainly fails to account for the responsiveness of organisms, including their genes and genomes, to environmental and physiological changes.[26] The stability of organisms and species is dependent on the entire gamut of dynamic feedback interrelationships extending from the socio-ecological environment to the genes. Genes and genomes must also adjust and respond, and if

necessary, change, in order to maintain the stability of the whole. As stated above, the stability of organisms is diametrically opposite to the stability of mechanical systems. Mechanical stability – which includes that of so-called 'cybernetic' systems – belongs to a closed, static equilibrium, maintained by the action of controllers, buffers or buttresses designed to return the system to set points. Organic stability, on the other hand, is a dynamic balance attained in open systems far away from equilibrium, without controllers or set points, but by means of intercommunication and mutual responsiveness. The stability of organisms depends on *all* parts of the system being informed, participating and acting appropriately in order to maintain the whole.

Organic stability is therefore delocalised throughout the system, via symmetrically commuting parts, each of which changes in response to all the others and to the environment. I am reminded of Cecil Balmond's constructions (see this volume), his 'free forms' which defy gravity. Organic stability is in the dynamic integrity of the whole. I can imagine the stresses and strains distributing and ever-shifting from one part to another in cycles of correlated reciprocity. If these forms were made of transparent, liquid crystalline material, as living organisms are, one might see a beautiful display of ever-changing colour patterns reflecting the shifting patterns of stresses and strains, as the structure communicates with its environment, just as one can see in real organisms.

Organic forms are supported and sustained by their relationship to the environment. Liquid crystals, in particular, are constantly evolving embodiments of their changing environments, their surfaces are invariably curved and flexible, hence the study of their structure is referred to as 'flexi-crystallography' by crystallographer Alan MacKay. Liquid crystals go through many abrupt phase transitions, each 'phase' being itself a continuum of more subtle variations. The phases are all minimum energy surfaces separating an 'inside' from the 'outside', though the inside and the outside can be so thoroughly interdigitated that it becomes a major problem in topology to disentangle them. The infinite variety of intricately sculpted exoskeletons of radiolarians are mineral deposits templated by different liquid crystalline formations. Liquid crystalline structures have already inspired certain architectural designs, such as the carpark in the National University of Mexico.[27]

Organic space-time and organic architecture

Whereas a mechanical form is located *in* space and persists (or not) in time, an organic form, by contrast, *is* a space-time structure; to be exact, a coherent space-time structure. An organic form *creates* space-time, increasing its space-time differentiation in the course of development and in evolution. Being *in* an organic form is to partake of its distinctive space-time, and its possibility for nonlocal interconnections over multiple dimensions. Jencks points out that virtually all those who referred to 'organic architecture', including classicists such as Vitruvius and Alberti, and modernists, such as Gropius and Wright, insisted on work that shows fractal self-similarity, or 'unity with variety'.[28]

I have proposed above that organic space-time *is* fractal because it arises out of natural processes which are fractal. Fractal architecture, therefore, is a unique creation of organic space-time that extends and enhances our experience as organisms. I am captivated by Bruce Goff's plan of his Bavinger House.[29] It exhibits the dynamic, nonlocal inter-connections and the multiple resonances of the fractal, organic whole, simultaneously unfolding and enfolding, diverging and converging in the gesture of life itself. I imagine sounds taking on added dimensions of musicality and coherence within this structure.

Another aspect of organic space-time is its complexity, or space-time differentiation.[30] This corresponds, I think, to Jencks' concept of the 'organizational depth' of an architecture – the 'density with which things are linked' – which counters the 'depthless present' of modernist architecture by 'building in time'. The depth of organic space-time is not just a nestedness but a special kind of superposition and entanglement. A fine example of space-time entanglement is Rem Koolhaas' library in Jussieu University, Paris.[31] It is a continuous linear route traversing a stack of near-horizontal planes connecting one level to the next; the whole floor is one unbroken multi-level ramp through which weaves 'a grid of columns and randomized incidents'.[32]

Of course, organic architecture is not restricted to fractal constructions, just as organic processes can undergo global phase transitions or catastrophic changes. In terms of space-time structure, phase transitions would correspond to major reorganisations of the system, giving rise to a new Schrödinger's wave or 'geodesic' equation. Jencks has explored nonlinear and catastrophic forms to much effect in his interior and exterior designs and in landscaping.

The integral delocalisation of organic forms and organic architecture

Finally, it must be stressed that an organism is an unique embodiment of its environment, that arises out of an uninterrupted act of 'prehensive unification',[33] a Bergsonian duration. Put in another way, the organism is an unique, integral space-time entangling a multitude of space-times. It simultaneously creates its own space-time while being constitutive of other space-times. As a work of art, the organic architecture is more than an icon or a symbol. It is a coherent superposition and entanglement that gives nonlocal access to the diverse multiplicity of space and times that constitute its integral whole. That may be the real challenge to organic architecture.

Bioelectrodynamics Laboratory, Open University, Walton Hall, Milton Keynes, MK 7 6AA UK.

Acknowledgments
This essay benefited from stimulating discussions with Charles Jencks and Cecil Balmond, and with Alan Mackay. Philipe Herbomel drew my attention to Nottale's papers on fractal space-time by kindly sending the xerox copies. Part of this article was first presented as a public lecture 'A theory of the organism and organic space-time' at a Conference on Time and Timelessness, Dartington Hall, April 9-13, 1997. I was much inspired by the occasion, by the responses of the audience, and by composer and scholar, Edward Cowie, who introduced my lecture. Julian Haffegee exercised great skill in preparing the colour images of figure 4.

Notes
1 A N Whitehead, *Science and the Modern World*, Penguin Books (Harmondsworth), 1925.
2 M Milner, *Not Being Able to Paint*, Heinemann Education Books (London) 1957.
3 H Bergson, *Time and Free Will. An Essay on the Immediate Data of Consciousness* (F L Pogson, trans), George Allen & Unwin Ltd (New York), 1916.
4 A N Whitehead, op cit.
5 See M W Ho, *The Rainbow and the Worm, The Physics of Organisms*, World Scientific (Singapore), 1993.
6 See M W Ho, 'The biology of free will', *Journal of Consciousness Studies* 3, 1996, pp231-44.
7 For details of this refer to M W Ho, *Genetic Engineering Dreams or Nightmares. The Brave New World of Bad Science and Big Business*, Third World Network (Penang), 1997.
8 M W Ho, *The Rainbow and the Worm, The Physics of Organisms*, op cit.
9 M W Ho (ed), *Bioenergetics, S327 Living Processes*, Open University Press, (Milton Keynes), 1995.
— 'Bioenergetics and the coherence of organisms', *Neural Network World* 5, 1995, pp733-50.
— 'The biology of free will', *Journal of Consciousness Studies* 3, op cit.
— 'Bioenergetics and biocommunication', in *Computation in Cellular and Molecular Biological Systems* (R Cuthbertson, M Holcombe and R Paton, eds) World Scientific (Singapore) 1996, pp251-64.
10 A N Whitehead, *Science and the Modern World*, op cit.
11 In M W Ho, 'The biology of free will', op cit; and 'Bioenergetics and biocommunication', op cit.
12 See M W Ho, 'Bioenergetics and biocommunication', op cit; and S Ross, R Newton, Y M Zhou, J Haffegee, M W Ho, J P Bolton and D Knight, 'Quantitative image analysis of birefringent biological material', *Journal of Microscopy*, 1997 (in press); and M W Ho, J Haffegee, R Newton, and S Ross (1995) 'Organisms are polyphasic liquid crystals' *Bioelectrochemistry and Bioenergetics* 41, pp81-91.
13 M W Ho, *The Rainbow and the Worm, The Physics of Organisms*, op cit; 'The biology of free will', op cit; 'Bioenergetics and biocommunication', op cit.
14 See M W Ho 'The biology of free will', op cit.
15 See M W Ho, *The Rainbow and the Worm, The Physics of Organisms*, op cit; and M W Ho, 'On the nature of sustainable economic systems', *World Futures*, 1997 (in press).
16 See M W Ho, *The Rainbow and the Worm, The Physics of Organisms*, op cit.
17 See M W Ho, 'On the nature of sustainable economic systems', *World Futures*, op cit.
18 See I Stewart, *Does God Play Dice: The Mathematics of Chaos*, Basil Blackwell (Oxford) 1989.
19 Ibid.
20 See M W Ho, *The Rainbow and the Worm, The Physics of Organisms*, op cit.
21 L Nottale, 'Scale relativity and fractal space-time: applications to quantum physics, cosmology and chaotic systems', *Chaos, Solitons and Fractals* 7, 1996, pp877-938.
22 R P Feynman and A F Hibbs, *Quantum Mechanics and Path Integrals*, MacGraw-Hill (New York), 1965.
23 L Nottale, 'Scale relativity and fractal space-time: applications to quantum physics, cosmology and chaotic systems', op cit.
24 See M W Ho, *The Rainbow and the Worm, The Physics of Organisms*, op cit.
25 C Jencks, *The Architecture of the Jumping Universe*, Academy Editions (London), 1995; chapter VIII, 'Self-similarity (fractals) and strange attractors' p43.
26 See M W Ho, *Genetic Engineering Dreams or Nightmares. The Brave New World of Bad Science and Big Business*, op cit.
27 Alan Mackay, personal communication.
28 C Jencks, *The Architecture of the Jumping Universe*, op cit, p43.
29 Ibid, p45.
30 See M W Ho, *The Rainbow and the Worm, The Physics of Organisms*, op cit.
31 See C Jencks, *The Architecture of the Jumping Universe*, op cit, p87.
32 Ibid, p88.
33 A N Whitehead, *Science and the Modern World*, op cit.

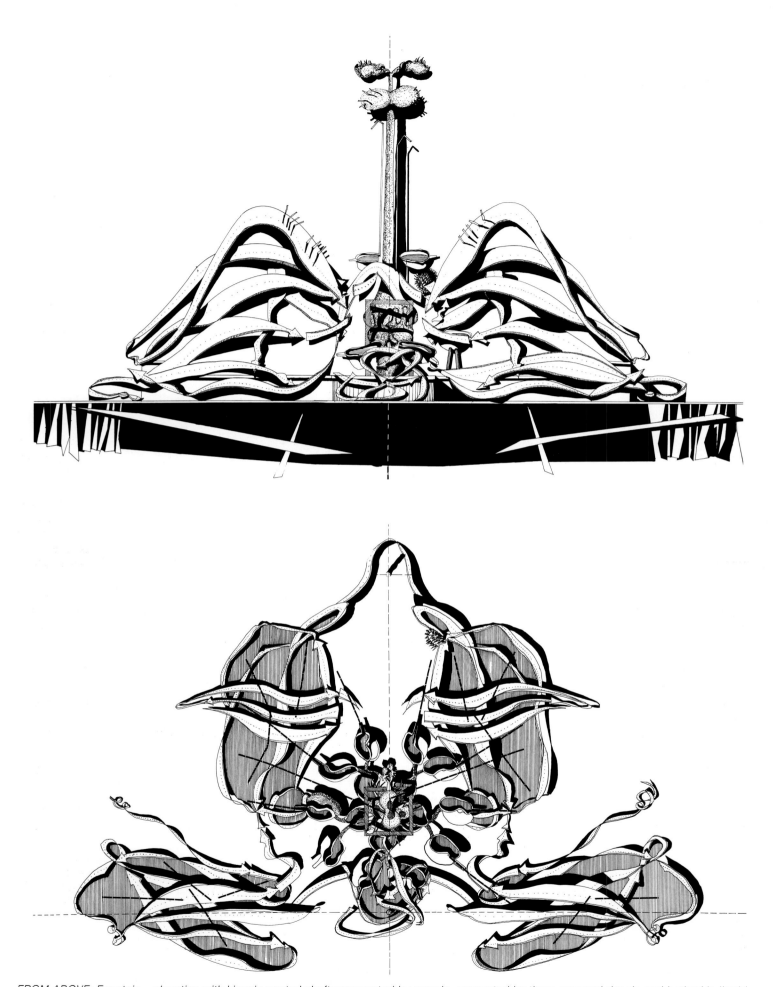

FROM ABOVE: Fountain – elevation with kinesin central shaft surmounted by myosin, supported by three-pronged dynein and bathed in liquid desire; model of EPO mimetic, cross-linked to form a covalent dimer with nested, spiky gooseberry and central antibody water butt feature

NEIL SPILLER
VACILLATING OBJECTS

Distended design through a Dalinian lens
It was an instrument of high physical poetry formed by distances and by relationships between these distances; these relationships were expressed geometrically in some of the parts, and arithmetically in others; in the centre, a simple indicating mechanism served to measure the saint's death-throes. The mechanism was composed of a small dial of graduated plaster, in the middle of which a red blood-clot, pressed between two crystals, acted as a sensitive barometer for each new wound.

In the upper part of the heliometer was Saint Sebastian's magnifying glass. This was at once concave, convex and flat. Engraved on a platinum frame of its clean, precise crystals could be read Invitation to Astronomy; *and beneath, in letters standing out as if in relief:* Holy Objectivity. *On a numbered crystal rod one could read further:* Measurement of the Apparent Distances between Pure Aesthetic Values *and to one side, on a highly fragile test-tube, this subtle announcement:* Apparent Distances and Arithmetical Measurements between Pure Sensual Values. *The test-tube was half full of sea water.*

'Heliometer for the deaf and dumb', from *Saint Sebastian*, Salvador Dali[1]

Flipping spatiality

The city is populated by limp and soft bags of liquid, mostly water, crowded between and within towers of metal, stone and glass. Some towers are tall and thin, some are very stubby indeed. These soggy, leaky bodies spend much of their day mumbling to each other through an invisible meta-skin, This skin, a skin of communication, is forever becoming hyper-sensitive and more able to trace itself. These beings pluck bits off themselves and other animate and inanimate material, which they farm and reinstall in the hope of damming their bodily leaks or unblocking their aneurisms.

The space-flight programmes of the 60s and 70s have been described as an exercise of putting 'spam in cans' and shooting them into space. Historically, there has always been a distinction between the 'spam' and the 'can'. The spam is wet, fragile, sensitised, the desiring observer and the conscious subject. The 'can' is bought, sold, slow, inert, often a hollow container and in thrall to its function. This is all changing; the stasis of the object is in question. Man-made constructions, the products of hard engineering, are starting to vacillate. The object is losing its pathetic impartiality. Objects have for too long floated in a sea of objectivity. Our technologies have developed a series of interlinked spatial fields, each with differing qualities with blurred boundaries. The objects that inhabit those fields are becoming schizophrenic. One of the tasks of the 'cyber-' or 'bio-tect' will be to design ecologies of what I shall call 'object fields', not just to define the definite object that operates in a uniform spatial field. An object will have many selves, many simultaneous forms. Technology is forcing the object to become a subject, partial and

anamorphic. The anamorphic object changes form when viewed from certain viewpoints, in different fields or in distorted mirrors. The new objects will have formal qualities that are determined by the virtual or physical terrain in which they are viewed or manipulated. Baudrillard has battled with the evil genie of the object and its destiny:

'Only the subject desires; only the object seduces'. We have always lived off the splendour of the subject and the poverty of the object . . . The fate of the object, to my knowledge, has been claimed by no one. It is not even intelligible as such: it is only the alienated, accursed part of the subject, The object is shamed, obscene, passive, prostituted, the incarnation of Evil, of pure alienation.[2]

The surreal object fascinated Dali. He described it in terms of its variations in an article entitled 'Surrealist Objects', in *Le Surrealisme au Service de la Revolution*. These variants included 'Symbolic Functioning Objects', 'Transubstantiated Objects', 'Objects for Hurling', 'Enveloped Objects' and 'Mould Objects'.[3] Dali also wrote of 'Edible Objects', 'Liquid Objects', 'Blind Objects' and 'Psycho-Atmospheric-Anamorphic Objects'. Whilst Dali's objects were often the product of automatic assemblage, it is clear that he could see the changing status of the object as crucial to society. His work often alluded to Freudian symbolism with which he was obsessed.

Whilst Dali's objects did much to further the Surrealist project, they are fundamentally different from the new vacillating, partial objects that are starting to populate our contemporary spacescapes.

Unhelpful topology

The new vacillating objects take no notice of topological distinction. Topology, as described by F David Peat, is:

concerned with boundaries, intersections and containment. It is more general than geometry and could be thought of as those relationships which survive being stretched, bent and twisted on a rubber sheet. Once lengths have been expanded or contracted, straight lines twisted into curves, and triangles transformed into circles or squares, all that remains are the more primitive, yet powerful relationships of topology. These are concerned with the way figures intersect and enclose each other and with how many holes pass through a figure.[4]

Topology, particularly of space-time, is an important mathematical idea and is useful in determining the similarity of objects across various distorted fields. One would think that on the surface the new objects would have topological similarity across their various spatial territories. This is not the case. The new spatial fields contort not only the object but also the 'rules' from which they themselves consist. The viscosity of a spatial domain can fluctuate. In the same way that 'virtuality' can be amplified along the Virtuality Continuum (see 'Unit 19: Restless Hearts and Restless Minds', p87), space can be reconstructed. The new

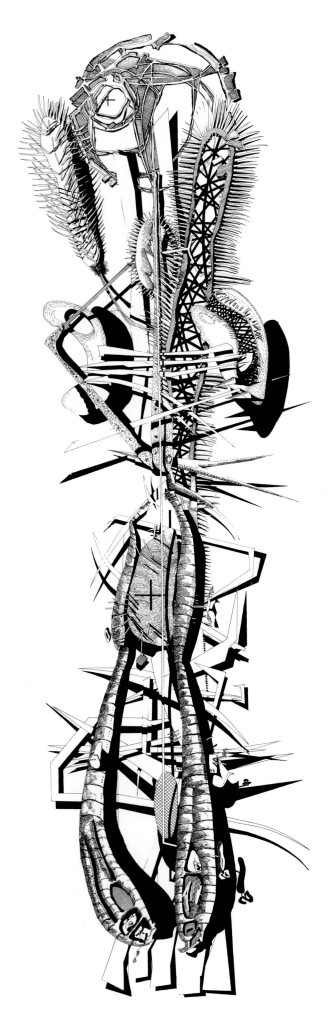

The Martydom of Saint Sebastian is the third panel of a triptych that illustrates some of the issues concerning the contemporary body and its relationship to technology. The first panel was published in AD 'Integrating Architecture' as 'Genesis to Genocide'; the second, 'Nativity in Black' as an illustration to the essay 'Vile Bodies', published in Ecstatic Architecture *(Academy Editions)*

spatial fields consist of a series of variable component fields: gravity, viscosity, spatial jump-cutting being but three simple ones. These optional spatial parameters will become ever more dexterously manipulable as our technologies become advanced and less confined to the virtual. One must not forget the morphological potential of biotechnological objects and nanotechnological objects.

Objects have always occupied worlds where the objects and spaces around them change geographically or in respect of their informational denseness, and can be forcibly and formally changed: some by way of distortion of the spatial field, others through the contortion of the object. The object has had an inability to respond to most spatial fields, and changing an object by force, whether heat or hammer, has normally resulted in the object ceasing to function. The new objects will suffer from none of this crippling inertia or pathetic entropy; they will work in mysterious ways. They will change their topologies not just across spatial boundaries but often within the same spatial field.

We must also not become fixated by the almost salacious attractions of 'function'. Dali saw the benefit of useless objects which perhaps have other meaning than the overtly mechanistic and functional;

> The museums will fast fill with objects whose uselessness, size and crowding will necessitate the construction, in the desert, of special towers to contain them. The doors of these towers will be cleverly effaced and in their place will an uninterrupted fountain of real milk, which will be avidly absorbed by the warm sand.[5]

In our hurried rush towards more responsive and networked environments we must not neglect the simple pleasures of the gratuitous. This extends to the decoration of our new 'spacescapes' with vacillating objects, some of which may just be useless.

Active sites

The new objects may have zones that are much more sensitive than other parts of their surface. These might be even termed erogenous. However I will borrow the term 'active site' from molecular biology. Active sites are defined thus by David Goodsell:

> Enzymes are large but inconspicuous molecules. They are typically globular in shape, most often with a cleft on one side. A few key amino acids, precisely arranged in this cleft, perform the chemical task. Three glutamates, each carrying a negative charge, may be arranged in a triangle to snare a magnesium ion, which carries a complementary positive charge. Large, carbon rich phenylalanines and tryptophans may line a deep pocket, forming a comfortable nest for a fatty tail . . . This cleft with its perfectly tailored arrangement of amino acids, is termed the *active site*.[6]

Active sites, as well as being a way to link objects together, could be the ports that one tickles to cause formal distortion or to coerce information from objects, or be a door to another spatial terrain.

An object that has representations in more than one set of spatial conditions may well have differing numbers and configurations of active sites. So, even in terms of information topology, the new vacillating object will not be a martyr to the tragic topological inertia. Objects will flit between topological orders as one chooses clothes. These objects may, of course, be wearable but quite often will also be 'of' the body, negotiating its many methods of excluding the foreign with disdain.

The jungle of blood

As we nourish and clog ourselves and our culture with more and more data, the object will become invigorated. It will think, desire and swerve. It could be that the object is capable of a type of superposition, a quantum indeterminacy, being everywhere and nowhere at once. All this is very well if these special turbo-charged objects remain digital, virtual, and somehow contained in cyberspace. It is once the object learns some of the lessons of, as Lorca calls it, the 'jungle of blood', once it appropriates animal reproduction procedures that it is finally free.[7] It will smear itself in the viscera and its tactics of self-replication; its specialised proteins, its finely perforated lipid membranes and its genetic periodic table. It is here that pure evil lurks; it is here that the line is crossed. The machine, the dumb object will become fleshed, biologically 'other'. There was a time when machines, were deified, mimicked in art and sociology. It was easy then. Machines allowed us to keep the jungle of blood at armature's length. Now the new vacillating object's armatures can be gened. We used to mimic machines; now the machine is not only mimicking us, it is making cocktails of us.

These observations on the role of the new wet biotech objects are the subject of a humorous scenario in Jeff Noon's 'Automated Alice'. Alice encounters a character, Pablo Ogden, who is a 'reverse butcher'. He is busy constructing his greatest work, James Marshall Hentrails, Jimi for short. He tells Alice of the Newmonia.

'Newmonia!' Pablo screamed at Alice, 'not *pneu*monia! You silly creature! There's no P in Newmonia . . . Why can't you listen properly, Alice? The Newmonia is a terrible disease that allows animals and humans to get mixed in new combinations.'

Later Pablo tells Alice, 'A reverse butcher is an artisan of the flesh who reconstructs creatures out of their butchered parts.'[8]

Nonetheless, it is clear that the new objects may sometimes be clothed in flesh, protein and bone, sometimes operating in deep visceral space, often at a microscopic scale. These guises may not necessarily be human in origin but are often transgenic.

An example of a new object that is soft engineered is the Bony Object. Some recent research has suggested that bone can be tissue-engineered in designer moulds. Currently these moulds mimic the contour of skeletal bones, such as the femur. These are also characteristics of the new objects, camouflage and stealth. However, it could be that these moulds could grow bone that has a variety of other forms. These bones may be linked to all manner of virtual objects that in themselves are linked to other objects, both virtual and real. These objects will help us operate in the growing ecologies of spatial fields.

With objects of this type we are able to create Bolas Objects that shift across spatial divides, reconfiguring yet maintaining a type of informational orbit. It is possible to prescribe some relationships whilst still navigating the cloud of the 'object field'.

We should return to Dali and Saint Sebastian. As Ian Gibson writes, Dali sees the saint as 'an embodiment of the objectivity to which he had come to believe contemporary art should aspire. The Saint's impassivity, serenity and detachment as the arrows sear his flesh . . .'

It's marvellous no longer to feel the necessity of indulging in everything, the nightmare of being submerged in *nature* that is in mystery, in the imprecise, in what cannot be grasped; marvellous to be centred at last, limited to a few simple truths and preferences, clear, ordered sufficient in my spiritual sensuality.[9]

This is where we lose Dali. Seduced by the inertness of the metallic machine, he searched for objectivity. The Saint Sebastian of today is all that Dali's depiction, and those of the Renaissance, is not: porous not impervious, vacillating not static and networked, not detached.

The new virtual, vital, viral and visceral spaces within which the new objects will operate will be infinite; variegated, variform, ventral, varicose, vitrified, vomiting, velutinous, venereal, versicoloured, ventripotent, vascular and versatile will be just some of their qualities.

The Object is dead. Long live the Object.

Notes

1   Ian Gibson, *The Shameful Life of Salvador Dali*, Faber and Faber (London), 1997, p157.
2   Jean Baudrillard, *Fatal Strategies – Crystal Revenge*, Semiotext(e) (New York), 1990, p111.
3   Gibson, p 293.
4   F D Peat, *Superstrings and the Search for the Theory of Everything*, Abacus (London), p25.
5   Gibson, p293.
6   David S Goodsell, *Our Molecular Nature – The Body's Motors, Machines and Messages*, Springer-Verlag (New York), 1996.
7   Gibson, p165.
8   Jeff Noon, *Automated Alice*, Doubleday (London), 1996, pp82-83
9   Gibson, p143.

BERNARD CACHE/OBJECTILE
TOPOLOGICAL ARCHITECTURE AND THE AMBIGUOUS SIGN

The work of Objectile (Bernard Cache, Patrick Beaucé, and Taoufik Hammoudi) utilises design strategies situated within contemporary modes of production as a means to effect critical practices. Cache's development of the implicit relevance that materiality and fabrication have for architecture is significant, derived from the thought of Gilles Deleuze: particularly with respect to topology, the fold and planes of immanence. In *The Fold*, Deleuze refers specifically to Bernard Cache, a theorist in his own right; the closest evidence perhaps of Deleuze's proximity to architecture.[1]

Cache's theories are a rigorous source of what may be called the 'topologising' of architecture: a trajectory that is disseminating within the architectural field, not only as a result of the increasing presence of computer technology but due to the increasing complexity of contemporary life. It is ironic, yet interesting, that Cache's applications and implementations put the issue of authorship in architecture at risk.

Drawing upon a variety of scales and design problems, Cache's theories have reworked the classical tenets of architecture, stemming from Vitruvian theory with its basis in Platonic form. Translating Deleuze's rereading of Leibniz and the Baroque, Cache reworks the fundamental geometry of architecture: substituting the square, circle and triangle, with the frame, vector and inflection, which have tremendous import through their generative dynamics, in contradistinction to the combinatory logic of Platonic forms.

Cache's fundamental argument that all form consists of either convex or concave curvature, stems from his analysis of inflection – what Leibniz calls an 'ambiguous sign'. For Cache, an inflection has the characteristics of a geometric undecidable, which works outwardly from its centre. This is defined as an 'intrinsic singularity'.[2] The inflection works in a generative way, disseminating a geologic of openness and responsiveness to the potentials of an encounter.

Cache translates the fundamental dynamics of curvature, situated between the earth and the sky, describing topological relationships between geography and architecture, inside and landscape: filtered through a complex double frame. This is reflected most clearly in his furniture designs which are predominately of wood, exploiting the inherent contours of the material.

Much of the work of Bernard Cache and

Objectile is achieved through computer milling. Computer programming is just one of the many sites of inquiry of this philosopher, mathematician and businessman, whose theories are also insinuated in information technology. Cache has evaluated three computer-modelling paradigms that effect the discipline of architecture; one of which, he insists, architects have not, as yet, considered. While well-known to architectural practice, the dominant softwares are specifically avoided for being too inflexible.

At the other end of the spectrum is the higher-end, animation software. Although this is easily capable of creating fluid forms based upon animation and radical deformation, it is not geared towards full-scale fabrication. Instead, Cache chooses to rework software which is more familiar to industrial designers, who create precise components for mass production. It is the 'exact-modelling' software environment, Cache argues, that has the greatest potential for architectural variegation. This represents an interesting alternative to much of the content in this volume on hypersurface theory, whereby radical image-forms generated by high-end computers translate algorithmic data into complex configurations, exemplified by the work of Marcos Novak.

The overall objective of hypersurface theory is to allow for Other forces – cultural forces or subtle, sub-dominant forces – to influence, determine and destabilise the pure authority of the author/architect. The exact modelling of Cache's work is an interesting foray into an already dominant mode of production (manufacturing industries), where the generation of materialised form is determined by profit motivated, consumer-driven corporations. The mainstream corporation is what Cache, in his most Marxist moment, seeks to displace. Therefore Cache's work is, indeed, a strategy that calls into question the dominant powers, but by working within these powers seeks to challenge them, as close to the heart of the tradition as is possible (hence his close reading of Vitruvius).[3] This raises the issue of how other practices interpret the complexities of the contemporary world and how one may work within that complexity to further its chaosmotic potential.[4]

The ability of Cache's middle-range, modified software to produce the necessary tolerance for industrial design production is significant: taking

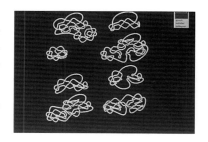

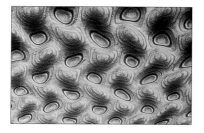

FROM ABOVE: Algorithmic knots; artificial landscape; non-standard bistro table

128

what used to be the parameters of the Industrial Revolution and mass production and reworking the systemic to accommodate infinite variation. This procedure has the potential to reconfigure a determinant that has a considerable impact on our built environment. Even though this places Cache's modus operandi on a middle scale, in terms of architecture (furniture, body, ornament and so forth), it is here that he establishes an important connection between Deleuze and Guattari's theories of indeterminacy and the very forces of capitalism; and here that he locates a critical schema within an inhabitable plane of immanence.

Cache is intent upon forging a direct connection between the multiplicity of consumer desire and the dominant modes of production that drive capitalism. He wants the mode of production to be placed in the hands of the consumer, a tactic that presents a significant challenge to the corporations of sameness that shape cultural identity. His interest here is in liberating the consumer from the repressive forces of consumer culture, seeking instead to celebrate alterability that can become an inherent feature within aggregate production.

Cache wishes to maximise the flexibility and variability available within the mode of production; an ability that goes much further than mere self-determination. If infinite variegation is a fact of production, then identity as such is rendered in a far more complex way, leading us back to Cache's theories of Subjectiles and Objectiles. The scope of these theories is extensive, offering a substantial contribution to a theory of hypersurfaces.[5] His most recent project for a Textile Museum is outlined as follows.

Notes

1 Gilles Deleuze, *The Fold: Leibniz and the Baroque*, Tom Conley (trans), University of Minnesota Press (Minneapolis), 1993, p14.
2 Bernard Cache, *Earth Moves: The Furnishing of Territories* Michael Speaks (ed), Anne Boyman (trans), The MIT Press (Cambridge, Mass), 1995 , p34.
3 Bernard Cache presented a lecture at Columbia University during the Fall of 1997, where he unfolded a specific attachment to and interrogation of Vitruvian theory. A transcript of that lecture is to appear in the forthcoming, *Columbia Documents of Architecture and Theory,* vol 7.
4 Félix Guattari, *Chaosmosis: An Ethico-Aesthetic Paradigm*, Paul Bains and Julian Pefanis (trans), The University of Indiana Press (Bloomington), 1995.
5 Ibid, p92; in particular, his discussion of half-object, half-subject.

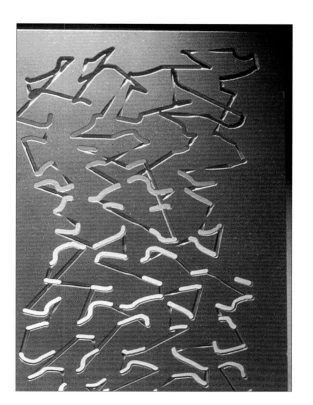

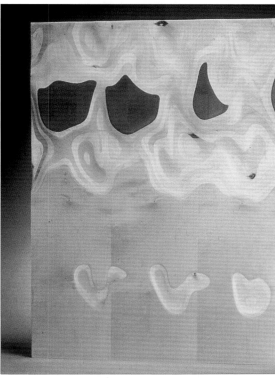

FROM ABOVE: Acoustic wood panel; decorative wood panel

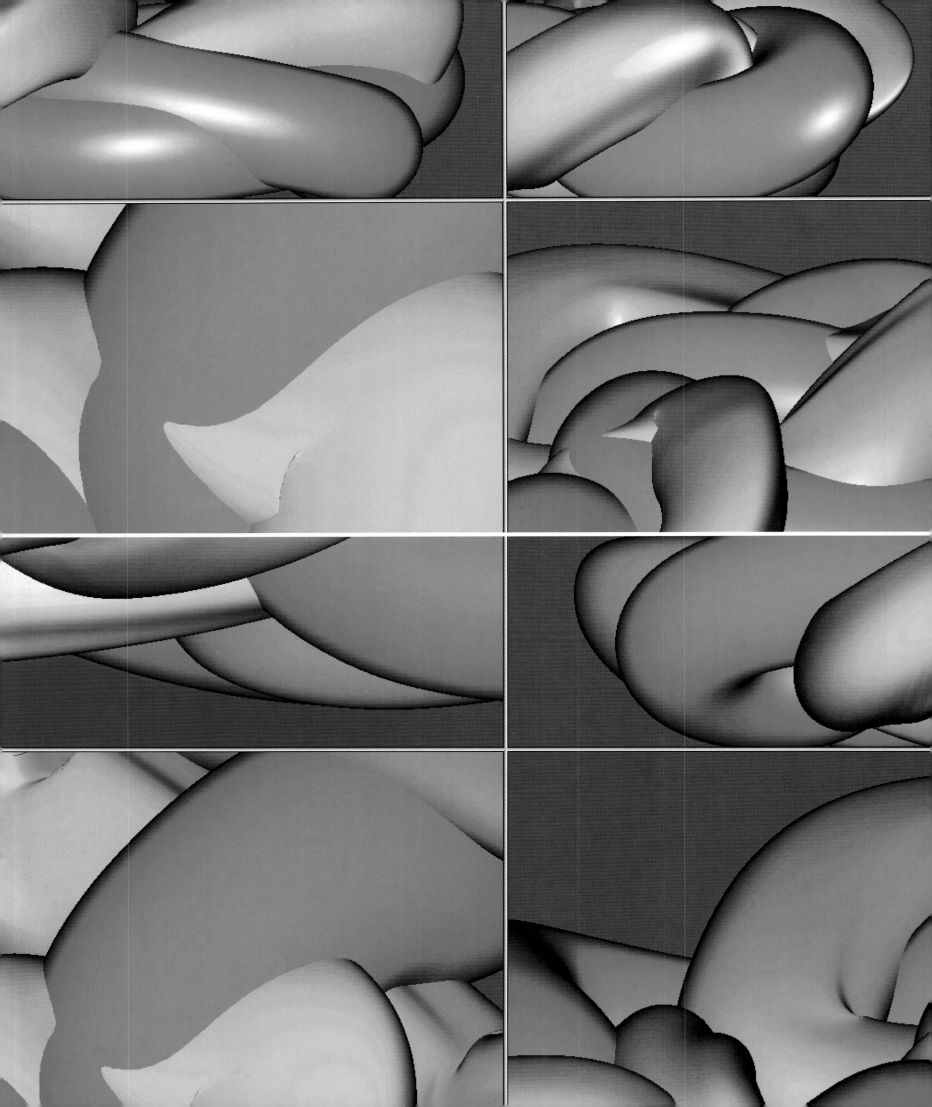

Textile Museum

This project investigates knot and string theory, questioning how a knot can be obtained when the inflexion loops onto itself, or how to escape from organicism when the open surface closes itself to form a solid. The question arises from the structure of the mathematical functions we use when we design 'objectiles' as opposed to 'subjectiles'.

In a Semperian mode, structure is subordinated to cladding. Thus textile technology comes prior to tectonics, ceramics and stereotomy.

The key element of textile is the knot. Our software development of knot generation provides very different results starting with traditional patterns, ie Arabic, Celtic, and so forth, and then developing them further with Penrose spatial structures, and then finally becoming the building itself.

Knot models are being used in various human sciences. For Gottfried Semper the knot was much more than just a technical element: it deals with a basic sense of corporeity, hence our detailed images. However, these images also allow us to study architectural detailing, like the lines of intersection between the several interlacing elements. The knot also works on the architectural pattern of the patio, which until now we considered as a horizontal torus. With the use of an interlace the different patios are perceived as overlapping one another.

Such architecture can only be built with the support of good non-standard technologies. The interesting problem of establishing a horizontal floor within this building may be considered.

Finally, this knot architecture plan seems particularly well suited to a museum with different sections. These can become circuits which are bifurcated at the crossings.

Stephen Perrella

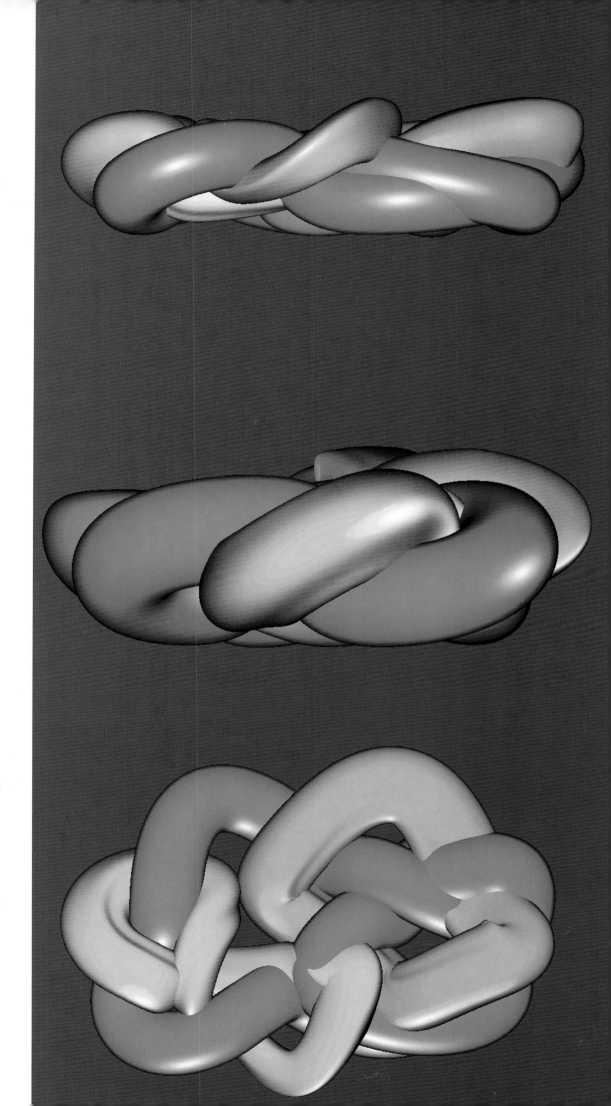

OPPOSITE: Details of intersections; RIGHT, FROM ABOVE: Front elevation; side elevation; plan

STEPHEN PERRELLA
COMPUTER IMAGING
Morphing and Architectural Representation

When one considers the complex spatiality described in the following interview involving the film *Terminator 2*, it is conceivable to maintain that such advances in digital technology affect cinematic temporality and enable new forms of spacetime. Suspending but not dismissing an analysis of the movie's technophobic/fatalist narrative, a closer consideration of its production techniques may reveal astonishing possibilites for contemporary architecture. The technology available to achieve cinematic effects has developed rapidly over recent years and instigates questions about culture, desire and its implementation in electronic technology, especially since many advances originate in the military industrial complex's research and development. The complexity made possible by these new practices may constitute an uncanny convergence between non-foundational theory and ordinary imaging practices. Considering modern culture's emphasis on visuality, 'everyday practices' as it is used here is fairly inclusive.

The context for this cinema/computer/body interface analysis begins with the cinematic fundament of 24-40 or more frames per second to create real time illusion. Innumerable theses exist surrounding the technical circumstances that constitute cinematic temporal illusion but for the purpose of this discussion it is consequential to examine such basic technical facts and their impact on the illusion of reality given their geometric relations to time. Much theory has also been spun around the possibilities of superposition and montage as a means to surpass the limitation of the frame-gap-frame production sequence of film, avant-garde film of the 30s, through to contemporary French new wave and new German film notwithstanding. These genres reveal specific attempts to emphasise structural transparency or the superposition of one image over another, creating shocking or abrupt juxtapostions. Architect Stanley Allen recently described this condition paradigmatically as *The Cinematic Eye:*

The engineer-monteur is an architect who builds with images. Place is created out of fragments distant in time and space: by constructing 'with intervals' he recognises the gap, the lag, which must now be built into the fabric of time and space. The metropolis produces a new subject: the montage eye capable of constructing a new reality out of the barrage of fragmentary, contradictory and obsolete information which characterises the modern city.'[1]

Between the spaced configuration of modern cinema, a transitional technology with a long and perhaps marginalised significance involves cartoon animation. Brian Boigon, from the School of Architecture, Toronto has argued for the inclusion, into architecture, of qualities of animism such as those which may be found in cartooning. This is made possible by the cartoonist imparting an intuitive connectivity contingent with the violated laws of realism. A further analysis of the geometries of cartoon animism would reveal glimpses of what is currently available to the mutations of realism.

The repressed phenomena excluded from each frame in the characterisation of modern film include change, time and *becoming.* Philosopher Mark Taylor eloquently unfolds this struggle between identity and difference in philosophy since Hegel (albeit in a critique of Structuralism) explaining that, 'since temporal change resists systemisation, systems can be constructed only by *excluding* time.'[2] The breakthrough achieved in *Terminator 2*, is an interframe, interstitial geometry-morphing. The importance of morphing lies in the capabilities of mutation and the transplacing of one image into another. The meta complex encompassing the interstitial geometry/smooth space involves the derivation of geometry from the actor's body with that of a virtual actor in the computer, which is then mapped into the cinematic frame-by-frame structure. This special effect construct has strong resonances with the problematics facing architectural representation and realisation (in that the architect transforms thoughts

into two dimensional form then into three-dimensional form). A similar difficulty arises in the gaps between the systems of representation. This brief outline suggests one possible connection between the new interstitial geometrics described in contemporary morphing and architectural practices. It seems reasonable to suggest that as technology affords increasingly sophisticated methods of complexification and pervades more deeply into everyday imaging practices, the boundaries between the real/architectural terms and image/effects will become further delimited.

Notes

1 Stan Allen formulations, 'Projections: Between Drawing and Building, Part II: Four Paradigms of Seeing', *A+U Architecture and Urbanism*, London, April 1992.
2 Mark Taylor, *Deconstruction in Context: Literature and Philosophy*, University of Chicago Press, Chicago and London, 1985, p13.
3 Peter Coveney and Roger Highfield, *The Arrow of Time*, Ballantine Books, New York, 1990, p82.

STEPHEN PERRELLA
INTERVIEW WITH MARK DIPPE
Terminator 2

Stephen Perrella: To learn more about geometric complexity we are interested in the computer software that Industrial Light and Magic (ILM) developed for the liquid metal sequences in *Terminator 2* and the 'morphing' effects in Michael Jackson's current video *Black and White*. We understand morphing as the grafting or the superposition of faces/images with a specified number of intermediate frames, but the *Terminator 2* sequences are certainly complex. In the documentary *The Making of Terminator 2* , laser scanning techniques and grids applied to the actor's face and body are the interface between 'reality' and the computer. Could you describe in detail these techniques and focus on their implicit geometries?

Mark Dippe: Morphing as you describe it was developed at ILM for the film *Willow*, for the sequence in which the Willow character tries with a magic wand to reconstitute a good witch who's been turned into a goat. In the sequence she transforms from a goat into an ostrich, a turtle, a tiger, a young woman and finally an older woman. Morphing involves a transformation between objects of completely different shapes, sizes and forms. A traditional technique like the typical wolf/man dissolve isn't enough. In the digital realm we now have the freedom to change the shape of the picture while simultaneously dissolving. That's the essence of the morphing technique, taking two images that are shot separately and, while performing a cross-dissolve between them, changing the shape of both to improve the illusion of transformation.

SP: Does one select particular control points on the first face/image and then determine their counterpart control points on the next sequential image, with an interstitial range of 50 to 5,000 frames?

MD: Yes. We talked earlier about the role of a grid in the original morph technique, and although it has evolved over the years, it is based on a grid of points. To take an image

of a square, for example, to a circle, a grid of points is imposed over the picture containing the square and a similar grid over the picture containing the circle. That gives you a correspondence between points on each.

SP: The grid is the controlling geometry for the linkages?

MD: Exactly. But to continue, if I take a certain grid point in picture A and move it and leave the corresponding grid point in picture B alone, that will determine how picture A will be distorted as it turns into picture B. That is a direct correspondence and becomes a unique mapping between the two images. This is how the original morph worked: a point-by-point grid correspondence with the freedom to move any of the points in picture A or B with the computer distorting them back to the ideal grid, which can then be cross-dissolved. That correspondence and manipulation give you the changing form. It's mostly moving the grids. The computer doesn't know what the picture is, it has no knowledge of the image. It only knows grids, and as the grid points move it takes the underlying picture and distorts it as the grid is distorted.

SP: How is the liquid metal effect more complex than this?

MD: We now have a whole new generation of morphing ability. The basic principle of morphing as it was used in *Willow* around 1988 has been used repeatedly and is now just one small tool in our spectrum of capabilities. We use the previously described morph all the time but now it's rarely the only thing used to accomplish an ILM effect, and in fact determines a rather small proportion of the total effect. *Terminator 2* is a good example of the next level of what some people call morphing; we don't call it morphing because it's really more distinct. *T-2* involved creating a believable, life-like human form. One quality of human forms, of any living form, is that they are

difficult to represent in traditional computer animation because they are soft and have tissue that reacts and changes in very subtle ways. For instance, when we run, our muscles shake each time our feet hit the ground and impact our thighs. These soft-tissue, muscle and bone dynamics of living creatures in motion are very difficult to model because conventional computer graphics are essentially Euclidean; everything is rigid, polygonal and flat.

SP: Current architectural researchers are interested in the middle ground between the organic and the Euclidean that is considered 'supple.'

MD: Organic forms don't obey the Euclidean rules in which computers excel. Computers can calculate perfectly straight lines but with human forms nothing is perfectly straight; there are only recognisable unique shapes. The other side of the coin is that people can recognise a real human face, even though they can't describe it. We might be able to draw it, but we can't quantify the shape easily.

SP: One might add that living organisms have a certain vitality over anything mechanical that furthers the computer modelling problematic.

MD: One of the aesthetic dilemmas in computer animation is that an algorithmic process can be stiff and inorganic. In *Terminator 2* we were very aware of these limitations and even the movement of the chromed liquid-metal man with a metallic feeling had to be life-like. The principle used here also relates to the grid. We knew that if we projected a perfect grid on our actor Robert Patrick's body and filmed him moving with a painted grid on his body, the grid would distort in the same way as his body tissues did when he walked, ran or performed. So he was made to stand still for hours like a figure on a crucifix while we projected grids on him and then make-up artists copied them meticulously around his body; parts of which the projection didn't cover, so the make-up artists interpolated them. We then took Robert into daylight to analyse his motion again. This became our reference to study how his tissues moved in an organic, supple manner. Our digital actor would move the same way. We worked with an analogy between the real world and our virtual world. With a real set, a real camera and a real actor on the one hand; and on the other a computer camera, a computer set and computer actor. Our objective was to make them match perfectly. We can put a computer actor into a real set or a real actor into a computer set. We're good at creating computer cameras that match real cameras and computer sets that match real sets. Things that are man-made, like buildings and chairs, are easily handled; but trees and flowing water are more difficult. We had our actor perform many different movements – running, walking, dancing and fighting scenes: different dramatic actions that were to occur in the film. They were filmed with two cameras simultaneously from two perpendicular views, a front view and a side view. The cameras were synchronised to photograph frames in unison. We then took the two pieces of film and input them into the computer to produce perfect side and front views. We also had all the data on the cameras and the lenses and built an exact duplicate on our computer of the real filming situation. We had two computer cameras with exactly the same lenses etc, then we placed our computer actor the same distance from the two cameras, made him walk and run at the same speed as the real actor, and then finally compared the two.

SP: So you built an interstitial model in virtual reality.

MD: We concentrated here on the mixture of reality and virtual reality. For me that's almost natural. We've always concentrated on augmenting things or growing them. Greater percentages of an image are being generated on a computer, but still there's always a portion that is photographed or obtained by some other means.

SP: Your work can be looked at in another way, in that it problematises real perception – what we see in the movies and in natural perception is altered by virtuality. We might also consider the space between virtual and real as one of displacement: where neither the virtual nor the natural remains intact but each problematises the other.

MD: Lately, images are no longer pure – in cinema, photography or almost anywhere. The camera itself is of course an interpretation of reality, but images are being manipulated further. There used to be a notion of the image as truthful, the veracity of photographs. It's a moot point now because they are always manipulated. The idea of special effects seems anachronistic; eventually it may be accepted as natural. This seems unusual because all images are 'real'. They are always manipulated or created, changed or altered, yet somehow real.

SP: That is a condition that we might consider as hyperreality .

MD: In this hyperreality we built our virtual man in a virtual set, with a set of references to make sure our digital actor behaved like the real actor. Having completed his model we had essentially created the character of our digital actor including his animation and behaviour. We knew what he would do in any situation, just as a writer would. We were able to anticipate how the T-1000 would sit, walk and get up and how his head would rise out of a floor. At that point we began working on the actual shots, and the initial phase of creating the T-1000 lasted at least two months.

SP: Did the research that you were doing in any way influence the script?

MD: No, but I would say we had a great impact on the film's look. In film-making the content must always come from the story. The director, James Cameron, was and still is the only major director who has any sort of sensitivity to, or compassion for, the new aesthetic possibilities of digital film-making.

SP: The documentary on the film portrayed the director's vision of how to go further with the man-machine relationship. Can you articulate the liquid-geometry sequences?

MD: We had created the T-1000 character to go through a transformation that breaks down into five stages, each with its own model that could be transformed or morphed, from one to the other. This is different from the morph we talked about in *Willow* because it's a 3-D shape: it's actual geometry, an architectural form in 3-D that can now transform or evolve through five stages. First, was the blob stage: the amorphous, molten liquid blob-form. Second, was the 'silver surfer' form: a very

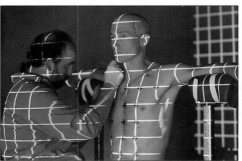

soft, man-like form; smooth like a sand-blasted figure, like the silver surfer in the comic books and like an Oscar award. The third phase we called the soft T-1000: the image of the actor smoothed down but with distinctly recognisable contours of clothing and detail. The fourth step was completely defined metal: he had all of the detail, minus skin or clothing. The fifth stage was reality: the real, skin and flesh actor.

SP: How many interim frames were used between phases?

MD: That depended on the action. The character might take at the most a couple of seconds to transform from one stage to another. Transforming from the stage-one blob to stage five, in the big, grandiose scene where he's a blob on the floor and the camera pulls up and he's slowly changed all the way to the man, took at least five seconds. It varied in the action scenes and he rarely went all the way between the two extremes. He typically went from stage two to stage five. That's how we broke it down. After working with it a while, we noticed there were distinct stages, even a certain logic to it. If he was going to perform a certain action, he had to go through a certain stage.

SP: What kind of geometry occurs in these five phases?

MD: We reduce our models of the actor to a great interconnected web of points, and those point meshes transform in shapes between the stages.

SP: Are those alpha-numeric trajectories, or do you actually see these geometric trajectories connected?

MD: On the computer you can see the model at stage one, then at stage two; and then you can run the animation and watch the model transform and all the points move in space from stage one to stage two. We have an interactive animation system for those views.

SP: You have software that helps you see the phase interfaces?

MD: Yes, we can bring up the point mesh visually on the screen. The ability to bring up these point mesh models interactively on the screen is becoming more common and you can buy various computer modelling systems that do that. The models we

work with are very dense and complex, so our systems are more high-end than most.

SP: Did ILM develop this software, or do you use standard authoring programmes? How deeply do you get involved with programming?

MD: It is a combination. At ILM we have a software staff of about six people and we combine the best of everything. There is no necessity to invent new programmes, we use whatever will give the best visual results. We have a combination of off-the-shelf software and custom software. The work we do could not be done without custom software. In some sense we are forced to write software to create these kinds of images. I'm an effects supervisor and I sometimes get involved in the design of our software in terms of the functionality needed to achieve the image. To me a central problem is the metamorphosing of 3-D forms. That's the key. Like muscularity, it's transforming in shape and function; but it's moving. It's a living organic being, a character. These things are very complex and many other things also take place. The surface quality changes: maybe from a very shiny metal to a dull, pitted, worn surface; or to a more diffused or a matte, skin-like surface; or even to clothing. The computer can transform very easily between two states. Animating all parameters or all aspects is a natural computer function and very difficult to do physically. In real life a morph like equivalent requires a dissolve between two stages or a very complicated and unique animatronic puppet. That puppet is only capable of a few things — maybe its fingers can grow longer or something — but with a computer it's very easy to transform shapes, colours and everything else.

SP: I've heard rumours that there is work on a virtual reality theme park and also about developing virtual space for audience interaction in movie theatres. When I saw the T-2 video arcade in the theatre lobby, I realised that project was already underway.

MD: They were working on the game when we were working on the set. It was interesting. They took some of our grid ideas as a clue. In fact, they had seen the two-camera shot and set-up and the grid on the actor, and they worked with similar ideas for the game designers. They were shooting from two simultaneous cameras to give the game designers references as well. Soon there

will be virtual reality thatchers, where each audience member has virtual reality headsets and can walk around and experience the movie as they like and perhaps be a part of the action. In the San Francisco Bay area there are performances groups like Antenna Theatre where the audience members actually walk around with little FM headsets and are part of the performance. As time goes on the difference between what is real and what isn't real is breaking down. For instance, we can extract something someone didn't like out of an existing film or take an actor out of an old film and put him in a new one.

SP: Can you mention any of the software that you used in the T-2 movie?

MD: For the 3-D morphing or the 3-D transformations we developed a technique called 'make sticky' – similar to Disneyland's Haunted House effect where live-action film is projected on a bust to simulate the act of talking. We have the same idea in 3-D computer graphics. We can make a figure of a man walking and then project a film of a walking man in the computer, where it becomes a virtual projection. The film projection on our computer model resembles the same man walking in the computer. 'Make sticky' entails sticking the picture onto an object. Another technique we developed was called 'sock' in order to create a flexible, supple tissue base for muscular form. We thought of it as elastic bandages vacuformed over a basic constructed rigid form. Workable elasticity was provided, hence the name 'body sock' – now developed into a system to create supple, muscular forms for human bodies, animals or anything. For modelling and animation we use off the shelf Alias software, along with custom software; for rendering we use Renderman. Silicon Graphics workstations we use exclusively – the same company that makes Iris, Indigo. When T-2 came out the Indigo wasn't around but we have a lot of their machines which vary in price from $30,000 to $250,000. Macintosh is used for paint touch-up. We also use a programme called Photoshop.

Mark Dippe was assistant effects director on Terminator 2. *Dennis Muren, who has won many Academy Awards, was effects director and Steve Williams was principal animator*

135

AMMAR ELOUEINI

Abstract machines

Over the last decade, radical changes both in methods of production and design in the architectural field have been effected through the integration of digital technologies. Replacing real experience with simulated worlds, and conventional relationships between 'function–form–structure' with 'information–field–interaction', new methods and techniques of operating within these emerging forms of production can be investigated.

The use of computers as 'abstract machines' to investigate new design strategies involving dynamic organisations and repetition with differentiation is part of the reality now considered by architects. A shift from the Cartesian to the topological definition of geometrical entities allows more complex and dynamic organisations to be produced through the integration of notions such as force, vectors and inflection.

This evolution in architectural practice can be described as endogenous in the sense that it is the fundamental ideas which define it that evolve. It is about redefining established and accepted terms such as dimensions, spaces, structures, etc, or perhaps inventing new ones that are more suited to expressing the changes. We do not operate any longer in a system that is limited to three dimensions but in a hyper-space which calls into question the space we are used to perceiving and imagining.

We are induced to work in an environment that requires less abstraction than representation, while more abstraction in the conception process becomes conceivable. This 'sliding' renders representation less abstract and the environment of the conception process more abstract. An experimental approach is indispensable in exploiting technological means which today are inseparable from all architectural thinking. An approach based on representation is therefore simplistic. Space reduces these dimensions, whereas we have a field of perception and action that is larger. Our perception deepens, which allows us to conceive of another space that would add itself to the one in which we evolve.

The new technologies we currently have at our disposal enable us to explore and exploit dimensions that were previously vacant. An architectural, conceptual, and projectual non-linear approach based on dynamic and evolutionary systems, responding to an architectural and urban complexity, can be both developed and applied.

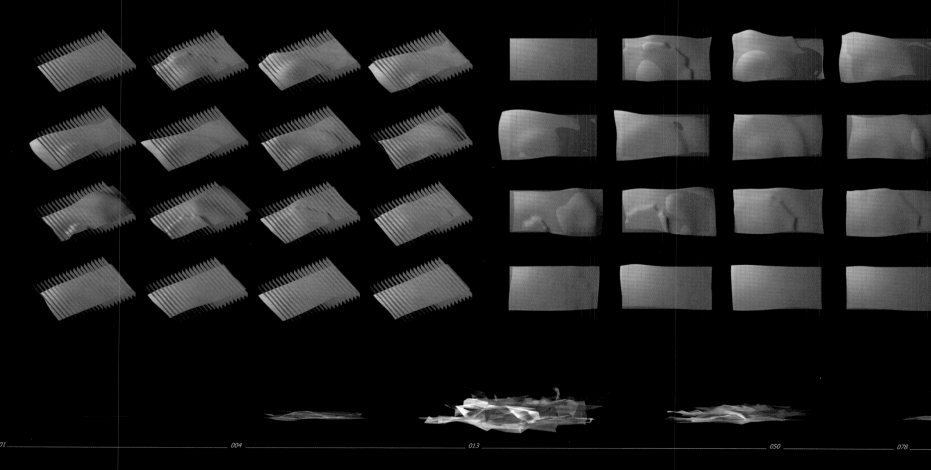

THE ROPPONGI
Tokyo

Fields and forces

With the use of animation-based software to visualise the temporally fluctuating forces associated with the city, urbanism was investigated as a network of interacting fields and forces which can be exchanged and replaced rather than a tableau of inert objects. The resultant image was of a new urban condition where programs mix and evolve in a supple way.

The approach was to analyse developments that occur in a very short period of time. This suggested attention to more local and ephemeral urban situations rather than monumental civic expressions and the use of fields and forces to shape and engender discrete, concrete forms of organisation, architectural spaces, without dealing with architectural forms or objects.

Layering

The program was divided into different layers to which forces were assigned, reflecting the unique conditions of the site. This related to a 24-hour cycle representing all kind of activities, flows and singularities. Layers folded and unfolded, forming a heterogeneous mosaic; an unstable, unpredictable fabric of programmatic connections and conditions. The forces attracted or repulsed the layers, depending on local events and global behaviour. Each layer was given the potential to develop autonomously, allowing intermittent correspondences to emerge. The Roppongi 'breath', a structure of motion, of conflicting forces effecting layers, created an urban dynamic structure of flows, and complex, oblique orientations between programs.

OPPOSITE, FROM ABOVE: Forces applied on surfaces; section of different program layers; BELOW, FROM ABOVE L TO R: Exterior; perspective; section; model views

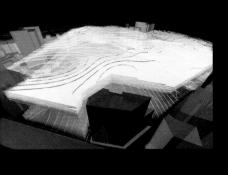
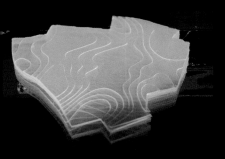
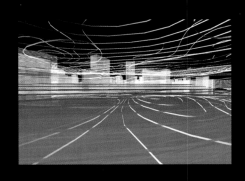
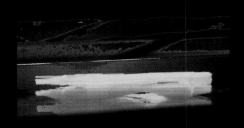

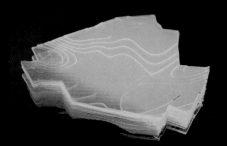
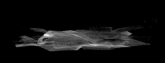
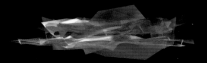
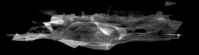
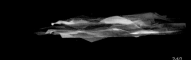

105   116   211   240

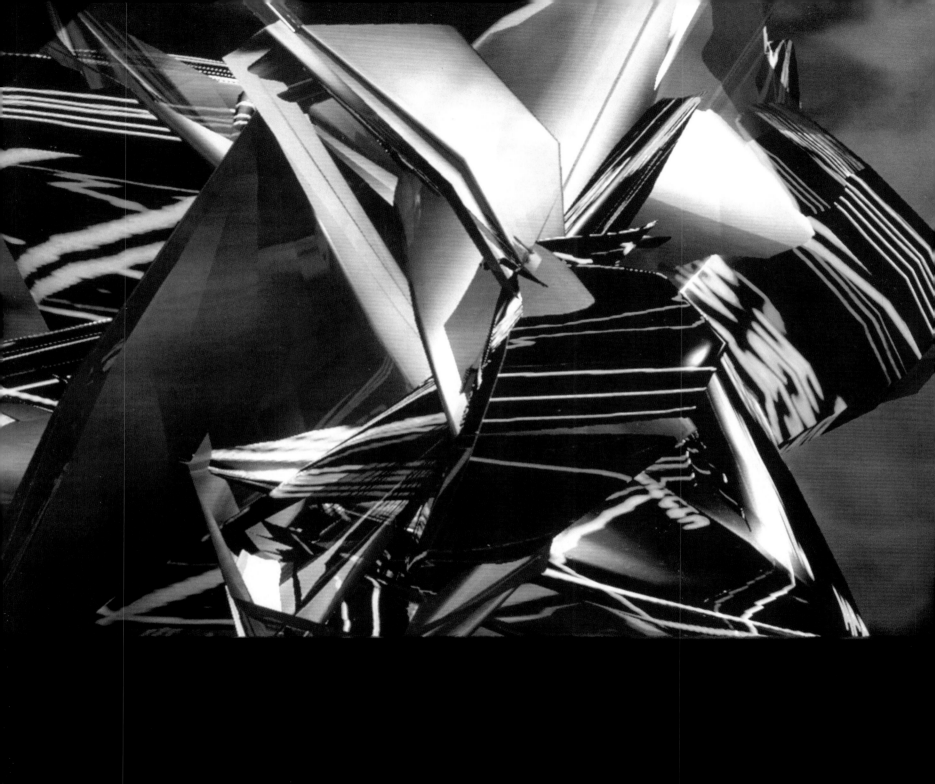

Stephen Perrella, Studio AEM, The Institute for Electronic Clothing, 1990 (with Anthony Wong and Ed Keller).

STEPHEN PERRELLA
HYPERSURFACE THEORY: ARCHITECTURE><CULTURE

Nike's marketing strategy develops both form (product development), follows market and the reverse – first the creation of image and lifestyles (creating the market) and then the design of the products that support that lifestyle change. For example, a kid in Harlem plays basketball, Nike re-presents that image, markets it and that image comes back to the court, and now the kid is wearing Nike shoes.   John Hoke, Nike Marketing Strategist[1]

In curved space, the shortest distance between two points is a curved line.   Albert Einstein

E-mail (excerpt) to Brian Massumi, September 1997
In architecture, there has been a tendency to eschew vulgar capitalist programmes: that is, to avoid the contamination of everyday consumer praxis, to stand-off from it, and somehow establish higher cultural ground. This, of course, describes a specific course through the last 60 years of modernism but is generally a basic aspiration. Over the last 10 years or so, with the advent of Derridean and post-structuralist thought, architecture, through a discourse established by only a small group of critics, has exacted a questioning of architecture's logocentrism leading to the movement known as 'Deconstructionist architecture'. Although the effect was pervasive in academia, a few of the architectural theoreticians were unsatisfied, believing that architecture still possessed a material presence that was not accommodated by the language/textually oriented philosophy of Derrida. They therefore moved towards the thinking of Gilles Deleuze and Félix Guattari, to improvise a radical theory that addressed architecture in its materiality. My sense all along has been that these improvisations are too narrow a reading of Deleuze, reflected in the theories of Greg Lynn and Peter Eisenman. However, as Deleuze's concept of The Fold became the main focus of theoretical architecture and computer technology became pervasive, we began to see in architecture, a clear move into topology. Many of the designs produced (especially here at Columbia GSAP) assumed smoother and more landscaped forms.

My concern with this was that it still continued an Enlightenment modernist tendency to avoid the messiness and vulgarity of everyday consumer praxis, an issue that Robert Venturi and Denise Scott Brown tried to bring into the consciousness of architecture. And so, the saturation of the Internet and the spread of teletechnology into regular business practices were not quite able to find their way into these topological, architectural design processes. However, as a journalist-architect, I am more inclined to embrace the radical proliferation of everyday advertisements or sign-culture as they connect to ever greater interfaces, or what we now witness as the emergence of a media culture. I also wondered how architecture's reading of Deleuze could possibly accommodate these semiotic mutations from everyday praxis, inasmuch as Deleuzean thought is concerned with opening boundaries and unfolding surfaces into conditions

of pure exteriority. Having a Heideggerian/Derridian background, I interpreted the media proliferation as an auto-deconstruction; that is, the deconstruction of the capitalist subject through the very modes of production and technologies that proliferate due to the instrumentalism inherent in consumer economics. Therefore, it seems the action at the level of the street, a hitherto neutralised element of the architectural problem, is becoming a contaminating factor, and the problem is that architecture, because of its formalist tradition, does not know how to respond to or embrace the technologically deconstructed or deterritorialised consumer subject. Yet arguably, these 'media' forces are pressurising the sanctity of elite architecture (and of course every other discipline) to enter into formative processes. This is why I am attempting to conjoin these two trajectories – mediatised culture and topological architecture – into an intertwined dynamic, one that I have come to call hypersurface. Your writings in *Capitalism and Schizophrenia: A User's Guide*, and Gary Genosko's readings of Félix Guattari, convinced me that there was, in fact, a semiotic and experiential dimension to Deleuze and Guattari that was missing from the initial and perhaps biased reading by architectural theorists, which resulted in a privileging of unadorned topology. While I truly support the topological impulses, I also realise that unless architecture is connected to everyday life, it is not alive, or even animate. For this reason I seek your consideration, and Gary's, to assist me with this second reading, so that architecture does not miss all the rich effects of a radical empiricism, as it concerns new forms of experience.

Hypersurface: architecture><culture
Hypersurface is an emerging architectural/cultural condition that is effected through an intertwining of often opposing realms of language and matter into irresolvable complexities that create middle-out conditions. In an effort to avoid thematising this effect and to consider it in its fullest complexity, the term hypersurface is introduced, to describe and render productive an Otherness that resists classical definitions but that is simultaneously produced by the tenets of traditional culture. As a verb, hypersurface considers ways in which the realm of representation (read images) and the realm of instrumentality (read forms) are respectively becoming deconstructed and deterritorialised into new image-forms of intensity. Hypersurfaces are an interweaving and subsequent unlocking of culturally-instituted dualities. Hypersurface theory is not a subjective invention, in contrast to what seems an unending foray of 'isms' attempting to explain postmodern culture (for instance in the efforts of Charles Jencks). Instead, this research suggests that there are self-generating and auto-emergent forces deeply insinuated within cultural historicity that are being unleashed by the machinations of contemporary praxis, and which already present a formidable challenge to the authority of the designer. Binary relations in

Western culture, as in the relationships between image and form, trace a long tradition leading to schizophrenic dichotomisation. Hypersurface theory may work productively with the effects and mutations that occur as a result of an accelerating capitalism. Hypersurfaces are configured, immanative topologies constituting nondialectic image-form interfaces into which intersubjectivity is being absorbed, only to re-emerge autopoeitically.

Hypersurface is a reconsideration of often dichotomous relationships existing in the environment. These binaries include: image/form, inside/outside, structure/ornament, ground/edifice and so forth; not as separate and hence static entities but as transversally-constituted fabrics or planes of immanence. Hypersurfaces are generated in the problematic relationships that occur when binary categories conjugate because such divisions can no longer be sustained in isolation through either linguistic or material divisions. Categories of the Real and the Unreal, for instance, are insufficient today because each is infused within the other. The reality of a Disney phantasm superposed with the unreality of media constructs, such as the O J Simpson incident, begin to describe a process of debasement brought about by deeply-rooted cultural contradictions – indeed, a schizophrenia.

The mechanisms that drive the real through the unreal and vice versa, impairing both, stem from the accelerating force of ubiquitous, everyday consumer-culture. This is what leads such theorists as Frederic Jameson and Mark Wigley to describe our contemporary condition as one of being 'lost in space'. A more accurate description, however, would be that we are 'lost at home', because there are no longer clear insides or outsides, and it is from the contortions within this context that immanent forces now issue forth. Such events are described here as hypersurfaces, producing intensities that are tangible, vital, phenomenological (or proprioceptive) experiences of space-time-information.

AntiTRANSCENDENTal defections

In mathematics, a hypersurface is a surface in hyperspace, but in the context of this journal the mathematical term is existentialised. Hyperspace is four + dimensional space, but here hypersurfaces are rethought to render a more complex notion of space-time-information. This reprogramming is motivated by cultural forces that have the effect of superposing existential sensibilities onto mathematical and material conditions, especially the recent topological explorations of architectural form. The proper mathematical meaning of the term hypersurface is discussed here as being challenged by an inherently subversive dynamic within capitalism. While in mathematics, hypersurfaces exist in 'higher', or hyperdimensions, the abstractness of these mathematical dimensions is shifting, defecting or devolving into our lived cultural context. Situated in this newly prepared context, hypersurface comes to define a new condition of human agency, of post-humanism: one that results from the internal machinations of consumer culture, thereby transforming prior conditions of an assumed stability. Instead of meaning higher in an abstract sense, 'Hyper' means altered. In both contexts, ideal abstraction and the life-world, operation is in relation to normal three-space (x, y, z). In mathematics there are direct, logical progressions from higher to lower dimensions. In an existential context, hyper might be understood as arising from a lived-world conflict as it mutates the normative dimensions of three-space, into the dominant construct that organises culture. In abstract mathspace we

have 'dimensional' constructs, in cultural terms we have 'existential' configurations; but the dominance of the mathematical model is becoming contaminated because the abstract realm can no longer be maintained in isolation. The defection of the meaning of hypersurface, as it shifts to a more cultural/existential sense, entails a reworking of mathematics. (This is similar to what motivates Deleuze to reread Leibniz.) This defection is a deconstruction of a symbolic realm into a lived one; not through any casual means: it arises and is symptomatic of the failure of our operative systemics to negotiate the demands placed upon it. If one could describe an event whereby cultural activities could act upon abstractions so as to commute the normative, etymological context into a context of lived dynamics, what activity has that capability? The term hypersurface is not simply attributed new meaning, but instead results from a catastrophic defection from a realm of linguistic ideality (mathematics). If ideals, as they are held in a linguistic realm, can no longer support or sustain their purity and disassociation, then such terms and meanings begin, in effect, to 'fall from the sky'. This is to describe the deterritorialisation of idealisation into a more material real. In the new sense for hypersurface, 'hyper' is not in binary relation to surface, it is a new reading that describes a complex condition within architectural surfaces in our contemporary life-world.

Capitalism and schizophrenia

The cultural forces leading to conditions that now evoke hypersurfaces are complex but may be traced through one main bifurcation in particular, one among many, that is formative in the history of Western culture. The division is between architecture as a formal practice and the practices of everyday life. Theorist-historians Alberto Perez-Gomez, Christian Norberg-Schulz and Robin Evans offer some of the most compelling accounts of the constellation of issues that this bifurcation involves. The overt result is that architecture comes to sustain an idea about form based upon its own internal discourse, one increasingly disassociated with the meaning structures constituted in the everyday world of commerce and material practices.

Our current architectural values tend to continue the division between the (capitalist) programme on the one hand, and (elite) form-making on the other. There have been many attempts to overcome this division within modern architecture. Strategies such as the 'form follows function' dictum stemming from Mies van der Rohe, while affirming everyday activities, remain complicit with the assumptions of capitalist progressivism prior to any interpretation of function or programme (one merely accepts the capitalist programme and expresses it). The modernist tactic privileges one oppositional term over another (driven by the obvious instrumentalism in the term 'follow') and is how binary thought works in the service of transcendentality. (In typical dialectics the synthesis of binary oppositions aspires to ascend to an ideal, one attended to by an ideality, like God.) But any process that assumes an ideality as an ultimate end is doomed to failure, inasmuch as it is ultimately unattainable. Yet this has remained the mandate of Western thought and has pervaded every value structure. Thus schizophrenia, sustained by capitalism, is continually forwarded by any attempt to synthesise a resolution with which to heal the fundamental split between form and programme. One of the least-considered strategies with which to negotiate perpetual dichotomisation (as it is reinscribed in the built environment) is to accept the schizophrenic condition, instead of attempting incessantly to overcome or transcend it with further, rational methodologies.

Dichotomisation can easily be read in the architectural cladding of Western culture. If we consider what architecture has historically symbolised – that is, what its form/surface relation has signified – it could be argued that form-surfaces (a prioritisation of structure over skin) have been at the service of the institutional power or a metaphysical belief behind a particular architectural institution. Architectural surfaces (of a religious, public or private institution) are thoroughly coordinated representations whether they are structurally expressive as in the case of Gothic architecture, or metaphorical as in the case of recent postmodern styles. Again, what seems most characteristic of modernism, in many of it manifestations, is that its system of representation is one of instrumentality; form-follows-function structures signification to be subsumed within the form. This is precisely how the realm of signification or signs are interpreted for the sake of form (where geometry becomes a scaffold for a transcendental belief structure). But signs have another meaning and another context; one that is normally superposed over construction. The vulgar programme of architecture simultaneously sustains a signification system, better described by Jean Baudrillard and Umberto Eco. And so, this doubled systemic of structure and sign commingle, leaving us to construct identities within schizophrenic contingency.

In an attempt to supersede the hierarchy of structure over surface, architect Bernard Tschumi used structural glass in his Gröninger Museum video gallery, employing tactics of reversal and dynamisation. Inside, the video columns displace the traditional meaning of a column as body, into flickering signifiers adrift upon the gallery's night surface. This project is seminal in a move toward hypersurfaces: in particular, through the way in which it reconfigures traditional architectural assumptions. In Tschumi's work, form is negated in order to celebrate programme in a tactic of negative modernism that affirms the deterritorialised consumer-subject as an ornamented membrane. Tschumi's deconstruction of traditional hierarchies in architecture reveals the latent potentialities of consumer praxis into an event space. His sensibility remains distinct, however, from the topological strategies of form that might carry his deconstructed and disseminated signifiers into contiguous surfaces. This possibility is taken up by other practices, notably in the work of Toyo Ito and Studio Asymptote, as well as Coop Himmelb(l)au. These are examples of architecture reaching towards consumer culture, remaining distinct from everyday consumer praxis reaching into architecture (unmediated by a designer). This is a propensity that architects may strive to engage, but in so doing may need to relinquish further degrees of authorship, as in the work and strategies of Bernard Cache, whose work raises the issue of the obsolescence of the architect altogether.

What appears to be a spreading trajectory is the further decentralisation of commercial representational systems unleashing new forms of human agency, in the guise of interactive information-play within the material surfaces of architecture. Nowhere is the possibility for such a transformative liberation (radical democratisation) so blatantly evident as in the electronic displays of New York's Times Square and Las Vegas (in particular the Freemont Street arcade). These are sites that Robert Venturi and Denise Scott Brown, Rem Koolhaas and philosopher Mark Taylor and numerous others have already investigated with varying degrees of architectural and philosophical import. (And it seem that the original impulse of Venturi/Scott Brown and

FROM ABOVE: XS cyber-arcade, Times Square – the schizophrenic condition between the real and the virtual; Steven Lisberger, Disney's Tron, 1982 – landscape with imbedded lines of information; Klein Bottle – topological space

Izenour – that is, to embrace the authenticity of vulgar culture – was quite prescient. Venturi's recent attempts, in his book *Iconographics and Electronics Upon a Generic Architecture*, to once more make architecture relevant to those who use it, was a move to embrace the dominant modes of signification for architecture. It was a move to democratise the discourse of architecture as walls to be written upon by those who inhabit it.) But while each, respectively, notes an underlying impetus within these deterritorialising contexts, their descriptions continue to embrace the extreme manifestations of capitalist culture as authentic and exhilarating (as almost all right or delirious). Yet we may ask what is offered in their descriptions to adequately negotiate a more deeply ingrained schizophrenia? The question is, to what extent do architects, who in an attempt to absorb 'vulgar' culture into the elite realm of architecture, only further subjugate capitalism's uncanny vitality into the formalisms of architectural discourse?

Hypersurface theory argues for planes of immanence (not planes of reference) whereby a vital relation between form and programme is a play of intensities (becomings) that are not commodifiable. Whether we are learning from (VSBA), delirious of (Koolhaas), or hidden because of (Taylor) the excesses of capitalism, the phenomenon and radicalisation of consumption in relation to the graphic sign (whether print, electric or electronic) can be seen as an activity that takes on self-transformative power; much in the manner of the Nike marketing strategy in the opening quote, but further accelerated. It is transformative in the way that older systems of representation used to work for institutions and the way that hyperconsumptive semiotics can serve to refigure an intersubjective self-image in an endless process of reconfiguration – indeed, disfiguration.

Incommensurates: architecture/culture

Hypersurface is an effect that occurs within the interface between two hitherto disparate trajectories of culture: in this case, the division between the aesthetic culture and academic discourse of architecture as distinct from the operations and machinations of everyday consumer culture. This is not an improvised separation, nor is it a forced dichotomy for argument's sake. Moreover, it is an attempt to identify and characterise the intertwining of two entirely different systems of subversion – one, avant-garde; the other, ordinary culture – taking place in two entirely different realms of culture but interfacing on the surface of built architecture. 'Hyper' implies human agency reconfigured by digital culture, and 'surface' is the enfolding of substances into differentiated topologies. The term hypersurface is not a concept that contains meaning, but is an event; one with a material dimension. We are currently at the threshold of this new configuration as a site of emergence for new intensities of culture and intersubjectivity. Toto Ito has recently written:

> Through the penetration of various new forms of media, fluidity is once again gaining validity. As more urban and architectural space is controlled by the media, it is becoming increasingly cinematic and fluid [. . .] On the one hand our material bodies are a primitive mechanism, taking in air and water and circulating them. On the other hand there is another kind of body which consists of circulating electronic information – the body that is connected to the rest of the world through various forms of media including microchips. Today we are being forced to think about how to architecturally combine these two different bodies and find an appropriate space for the emerging third body.

The third body that Ito describes is what is meant here by hypersurface. However, the body does not remain an operative metaphor going beyond what Deleuze and Guattari have called a 'body without organs'.

On the side of materiality, form has been pushed out of relation to function, programme has been dissuaded from context, and structure is disjoint from signification in any given architectural nexus. (This is clearly the impetus for the project presented here by Jesse Reiser and Nanako Umemoto – a seminal project that depicts more accurately the schizo-genesis that architectural problems seem now to require.) Architecture may now be explored as a condition of variant (human) agencies playing through, about and within one another; singular, yet connected and in a state of flux.

Provisionally, this may be called a condition of hypersurface. This trope serves only to accrue, absorb and resonate meaning, acting as an infrastructural term, a gesture toward a new middle ground between the traditionally conceived body/object duality. 'Hyper' suggests an existential eventualisation of the consumer-subject and 'surface' entails the new conditions of an object-in-relation. This is another way to consider Bernard Cache's theorisation of Subjectiles and Objectiles but with an added layer of complexity, in the incommensurate condition in which the two dynamised polarities commingle. Grafted, conjoined and co-determining the existent (the ecstatic subject) and the object-in-relation or hypersurface (dis)resonate together in a highly problematic, inflected condition.

Two main impulses operate simultaneously and contribute to the dynamic of hypersurfaces in architecture/culture. These two streams are reflected in elite architecture, predictably mapping the schizophrenia from the larger cultural context. The weaker trajectory (weaker because it goes against the dominant values of architecture as materiality, and the modernist subsumption of the sign within form) within the discipline of architecture is what has been elsewhere called 'pixel' architecture, that has been an attempt to manifest information space. In the current collection of projects, this trajectory is presented in the work of Bernard Tschumi, Hani Rashid and Lise Anne Couture (Studio Asymptote), and Toyo Ito among others (in a more modernist vein one must include Jean Nouvel and Jacques Herzog and Pierre de Meuron). Historically, in architecture, the sign or image has been relegated to a secondary, less functional or ornamental role. In the past century in modernism, signification has been subsumed into form and divorced from everyday activities while form (and its idealised use of geometry) has sought transcendence. Pixel or media architecture has sought to bring the vitality of the electronic sign into the surfaces of architecture, but in order to achieve this has negated or neutralised form. This strategy threatens to maintain signification in the role of ornament (see Gary Genosko's response overleaf) and is thus susceptible to commodification. However, media architecture helps to establish an infrastructure for hypersurfaces only without its material aspect. Hypersurface is fully intense when both surface/substance and signification play through each other in a temporal flux. For instance, if we could strip away all the electronic signs in Times Square, we would find a cacophony of material surfaces, each working to maximise the potential readability of the sign. It is this sort of drive, motivated by economic concerns, that differentiates surfaces, and that will propel the surface into the sign, and the sign into the surface. This 'vulgar' impulse exists outside of the discipline of architecture in terms of pure commercialism even though it has been acknowledged in the media architecture trajectory. The media complex (as Paul Virilio continually describes it and how Brian Massumi describe its relations to capitalism) involves an impetus of consumption through distended impulses that emerge from everyday life which are becoming transliterated into global digital networks. This dispersion of data is a body without organs. Information culture is spilling out into the built environment, creating a need for surfaces through which data may traverse (hypersurfaces).

Simultaneously, in architectural design, an unprecedented plasticity of form deriving from computer technology is generating new explorations of form. As a result, there is a general topologising of volume-space into activated surfaces, as can be noticed in the work of a number of leading and highly influential practitioners. This second impulse, from within 'proper' confines of the elite practice of architecture, is the deconstruction of Platonics in architectural form into enfolded, radical deformations. Avant-garde architecture, as it is explored and fostered within the academy and which to an extent defines future trajectories, has moved through a phase of self-critique, an inward interrogation of architecture's historical assumptions motivated by poststructuralism. Topology in architecture comes about due to a shift from an interest in language theories (Derrida) to matter and substance (Deleuze) in its theoretical discourses. The topologising of architectural form may be taken as a state of preparation for the reception of the flow of data as it overspills from contemporary cultural activities. A main effect of this transformation entails interconnectivity and continuity among previously systematised categories of architectural technics and production. The malleability of form and programme influenced by newly available technologies also makes possible the realisation of highly differentiated, topological architecture. The same impulses that bring technology to architecture occur throughout and across every facet of culture. An influx of new digital technology interconnects with other transformations taking place in global economic, social, and scientific practices cultivating fluid, continuous and responsive manifestations of architectural morphogenesis.

Architectural topology is the mutation of form, structure, context and programme into interwoven patterns and complex dynamics. Over the past several years, a design sensibility has unfolded whereby architectural surfaces and the topologising of form are being systematically explored and unfolded into various architectural programmes. Influenced by the inherent temporalities of animation software, augmented reality, computer-aided manufacture and informatics in general, topological 'space' differs from Cartesian space in that it imbricates temporal events-within form. Space then, is no longer a vacuum within which subjects and objects are contained, space is instead transformed into an interconnected, dense web of particularities and singularities better understood as substance or filled space. This nexus also entails more specifically the pervasive deployment of teletechnology within praxis, leading to an usurping of the real (material) and an unintentional dependency on simulation.

While the two impulses – pixel and topological architecture – have been separated categorically, at this juncture, overlaps are emerging as a direct result of respective deterritorialisations and auto-destructurations (clearly evident in the recent work by Coop Himmelb(l)au presented in this volume). The events of overlap mark the beginning of more complex interrelations that may provide an opportunity to explore more rigorous and intense manifestations of Otherness. Hypersurfaces may be significant in

FROM ABOVE: Venturi and Scott Brown Associates, Whitehall Ferry Terminal, Staten Island Ferry, 1997 – rejected proposal for a media surface on ferry terminal water side; Frank O Gehry, Guggenheim Museum, Bilbao, 1993-97; Bernard Tschumi, interior of Video Glass Gallery, Gröninger Museum, Gröningen, The Netherlands, 1990; Freemont Street, electronic arcade in Las Vegas – 2.1 million LEDs connected to a computer animation. This condition equivocates a built surface to a computer screen

the manner in which traditional assumptions are re-routed or are self-configured. Hypersurface is the activation of latent or virtual potential within forming substrates, membranes, surfaces, as an interstitial relation between bodies and objects; each distended as language/substance-matter. This does not occur as an intervention into an existing context, but becomes manifest due to complex interactions between technological manifestations and our media saturated background.

A hypersurface in architecture is elicited by incommensurate relations between form and image. The effects of hypersurface are also Other than that of either form or image. This is not the classical application of image or ornament to form, or the reverse: it is a superposed image, thereby creating a semi-autonomous form (through decontextualisation) and in turn, incompleteness or lack. Both image (programme) and form become part of each other and part of larger and other logics. For example, the presence of an advert on a billboard creates an incompleteness in its connection to a context (as in Guattari's notion of the machinic). Even though a hypersurface is an effect created by an incommensurate form-image relation, this condition creates a continuity and thus promotes a fluidity of interrelationships. When an image of an advert is screened over the form of a bus, the ad-graphic both accepts and denies the bus form. The advert parasitically appropriates the generally readable surface over the side of a bus. But the bus has other qualities that make it a graphically-charged surface, such as mobility. It is a surface that is latent with the potential to pass innumerable readers (willingly or not). The bus can remain fully functional and is unimpeded in having become fully appropriated by this ad-graphic. We may notice that the presence of the advert is connected to the forces of consumption giving the use of this form-surface a commercial value.; a value that is also calculated by the consumablility of the surface. An advert must be brushed-over by reader-bodies to have worth. This is a rudimentary formulation of what may be considered a haptic tangibility, or how the dynamics of consumption lead to such qualities of space.

Architecture configures subjectivity in a process that does not determine either polarity in the traditional subject-object distinction. Instead, we might describe a process that works over and throughout a plane of immanence from the middle-out. In the contemporaneous nexus of culture, human agency is evermore defined through technological interfaces. Subjectivity co-figures architecture in a complex way. This activation of the vitality of a constitutive middle-zone is neither understood solely as architecture nor as subjectivity, as *de facto* determinants in a co-constitutive dynamic. We will need to leave behind the dialectic constructs of habit – a middle-out logic, one of unfolding and enfolding; of proliferative differentiation.

E-mail from Gary Genosko, February, 1998
Dear Stephen, Your critique of dichotomaniac thought by way of the collapse of dominant dualities, which reveals their transversal connections on a plane of immanence, strongly suggests that the dominant generative force is consumer society. This ties hypersurface phenomena to capitalist codes, reinstating a dominant semiology on the plane of immanence and more or less defeating the purpose of your critique. The idea that hypersurfaces produce intensive effects must mean that singular traits of these effects are maintained against capitalist translations of them. This means that a certain amount of a-signifying semiosis must be at work in hypersurfaces: the relation between formal and

material fluxes must in some manner elude capitalist representations of them (if they fail to do so they will cancel each other out). Of course, hypersurface phenomena need to borrow capitalist semiologies, but they also need to retain some autonomy from them. I suppose, all that needs to be admitted is that hypersurface semiotics eludes the dominant meaning-giving formalisms of a signifying regime based on dichotomies, that they cannot be captured as a language (architecture is not a language!). What is hypersurface architecture? Well, it is not a pure signifying semiology, for one thing; it engages semiotic substances that are non-linguistic, especially tactile, which are relatively untranslatable into language, which is one of their virtues; and this tactility cannot be reduced to visual coding.

Response
Dear Gary, I am suggesting that hypersurfaces are an incommensurate complexity conjoined by a number of simultaneous impulses stemming from schizo-culture. One is from a Heideggerian/Derridean trajectory, whereby capitalism brings about a deconstruction and deterritorialisation of subjectivity through its modes of production. This is almost a Walter Benjamin thesis, but one needs post-phenomenology to talk about 'hyper' as flickering signifiers floating through material surfaces. This trajectory is the vulgar culture side and the material part is found in the architecture context, which has led to the topologising of form into surfaces. I think that when these two incommensurates conjoin: hyper-to-surface, they are not aligned, bringing about intensive effects that are not reducible to language. Indeed, they resist such consumptive subsumption, manifesting themselves instead as generative or autopoeitic.

As with a Jackson Pollock painting, there is no possible reduction. It is a field that only opens to greater complexity; a nexus of interweavings. Hypersurfaces result from the messiness of everyone's lines of communication criss-crossing over one another leading to disfiguration, with the architects trying to supply a membrane with which to support such crossings. They never can because the excess of media is too great, thereby contributing to the fluctuation of it all. The entire scene is one of autopoeitic emergence. Like randomly generated noise that has moments of clarity; a productive schizophrenia. Such effects are not reducible to language because they are merely effects that are shifting back and forth between the material and the immaterial; generated by consumption yet not providing a common ground upon which to build a socius. Gary, this is a main point about hypersurfaces: a material/immaterial flux of actual discourse (partially constituted by commerce) that cannot result in a political collectivity. Hypersurfaces are socius fluxus; a transversal of intersubjectivity. No governing consciousness, no material foundations – all middle. Out.

Productive schizophrenia: hypersurfaces from the middle-out
Hypersurface theory involves the simultaneous holding of a Heideggerian effect with a Deleuzean effect. Both conditions have become relevant because of the way culture has unfolded and embraced technology. The two trajectories are somewhat incommensurate: one is phenomenological and one is proprioceptive. This is why hypersurface theory is not a fusion of the two, but a theory that allows for both simultaneously. This is the basis for a productive schizophrenia. This is why an incommensurate effect is now resulting in architecture/culture. How will this schizo-doubling be productive? The strategy within a term like

'hypersurface' is to suggest that architecture is an inhabitable envelopment of between deterritorialised subjects and objects. Deleuze argues that everything is connected prior to divisions, thus subject and matter are fundamentally linked. What is described in this document is the complex of forces that are evacuating the dualisms that have categorically kept subjectivity and materiality apart. They are forces that undermine the tenets of separation and come from the machinations of our everyday life, which is now interconnected by digital teletechnology.

Hypersurface theory acknowledges that prior to experiences with the contemporary built environment, one is already affected by the media complex. This techno-existential condition situates us in an inescapable relation to media (here media meant to be broadly inclusive of all modes of representation in culture that are facilitated by technology). Activity in the contemporary milieu triggers associations that resonate within a partially constructed subject. The co-presence of embodied experience superposed upon mediated subjectivity is a hypersurface. The manifestation of this construct in the built environment is a reflection of this. If we are part-media constructs then it will be manifested in the built environment, an inflected place where we encounter ourselves, but as technology. Hypersurfaces appear in architecture where the co-presence of both material and image upon an architectural surface/membrane/substrate such that neither the materiality nor the image dominates the problematic. Such a construct resonates and destabilises meaning and apprehension, swerving perception transversally into flows and trajectories.

The purpose of hypersurface theory is to describe an emerging phenomenon in architecture and culture as a means to go beyond schizophrenic or nihilistic interpretations that contribute to the dynamics occurring in our complex world today. Prior to the divisions between things, there is a more pervasive connectedness. There are many approaches to this impossibly complex configuration but a few themes may be explored to uncover the underlying dynamics of connection before division. Hypersurface theory suggests an architecture/culture from the middle-out. What is a middle-out architecture and how does it stand in opposition to other theories about architecture? What would it be to think architecture from the middle-out? To what end?

Firstly, it would not be an end. Middle-out works in an alternate way from our more dominant tendency to think of oppositions and privileging one or other entity. This is what we learned from deconstruction: that binary oppositions operate to create frameworks for all that is meaningful. Does this mean that we are interested here in a meaningless architecture? What situation are we confronted with at the beginning of a new millennium?

Hypersurface architecture is the simultaneous and incommensurate action of human agency over a material topology. A hypersurface is the co-presence of the activities of human agency taking effect in a form-substance of force, or linguistic signifier as it occurs in a plane of immanence relative to another plane of immanence whose form-substance is that of matter. Intensities occur where these two planes of immanence create new planes of immanence – none of which participates in any absolute or transcendental logics. Hypersurface is that condition made possible as a result of the forces effecting both human-becoming and form-matter, such that these two polarities are no longer apposite and isolated. They each instead commingle and proliferate, establishing the rudiments of what may soon become an intersubjective plane of immanence. Mind and body meet in hypersurface in a conjunction with the realm of form-substance

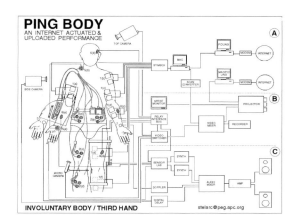

FROM ABOVE: Toyo Ito, Noh Theatre, model, 1987; Stelarc, Ping Body, 1996 – 'pinging' employed as a control mechanism for the body, the Net becoming the external nervous system; Serge Salat, Aleph I, Palais National de la Culture, Sofia, 1989

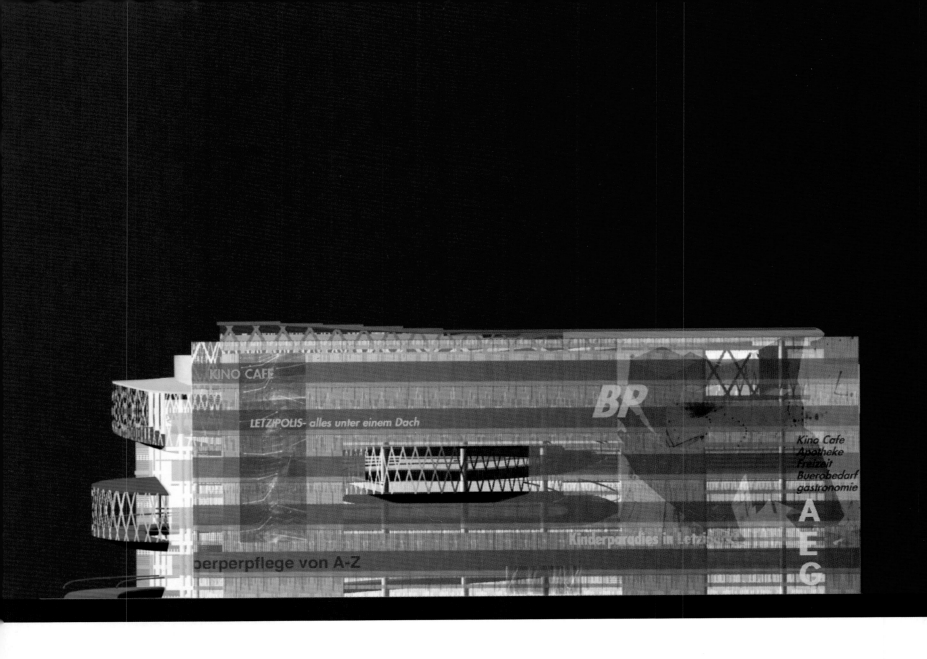

KINO CAFE

LETZIPOLIS- alles unter einem Dach

BR

Kino Cafe
Apotheke
Freizeit
Buerobedarf
gastronomie

Kinderparadies in Letzi

berperpflege von A-Z

A
E
G

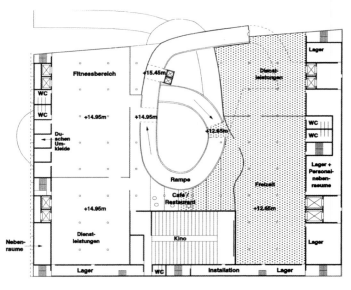

*Bernard Tschumi, Zurich Department Store, 1995.
FROM ABOVE, L TO R: Model; computer-generated image;
plan. This competition entry reveals an attempt to express
the dance of consumer-to-object, object-to-consumer*

and are let-to-flow as planes of immanence in a hypersurface architecture. Our bodies are hypersurfaces, convex and concave surfaces over and through which sense flows. This is an irreducible condition having neither an absolute inside nor outside.

Inside must reconnect to the outside through imagination, but one that is configured by a highly problematic intersubjectivity. Hypersurface is the activation of those latent potentials within substrates, membranes or surfaces that constitute the interstitial relations between bodies (distended as language) and substance-matter. This does not occur as an intervention into an existing context but becomes manifest due to complex interactions between technological manifestations and our background and past that is latent through having been saturated with the media. The unconscious always exits in the background, underlying human motives, operating just beneath apprehension. Psychoanalytics brings an interpretation of these operations to the surface but not into any full framework of understanding. The effects of hypersurface are beyond that of either form or image. Generally, a hypersurface has a range of effects, including and most significantly a surreality or hyperreality; a realism that is simultaneously uncanny, incomprehensible and therefore a catalyst or provocation, but not in any overt way. Being neither in the context of the purely conscious or unconscious, hypersurfaces slip readily between these realms, in the seam between the two. A hypersurface is the informed topology of an interstitial terrain between the real and unreal (or any other binary opposition) which then flows transversally into a stream of associations. Our current condition of stasis in an audio-visual world is what Virilio means by the 'last vehicle'. But it is a condition that will be overcome as our mediatised sensibilities begin to flood into the new proliferation of architectural forms being transformed into topological hypersurfaces.

Note

1 Quotation from the studio pamphlet developed by Steven Izenour for a studio at Yale University, 1995.

References

John Brockman, *The Third Culture*, Simon & Schuster (New York), 1995.

Hal Foster, *The Return of the Real*, The MIT Press (Cambridge, Mass), 1996.

Denis Hollier, *Against Architecture: The Writings of Georges Bataille*, Betsy Wing (trans), The MIT Press (Cambridge, Mass), 1989.

'Architecture After Geometry', *Architectural Design*, Academy Group Ltd (London) 1997.

Looking Back on the End of the World, Dietmar Kamper, Christoph Wulf (eds), David Antal (trans), Semiotext(e) (New York), 1989.

Todd May, *Reconstructing Difference: Nancy, Derrida, Levinas, and Deleuze*, The Pennsylvania State University Press (University Park), 1997.

Avital Ronell, *The Telephone Book: Technology, Schizophrenia, Electric Speech*, The University of Nebraska Press (Lincoln), 1991.

Immersed in Technology: Art and Virtual Environments, Mary Anne Moser with Douglas MacLeod (eds), The MIT Press (Cambridge, Mass), 1996.

Gilles Deleuze, *The Logic of Sense*, Constantin V Boundas (ed), Mark Lester with Charles Stivale (trans), The Columbia University Press (New York), 1990.

Anne Friedberg, *Window Shopping: Cinema and the Postmodern*, The University of California Press (Berkeley, California), 1993.

Robert Venturi, *Iconography and Electronics Upon a Generic Architecture: A View from the Drafting Room*, The MIT Press (Cambridge, Mass), 1996.

J Abbott Miller, *Dimensional Typography*, Kiosk Report (Princeton), 1996.

Gianni Vattimo, *The End of Modernity*, J R Snyder (trans), The John Hopkins University Press (Baltimore), 1988

Paul Virilio, *The Vision Machine*, Julie Rose (trans), The Indiana University Press (Bloomington), 1994.

Gilles Deleuze, *Cinema 2: The Time-Image*, Hugh Tomlinson and Robert Galeta (trams), The University of Minnesota Press (Minneapolis), 1994.

Gilles Deleuze, *The Fold: Leibniz and the Baroque*, Tom Conley (trans), The University of Minnesota Press (Minneapolis), 1993.

Gilles Deleuze and Félix Guattari, *A Thousand Plateaus: Capitalism and Schizophrenia*, Brian Massumi (trans), The University of Minnesota Press (Minneapolis), 1987.

Bernard Cache, *Earth Moves: The Furnishing of Territories*, Michael Speaks (ed), Anne Boyman (trans), The MIT Press (Cambridge, Mass), 1995.

Brian Massumi, *A User's Guide to Capitalism and Schizophrenia: Deviations from Deleuze and Guattari*, The MIT Press (Cambridge, Mass), 1992.

Tony Fry (ed), *Heidegger and the Televisual*, The Southwood Press (Sydney), 1993.

Félix Guattari, *Chaosmosis: An Ethico-Aesthetic Paradigm*, Paul Bains and Julian Pefanis (trans), The University of Indiana Press (Bloomington), 1995.

Ada Louise Huxtable, *The Unreal America: Architecture and Illusion*, The New Press (New York), 1997.

Gianni Vattimo, *The Transparent Society*, David Webb (trans), The John Hopkins University Press (Baltimore), 1992.

Mark Wigley, *The Architecture of Deconstruction: Derrida's Haunt*, The MIT Press (Cambridge, Massachusetts), 1993.

Mark Wigley, *White Walls, Designer Dresses: The Fashioning of Modern Architecture*, The MIT Press (Cambridge, Mass), 1995.

Stephen Perrella with Rebecca Carpenter The Möbius House Study

STEPHEN PERRELLA
ELECTRONIC BAROQUE
Hypersurface II: Autopoeisis

'Our perceptions give us the plan of our eventual action on things much more than that of things themselves. The outlines we find in objects simply mark what we can attain and modify in them. The lines we see traced through matter are just the paths on which we are called to move. Outlines and paths have declared themselves in the measure and proportion that consciousness has prepared for action on unorganised matter – that is to say, in the measure and proportion that intelligence has been formed.'

Henri Bergson[1]

What's a hypersurface?[2]

The projects produced out of the general thesis of hypersurface architecture entail new relations and affects between media (inclusive of both print and the electronic) and topological surfaces in architecture. As stated in the first issue of 'Hypersurface Architecture', published last year, experimentation a decade ago with computer workstations using animation software, revealed uncanny possibilities for the relations between form and image. Any form whatsoever could be textured with any image – whatsoever. It seemed imminent that a widespread use of this new technology would unleash a new dimension of effects because there is realm of potential relations between image and form. Currently and historically, however, the relations between image and form are superposed schizophrenically.

An analysis of the built environment reveals a systematic deployment of commercial images connected and controlled by the interests of consumer capitalism leading to a system of representation. The media image is a logic that has little to do with architecture and the way architecture thinks about itself. On the other hand architecture as a discipline has varying schools of thought on how architectural form is an image, but for the most part, architecture is about form. Over the last decade or so, the electronic era is transforming these two polarities: image and form, each from within its own context. While new technology is taking media into an unbounded zone we know as cyberspace, architectural form is also coming to question its Cartesian foundations. These two simultaneous trends, what may be called 'hyper' (media) and 'surface' (topological architecture), have not yet been considered in relation to one another. This is because each calls the other into question. If each dimension, image and form comes with its own disciplinary logic, for example two-D and three-D, then when each questions the other, neither two-D or three-D are adequate concepts to explain the new interdynamic. This is why hypersurfaces may be important to many of the new effects that we are seeing today, as the unravelling of the world of the image enmeshes with the unfolding of form into the image. When I least expect it, I notice minor, sporadic developments of hypersurface in precise surroundings in variegated contexts. It subtly slips into everyday life and is hardly perceptible. One

almost has to work backwards to see from where hypersurfaces are being initiated, but it seems to be enlivened by the implosion of three-dimensional action, fuelled by the density of commercialism, (the onrush of consumerism-as-force) coupled with the connections, lightning-like, between things.

For instance, the other day when I went looking to purchase a camera, a film shop that I ventured into had one specific camera announcing a new advanced film system. Being a bit fussy, I made them explain the significance of this film as opposed to going with a digital camera. The shop owner enthusiastically brought out a large glossy image that was fairly impressive in its clarity and depth. He said it had to do with a three-dimensionality within the chemical make-up of the film. Quietly stunned, I noted this prime example of how, in everyday consumerism, and with the incessant march of the development of technology, hypersurfaces unfold. This seemingly minor evolvement of the three-D within the realm of two-D imaging establishes a new layer of connective dimensional infrastructure and is how hypersurfaces are filling out the middle. What is really remarkable about the example though, is that it was in the chemistry. In retrospect, it seems foolish to argue for any kind of foundationalism in the face of this phenomenal infilling, especially since it seems so difficult to make anything meaningful in architecture today. It is not surprising also, that I find examples and developments contributing to ways of working with hypersurfaces among a selection of our colleagues's work. What I value in their work are the careful progressions they are making in finding ways to make this new 'withinness' more vigorous, more engaging.

It strikes me too, that if I am rigorous about this infilling of the middle, that there might be enough 'flesh' in what was once a dialectical void for there to be another way for us to begin considering how things become meaningful. In other words, if all modes of connections are being made, in multiplicate contexts within our world, then at a certain point, there might be a logic of connections superseding the mostly polarised logics that currently exist. An almost mundane example would be the links between sites within the worldwide Web, where amid the density of content and language, exists this immense web of connectivity. The associative drift (surfing) that occurs as a result becomes a way of being on the web. But because this emergence-of-connection occurs on many different levels, what may be most significant for architecture might be what occurs between the realms of media and of materiality.

So, without sounding too apocalyptic or even delirious, it seems to me that what may be building-up within this in-between zone that we have been calling hypersurface, is a more direct interface between thought and matter. Could it be, that we are working here to describe minute transitions leading to a switchover point, whereby new relations between media and matter change the possibilities for thought? If so, then consider the detrimental role that architecture will play in that. Martin Heidegger

Stephen Perrella with Tony Wong and Ed Keller, Studio AEM, *Institute of Electronic Clothing, 1990*

Marquee at 1500 Broadway in Times Square. Photo by S. Perrella, 1999

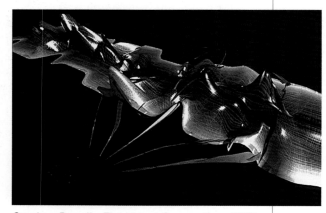

Stephen Perrella, The Virtual Corporation, *1993*

once called language the 'House of Being'. That describes 'Being' nicely, but it rather privileges an immaterial realm. So today we might ask, what is the 'House of Being' if the material house is infused and interfaced with language?

Why is the world of the sign so disassociated from the world of materiality? How is it that these two realms run parallel to each other, having little actual relation, yet creates what is essentially our built surround? Is it that everywhere we look there is this division, or is it in our way of looking that constitutes it? Can we approach this another way?

With varying degrees of inhabitability, a hypersurface is the envelopment of exchanges between human agency and matter. Hypersurface is a zone of exchange between consciousness (language or text) and levels of the inorganic. Hypersurface requires reciprocal relations where exchanges are the operative principle. These exchanges are intensities stemming from multiple planes of imminence. Considering that the gene and the bit are not yet and may never be unified, we must settle for relations between these two worlds, and there are all manner of relations. There are innumerable ways of considering the interweavings between media and matter but the predominant logics are dialectically and dualistically divided, something deeply written into cultural habit.

What can be made of these divisions? Are they harmless or are they denigrating? Where to begin in asking this question? Answer: in the middle, middle-out. What middle, middle of what? Answer: any place is already the middle, the middle is always already presupposed in the framing of the question. How to work from the middle-out? Answer: focus on the issue of relations and forget the frame, remember there is no originating point to the middle to adhere to or give reference. This is to speak of a plane of imminence. A surface whereby effects are completely determined through systems of exchange.

Hypersurface is the word we are using to describe any set of relationships that behave as systems of exchange. A system of exchange that when physically constituted as the present is the presupposition of one set of points or the dynamic deformation of the space of one set of points into the adjacent set of points in the production of the new. The presupposition of the set of points is not simply a construction of successive points but the coexistence of the two. The coexistence of the two means that both stretch out alongside each other disassociated but always in combination when they emerge into the present. We can write pairs of points that describe this dynamic; past–present, image–form, two-D/three-D, memory/matter and so forth. Animation offers the potential to actualise these constructions as the present by stopping time in a two-D frame, yet it also offers the potential to experience the surplus space of its transformation, the literal coexistence of differential geometries as movement, like image and form.

This is the geometry of topological transformation where all the complexity of the coexistence of relations is held within the singular flatness of a vertical plane, a plane loaded with excess experience, overly abstract and abundant with information. We can pull-out, pop-out, leave-out, splice out, but the moment we do we are not describing hypersurface any more we are talking about a static figure, definable in relation to, but not the fullness of the shared figure. Hypersurface is after the shared figure, the set of relations in their coexistence, the excess and the experience of this excess.

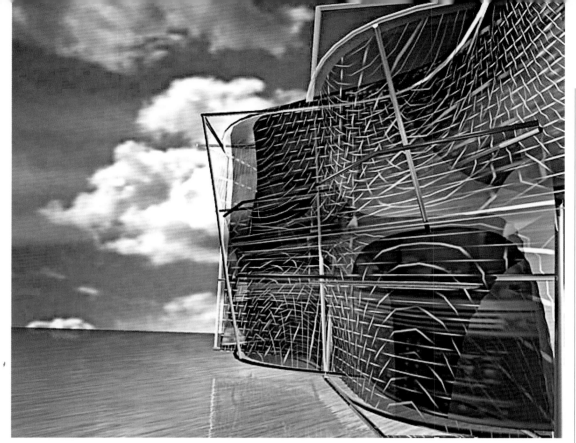

Stephen Perrella, Us, *1998*

Notes

1 *Creative Evolution*, Arthur Mitchell (trans), Dover Publications (Mineola, New York), p188.
2 Quoted from a check-out clerk at a local foodstore upon reading the company name on my credit card.

References

Beckmann, John (ed), *The Virtual Dimension: Architecture, Representation, and Crash Culture*, Princeton Architectural Press (New York) 1998 (see my essay, 'Socius Fluxus').

Braidotti, *Rose Patterns of Dissonance: A Study of Women in Contemporary Philosophy*, Routledge (London and New York), 1991.

DeLanda, Manuel, 'Non Organic Life', ZONE Incorporations.

Dienst, Richard, *Still Life in Real Time: Theory after Television*, Duke University Press (Durham and London), 1994. See chapter two on 'Image/Machine/Image: Marx and Metaphor in Television Theory' is very good on Marx and 'machinery' 'value,' and 'circulation'. The last chapter 'Ineluctable Modalities of the Televisual' is on Deleuze and Guattari.

du Gay, Paul (ed), *Production of Culture/Cultures of Production*, Series: Culture, Media and Identities, vol 4, SAGE Ltd. Published in association with The Open University, 1997.

Hartz Michael and Gilles Deleuze, *An Apprenticeship in Philosophy*, Univ. of Minnesota Press (Minneapolis), 1993 (see last chapter 'Parallelism').

Holland, Eugene, *Deleuze and Guattari's Anti-Oedipus: Introduction to Schizoanalysis*, Routledge (London and New York), 1999.

Lazzarato, Maurizio, 'Immaterial Labor', Paolo Virno and Michael Hardt (eds), *A Potential Politics: Radical Thought in Italy*, Theory Out of Bounds Series, vol 12, University of Minnesota Press (Minneapolis, London).

Levy, Pierre, *Becoming Virtual: Reality in the Digital Age*, translated from the French by Robert Bononno, Plenum Press (New York),1998.

Jameson, Frederic, 'Marxism and Dualism in Deleuze', edited by Ian Buchanan, *A Deleuzian Century?* South Atlantic Quarterly 96:3, Summer 1997. This is useful for an understanding of 'axiomatic' and flux/flow and code.

Massumi, Brian, *A User's Guide to Capitalism and Schizophrenia: Deviations from Deleuze and Guattari*, The MIT Press (Cambridge, Mass), 1992.

Morse, Margaret, *Virtualities: Television, Media Art, and Cyberculture*, Theories of Contemporary Culture, Univ Press, 1998.

Riley, Terrence (ed), 'The Un-Private House', catalogue to the exhibition at The Museum of Modern Art, 1999.

Rodowick, DN *Gilles Deleuze's Time Machine*, Duke University Press (Durham and London), 1997.

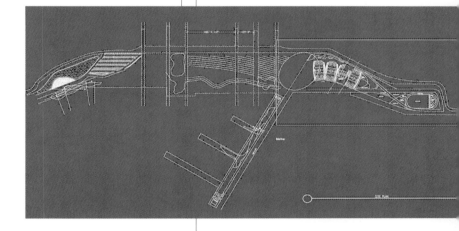

Stephen Perrella with Louis Wein, Henry Wojdyla, Dennis Pang, Paul Cumming and Frank Scicchitano of Ellerbe Beckett, Staten Island Homeport Redesign/HarbourFest, *1998-99*

ACKNOWLEDGEMENTS

I am grateful for the continued encouragement and support of Bernard Tschumi and the Columbia University GSAP. The kind efforts of Karen Ocaña who translated the Bernard Cache's text is greatly appreciated. I thank Louis Wein for his efforts in the Staten Island homeport project, toward actualizing hypersurface architecture. And to Sara Foster of Rhythm & Hues for her extraordinary concerns and effort in helping out with our Mazda, Cool World collaboration. To Rebecca Carpenter for her belief in my ideas. Rebecca, this issue is dedicated to you. To Ciro Asperti, Clair Cipriani for their friendship and undying support. To Daniel Pavlovits, Henry Wojdyla, Dennis Pang and Paul Cumming for their service as assistants and for their energetic investments in my theoretical project. To Stelarc for his interest in future collaborations. To Jose Sanchez for his assistance with computers. To Susan Sanders, Greg Siegworth and Leonard Ragouzeos and Pia Ednie-Brown for their interest and support in my recent lectures that helped to clarify my ideas. And most recently, thanks to Lori Andreozi, for her ability to help take hypersurface theory into the marketplace.   *Stephen Perrella*

MARCOS NOVAK

TRANSARCHITECTURES AND HYPERSURFACES
Operations of Transmodernity

Transmodernity: becoming alien

After modernity, virtuality: all that is solid melts into information. Between modernity and virtuality, transmodernity. As we all know, definitions, disciplines, institutions have all become unstable and inadequate, and everywhere there are re-evaluations of the structures by which we comprehend the world. These changes are not formless. They are characterised by the aspects of metamorphic change clustered under the prefix 'trans': transformation, transmutation, transgression, etc. Everywhere present, this kind of change is most evident in the structures of our quest for knowledge.

Historically, guilds became epistemes, specialisations and disciplines only to reach an impasse of isolations. In stages, their boundaries softened, merged and collapsed. From separate disciplines (degree zero) we ventured to multidisciplinarity (degree one), interdisciplinarity (degree two) and finally trans-disciplinarity (degree three), spawning new sciences rooted in, but utterly unlike, previous explorations. Like the situation that arises in the collision of black holes, the event horizons of separate views on the world touched, merged and became one, but not merely as a Hegelian synthesis of thesis and antithesis moving onto some next 'higher level', but as a metamorphosis into conditions that are unprecedented rungs on the ladder, taking us from a centuries-long outlook called modernity to another stage called virtuality. In-between modernity and virtuality spans the transversal link we are crossing: transmodernity.

Firstly, every path, bridge or ladder fulfils a role of passage, but simple linear movement is not yet full 'transport' in that it merely propels something along a single, unaltered and unchallenged line of development, providing incremental progress without qualitative change. Transmodernity is not about incremental progress but about transformative exponential change. Secondly, some transmissions occur not as simple linear sequences, but as operations of multi-threading: transversal weavings and warpings of initially disparate strands. It is the proliferation of these conditions of transversal weaving and warping which characterises transmodernity. Thirdly, these admixtures result in conditions that are not merely collages or juxtapositions, as would characterise modernity, nor morphings, blendings or folds, nor even formations of monstrosities that are still terrestrial, as would characterise recent postmodernity, but transmutations into unpredictable conceptual spaces, completely new states of being. This is, of course, very rhizomic and could be described in terms of lines of flight, de- and re-territorialisations, and the full conceptual mechanism of 'A Thousand Plateaus'.[1] This is no surprise: transmodernity is about becoming: becoming *alien*.

Conceivable/presentable

In his essay 'Answer to the Question: What is the Postmodern?' Jean-François Lyotard posits that both modernity and postmodernity are responses to the problem of 'the sublime relationship between the presentable and the conceivable'.[2] He mentions two responses, varying by where they place the accent of the failure to make the conceivable and the presentable coincide. On the one hand, 'the accent can fall on the inadequacy of the faculty of presentation'; on the other hand, 'the accent can fall on the power of the faculty to conceive, on what one might call its 'inhumanity'. Modernity, he claims, is a nostalgic invocation of the Kantian sublime as absent content, while postmodernity is a concession to the pain and pleasure of inexpressibility but a refusal of the nostalgia of correct form.

The transmodern stance I am articulating takes a different position. Whereas Lyotard's positions both assume the 'human' as fixed, transmodernity accepts as given the technological augmentation of the human, either as the cyborg or as the 'transhuman'. Accepting that we are using technology to increase constantly the 'visible' portion of the world means also that even if the distance between the conceivable and the presentable remains unchanged, the interval between them advances in direct proportion to our technological progress, revealing uncharted territories of the newly presentable. We can register this advance without judging it to be progress or regression, without calling upon Utopia and totalisation. When this interval has moved sufficiently far away from any given position, we are transformed. Exponential change means that we are transformed ever more frequently.

Screens and manifolds

Space, as we know it, is both non-Euclidean or curved and multidimensional, containing more than three spatial dimensions. Curvature and multidimensionality are separate issues. A space can be Euclidean and four dimensional, for example, or three dimensional and non-Euclidean. Membrane theory, the present outgrowth of string theory, places the number of spatial dimensions at 11 and replaces the 'string' with the 'membrane', itself a hypersurface affectionately called a 'p-brane' (to indicate its inherent multidimensionality), as the fundamental building element.[3] In the last century, the discovery that different axiom sets produce viable alternative conceptions of space – positively curved, negatively curved or flat – created a bifurcation in the study of the nature of space. Since then, one strand is concerned with the study of physical spaces and the other strand is concerned with possible spaces; each strand subject, respectively, to empirical or logical rigour. In either case, we now think of n-dimensional manifolds. Space and surface are thus intertwined: both are manifolds, the difference between hyperspace and hypersurface being that a hypersurface of a hyperspace of (*n*)-dimensions is a submanifold of *(n-1)* dimensions. Thus the hypersurface of a hyperspace of four spatial dimensions is a space of three spatial dimensions, produced by an act of projection or section or screening.

The economies of discernment, at each level of sensing-perception-cognition-formation-creation, dictate that we come to know through a logic of selective reduction: screening. In a multitude of ways, what is known appears on or through screens that are simultaneously reductions and clarifications of worlds-at-large with which we never have direct contact. All reality, including self-knowledge, is available to us only through the mediations of screens: projections of meaning, sensory and hermeneutic filtrations, personal and political veilings. The question of the conceivable and the presentable is already a question of incommensurable screens.

To begin, there are the screens of our senses, consisting of neural arrays, synaptic nets, filters, and membranes, each receiving a narrow range of a wider spectrum, already paring off the larger portion of the raw data of the world. Then there are the cognitive screens of our interest in the world, registrations of Gibsonian affordances, themselves constrained by the lenses and filters of momentary attention. Following these are the screens of faciality, self-knowing and self-presentation. Our faces are screens, concealing and revealing identity, character and expression in double articulations of masking and becoming, veiling and viewing; so too our skin and its echoes, our clothings, architectures, avatars.

A review of literal screens would include mirrors, shadow theatres, zoetropes, cinema, television, computer monitors and the cluster of technologies pertaining to virtual reality. These are screens once removed from how we experience the world, marking the beginning of world making rather than world knowing. Here also are the psychological screens of interpersonal and social mirroring, identity formation, and political representation.

More abstract screens surround us: Stuart Kauffman's 'fitness landscapes' are the invisible hypersurfaces along which evolution and the emergence of order perambulate, climbing gradients in higher-dimensional spaces. Embedded in Minkowski's four-dimensional spacetime are three hypersurfaces defined by three kinds of 'separations': 'spacelike', 'timelike' and 'lightlike'. Two hypercones, meeting at a subjective present moment, chart out the territories of a subjective past and a subjective future. The 'lightlike hypersurface' of the cones defines all that can be reached by light emanating from the present and dictates the precise limit of causality. All that is outside the cones is the unknowable zone of indeterminate causality that is simply referred to as 'elsewhere'.

The 'spacelike hypersurface' that contains the subjective present is perpendicular to the axis of time and holds all of our familiar three-dimensional space in a conceptual but completely inaccessible universal simultaneity. That is to say, although we can conceive of a plane of pure simultaneity, no such relationship can actually exist unless the hypercones are coincident and, hence, tautological: the hypersurface screens that chart the extent of all that is in any way accessible also act as screens of exclusion of all that is 'elsewhere'.

Examining these varied manners of understanding screens, we see that they can be conceptualised into several variants: *projection* (screens proper), *protection* (screens as veils) and *selection* (screens as sieves). Screens of projection are the most familiar and are of two kinds: projections of presence (movies, television) and projections of absence (shadow theatre, shadow masks). Screens of protection include not only literal veils but all manner of costume and clothing. Screens of selection are simultaneously the most basic and the most advanced screens: at the most basic level they are articulated as the basic senses by which we detect the world within small portions of wider spectra. At the highest level they are constituted as material and conceptual technologies of sensing and effecting, enciphering and deciphering, expert systems, search engines, data mining, autonomous agents, genetic algorithms and artificial intelligences. Theories, ideologies, legal codes, value systems etc, constitute selection screens just as surely as do our senses of sight or hearing.

Transmodernity, in tracking the transformative effect of the moving interval between presentable and conceivable, is concerned also with how screens conceal even as they reveal.

Eversion: the fifth virtuality

The discussion of screens and hypersurfaces leads to questions of the nature, kinds and degrees of virtuality. We can distinguish five degrees of virtuality, as related to screens and hypersurfaces: *light and shadow*: projections of absence and presence: mirrors, shadow theatres, Plato's Cave; *sampling and statistics*: constructions of continuity from discontinuity, connotation from denotation: zoetropes, cinema, television, digital sound, transitions from discrete to continuous space and back by processes of digital-to-analogue and analogue-to-digital conversions; *inversion*: computation and epistemology, seeing through knowing, scientific visualisation, simulations, computer graphics, special effects; *immersion*: alteration, cyberspace, virtual reality, casting the world into the virtual; *eversion*: casting the virtual unto the world, multi-threading virtual/real and actual/possible.

Eversion, as the name implies, is the turning inside-out of virtuality, so that it is no longer contained in the technologies that support it but is cast into our midst and projected onto our architectures and our cities.

If screens are related to how we understand the interval between conceivable and presentable and transmodernity urges this interval forwards to the zone of transmutations and transfigurations, then everted screens become instruments by which to glimpse and enact that which is barely within perceptual or conceptual reach.

Augmented spacetime

Architecture has employed many of these screens in one way or another in its long history, but it has yet to fully comprehend and embrace screens of selection as a tectonic issue. To understand this we must register that we have entered an era in which space has lost all its innocence: we live in augmented spacetime.[4] By this I mean that space is already intelligent and imbued with nonlocality, not only theoretically but in actual practice. Technologies such as the Internet, cellular telephony, the Global Positioning System and satellite-based telecommunications have created a condition in which every point in space is activated and ready to take on different roles at any instant and for any person. Augmented spacetime is characterised by the fifth virtuality, 'eversion', but since each degree of virtuality contains the previous, all aspects of virtuality come to play in new space.

To understand this condition, it is helpful to realise that we have already constructed pockets of intelligent space on our computer monitors. A computer screen can be seen as a two-dimensional prototype of a space whose extent is fixed but whose partitions and functions change as needed or desired. This space, once confined to the user-interfaces of our computers, has already escaped the monitor and has entered the three-dimensional world at large. The language of windows, menus, icons, tools and sundry controls to which we are already habituated is being extended to the third dimension. Whereas on the two-dimensional computer screen we are embodied only as cursors and icons, in augmented spacetime we participate with our entire bodies. Just as a region of a computer monitor can take an infinite number of forms according to the software that commands it, so too can physical space adopt an infinite number of virtual architectures within the confines of a single physical space. The design of these non-retinal architectures as architecture proper is a problem we have yet to acknowledge fully, let alone master.

In the example of the computer screen as a two-dimensional prototype of augmented spacetime, the relationship between hyperspace and hypersurface becomes clear. The screen is a highly interactive, intelligent surface, a hypersurface. At first glance it has two spatial dimensions, a temporal dimension and a variety of space-related attributes such as colour, resolution and refresh rate. Its main interest, however, comes from the complex behaviours and relations it enables by being connected to the hyperspaces created by the computer that drives it and the network within which it is located.

Retinally, a two-dimensional graphical user interface will differ from the physical screen primarily on the basis of its mutability, since both physical screen and virtual interface have the same number of dimensions, while a representation of a three-dimensional real-time walkthrough will begin to depict virtual dimensions over the matrix of physical pixels, initiating the process of casting the screen into hyperspace. This process continues non-retinally, as all the behaviours of the screen are indexed into the otherwise invisible spaces of hyperlinked information and computations. The hypersurface of the screen is thus our interface to otherwise inaccessible hyperspaces. If these are not just inaccessible but also at the edge of the presentable, leaning into the inconceivable and pushing forwards, then they partake in the transmodern.

When we imagine the computer screen as a plan-view and the cursor as an avatar of our presence in an intelligent and hyperactive, transactive space, we see a premonition of the nature of our interactions, via hypersurface interfaces, with the transarchitectures of augmented spacetime. This premonition is waiting to be raised off the screen and everted into the everyday space of our embodiment.

Camera cognita

In his book *Camera Lucida*,[5] Roland Barthes, seeking the distinguishing characteristic of photography, its 'stigmatum,' explores the notion that photography records that which has been – that it is evidence that something has existed, that some event has transpired. He presses his definition further to conclude that photography articulates a double catastrophe: that something is to happen (the future implied in the photograph) that has already happened (the photograph as record of a future now past). As we know already from digital photography and special effects of all sorts, the hypersurface screens of virtuality give different testimony: to see an image is not to know that some event has transpired but that the constitutive elements of that event are known well enough to have been involved in an explicit computation. Where 'camera lucida' gives testimony to existence, the digital visual asserts a 'camera cognita' in which to see is to know. The shift from screen to hyperscreen is a shift from ontology to radical epistemology.

Within the 'camera lucida' was a screen – or hypersurface – of recording. Within the 'camera cognita' is a screen – or hypersurface – of knowing. Applying the fifth virtuality, eversion, to the third virtuality, epistemology through computation, implies turning the 'camera cognita' inside out, casting the hypersurface of knowing onto the world at large.

Transarchitectures and hypersurfaces

'Hypersurface architecture' and 'transarchitectures' are complementary concepts. While they are not identical, pursuing one soon leads to the other. Transarchitectures are permeated by hypersurfaces in both literal and metaphoric senses, and theorising and practising hypersurface architecture would lead to the radical transformations that the construct 'transarchitectures' articulates for the evolving conception of architecture.

Transarchitectures

I coined the terms 'transarchitecures', meaning the architectures of transmodernity, and 'transmodernity' in order to provide a way to discuss the overall cultural condition we find ourselves in and the overall architectural possibilities that we face. The cultural condition we witness is no longer merely modern, postmodern, poststructural, or most of the other appellations attributed to it in current discourse. Like the modern, it is a condition fully conscious of change; like the postmodern it finds all Utopias suspect, but change is now recognised as bringing forth conditions that are alien and 'trans' so that neither a romantic modern nor an ironic postmodern stance provide sufficient responses to the new problems and possibilities arising daily.

Within the overall notion of a transmodern condition, 'transarchitectures' articulates the full scope of architectural possibility at the beginning of a new millennium. In short, this is as follows: we conceive algorithmically (morphogenesis); we model numerically (rapid prototyping); we build robotically (new tectonics); we inhabit interactively (intelligent space); we telecommunicate instantly (pantopicon); we are informed immersively (liquid architectures); we socialise nonlocally (nonlocal public domain); we evert virtually (transarchitectures).

This list is doubled by the construction of an electronic, fully spatialised public domain, which is also conceived algorithmically, also modelled and simulated numerically, also built by software 'bots' and agents, inhabited interactively, used for instant telecommunication and telepresence, and within which we and our avatars are immersed in virtual spaces. These two worlds are already threaded into a new spatial continuum that, as a whole, constitutes the domain of transarchitectures. Consistent with the notion of 'transmodernity', the term transarchitectures registers this cascade of changes and points to the radical nature of the transformations facing architectural and urban theory, practice and so on, admitting, as Archigram did, that the best responses to any or all of these may soon not be recognisable as conventional architecture, but may fork into a multitude of new transdisciplines. While much of the advanced architectural debate has disengaged itself from the world that we are so fervently building, transarchitectures seek to be visionary, relevant, and open to unforeseen modes of theory and praxis. At a time when the rate of change is such that conceptual dislocation is inevitable, theorising metaphysical dislocations, while maintaining conventional practices and building wonderful but ultimately static and localised edifices, is not avant-garde, it is derivative and conservative. The links on the chain of conceptual fascinations of recent years, as potent as they promise to be, become derivative and fail to meet their promises when linked to incestuous modes of discourse, conservative modes of practice, and intolerant, reactionary and exclusive holds on power.

To a great extent, such failures are caused by the refusal by portions of the architectural theoretical establishment to acknowledge the depth of the transformation that the accelerating rate of scientific and technological advances have brought upon us – the transmodern condition – and the most radical architectural innovation of the century: the invention of virtual space in augmented spacetime.

Transarchitectures are the architectures of transmodernity in augmented spacetime, both immersive and everted.

Hypersurfaces

The cave paintings at Lascaux, Egyptian hieroglyphics, Byzantine hagiographies, Muslim calligraphies, Hendrik Willem Mesdag's panorama at The Hague, the multiple exposures in stone of the Sagrada Família, the reflective titanium skin of the Bilbao Guggenheim, cinematic projections, virtual-reality environments known as CAVEs, crystal balls and talking mirrors, and eventually, the fiction of the holodeck, all anticipate a time when surface becomes viewport, an eversion of the retina into the world, not as fantasy, but as accurate prefiguration of a condition already near at hand.

Stephen Perrella's hypersurface concept resonates with this rich history of efforts to produce depth on architectural surfaces, an effort to see surface not as an Aristotelian delimiter of space but as the portal between worlds through which subjectivity emerges. Perrella writes: 'Hyper is the existential dimension and Surface is the energy-matter substratum', parsing 'hypersurface' into an aspect of presence and an aspect of material form.[6] In his own work, this is made manifest as the culling and superposition of electronic imagery upon surfaces of differential geometry as a proposal for a concrete architecture, anticipating technologies of architectural luminescence that allow buildings to become displays, and hence, living signs. The utility of Perrella's compelling conception of hypersurface does not stop here. Akin to the notion of 'liquid architectures' but focused more closely on the built in physical space, his conception aims at the bringing together of form, presence, and information into conceptually clear formulation. Once this cluster is grasped, other ways of achieving the same consolidation are opened.

Instantiations

'Poéme Electronique', the 1958 Philips Pavilion by Le Corbusier, Xenakis, and Varése is perhaps the strongest modern precursor to transarchitectures and hypersurfaces. Integrating architecture, mathematics, music and technology, this building was formed by two surfaces: an exterior hyperbolic paraboloid similar to the one Xenakis used for his musical composition, 'Metastasis', and an interior surface likened to a 'cow's stomach'. This curious duality of mathematics and viscerality characterises the scope of the transarchitectural. Within the building, 400 speakers and a multimedia presentation consisting of projections of images from sources as varied as mythology, science, world news, art and popular culture, liquefied the space into an inhabited spectacle.

In the Cité Médiévale des Baux de Provence, in an abandoned quarry, Albert Plécy created in 1977 the 'Cathédrale d'Images', a space of subterranean projections that anticipates both transarchitecures and hypersurface architecture. Forty-six light-valves project over 2,800 slides onto 36,000 square feet of quarry surfaces every half-hour. Artists such as Hans-Walter Muller create programs of images and sounds that abduct the space and superpose a myriad other architectures upon the solid physicality of the vast quarry chambers.[7] What is most striking is how many spaces a single space can become, confounding conventional distinctions of real/virtual, actual/possible, material/immaterial. This is all accomplished using technologies that do not yet engage the computer fully, but the anticipation of the issues discussed here is unmistakably present. At some point in the program, images of architectural interiors are projected onto the quarry walls, making evident the extent of present possibility. A giant window of a Parisian apartment appears and we realise that we have come to the point of projecting onto the wall not only the image of that window but also its function. Bentham's panopticon has become what I call the 'pantopicon'. We have come to the point where we can arrange our technologies in a manner that allows us to project a virtual window where no window exists and see out of it, looking through to any place where a camera can go, or to places where cameras cannot go but computations can. The virtual window on the blind walls of the quarry can look onto the surrounding landscape, a street in Paris, the bottom of the ocean, the news on CNN, the terrain of Mars, a real-time scan of someone's brain, or into AlphaWorld on the Internet, three dimensional and inhabited by 200,000 'netizens' and their avatars.

The makers of this 'Cathédrale d'Images' belong to a generation that reached its prime before computers became ubiquitous. In the end this is a glorified slideshow, but this is no criticism, since what is presented is a clear, strong vision pertinent to the problems and possibilities we face. We can replace the slides with live video, computer animations, virtual realities; we can move out from the surface of the walls and into the volume of the quarry and make the space intelligent and interactive; we can link image and space to the Internet and to other quarries and buildings in other parts of the planet. We can take the next step, and the next, and the next.

Combining aspects of the 'Poéme Electronique' and the 'Cathédrale d'Images' with an openness to present transarchitectural possibilities, Kas Oosterhuis and Lars Spuybroek, the architects of the Janus-like Water Pavilion near Rotterdam, have begun to take such next steps. This dual building is dedicated to water, consisting of a Fresh Water Pavilion (Spuybroek) and a Salt Water Pavilion (Oosterhuis). Each in his own way, the two architects have built the first building to take mutated, augmented, transactive space as an architectural given of our times, creating an edifice in which graphics workstations are part of the architecture and real-time sensors and effectors, and interactive projections and sounds are integral to the architectural intention. Engaging the concept of 'liquid architectures' not only for its obvious proximity to the programme of a 'water pavilion' but, more importantly, as a statement of radical variability and openness to unexplored architectural potentials, they have produced the best built example of transarchitectures, a work that at once transcends categories and sets new standards for the incorporation of computation in a design. The fact that this is a dual building is important; the concept of liquid architectures is always plural and inclusive (by tolerance, not consensus), as 'transarchitectures' aims to be. The conception, design, execution and inhabitation of both parts of this building are fully transarchitectural. All of the levels of transarchitectures described above are engaged, except perhaps the last, the level of architectural nonlocality. They are already poised for breaking through this important threshold as well. The two sides of this linear building meet near the centre, at an agreed common plane, a physical section; otherwise they are quite distinct. One can imagine a pair of other planes, each one a laminar half of an interactive hypersurface encountered at the far ends of each half of the Water Pavilion, planes that become virtual portals into the other part of the building, warping the long linear space into a Möbius strip that allows people to interact with each other at opposite ends. Once in place, this short-distance nonlocality can be extended across the globe and into virtuality.

Algorithmic spectacular

As science and technology shift the conceivable, the presentable also is altered. The moving span between the conceivable and the presentable can be mined for new transarchitectural potential. In my work, this kind of mining is pursued as a research into pure tectonics. I construct mathematical models and generative procedures that are constrained by numerous variables initially unrelated to any pragmatic concerns. Even so, there are sites into which external influences can injected. Each variable or process is a 'slot' into which an external influence can be mapped, either statically or dynamically. Because the models are mathematical and algorithmic, they offer maximum compressibility – all that needs to be transmitted is the mathematical formula and the algorithm by which to unpack it, not the apparent data – and are therefore eminently suitable for transmission, either across the Internet to a virtual polis, or across the city to the office of a consultant or to a fabrication bureau.

Once the model is constructed, an iterative evolutionary process locates a set of values that fits into the variable slots and instantiates a design. These values can be derived from the particulars of the real world, from data and processes of the virtual world or from numerous techniques of capturing the real and casting it into the virtual, motion-capture, for instance. Since time is a feature of the model, if the model is fed time-based data, the form becomes animate, the architecture – liquid.

Topology does not mean curved surfaces, as the current discourse would have it, it means simply the study of those relations that remain invariant under transformations and deformations. A notion of continuity is indeed implied in this definition, but the continuity is abstract. A cube is not less topological than a blob. However, when working algorithmically, what remains invariant is the algorithm, so that a new notion of topology, 'variable topology' is introduced. While the variations in the space of the parameters and control structures that implement the algorithm may be continuous, the product of the algorithm may be to show tears and discontinuities and ever fracture into a cloud of particles or an explosion of shards. Like Raymond Roussel's method for writing, 'certain of his books',[8] the variable topology of the algorithm can take us to the alien edge of the moving transmodern presentable/conceivable interval.

My algorithmic explorations of tectonic production are concerned less with the manipulation of objects and more with the manipulation of relations, fields, higher dimensions, and eventually, the curvature of space itself. Once the architecture of objects has been set aside in favour of an architecture of relations, the notions of hyperspace and hypersurface become natural. In working with fields of force or fields of data, the notion of the isosurface is necessary; in working with hyperspaces of higher dimensions, visualisation itself requires the extraction of three-dimensional subspaces or submanifolds, which are, as mentioned above, hypersurfaces of the hyperspaces within which the designs evolve. Finally, in the case of the curved space, it is the space itself that is understood as a hypersurface that is modulated in a way that warps everything within its purview.

Typically, I compute or find a field of forces or data, scan it for isosurfaces, extrude the isosurfaces into a hyperspace of higher dimensions, transform the new higher dimensional hyperobjects in the hyperspace, project the object in a space of fewer dimensions – a hypersurface of the hyperspace – and then, finally, warp the spatial matrix itself into a new curvature of space. This elaborate process is repeated to produce alternative 'voices' to be used in a spatial polyphony. Some aspect of hypersurfaces is implicit at each step of the way, even at, but not limited to, the level of form. These forms are cast into the space of transarchitectures, the intelligent, augmented spacetime both within and outside cyberspace. This means that the design does not end with form; rather, it is the hypersurface of interface that animates the design. Each point and polygon is a known index into a body of information, placed in space and time by a known algorithm and, hence, interactive, transactive and intelligent.

The formulation of hypersurface as the 'hyper' of presence and the 'surface' of the matter/energy substratum applies, not as a description of the building-as-television, but as part of an information ecosystem of dynamically balanced constraints. Given enough computational power, connectivity and human presence, these models transform in real-time in registration with human action. In the absence of such power, or in the absence of inhabitants, they are rendered as reflective surfaces, empty virtual mirrors.

Form follows neither function nor form; rather, I am concerned with what the Situationists called the 'psychogeography' of these emergent spaces.[9] Moving from algorithmic derivations to the Debordian 'derive', from the 'naked city' to 'naked transarchitectures'. I am interested in drifting through these spaces in a condition at least momentarily uncontaminated by the spectacle. No purpose is needed; indeed to the extent that the spaces that are formed are fundamentally unfamiliar, it is possible to savour their inherent psychogeographic content in a moment of surprise just prior to the onslaught of references. Just as the invention of electronic instruments and the parallel emancipation of noise brought forth musical materials that exceeded the theoretical frameworks of their times, so too do these explorations reveal tectonic materials whose potencies and valences cannot immediately be comprehended.

Adopting pure spectacle within Debord's 'society of the spectacle' may be the only form of resistance to the omnivorousness of late-capitalist appropriation, since the imposition of any purpose instantly becomes figural and visible as a tactic or target of takeover. The alternative is to learn from the world itself: to produce an endless and unjustifiable proliferation of alien variety, within which local purposes can emerge, flourish and disappear, always pushing the very transmodern edge of (trans)evolutionary transmutation.

Notes

1 Gilles Deleuze and Félix Guattari, *Anti-Oedipus: Capitalism and Schizophrenia*, Robert Hurley, Mark Seem, Helen R Lane (trans), Viking (New York), 1977. See also *A Thousand Plateaus: Capitalism and Schizophrenia*, Brian Massumi (trans), University of Minnesota Press (Minneapolis), 1987.

2 Jean-François Lyotard, *The Postmodern Explained*, Julian Prefanis and Morgan Thomas (trans), University of Minnesota Press (Minneapolis), 1992.

3 Michael Duff, 'The Theory Formerly Known as Strings', in *Scientific American* (New York), February 1998, vol 278, no 2, pp64-69.

4 Lawrence Sklar, *Space, Time, and Spacetime*, University of California Press (Berkeley), 1977.

5 Roland Barthes, *Camera Lucida: Reflections on Photography*, Hill and Wang (New York), 1981.

6 Stephen Perrella, 'Hypersurface Infrastructure', in *Fisuras: On Interzones and Unplaces*, Banigraf (Madrid), vol 3, no 3, 1995, pp112-35.

7 François Seguret, *L'Entretien Des Illusions: Hans-Walter Muller, Claude Giverne, Xavier Juillot*, Editions de la Villette (Paris), 1997.

8 Raymond Roussel, *How I Wrote Certain of My Books and Other Writings*, Trevor Winkfield (ed), Exact Change (Boston), 1995.

9 *Theory of the Dérive and other Situationist Writings on the City*, Libero Andreotti and Zavier Costa (eds), Museu d'Art Contemporain de Barcelona, 1996.

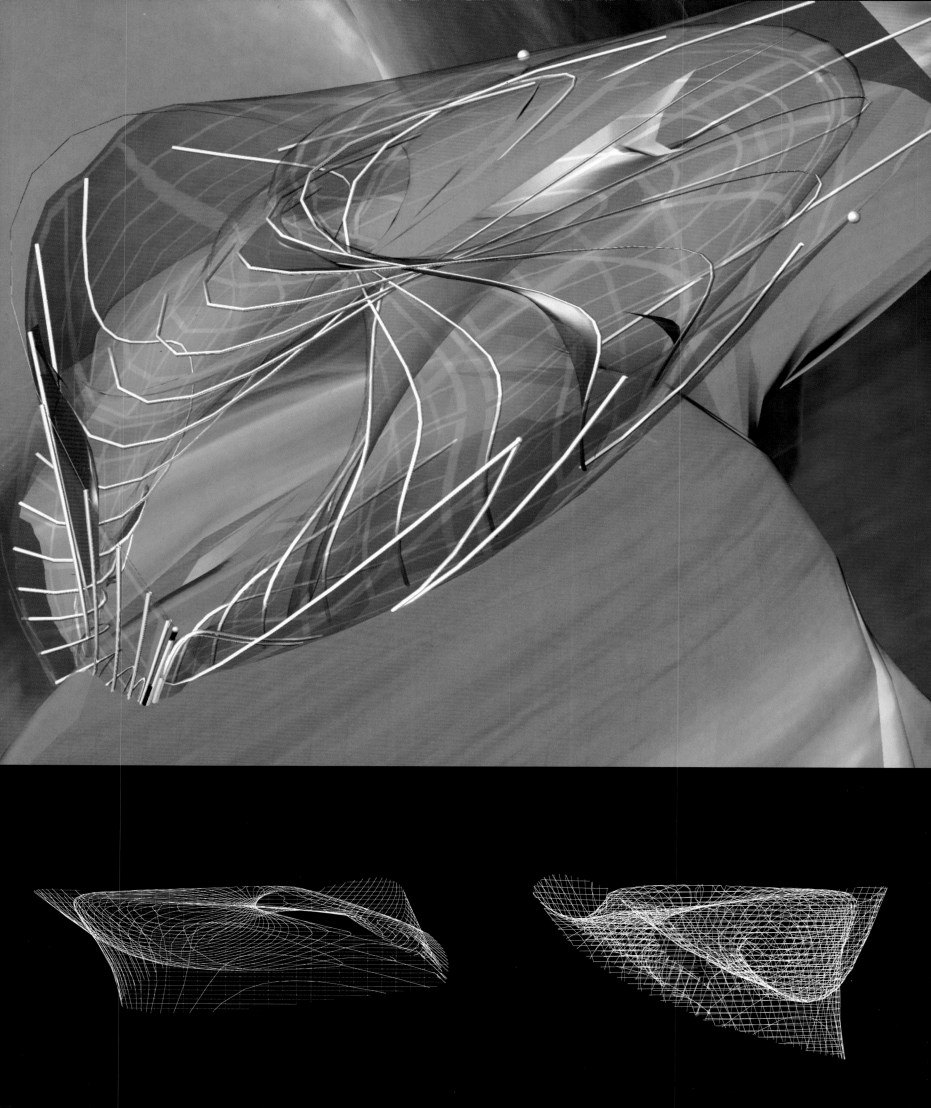

STEPHEN PERRELLA WITH REBECCA CARPENTER
THE MÖBIUS HOUSE STUDY

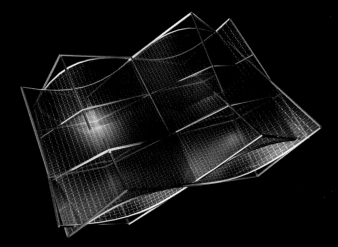

This study (1997-98) is an investigation into contemporary domesticity to reconsider dwelling for the new millennium. A preliminary analysis revealed that the pervasive use of technology in the home presents an ontological dilemma. Current house formats are no longer tenable because space and time are reconfigured by a lived informational geometry. Dwelling has become problematic solely in terms of Euclidean space as a result of media infiltrations – a force that implodes distance and then perplicates subjectivity as it enfolds viewer perception into an endless barrage of electronic images. This occurs in combination with, and yet is dissimilar to, the dynamics of teletechnology and computer-to-Internet connectivity. As home-viewing narrows onto the TV surface, it fuses with an image-blitz into a perpetual present.[1] Teletechnology contributes to a burrowing effect, altering the home as an exclusively interior condition. This battlefield of intersubjectivity problematises the dweller-consumer as an ego-construct-identity, traditionally based upon an interiority divided from an exteriority and governed by an ideality.

The Möbius House study diagram for post-Cartesian dwelling is thus neither an interior space nor an exterior form. It is a transversal membrane that reconfigures binary notions of interior/exterior into a continuous, interwrapping median – it is a hypersurface. The current phase of the study presents a fluxing diagram-membrane generated by an animated inflection. It is a hypersurface generated by first deconstructing the supporting geometry of a NURB (non-uniform rational B-spline) curve in the animation software by Microsoft/Softimage. Each singular control point that governs a five-point NURB was animated along the path of a Möbius surface, generating a topology that cannot be understood by either Euclidean or Cartesian geometry. Within the animation sequences, temporal delays are programmed to avoid determinate, linear form: what is otherwise known as 'the stopping problem'.[2] The Möbius House study is thus irreducible, rendering it open to complex, temporal experience: it is architecture that is not based upon fundamental form or space and therefore, in part, constitutive of experience; not an attempt to contain or act as a plane of reference. It is a transversal construct.[3] A domestic hypersurface program thus emerges immanently from the diagram-substrate, facilitating proprioceptive experience, a radical empiricism more commensurate with the complexities of new-millennial modes of inhabitation.[4]

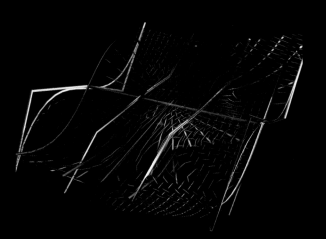

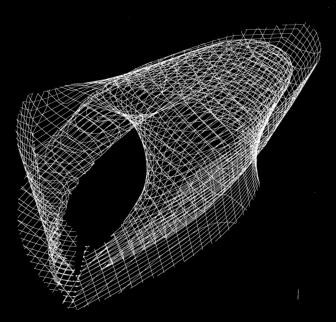

Notes

1 In *Blue Sky* (Verso, 1997) Paul Virilio discusses the notion of pyknoleptic from pyknolepsy, a medical term denoting childhood avsence epilepsy.

2 In the 'Emerging Complexities' Symposium at Columbia University GSAP, Spring 1997, theorist-economist Akira Asada raised the issue of whay he called the 'stopping problem' – a way of describing work that attempts to bring temporality into architectural form. He noted that at a certain phase of design development, the form must be frozen and then conceivably built as such. Hypersurface theory and the Möbius House study argue that if the constituting or governing structures of form are considered separately from a lived program, then 'animate' form will exist only in the realm of materiality. What is most significant about the work of Deleuze and Guattari is that they ofer a means to evacuate such dualities.

3 See Gary Genosko's essay in this volume, pp32-37.

4 See Brian Massumi's essay in this volume, pp16-25. His thesis on proprioperception entails an enrichment of experience that embraces but reworks the impoverishing dynamics within the schizophrenia that stems from capitalism.

OPPOSITE: X, Y, Z sections; FROM ABOVE: Hypersurface panel studies 1 and 2; X, Y Z axonometric

FROM ABOVE: Théâtre Oblique
dans une structure, *1972;* Surface
en X, *1966*

CLAUDE PARENT

THE OBLIQUE FUNCTION MEETS ELECTRONIC MEDIA

My approach as an architect was characterised, as early as 1950, by the professional interest I had in the media at the time (in particular with the collaboration of Ionel Schein). This approach towards the press and cinema, and later towards television, was so unusual that it has been criticised by my peers. One should not forget that in France, in the 1950s, it was forbidden by the Architects' Chapter to sign a building or to publicise one's work in a way that would give its presentation a commercial quality.

Therefore, right from the beginning, I was not well accepted by my professional colleagues as an architect who publicised his work and his ideas with the support of the press; quite laughable, I suppose, to the eyes of the Anglo-Saxons. Magazines like *Elle*; *Paris Match*; François Lazaroff's group *France Soir*; *Jardin des modes*; *Science et vie*; *Realités*; *Plaisirs de France*; *Femina*, and of course *Architecture d'Aujourd'hui* – in addition to the art press – became champions of my work, and moreover, keys to opening my mind to architecture and projecting my ideas towards the future.

My research was influenced very early on by its relationship to the world of news through the popular press and by a fusion with the artistic world via André Bloc.

The study of the 'Spaciodynamic City' with sculptor Nicolas Schöffer in 1954 is an idiosyncratic example of this mind-set. 'Utopian City' (1954) was certainly related to the 1917 Russian Constructivists' essays/experiments but it already linked up with all kinds of communication systems expressed by architecture up to its theoretical limits.

A 1955 project consisted of the realisation of a full-sized model at the 'Construction Show'. This depicted the way in which the facades of buildings, instead of being simple enclosures, would interact like real urban transmitters, allowing for exchanges, as permanent sources of information creating animation in the city.

Nicolas Schöffer and myself had already realised image screens projected on to mobile sculptures on commercial billboards, and through this 'light dynamism' we were to create alive and expressive facades of the spacio-dynamic city which would become 'cybernetic'.

Finally, however, the press group originally interested in this urban setting of information withdrew because of all the technical problems. In fact, our demands were too advanced for the ambitions and state of the media at that time.

The power and the wealth of the written press prevented them from anticipating the transformation that we were witnessing. A transformation as rapid as it was unavoidable. The important fact to remember was that in 1955 an architect and a sculptor had tried to create an architecture in close relation to the development of the media.

At the same time, Nicolas Schöffer designed the 'Key Hole' House which subjected visitors to a 'cold' space and a 'hot' space communicated through pictorial and dynamic means which did not need to be interpreted intellectually by visitors. The information was sufficient to enable understanding by all visitors, whether educated or uneducated.

Ten years later with Paul Virilio, we dealt with this problem in a different way through our proposal of 'inclined planes' or the oblique. The foundation of life was not neutral any longer but active, and the disruption caused by the inclined plane could not be misunderstood since it was addressed to obvious human attitudes like balance and imbalance (stability, instability, shift of references). It used indisputable means of direct information such as tactility. The non-coded 'foot' and the non-coded 'hand' also became foremost and unquestionable information sources and superseded the eye and the logical intelligence, which are considered usual filters of the understanding of space.

In order to explain the introduction of 'topology' into the discourse on space (to the detriment of form which at this point in time was predominant), I took a simple and ordinary tactile image which has never been appreciated by architects. I said that architecture was like knitwear, that one would start the sweater at one end and would finish it at the other extremity without defining its limits.

This prosaic way to consider space in its continuity and in its deformation was too natural to be convincing, although it was extremely genuine as well as popular. I continually reasserted that the oblique was not an architecture proposing a new language, but rather a tool. This approach always prompts fresh is-

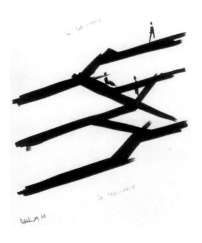

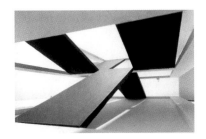

FROM ABOVE: La Carapace – surface en X, *1966;* Sur-face/Sous-face, *1972;* Théâtre Oblique, *1972*

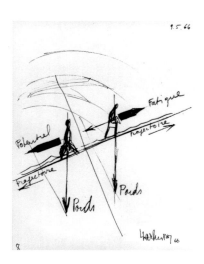

sues to be raised, leading to the discovery of new solutions and relations to the space, and finally the creation of new spaces which would have been unimaginable through traditional methods of creation.

This part of the research has been denied by French architects, and this is where the sadness lies in not having been understood. However, I am convinced that as a result of the dazzling development of contemporary electronic media that we have witnessed, and the newness and power of means that researchers benefit from today, the oblique is gaining the place it originally deserved.

It is linked naturally to the research that Stephen Perrella calls Hypersurface. One of the paths that the oblique had hoped to explore was the notion of limit, a notion which now becomes important when exploring topology. The oblique had explored the absolute necessity of a threshold of restoration when one wants to pass from, or more exactly jumps from, one continuity to another. In mathematics there is the notion of solution of continuity which allows, while breaking up mathematical space, for the passage of one element to another within the continuity of a topological space and thus, despite the excessive deformations of space.

Let us not forget that architecture lives only in the revelation of the limits it conceives. In the past, the wall was its recurrent image. The

adventurer was the one who pushed away limits of knowledge; who moved away the wall.

As a result of electronic media, the architect experiences spaces which were never conceived before. He discovers them and at the same time pushes away the limits of form. The 'media' wall still remains to be invented as a modern notion of 'enclosure' which undoubtedly will include the intervention of time.

Meanwhile, let us hope that Hypersurface architects opt for good choices within the infinity of possibilities that the new technology of the machine can offer them. In any case, whatever the resulting quality, it should be acknowledged that electronic media enabled new methodologies to be invented, and that it is only through such imaginative approaches that one will be able to improve architecture. Without a fresh approach, it is not possible for creation to be improved.

The relevance of the computer tool we use, thanks to the strength of today's new technologies, directly stimulates our 'imagination' – to a point that it could help solve a fundamental question which seemed insoluble: how one can keep the modern quality of continuity ('vanishing spaces') and preserve the ancestral notion of enclosure ('limit'). How shall one make these two architectural poles reconcilable?

Translated by Laetitia Wolff

Important note

Important in our understanding of the 'oblique function' is that for the first time it has substituted the notion of surface for one of volume in the definition of space.

Thus, in relation to the 'oblique function' one cannot speak about interior and exterior, or of enclosure-envelope realising the distinction, one could say the discrimination, between internal space and external space. This distinction describes architecture through the limits between the two, and thus whatever ingenuity an architect needs to make it as non-existent as possible (Richard Neutra for instance), even virtual (actuality).

In the oblique function, this research around the notion of enclosure which had agitated the architectural milieu does not need to be, because it does not exist. Indeed, the enclosure is linked to the notion of volume (distinction container-content) whereas the oblique function materialises the structure of space, by the surface under and over, both creating more or less parallel layers, whose meeting and interpenetration creates limits allowing for the inhabit-ability and the use of these surfaces.

Everything resides in this major principle of the oblique function. There is no such thing as interior (circulation) and exterior (shelter) but an ensemble of surfaces developed and associated so that, while creating a coverable totality, they determine endless protected surfaces or open-air surfaces ('inhabitable circulation').

The word limit is therefore wrong because it is unadapted. One has to invent a new word, a novel expression to define the progressive penetration towards protection, the fact that enclosure is not formulated architecturally by a specific element but becomes virtual, imprecise, indecisive, maybe even a tangibly and not illusory virtual through the transparency of glass: an illusion.

Historical note

From the 1920s throughout the 1930s, there was an attempt to destroy volume via the decomposition and *mise en scène* of plans (Rietveld). However, imprisoned in the orthogonal (and in its constraining system), the attempt was limited to an aesthetic change and never reached further than a fashion, whereas in fact it dealt with a very innovative doctrinal point. What a pity!

FROM ABOVE: Les Grandes Oreilles, *1966;* Premier croquis sur le Potentialisme, *1966;* Untitled, *1970; OPPOSITE:* Intérieur, *1973;* Espace de Rencontre, *1973*

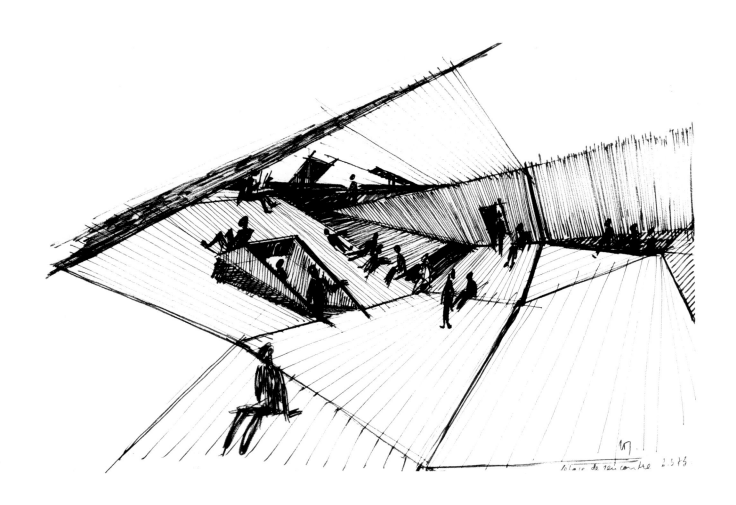

LARS SPUYBROEK
MOTOR GEOMETRY

'There's this *thing*, this ghost-foot,' said one of Oliver Sacks' patients. 'Sometimes it hurts like hell. This is worst at night, or with the prosthesis off, or when I'm not doing anything. It goes away when I strap the prosthesis on and walk. I still feel the leg then, vividly, but it's a *good* phantom, different – it animates the prosthesis, and allows me to walk.'[1]

What is it that animates a mere mechanical extension? How is it that the body is so good at incorporating this lifeless component into its motor system that it recovers its former fluency and grace? The body does not care if the leg is made of flesh or of wood, as long as it fits; that is to say, it fits into the unconscious body model created by the different possible movements. Proprioception, the neurologists term it: the body's power of unconscious self-perception. Our legs are a 'comfortable fit' by their very nature, but only because the leg coincides exactly with the ghostly image invoked by the automatism of walking.

Once a leg is frozen in immobility, however, it very soon no longer 'fits'. Sacks reports one such instance: 'When, after a few weeks, the leg was freed from its prison of plaster, it had lost the power to make all kinds of movements that were formerly automatic and which now had to be learned all over again. She felt that her comprehension of these movements had gone. [. . .] If you stop making complex movements, if you don't practise them internally, they will be forgotten within a few weeks and become impossible.'[2] With practice and training, the movements of the prosthesis can become second nature, regardless of whether it is of flesh, of wood or – a little more complex – of metal, as in the case of a car. That is the secret of the animation principle: the body's inner phantom has an irrepressible tendency to expand, to integrate every sufficiently responsive prosthesis into its motor system, its repertoire of movements, and make it run smoothly. That is why a car is not an instrument or piece of equipment that you simply sit in, but something you merge with. Anyone who drives a lot will recognise the dreamlike sensation of gliding along the motorway or through traffic, barely conscious of one's actions. This does not mean that our cars turn us into mechanical Frankensteins but that the human body is capable of inspiriting the car and making its bodywork become the skin of the driver; this must be true, otherwise we would bump into everything. If we did not merge with the car, if we did not change our body into something 4 x 1.5 metres, it would not be possible to park the car, take a curve, or overtake others. Movements can only be fluent if the skin extends as far as possible over the prosthesis and into the surrounding space, so that every action takes place from within the body, which no longer does things consciously but relies totally on 'feeling'.

When this haptic sense of extension is taken seriously it means that everything starts inside the body, and from there on it just never stops. The body has no outer reference to direct its actions to, neither a horizon to relate to, nor any depth of vision to create a space for itself. It relates only to itself. There is no outside: there is no world in which my actions take place, the body forms itself by action, constantly organising and reorganising itself motorically and cognitively to keep 'in form'. According to Maturana and Varela: there is no structured information on the outside, it becomes information only by forming itself through my body, by transforming my body, which is called action . . .[3]

'Hey, we are lost!' Michael said to his guide. The guide gave him a withering glance and answered: 'We are not lost, the camp is lost!' In a flash Michael realized a very important aspect of what separated his vision of the world from that of his guide: for Michael, space was fixed, in which a free agent moved around like an actor on a stage, a vast space in which you could lose your way. The guide however saw space as something within, rather than outside the body, a fluid and changing medium in which one could never lose one's way when the only fixed point in the universe consisted of himself, and although he might be putting one foot in front of the other he never actually moved.[4]

This, of course, is a nomad's view of the world; the view of somebody on the move, because only by the prosthetic act of walking does the whole space become one's own skin. The tent nomads carry with them is part of that walking; it never interrupts space, as a house does. So every prosthesis is in the nature of a vehicle, something that adds movement to the body, that adds a new repertoire of action. Of course, the car changes the skin into an interface, able to change the exterior into the interior of the body itself. The openness of the world would make no sense if it were not absorbed by my body-car. The body simply creates a haptic field completely centred upon itself, in which every outer event becomes related to this bodily network of virtual movements, becoming actualised in form and action.

Where there is close vision, space is not visual, or rather the eye itself has a haptic, non-optical function: no line separates earth from sky, which are of the same substance, there is neither horizon nor background, nor perspective nor limit nor outline of form nor centre; there is no intermediary distance, or all distance is intermediary.[5]

In Tamás Waliczky's short film *The Garden* (1992), made with video manipulation and computer animation, we see a little girl running around a garden, extending her hands towards a dragonfly, sitting down under a big tree, climbing up the ladder of a slide, and then sliding down. We see all this and at the same time nothing like it. In fact, during the whole movie the little girl does not move at all, or rather, she moves her hands and feet, but her head never leaves the centre of the screen. We see the tree folding under her legs, we see the rungs of the ladder shrink and bulge under her feet, we see the slide deform under her body. Nothing moves, but everything changes shape. As the girl reaches her hand out to the dragonfly, we see the insect grow disproportionately large then shrink and disappear the moment she shifts her attention.

OPPOSITE: Nox Architects, interior of FreshH₂O eXPO (Fresh Water Pavilion), The Netherlands, 1997

The girl does not move around in a perspective world where things are between the eye and the horizon; rather, through her actions she is in perfect balance and stays fixed on the vertical axis: she has become the vertiginous horizon of things, the vanishing point of the world. Things become part of her body by topological deformation, not by perspective distortion. She has become the gravitational centre of a field, or better, a sphere of action – a motor field – her own planet . . . This is not perception but proprioception. Everything immediately becomes networked within the body, where the seen is the touched and the felt, where no distinction can be made between the near and the far, between the hand of manipulation and the sphere of the global.

An eye acts as if it were a hand; not as a receptive but as an active organ, and what is at hand is always nearby and close, without any sense of depth or perspective, and without background or horizon. So every action becomes prosthetic because it extends the feeling reach of the skin, and, vice versa, every prosthesis, and I mean every technological device, becomes an action, a vector-object, a twirl in the environmental geometry. Every change of muscle tone in the motor system has its topological effect, because outside and body are networked into one object with its own particular coherence, where seeing and walking and acting are interconnected in one (proprioceptive) feeling skin, without top or bottom but with an all around orientation; without the orthogonality of the vertical and gravitational axis of the body's posture in relation to frontal and horizontal perspective, but a three-dimensionality where images and actions relate to one and the same geometry, without any X, or without any Y, or without any Z.[6]

FreshH$_2$O eXPO, Zeeland, The Netherlands, 1994-97

Liquid architecture is not the mimesis of natural fluids in architecture.[7] First and foremost it is a liquidising of everything that has traditionally been crystalline and solid in architecture. It is the contamination of media. The liquid in architecture has earlier been associated with the easing back of architecture for human needs, of real time fulfilment. This soft and smart technology of desire can only end up with the body as a residue, where its first steps in cyberspace will probably be its last steps ever. But the desire for technology seems far greater and a far more destabilising force, since our need for the accidental exceeds our need for comfort.

FreshH$_2$O eXPO (as our design office NOX named the project),

generally known as the Fresh Water Pavilion, has been seized by the concept of the liquid. Not only its shape and use of materials but the interior environment tries to effect a prototypical merging of hardware, software and wetware. The design of this interactive installation was based on the metastable aggregation of architecture and information. The form is shaped by the fluid deformation of 14 ellipses spaced out over a length of more than 65 metres.

Imagine the curves connecting all the ellipses being torn apart, bent and twisted again by outside forces – the wind, dunes, ground water, the Well – while internal forces try to maintain the ellipses; that is, attempt to stay smooth. The basis of the geometry is the vector-based changing of splines linking the ellipses. In this way, line and force become connected. The spline with its control points and tangential handles in 3D modelling software derives from naval architecture where a curve was created by a wooden spline bend by the positioning of several weights at the 'control points'. Line is not separated from point, but every vertex is the basis of a vector. If one changes the position or direction of the vector, the others change in accordance with their mutual dependency. In this case, the line becomes an action, and not the trace of an action. H$_2$O eXPO is a bundle, a braid of splines. It derives its coherence from movement. In its soft network no distinction is made between form and deformation.

From the beginning, we wondered if we could design something that was completely in line with the law governing wheelchair accessibility (eg the steepness of ramps) while at the same time devise a prosthetic geometry, a geometry of wheels, a geometry of speed and imbalance? Not one part of the building is horizontal, no one slope stays within the same gradient. Conceptually, the building has not so much been 'placed on' the ground as 'dug out of' the ground. The essential instability is achieved through the concept of the ground as being 'all around'. The floor becomes hyperdimensional and tries to become a volume.

When dealing with a haptic, three-dimensional body – a body without the distinction between feet and eyes – the difference between floor and ceiling becomes irrelevant. With this kind of topological perception action is no longer ground-based, with your eyes transported blindly. Buildings are generally guided by this dichotomy of transport and vision, where the programmatic is on the floor and the formal is in the elevation. In this building, the information on the floor is blended with the deformation of the volume, to paraphrase Jeffrey Kipnis.

In H$_2$0 eXPO there is no horizon, no window looking out. There is no horizontality, no floor underlining the basis of perspective. This is, of course, the moment of dizziness, because walking and falling become confused; or, as the manual for 3D Studio MAX observes in the chapter on animation: walking and running are special cases of falling . . . This imbalance is the very basis of this building, and also the basis of every action, because not one position is without a vector. This building is not only for wheel-chairs and skateboards, it is also for the wrong foot, the leg one happens to stand on . . . That is why, instead of a window, there is a well. The Well is another kind of horizon, more like a window to the centre of the earth: a hidden horizon, not horizontal, but vertical, on the axis of vertigo, of falling.

Where, then, is the point of action. Where is the source of the Well? Here, just like a surfer, the body is placed on a vector and obliged to react to that outer force, although it can change its direction or goal at any time. The architecture charges the body because its geometry is such that points become vectors. The source of the action in architecture that has become transported and moved – its geometry has become a prosthetic vehicle by contamination – is exactly in-between body and environment. This is not subject versus object, but an interactive blend. Part of the action is in the object, and when this is animated, the body is too.

The interactivity is not only in the geometry: the action moves through the material – not a form with a certain speed or on the move, but action in the form.[8] The design does not distinguish architecture and information as separate entities, nor as separate disciplines. The project is not restricted to materials such as concrete and steel, which were considered to be liquid, but utilises cloth and rubber, ice and mist, fluid water (taking over the action and wetting not only the building, but also the visitor), in addition to electronic media, interactive sound, light and projections. The material is not separated from the so-called immaterial. There is only substance and action.

The continuous surface of the interior is covered with different

sensing devices. Imagine walking or running up the central slope towards a wire-frame projection on the floor. In the course of this you activate a series of light sensors and step right into the projection, where you are covered in a grid of light. The waves begin to run through the mesh. Now you start to run with the waves, activating more sensors and creating more waves . . . The vertigo of the motor system is inextricably linked to sensory hallucination.

At the same time, the pulse of light going through the sp(L)ine – a line of numerous blue lamps – is speeded up by the crowd activating the light sensors. When you dare to step on a touch sensor, ripples suddenly shoot out from your feet: circular decaying waves in the wire-frame projection. Somebody else jumps on to the second sensor, a few metres away from you. Ripples then shoot out from their feet too, interfering with your ripples halfway. As you both begin to jump up and down you are pushing away the sound and activating the light running along the sp(L)ine: suddenly a high level of blue light splits in two and slowly fades away. Further on, a sphere is projected in wire-frame on a steep slope between handles that are gently operated by four people. Their action causes the sphere to deform in as many directions, while at the same time 'pulls the sound' from the Well. With their hardest pulling action, the light on the sp(L)ine is frozen in its last position.

Why still speak of the real and the virtual, the material and the immaterial? Here, these categories are not in opposition or in some metaphysical disagreement, but more in an electroliquid aggregation, enforcing each other, as in a two-part adhesive; constantly exposing its metastability to induce animation. Where is the sun in all this? Excluded and reflected by the outer skin of stainless steel, it is left behind in a museum.[9] The building is lit from the inside out, by the endogenous sun of the computer. This must be why the light is so blue: making hundreds of thousands of real-time calculations, shining on everybody, and rendering the action; the motor systems of the shadowless, spectral bodies coinciding exactly with the reality engine of the computers.

Notes

1 Oliver Sacks, *The Man Who Mistook his Wife for a Hat*, Picador (New York), 1986, p66.
2 Oliver Sacks, *A Leg to Stand On*, Picador (New York), 1991, Afterword, note 2.
3 H Maturana and F Varela, *The Tree of Knowledge*, Shambala, 1984, chapter 7.
4 Derrick de Kerckhove, *The Skin of Our Culture*, Somerville House Books, 1995, p29.
5 Gilles Deleuze and Félix Guattari, *A Thousand Plateaus*, The Athlone Press (London), 1988, p492.
6 Maurice Nio and Lars Spuybroek, 'X and Y and Z – a manual', *ARCHIS*, 11/1995.
7 Marcos Novak, 'Liquid Architecture', in *Cyberspace: First Steps*, Michael Benedikt (ed), MIT Press (Cambridge, Mass), 1993, p 225.
8 Maurice Nio and Lars Spuybroek, 'De Strategie van de Vorm', *de Architect*, 57, 11/1994.
9 Paul Virilio, 'The Museum of the Sun', in *TechnoMorphica*, V2 Organisation, 1997; *The Art of the Motor*, Minnesota, 1995; 'The Function of the Oblique', AA Publications (London), 1996; and *ARCH+* 124/125, p46.

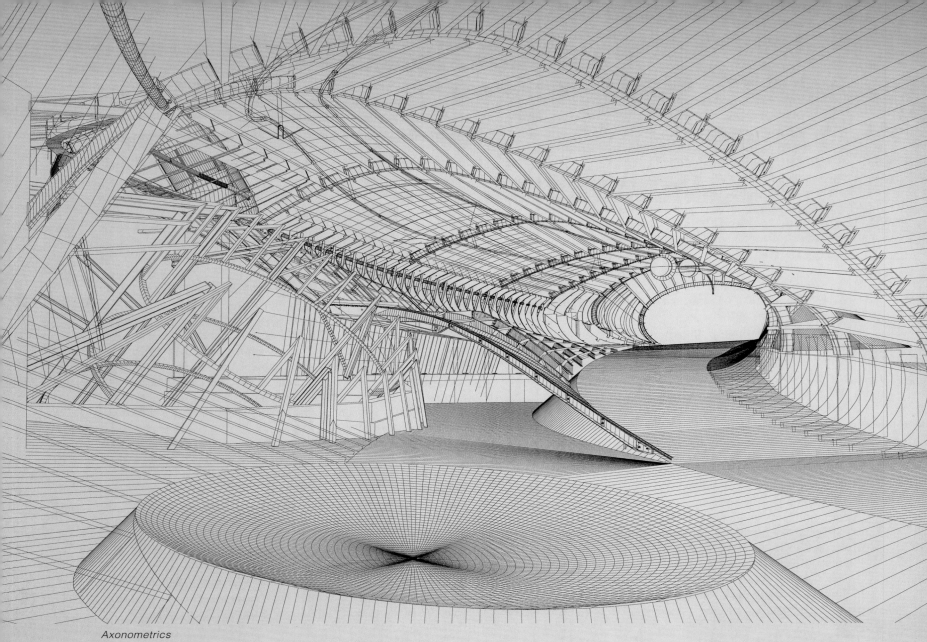

Axonometrics

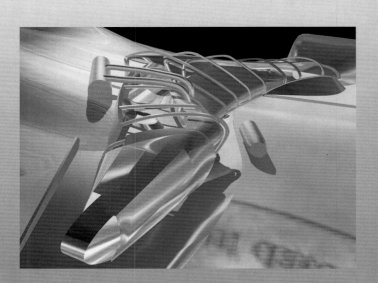

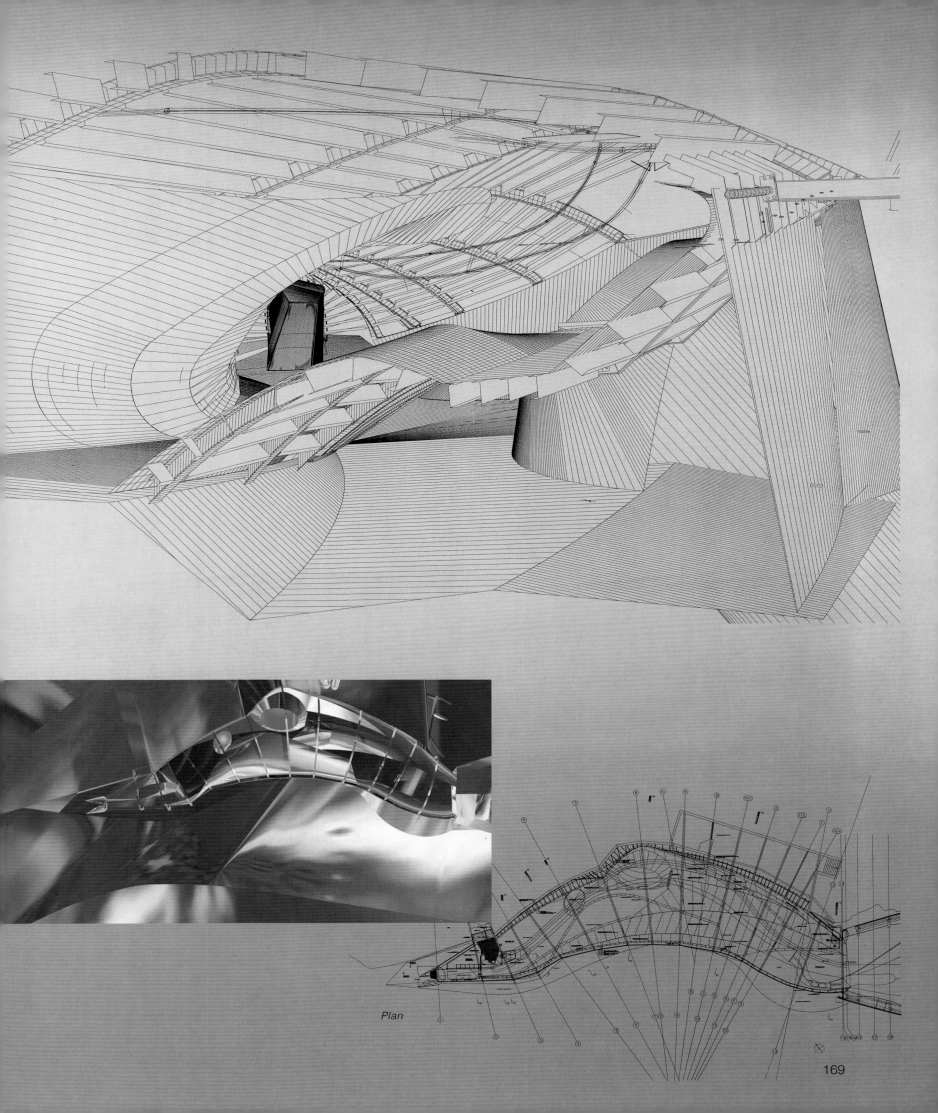

Plan

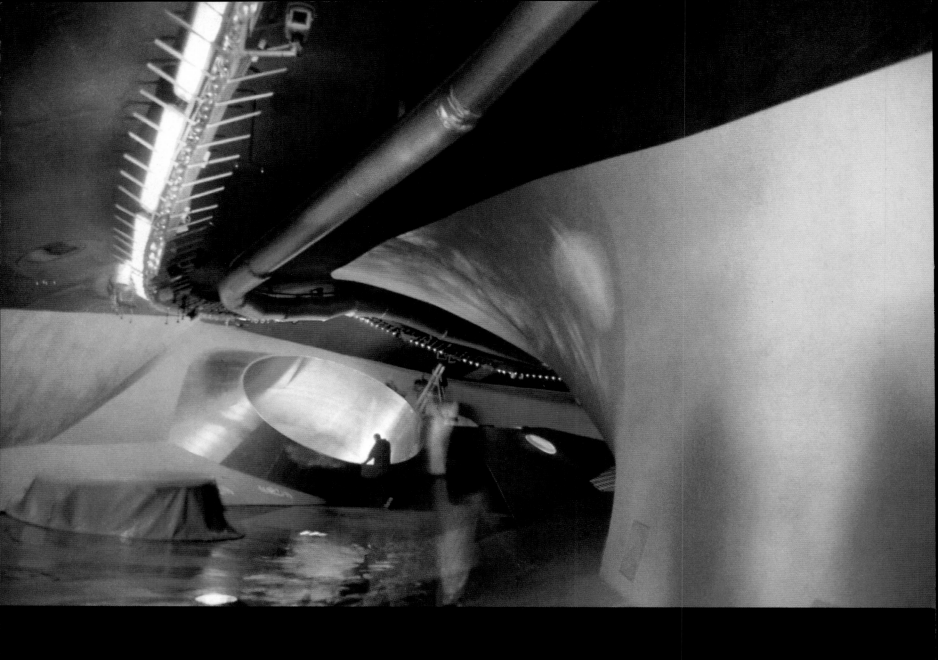

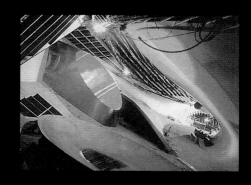

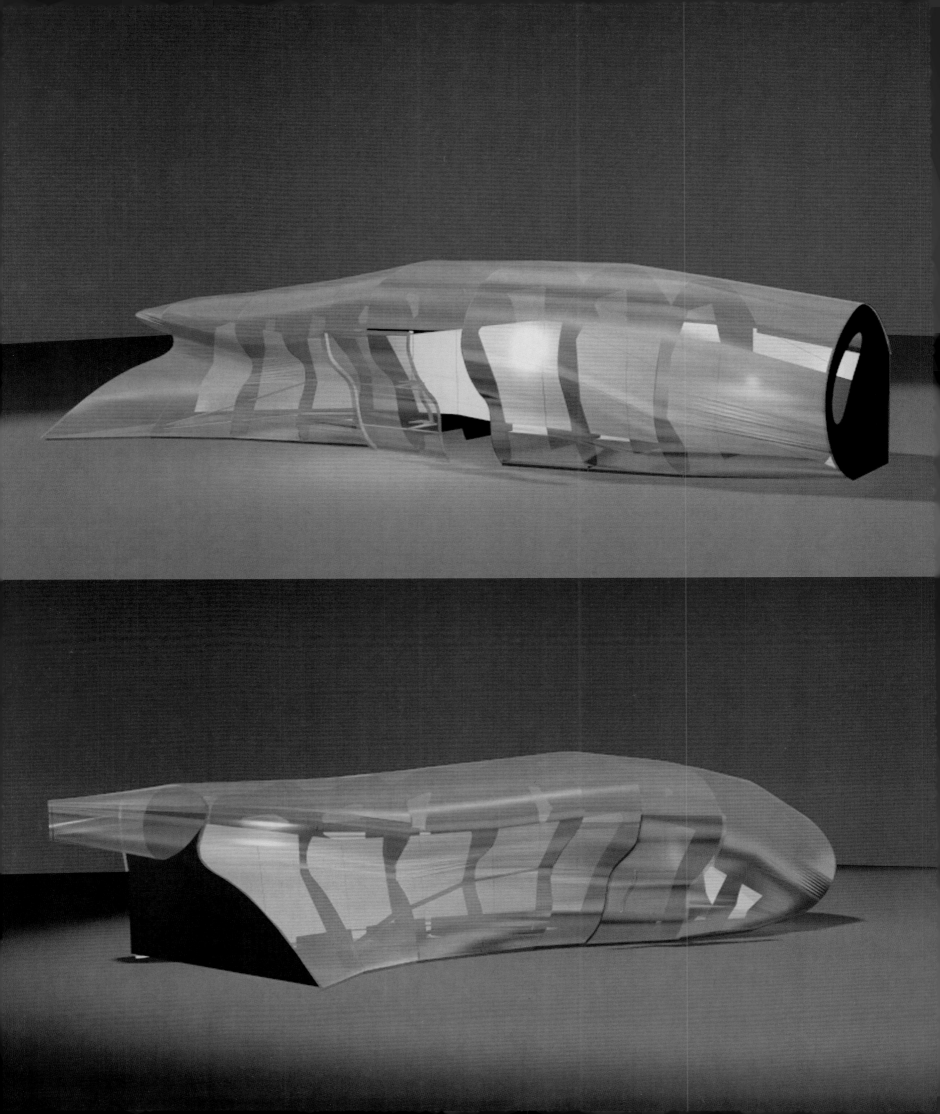

NOX/LARS SPUYBROEK WITH JOAN ALMEKINDERS

BLOW OUT

Wouter van Stiphout states, in *Rethinking the work of Frederick Kiesler*, that everybody seems to focus on Kiesler's 'organic', a-tectonic forms as something sculptural; while for him this architecture obviously clears the way to restoring the relation of the human body, vis-à-vis the furniture, the piles of papers, the table still being set, the odours, the other people, the cat, and so on.

Architecture steps aside by declining to frame events in perspective and tectonics, to have a direct, unfiltered and intimate connection with odour, body and image. Here, architecture does not frame furniture but becomes it: it is moveable, flexible, and consists of moving vectors. Architecture is deframed by the interactive mobility of topology.

This small building for a toilet block on Neeltje Jans in the Netherlands (1997), near the Water Pavilion, has a progressive geometry: it attempts to split up. At one end the building is curved, then halfway along its length it inflects heavily, and at the other end it splits into two distinct parts. The spline-trajectories containing the different sections divide: one dives into the earth, the other jumps into the air. The building resembles a dune that splits backwards into sand and wind, ground and sky.

The toilet block is entered at the centre. Its programme is simple: accommodating four men on the right (two standing up, two sitting down) and four women on the left; with space for a disabled person (sexless) in-between.

When a visitor leaves the Water Pavilion nearby, the 'pressure' within the body has built-up over a period of time. Rather than confront the visitor with a building that directly connects A to B, the direction of the toilet block is multiplied, bent and twisted by other movements. The visitor steps into another vector, of the wind moving through the interior at high speed.

The structure is opened-up on both sides, with a grille on the right-hand side and an extraction duct on the left. With the strong vector of the wind, a balancing act occurs while the lavatory is in use: the building establishes a dynamic equilibrium between internal pressure and external forces.

These external forces are not just another natural element of the architecture: they are media, furniture, mobility, a vector, carrying the acts of other people. The vector of the wind carries the odour and noise of others. This liquid machine connects one interior with another – it shapes intimacy, builds it up, and releases it. Sitting on the lavatory, perpendicular to the direction of the geometry, the visitor can finally relax.

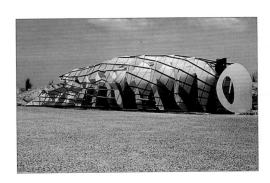

V2 LAB (PART OF V2 ENGINE)

*Renovation within the V2 Building,
Rotterdam, 1998*

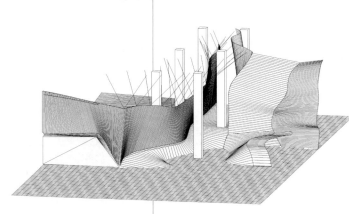

The V2 Lab is part of a larger concept, the V2 Engine. This project is based on the future renovation of the entire V2 building, which will include converting the facade and hall, as well as inserting an extra floor for public activities (bookshop, café and lecture area) in the large exhibition space on the ground floor. This concept has been entirely developed by computer, with animation software that allows for a non-linear, time-dependent architecture.

The V2 Engine consists of a central void, which will be partially finished with synthetic translucent fabric. This will protrude from the facade far enough to be visible from the Witte de Withstraat (a main street nearby). The space will be filled mainly with sounds and images generated by a specially developed software engine that will roam the Internet in search of webcam images of other facades around the world. These images will then be projected from the inside onto the fabric of the facade, together with other images: live portraits of people working at V2, pictures from projects being developed at the time within the V2 Lab.

This concept is not based on the classical distinction between media and architecture where the hole – the void filled with light – is positioned against the material – static and solid architecture. Nor is it based on the even cornier notion of architecture as carrier and media as image.

Instead, the concept is the result of a media criticism of architecture: within a medium, events progress by means of waves, not just within the topological continuity of the medium, but more to induce movement within this continuity by passing on forces within the field. The Euclidean distinction between a point and a line prohibits this, as each point effectuates the separation of lines rather than stimulates their joining. Therefore, with this project, the point constitutes a knot, capable of shrinking and expanding, scientifically known as a 'spring' – a non-static point able to pass on force. Within the computer model that has been developed for the V2 Engine, this spring is the place where the void – the three-dimensional window through which the audience will enter the building in the future – will be located, according to the organisational diagram. All forces within the spring are channelled towards the extremes of the building by way of 'strings', which will be located in the vicinity of the V2 Lab, the extra floor, the new hall and the facade. These forces from the

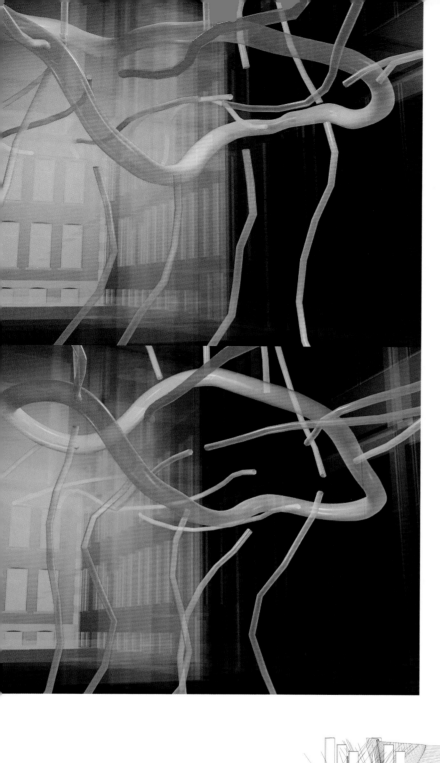
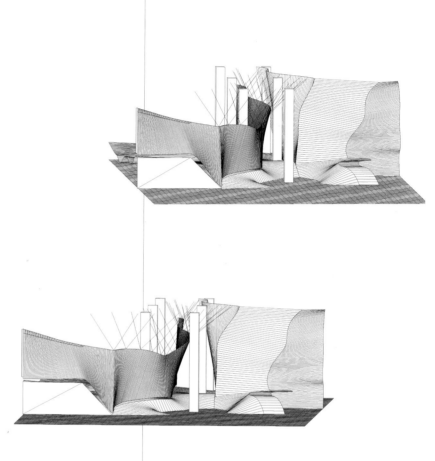
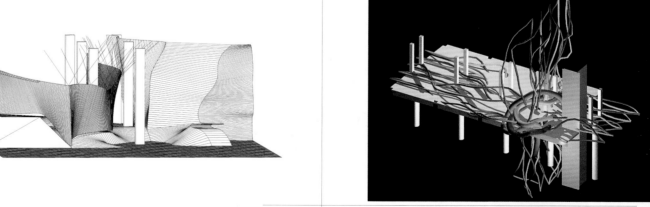
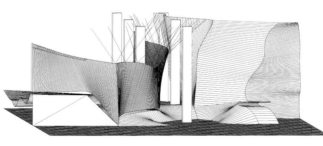
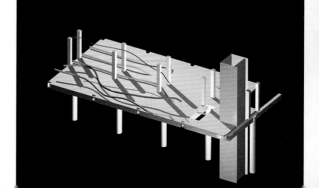
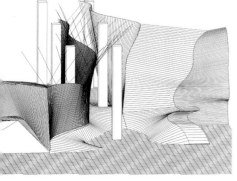

central projection space are transported to the extremes by waves, moving in four opposite directions through 20 strings. Continuously returning as waves, and interfering with new forces, eventually, in the topological continuity, active and reactive forces can no longer be distinguished and end up in a process where the inflections of the strings are no longer predictable. The resulting design ceases to be a form that can be overlaid on an organisational diagram, becoming a process in which topological coherence consists of the soft co-ordination of thousands of simultaneously operating diverse forces, making motion and time part of the organisation.

For the V2 Lab and the V2 Medialab – the international Lab for unstable media – this concept is an essential one. For here media are not perceived as belonging to a comfort-creating, servile instrumentalism familiar from engineers, interface designers and system operators, but as accelerators and destabilisers of reality. The virtual is not a so-called parallel world that exists safely on the other side of reality. It is something that continually charges up the present.

Instead of regarding the renovation as that which tranquillises the existing structure and refurnishes it to death, architecture here assumes the attitude of furniture and textile – as that which introduces movement into the existing situation, accelerating it, vectorising, seducing and flexing. In this way, we progress seamlessly from a computer-generated process of forces, vectors and springs, to inflections in plywood sheets and PVC pipes, to (literally) the vibrations in the tables, the undulations of the floor, to chairs with adjustable spring legs, to tensions in the 4-millimetre-thick plastic wall (stretched with steel cables and springs), to the flowing transition between floor and tables and then to the tensions within the human body: the arm and leg muscles that provide a constant neuro-electrical background to all human activity taking place here; a background that may fall outside the diagram, outside the concept of work; a background to all human media showing on the foreground, like piles of paper, coffee cups, old newspapers, the glow of computer screens, clothing, voices. In this sense, the design attempts to produce a shift from the optical domain where architecture is always judged, towards the haptic where everything is proximity.

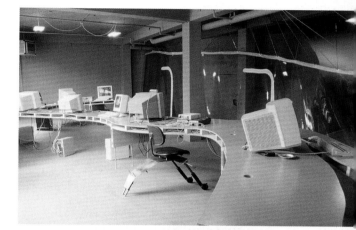

HARESH LALVANI
META ARCHITECTURE

Architect-morphologist Haresh Lalvani has developed a tech-nique to modulate sheet metal into a wide range of new configu-rations that can be easily manufactured using a patent fabrica-tion process he developed with Milgo-Bufkin. Here he discusses the development of his theory of Meta Architecture, his applica-tion of the term Hypersurface, and his work with Milgo-Bufkin which is currently launching his new design series.

Meta Architecture is based on manipulating morphologically structured information via algorithms and genetic codes that encipher the formal possibilities of architecture. These possibili-ties are determined by mapping them in a unified morphological universe,[1] a higher dimensional meta space, which (theoretically) encodes all past, present and future morphologies. It also maps all their transformations. The coding of structures within this universe leads to an artificial genetic code.[2] This is a universal morphological code[3] and acts as a driver for organising, shap-ing, building and transforming architecture over short-term and long-term time scales. Coupling the code with manufacturing processes, both at the macro level of current computer-aided manufacturing and the micro level of nanotechnologies and genetic engineering, enables the direct translation of the code into the physical process of building. Coupled with biological (DNA-based) or other (chemical, physical) building processes, the artificial genetic code enables growth, adaptation, evolution and replication of buildings, permitting architecture to design itself and eventually liberating it from the architect. Architecture as we now know it will end when self-architecture begins.[4]

Within this overall premise, several examples from my ongoing work in Meta Architecture, and the related visual product, Hyper Space Architecture (or Hyper Architecture), are presented. The work offers an alternative paradigm to 'digital architecture', which has emerged in the last decade. Increasingly sophisti-cated computer graphics tools have enabled architects to visual-ise relatively complex spatial environments in virtual space without recourse to physical models or, in some instances (as in Frank Gehry's museum at Bilbao), to digitise complex built models directly. These digital visualisations, all conceived in virtual space, are admittedly visually spectacular and are con-ceived 'top down', both visually and spatially. However, they are neither informed by construction methods or the properties of physical materials, nor by any morphological principles of space and structure, which impose strong constraints on architecture. Architecture, shaped by these constraints and modelled by morphological principles – including Meta Architecture – is architecture that proceeds from the 'bottom up'.

The works presented here exemplify the bottom-up approach in two different ways: one driven primarily by higher-dimensional geometry, and the other by combining geometry with manufac-turing process in making physical form out of real material. Both examples show the unprecedented possibilities for shaping architecture opened up by recourse to basic morphological principles (geometric, topologic, structural, etc). The images demonstrating the first approach are excerpted from my folio 'Hyperspace Architecture', which shows the various applications of higher dimensions for architecture,[5] and the second approach is from an ongoing experiment currently being carried out with Milgo/ Bufkin, a leading metal fabricator in New York.

Highly ordered geometry is used in the first approach (figs 1 and 2) as a basis for generating irregular hyperstructures; in this case, hypersurfaces. The term 'hypersurface' here is used according to its original meaning, defined in the strict geometri-cal (mathematical) sense: ie, having spatial dimensions greater than three. This definition contrasts with the usage in this and the previous special issue of *AD,* edited by Stephen Perrella, entitled 'Hypersurface Architecture', where the term 'hyper' is used as a meta-dimension of the surface and not its spatial dimension. Interestingly, in the first example shown here (figs 1a, b), the term has a double meaning. The two tiling designs are identical in their base geometry, which comprises an assembly of identical crescent-shaped tiles[6] based on two-dimensional projections from five-dimensional Euclidean space. The crescents are thus hyper-tiles. In addition, they have a superimposed pattern of dark lines, echoing the other meaning of 'hypersurface' (as used by Perrella). While the designs appear random, each tile is identically marked in both cases. The image captures the paradigm that irregular and random-looking designs can be constructed from identical modules, an idea of great significance for architecture as it visually blends order with chaos.

Another example (figs 2a–c) further exemplifies this juxtaposi-tion between order and disorder in a three-dimensional structure. The irregular surface, a true hypersurface projected from higher-dimensional space, hovers like a cloud over a space that, when extended, is non-periodic. The structure can be constructed from a single-node design,[7] a single-strut element and flat panels. Additional stabilising features would most likely be needed for its structural stability. This is just one example of the unlimited and varied architectural compositions that can be constructed from this new morphological invention.

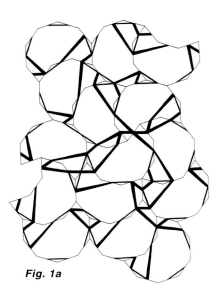

Fig. 1a

Fig. 1b

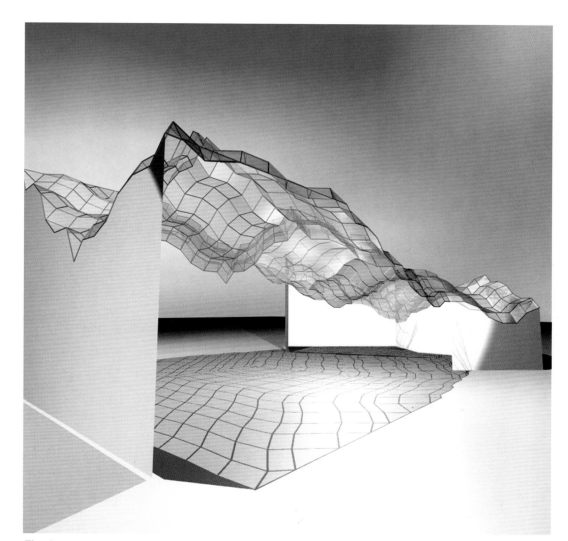

Fig. 2a

Fig. 2b

Fig. 2c

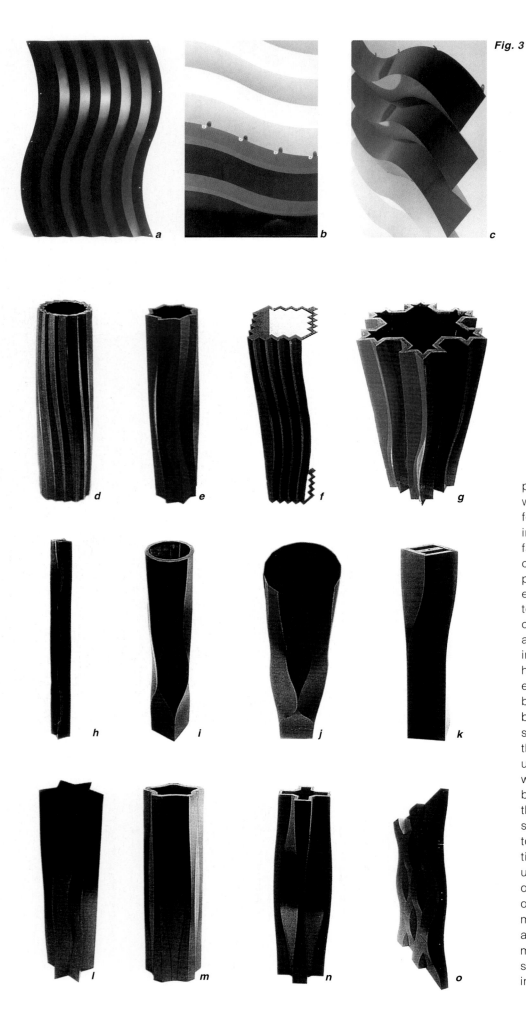

Fig. 3

The next group of images (figs 3a–o) exemplifies the second approach. The project deals with software-driven fabrication of sheet metal for architectural surface structures[8] and is being carried out at Milgo/Bufkin's manufacturing facility. Though columns, capitals, wall and ceiling panels are immediate architectural applications of concern for Milgo's business interests, the project provides a unique opportunity to experiment with broader Meta Architectural concepts, especially the relationship between an artificial 'genetic code' and the manufacturing process. All sheet-metal structures shown here were generated using a morphologically encoded algorithm, which provides the possibility to generate endless 'variations on a theme' by manipulating the code. As a result, no two structures need be alike, so each individual in the world, if desired, could have their own unique structure. A procedure was developed whereby single continuous metal sheets could be marked by computer-driven equipment and then folded (manually, for now). The resulting structures not only have a new look, but appear to be structurally advantageous at the same time. Architectural and industrial design products as well as complete environments based on these structures are currently being developed (figs 4-8). The algorithmic approach permits the structures to be modelled, transformed and fabricated with ease. We expect that the morphologic elegance in the shaping of these structures would also translate into an economy in building.

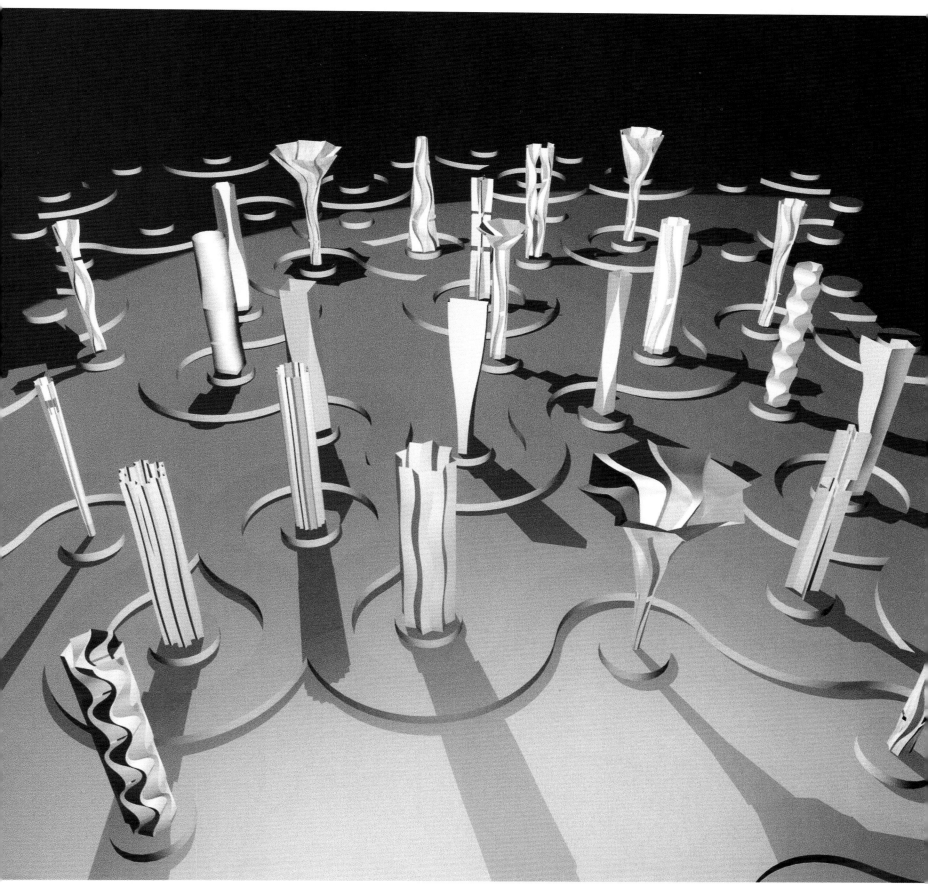

Fig. 4

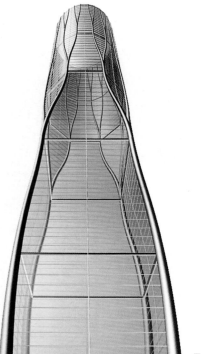

Fig. 5

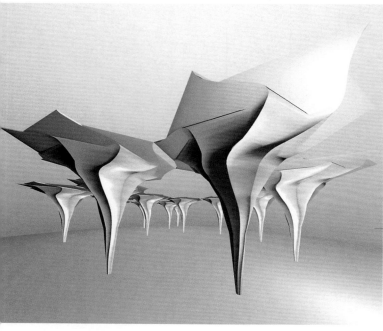

Fig. 6

Fig. 7

Column Museum (fig4) shows a sampling of the morphologically encoded columnar structures being prototyped and fabricated at Milgo. *Fractal High-Rise* (fig 5) shows a branched fractal column concept applied to a glass skyscraper. *Umbrellas* (fig 6) utilises the twisted fold for a freestanding structure in an open-air environment. *Transitions* (fig 7) shows flat, wavy and irregularly curved walls within the same spatial layout, using the same material and fabrication technology. *WaveKnot* (fig 8) employs a continuous rippled surface for a ceiling or roof, defined by a simple topological knot space.

The undulating look of these structures resulted from an interest in the fundamental behaviour of sheet material under forces. Material 'flows' under its own weight and other forces according to predetermined morphologic laws, which pertain more to fluid motion than to static objects. Constructing architectural elements from rigid rectilinear units (such as bricks and beams), has 'frozen' this inherent flowing nature of architectural envelopes. The wrinkles on our skin, the surfaces of plants and skins of animals, waves and cloud forms, display this fluid-like quality in nature. Curvilinear architectural forms constructed using standard building methods have usually raised concerns of economy.

However, our experiments at Milgo suggest that advanced software-driven manufacturing processes, coupled with powerful morphological underpinnings, can easily and possibly economically generate a wide repertory of new curvilinear vocabulary unavailable to architects in the past. Paradoxically, high technology, representing the opposite pole in the man–nature dichotomy, permits fluid shapes not possible earlier in a simple and elegant manner and, in doing so, brings us closer to forms in nature. This is true not only in visible forms, but also in the concept of the genetic code, which permits each one of us to be unique yet encoded by the same basic genetic alphabets (DNA bases). These sheet metal structures are morphologically coded in a similar way.

Notes

I am indebted to the following for their contribution to the project: computer modelling and rendering, Neil Katz and Mohamad Al-Khayer; photography, Robert Warren; product development, prototyping and fabrication, Milgo-Bufkin with Bruce Gitlin and Alex Kveton. More information on these projects with Milgo-Bufkin, Brooklyn, New York, can be found on their website <www.milgo-bufkin.com> from January 2000.

1   Haresh Lalvani, 'Morphological Universe, Expanding the Possibilities of Design and Nature', unpublished, 1998, based on a lecture presented at ACSA conference, Dalhousie University, Nova Scotia, October 1998, on the theme 'Works of Nature: The Rhetoric of Structural Invention'.

2   My interest in the genetic code of architecture dates back to 1975; my first published work on morphological coding was in the context of Islamic patterns (1982). In 1993, I proposed 'architectural genetics' as an emerging science.

3   I have been developing such a code for over two decades. Early interim results appeared in 'Multi-dimensional Periodic Arrangments of Transforming Space Structures', PhD Thesis, University of Pennsylvania (1981), self-published as *Structures on Hyper-Structures* (1982). Subsequent extensions of this work have been published in various papers, and applications to various structural morphologies have been in progress since the early 1990s.

4   For the origins of 'growing' architecture, see William Katavolos, *Organics*, Steendrukkirj de Jong & Co (Hilversum), 1961; Vittorio Giorgini, 'Early Experiments in Architecture using Nature's Building Technology', in H Lavani (ed), *The International Journal of Space Structures*, vol 11, nos 1, 2, special issue, 1997.

Fig. 8

My work in this concept came via genetic engineering and was proposed in 'Towards Automorphogenesis, Building with Bacteria', unpublished, 1974, the source of which goes back to the question asked by my thesis of 1967: 'Why don't we build with bone and spider silk?' In recent years, John Johansen has been proposing growing architecture using 'molecular engineering'.

5 Lalvani, 'The Architectural Promise of Curved Hyperspaces', 2nd International Seminar: 'Application of Structural Morphology to Architecture', University of Stuttgart, 1994; 'Hyperstructures', in P Dombernowsky and T Wester (eds), *Engineering a New Architecture, Conference Proceedings*, Aarhus School of Architecture (Denmark), 1999.
6 Lalvani, US Patent 4,620,998, 1986.
7 Lalvani, US Patent 5,505,035, 1996.
8 Patent pending. ·

MICHAEL SPEAKS

IT'S OUT THERE . . .

The Formal Limits of The American Avant-Garde

In an essay published last year, I proposed that a new image of architecture has begun to develop in The Netherlands.[1] This image, I suggested, is one whose Dutchness is fixed neither by national or professional identity, nor by ideology, but instead identifies a disposition towards the artificial urban milieu that today is The Netherlands but which is fast becoming the rest of the world. I went on to suggest that this new urban disposition defines what is fresh and exciting about an emergent generation of Dutch architects, and moreover, that it is what distinguishes them from their North American and European counterparts.

Two features of this urban disposition were identified. The first is a de-emphasis on form development and a renewed focus on the analysis and manipulation of material and immaterial processes such as those recognised by the Rotterdam Maaskant Prize jury in 1996: 'Rotterdam harbour is a particularly instructive and inspiring example of a "modern" environment, of a space whose organization is not so much dictated by traditional planning and urban design concepts as by the rapid and creative management and steering of trends, movements and forces in the field of transport and communication.'[2]

The second feature of this new disposition is a post-avant-garde attitude, which I named 'just there' modernism, after Joost Meuwissen of One Architecture, in Amsterdam. In the same essay, I focused especially on the implications of 'just there': on the banal, everyday reality at hand, and the way that reality is intensified and made to become something else, something unexpected, something new. 'Just there,' I suggested, focuses on the limitations and constraints that architecture necessarily transforms into conditions of possibility. 'Just there' is thus always connected to what cannot be 'just there': to what shapes what is 'just there', and more importantly, what also offers the potential that any architecture must exploit in order to transform what is 'just there' into something else . . . even if only by a thread, 'just there' is always connected to what is 'out there'. This was not only implicit in my previous essay, but it is what I meant to suggest by focusing on the 'urban disposition' of these fresh young Dutch architectural offices; for, in the words of a famous contemporary Dutch architect, it is this that allows them to irrigate their architectural intentions.

In what follows, I wish instead to focus on the contemporary American equivalent of these Dutch architects. However, as will become clear there is no such equivalent, for while the Dutch have moved beyond the constraints of the avant-garde, the Americans remain fascinated with its possibilities. Rather than focusing on the connection between what is 'just there' to what is 'out there', however, I wish to suggest that in the most advanced registers of contemporary American architecture there exists a kind of structural condition that makes impossible any connection between the latter. And that is because what is always 'just there' is form. Going from 'just there' to what is 'out there' one is

always stopped at the border, thinking it is possible to see beyond it, but what is seen is always defined by this border, by form itself.

Despite our collective boredom with ideology, politics, philosophical truth, and other such accounts of those larger realities which exceed the banality of everyday life, we Americans are nonetheless still interested in what is 'out there', as the popularity of the television series *The X Files* attests. Each episode begins with the teaser, 'the truth is out there'. The implication is that to find it we only have to follow the thread that leads from here to there. With its stylised banality, *The X Files* has set the 'just there' standard for a new inquiry into the vast array of forces that shape the everyday, and it has done so precisely by connecting the leaden normality of town life and petty criminality to paranormal events that make old fashioned conspiracy theory seem small indeed. More importantly, the programme's framing of what is 'out there' is consistent with a number of recent attempts to make the dark, unfathomable chaos lurking just outside our door comprehensible.

The explosion of postmodernist theories in the 80s and complexity theory in the 90s come to mind of course, as well as the now ubiquitous globalisation discourse. However, one of the most interesting, recent expressions of this desire to make comprehensible what is 'out there', is the increasing use of ecological models to explain the relationship between complex, dynamical systems and their environments. Take, for example, Noel Boaz's recently published *Eco Homo*, in which he argues for a climatological account of the emergence of the human species; or economist Alain Lipietz's use of political ecology to put forth a new post-left political agenda. Or the plethora of new management and scenario planning books such as Arie de Geus' *The Living Company* and James F Moore's 'national bestseller', *The Death of Competition*, on whose dust jacket internet guru Esther Dyson writes: 'Moore catches the fundamental shift in business thinking – and behavior – today: the economy is not a mechanism, businesses are not machines. They are co-evolving, unpredictable organisms within a constantly shifting business ecosystem that no one controls.' As the blurb suggests, what is especially appealing about ecological models is not only that they seem to offer a flexible means by which to deal with turbulent environments, but they also offer a way to think of seemingly lifeless, static forms such as corporations, economic communities, or political ideologies, as dynamic, living, changeable life-forms which interact with and alter their environments.

Although our objective is to discuss that life-form otherwise known as architecture, how we do that will depend on whether by architecture we mean a dynamic life-form open to external influences, or a lifeless object on and in which those influences are registered as avant-gardist gestures. It will also depend on what importance we attach to 'the new', whether it is the source of difference and new life or the source of sameness and decrepitude. Reporting on what appeared in 1995 to be renewed architectural interest in the ecological, *Assemblage* profiled two designs entered in the Cardiff Bay Opera House Competition, including Greg Lynn's formally inventive entry,[3] based in part on Gregory Bateson's book, *Steps to an Ecology of Mind*. In its editorial comments, *Assemblage* insists that what is not different or new about this project is its formal strangeness; that is, the fact that it looks so new. What is new, they suggest rather enigmatically, are the projects' 'ecological aspects', realised through '"process studio techniques" tempered by non-automatic generative rules and critiques of the competition brief'. They imply that this is connected to Lynn's interest in the problem of the supple, the fluid, and the body; all, in their view, pre-eminently ecological concerns.

Commenting on some of Lynn's source materials, they in fact remark that Bateson's book, on which Lynn draws, 'is not so much about the science of teratology and the rules for the mutation of form as a search for "an ecology of ideas" that can help us understand "man's relation to his environment"', adding, parenthetically, 'an architectural problem if there ever was one'. So it comes as something of a surprise when they conclude that 'the most amazing, and ultimately most persuasive, thing about these projects is that *nothing has ever looked like this before*'. They qualify this by observing that 'nothing looks different unless it is different and, further, it is virtually impossible to set out intentionally to find a "new look"'.

Perhaps this is so. Perhaps 'this look' and the design techniques used to generate it are part of something different, something new, but *Assemblage* is unable to define what that is. On the contrary, their focus on 'the look' and thus on the formal aspects of the relationship between ecology (understood here as one name for a renewed interest in the relationship between complex systems and their environments) and architecture, while not wrong exactly, does obscure what one might have thought were the real 'ecological aspects' or implications of Lynn's Cardiff Bay Opera House. Namely, that if taken seriously, an ecological disposition would require us to think in a new way not only about the 'ecological', biomorphic look of Lynn's project, but also, and more significantly, about the relationship between his practice of architecture (which includes 'the look' and the techniques used to generate it) and those larger forces external to architecture; as do, for example Reyner Banham's *Los Angeles: Architecture of Four Ecologies*, in which he describes, among other things, the conditions necessary for the emergence of new architectural life, or Rem Koolhaas' proto-ecologistic (in this larger sense) assertion of 'Bigness', that limit beyond which architecture becomes urbanism.

The need to rethink not only architectural forms but the forms of architectural practice becomes even more appropriate when we consider Lynn's accompanying text, 'The Renewed Novelty of Symmetry'. Here, Lynn follows Bateson's model of symmetry breaking as a way to introduce novelty into a system, novelty being the ultimate guarantor of continued existence for evolving life-forms. As Lynn points out, one of the fascinating insights offered by Bateson is that the introduction of novelty leads not to disorganisation but to greater, more complex organisation within the system. Surprisingly, lack of external information leads to a less ordered, less coherent system, which means a less adaptable and thus more susceptible system. When external information is introduced into a system it triggers sets of regulators that prevent default symmetrical arrangements with less organisation; this results in more complex, internally coherent organisation. The point is that diversity and external influence result in more internally coherent and fluid organisational structure. As Lynn writes in his concluding paragraph:

> Symmetry breaking is not a loss but an increase in organization within an open, flexible, and adaptive system. Symmetry breaking from the exact to the anexact is the primary characteristic of supple systems. These flexible economies index the incorporation of generalized external information through the specific unfolding of polymorphic, dynamic, flexible, and adaptive systems. Symmetry is not a sign of underlying order but an indication of a lack of order due to an absence of interaction with larger external forces and environments. Given this complex conceptualization of endogenous and exogenous forces, deep structure and typology are just what they seem to be: suspect, reductive, empty, and bankrupt. An alternative is an internal system of directed indeterminate growth that is differentiated by general and unpredictable external influences, producing emergent, unforeseen, unpredictable dynamic, and novel organizations.[4]

It would seem to require an extraordinary effort to stop at 'the look' when the very nature of these models requires that we move beyond this and think about architecture's relationship to its exterior, namely to the globalised urban world in which it must, as a practice, struggle to survive. Lynn's description of supple systems seems an excellent description of architecture if by that we mean not simply a supple form but a supple form of practice. Indeed, it seems an apt description of a practice such as Lynn's own, which takes in external information, such as the very Batesonian model under discussion, triggering a set of internal regulators which prevent the system from defaulting into a less organised, less adaptable system, inducing instead the emergence of a more complex, adaptable system.

But therein lies the problem: if, as *Assemblage* seems to suggest, it is only 'the look' that is new, then the only means by which Lynn is able to address the complexity of contemporary urban life is through form. All of the quite remarkable things Lynn attributes to supple systems are thus registered only on the forms themselves. The introduction of external information – Bateson – leads in that case not to a more complex organisation, a new practice of architecture able to adapt to this complex world, but only to a defaulted, less organised, system, or practice of architecture as form-producer.

Now it would be unfair to criticise Lynn for not applying this kind of metacritical position to his own work; that is, for not pushing the implications of his supple systems analyses past the form, and the design techniques which create them, to include an analysis of his practice of architecture itself. The same cannot be said for *Assemblage*, however, a magazine that stakes its reputation on its hypercriticality and sensitivity to external conditions. And yet it cannot really be faulted either, for there is a kind of structural condition that prevents *Assemblage* and Greg Lynn from exploiting the real 'ecological aspects' of his project. Despite being pulled out into the exterior of architecture by his stated interest in urbanism, and by theoretical models such as those of Bateson, Lynn is more powerfully drawn back into contemporary American architecture's most powerful interiority: form. And strange as it may seem, he is lured there (like *Assemblage*) by his search for the new.

The question of the new has been raised frequently in the last few of years, especially in the United States, where it always seems to be on the agenda. But more often than not, this interest in the new is a complicated and often contradictory affair. The 1988 MoMA Deconstructivist Exhibition, for example, gave the world of architecture a new, 'avant-garde' style, while its theoretical underpinnings mitigated precisely against style, and against the new. As Mark Wigley, associate curator of the exhibition, wrote in the *Deconstructivist Architecture* catalogue:

> Even though it threatens this most fundamental property of
> architectural objects, deconstructivist architecture does not
> constitute an avant-garde. It is not a rhetoric of the new,
> Rather, it exposes the unfamiliar hidden within the tradi-
> tional. It is the shock of the old.[5]

With the arrival of such news, many of those interested in little more than 'the new' moved on to other theoretical conceits, such as 'the fold', and on to other French theorists. Indeed, in the period between 1988 and 1994, there was growing and palpable disappointment with deconstruction, some of which was directed towards Derrida himself when, at the 1992 Anywhere conference in Yufuin, Japan, he refused to outline a project for the new, preferring instead to discuss deconstruction in terms of a formal structure he called 'faxitecture'. What this meant in practical terms was that Derrida did not offer the architects a clear way to convert deconstruction (as the theoretical protocol) into architectural form. Derrida's failure to offer a project of the new in fact became a kind of sour refrain mouthed especially by Jeffrey Kipnis during much of the conference.

Although it is impossible to know for sure, one can only imagine that Derrida's refusal (as well as the ascendance of Mark Wigley's more considered reading of Derrida as a Heideggerian) was one of the reasons for Kipnis' shift from deconstruction and its stated refusal of the new. Kipnis, you will remember, is a self-proclaimed Nietzschean. But, since this was the period in which Kipnis was becoming a designer and not merely a theorist (a larva to butterfly transformation that is virtually irresistible to architectural theorists), there are design implications as well. Writing in his now famous essay, 'Towards a New Architecture', collected in the *AD Folding in Architecture* publication, Kipnis decried what he called a general cultural disinclination towards the new: 'Briefly, it [this retreat from the new] manifests itself as a rationale which holds that the catalogue of possible forms (in every sense of the word form: institutional, social, political and aesthetic) is virtually complete and well-known.'[6] In an attempt to redress this situation, Kipnis offered a new set of design principles, all of which might be said to operate under the rubric of what he called intensive coherence, 'a coherence forged out of incongruity'. 'Intensive coherence,' he writes, 'implies that the properties of certain monolithic arrangements enable the architecture to enter into multiple and even contradictory relationships.'

Like Kipnis, Greg Lynn proposes to address the fluid and complex conditions of late 20th-century urban life by calling for architectural forms that are themselves more fluid and complex. Writing in the same issue of *AD*, Lynn criticises deconstruction's inability to produce new design techniques that might result in an architecture which is both internally coherent yet open to its exterior conditions. Instead, he suggests that deconstruction only gives us architectures which are incoherent and which have a conflicted, contradictory relationship with their contexts or exteriors. Deconstruction allows only static collaging of existent or rosterable architectural forms with existent contexts. Lynn wants an architecture, which, like those influenced by deconstruction, is heterogeneous, but he wants one that is also malleable, fluid and supple. Lynn thus looks outside architecture to the culinary arts, to Gilles Deleuze, René Thom, and other sources in order to develop new, folded, pliant design techniques which might result in architectural forms that are themselves pliant and fluid with respect to their external conditions.

Lynn has since developed more fluid and more temporally-based design techniques, including his impressive animation modellings enabled by Alias software, all of which, to cite his forthcoming book, seek to produce lifelike 'animate form'.[7] In essays such as 'Form and Field', first given as a lecture at the Anywise conference in Seoul, Korea, in 1995, Lynn argues that given the material and immaterial structural changes occurring today, architecture must become more animate – it must move! 'The classical models of pure, static, essentialized and timeless form and structure,' he says, 'are no longer adequate to describe the contemporary city and the activities it supports.' Lynn thus calls for motion-based design techniques, a new attention to 'shaping forces', and an anorganic vitalism, all of which are meant to engender a new relationship between a stable (as opposed to static) architecture as a producer of discrete form in productive tension with urbanism understood as a practice of shaping gradients within fields. Lynn argues that using animation videos to conceive the urban context as animate, as in-motion, allows us to understand the relationship between architecture and urbanism in a new way:

> Throughout history, movement in architecture has involved
> the arrest of dynamic forces as static forms through mapping.
> Thus urban fields and movements have been understood as
> the fixed lineaments upon which forms could be mapped.
> To work as an architect with urban forces in their nonformalized
> state it is necessary to design in an environment that is
> dynamic. Architects need to develop techniques like [D'Arcy]
> Thompson's model that relate gradient fields of influence
> with flexible yet discrete forms of organization. This means
> moving from an architecture based on the equilibrium of
> Cartesian static space to one designed within dynamic
> gradient space. Architecture will not literally move, but it
> must be conceptualized and modeled within an urban field
> understood as dynamic and characterized by forces rather
> than forms.[8]

Yes, absolutely, but one would want to ask why does architecture itself not move? Why is architecture itself not animate?

When asked this question by Jeffrey Kipnis at the 1995 Anywise conference, Lynn responded as follows:

Kipnis: Let me hold you accountable to the question, Greg. Because you stay at the level of dynamic animation, we could be fascinated by what we see, but because you do not resolve it as a fixed static object with materials, structure, and construction, at which point we see its real consequences, we're left fetishising the video rather than really understanding its design consequences. Is this true or not?

Lynn: I want to resist answering that question. In other situations in which I have shown material like this, the response has been, 'Well, are you saying architecture has to move in order for this to be an interesting design approach?' I would say no.

Kipnis: You say no, but you do not show us what happens when you take the motion away.[9]

If the urban context or field is a dynamic play of forces, as Lynn suggests, does this mean that architecture is no more than a static form that arrests those forces? Lynn states the opposite: that architecture should no longer be understood as static forms, but as stable forms which dynamically give order to an urban field. This is precisely what we see in his animations: architecture as a dynamic force shaping other dynamic forces. But when it becomes form, the audience asks, when it becomes architecture, does it remain dynamic? Lynn cannot answer: the implication is that when it is being designed it is animate, but not architecture; when it becomes architecture, however, when it becomes a form, it becomes static. Is this because for Lynn, as for Kipnis and *Assemblage*, architecture is only the object-form at the end of the process? If architecture is stable and not static, as Lynn insists it must be, and if it is temporally inflected, implying movement, why does his architecture not move? Why does it not flow like the urban context with which it presumably interacts? Why does the movement stop when it becomes form? Why does his architecture stop moving when it is no longer design technique and becomes architecture? The answer lies with Peter Eisenman.

Lynn's critique of static form in the above cited essay, and typology and deep structure in his Cardiff essay, is an implicit critique of Peter Eisenman, the unofficial dean of the American avant-garde, and Lynn's former employer and mentor. Lynn wants new forms which respond to the new, dynamic, fluid conditions of late 20th-century urban life; animate forms in particular. However, as we have seen, he is only able to offer animate techniques which produce, in the end, forms that seem no more animate than those he sets out to surpass. Eisenman, unlike Lynn, is not interested in new forms which might deal better with the new conditions of the late 20th century, but in dislocative forms which call into question what he calls the metaphysic of architecture. It is this activity which defines architecture for Eisenman. The essence of the act of architecture, he says, 'is the dislocation of an ever re-constituting metaphysic of architecture'. In his essay 'Misreading' he writes:

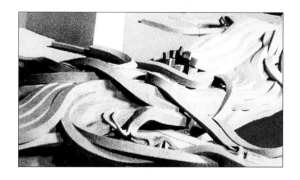

The history of architecture can be seen as the continual rereading, and misreading, of the metaphysic of architecture

Topological architecture – FROM ABOVE: Philip Johnson, Gate House, New Canaan, Connecticut, 1995 – exterior and interior; Peter Eisenman, Staten Island Ferry Terminal, winning proposal, 1997; Greg Lynn, Stranded Sears Tower, model, 1992; Rem Koolhaas, Kunsthal Gallery, Rotterdam, The Netherlands

through successive dislocations, and the subsequent institutionalization of each dislocation, which thereby reconstitutes the metaphysic.[10]

Eisenman's architectural project is consistent with Derrida's philosophical project; both are simultaneously transgressive and conservative in their respective discourses; and both dialogic with those discourses in the very terms given them by the discourse. For Derrida this is the language of Heideggerian metaphysics, and for Eisenman, this is form. I say this only to note the connection between Eisenman's dislocation and Derrida's deconstruction, both of which differ fundamentally from the work of Gilles Deleuze, whom Lynn often cites.

For Eisenman, the new is not even desirable in itself, and that is because it often conceals beneath its newness this metaphysic of architecture. Eisenman's critique of modern architecture takes precisely this form: while it seemed new and different from the *beaux arts*, modern architecture's functionalism is consistent with humanist or anthropocentric architecture dating from the Renaissance. Modern architecture, despite its new, technologically derived forms, still operated within the metaphysics of humanism, and so while new, modernism was not dislocative.

This metaphysic of architecture is arranged around what Eisenman today calls an interiority, or by any other name an epistemology or ideology. Much of his own work, from the early essays and houses, to his most recent projects, has attempted to destabilise the interiority of functionalist humanism that dominated modernism, and that, in his opinion, persists today in even the most sophisticated architectures. Eisenman argues that architecture should never, as modernism did, place itself in the service of any exterior discourse, such as politics, or philosophy, but should instead articulate itself as an autonomous practice of form following form. Even when architecture turns to its exterior, as Eisenman did with Chomskian linguistics, psychoanalysis, deconstruction, folding, etc, it must always do so with the aim of dislocating and relocating the interiority of architecture itself, and that interiority for Eisenman is always form.

Eisenman thus always carries out his project of dislocating the metaphysic of architecture on the object itself, or rather one should say that the mark of this dislocative project is always registered as form. For Eisenman, great architecture – characterised by what he calls 'presentness' – dislocates by its form a previous form or type, forever transforming that type. He often cites his own Columbus Convention Center in Columbus, Ohio, as architecture which, while it might be new and interesting, is not dislocative. His Wexner Center, also in Columbus, Ohio, on the other hand, is a form which he argues calls into question the museum type itself, and as such is architecture that is dislocative and not simply new. Ultimately, Eisenman insists that architecture will continue to evolve only by turning inward: by focusing on its interiority; that being for him, in the last instance, form.

Lynn and Eisenman are literally pulling form in opposite directions. Lynn wants new forms which answer to new, exterior conditions, but he neglects the critical question raised by Eisenman about the interiority of architecture; about, in other words, what architecture is and does. Eisenman calls into question architecture's humanist interiority – architecture, that is, as a practice of housing and making safe. But he does this only in order to establish a new interiority, that of form generation. Eisenman wants to replace the humanist, modernist, form-follows-function interiority with a form-follows-form interiority. Lynn, on the other hand, wants to move architecture away from this interiority to its exteriority, from static form – typologies, deep structures, etc – to stable form which interacts with the dynamics of its urban context. But he can do so only from within Eisenman's interiority of form; that is, he can only move to architecture's exterior, to something other than form, by way of form itself.

Thus, rather than questioning Eisenman's interiority of architecture, rather than questioning the status of architecture as a generator of form (as he does, for example with urbanism which he insists is an animate field of forces), Lynn accepts this interiority and takes form generation as far as it will go. He tries to make form animate, he tries to take form out to meet its urban exteriority, but in the end, he is only able to devise more and more animate techniques to design what are ultimately static forms. But if Lynn were to raise the question that Eisenman does, if he were to question architecture's interiority, he would then be able to move beyond Eisenman's interiority of form to a new consideration of architecture as a new kind of urbanism in-transit; something I have argued is at the centre of the work of a number of young Dutch architectural offices.

The real question not only for Lynn, but for this form-driven American avant-garde, is whether they will be able to discover a dislocative architecture that, rather than dislocating form or type, dislocates the form of architectural practice itself; that, in other words, calls into question the interiority of architecture as a practice of form production, opening it to the kind of expansion that has occurred in the Dutch context where the freshest practices focus on animate forms of practice, not on animate forms. Such a dislocation would necessarily take leave of the discourse of architectural interiority altogether and focus on architecture as a practice of fixity that manipulates or exploits movement in order to induce the production of new urban life. Architecture would then be able to become both a stabilising *and* an animating force in the metropolis without feeling compelled to make its forms move.

As Rem Koolhaas has observed in his distinction between Mies and Rietveld, there are practices which fix in order to open up avenues of freedom, and those that seem to offer an infinity of choice but which give no choice or freedom. Forms that 'look like' they are fluid with their urban contexts may in fact interdict, and forms which 'look like' they are interdictive may in fact be fluid with their urban contexts. If this were to be recognised, the question would no longer be 'what is the essence of architecture?', (form, light, image, etc) but 'what can architecture do' when it looks to its exterior, to the globalised metropolis?

This is a question that Eisenman, Lynn, Kipnis, *Assemblage*, and indeed the entire American avant-garde seem never to ask, and that is because they are always stopped at the border, stopped by form. Only such a dislocation can guarantee architecture continuous life in a world in which it seems to have lost its object, its mission and its way. Indeed, this is precisely what is at stake in Koolhaas' 'Bigness', in which the art of architecture must give way to a reduced, and interconnected set of practices that 'depend', as he says: on technologies, engineers, contractors, manufactures and currency markets. This is also what is at stake in the new practice of urbanism implied in 'What Ever Happened to Urbanism?', an approach and not a professional practice which takes up the problem of shaping the conditions under which new urban life can emerge and proliferate. Of course this is also what is at stake in Sanford Kwinter's 'new pastoralism', and Bernard Cache's insistence that architecture is the art of the frame, that it is the framing of the conditions under which life emerges.

Ultimately, architecture will have to develop a dynamism that matches that of the globalised metropolis. In order to do so, it must become, among other things, an animate form of form shaping, a practice of creating forms which themselves may not be animate, but which induce or create the conditions under which new urban life will emerge. The real implications of architectural ecologism, of which the work of Greg Lynn is just one example, will only be understood when we begin to think more clearly about how the practice of architecture can adapt to the turbulent conditions of late 20th-century life, how it can become something different, and yet remain the same, remain architecture. Perhaps *the practice of architecture* should become everything Lynn says about form and about technique: a pliant system, a blob, a semi-fluid/semi-solid practice, or even a body, as defined by Lynn in a recent text in which he again turns to the exteriority of architecture:

> For Margulis, a body is not an ordered whole but a provisional colony of previously discrete free-living entities that fuse together to live as a collective of organs able to reproduce and sustain themselves as a complex. These complexes can then become the organs of higher-order complexes through further linkages, exchanges, parasitisms, and codependencies. Instead of analyzing a body to find its essential structure, the insight resides in the functional and machinic behaviors of all the organs, in their ability to behave as an ensemble with the coherence and stability of a singular organism. The new concept of the organism resembles the definition of an ecosystem, which has no single identity but exhibits self-regulation and persistence nonetheless.[11]

Lynn cites this account of the body as a way to illustrate the new model of the body implied in his wonderful 'blob' architectural forms. But what if this model took him and us past those architectural forms, past the border of Eisenman's formalist interiority? If we were to understand architecture itself as a provisional colony of discrete practices, then urbanism might also be redefined as a dynamic body, corpus, or corporation made up of smaller bodies, or 'living companies', as Arie de Geus, past head of Scenario Planning at Royal Dutch Shell, says in his book of the same title.[12]

In *The Living Company*, an important new study of corporate life, De Geus develops the thesis that only those companies which learn can make themselves adaptable enough to survive in the turbulent commercial reality that exists today. Unlike 'economic companies', which close themselves off to this environment, preferring the guidance of shareholder profits and short-term gain, 'living companies' are open to their exteriors and are motivated not only by profit but by a desire to survive, to live on as companies. The 'living company' is thus defined not by its product, owners, profits, or even corporate ideology, but by its sensitivity to an ever-changing, fluid, commercial environment.

The Living Company, like the account of the body offered above by Greg Lynn and surprisingly like the body put forward in Gilles Deleuze's wonderful book *Spinoza: A Practical Philosophy*, is favourably disposed towards its chaotic exterior from which it gathers new information, or as De Geus says, from which it learns. As in Lynn's account of supple systems, this triggers sets of internal regulators which increase the order of the system, and make survival more likely. In De Geus' account, corporate learning occurs by way of scenario planning. Scenario planning attempts to project scenarios of possible futures that the company might find itself living; it does this in order to access and make visible virtual paths of company movement which are constructed from analysing the turbulent environment itself. Scenario planning is not predicative, however, not employed to reduce disorder, thus making the right path or plan obvious. Instead, scenario planning allows a company to increase order through learning, and as a result to enhance its own flexibility and adaptability to conditions over which it has no control.

To return more explicitly to Lynn's Cardiff text, 'The Renewed Novelty of Symmetry', the living company breaks symmetry and increases order as a way of enhancing its own survival, while the economic company, in a desperate attempt to find the right or correct plan, refuses to acknowledge its exterior. Now I do not want to push this analogy too far, but De Geus' book, *The Living Company*, might have something to offer architecture, something other than a new set of design techniques. In short, it might offer architecture 'a pass' across the border of form, and thus a ticket to a new life in the new metropolis. Nowhere is the need for such a pass more evident than in architecture's recent turn to ecologism and vitalism. Indeed, one can only hope that architecture will follow the path of the living company, corporation, body or practice. If, on the other hand, this new vitalism or ecologism, of which Greg Lynn's 'animate forms' are but one example, continues to follow the plan of the economic company, closed to what is 'out there', then it will profit only those CEOs and corporate board members for whom short-term profits made in-form-creation are the primary objective. If this occurs, it will only be a matter of time until Lynn and other members of the American avant-garde assume their places at the board room meeting tables of such companies. Perhaps they have already been seated.

This essay was first presented as a lecture at the Berlage Institute in Amsterdam, The Netherlands, on 28 October, 1997.

Notes

1 See Michael Speaks, 'Just There Modernism', in *Nine + One: Ten Young Dutch Architectural Offices*, NAi Publishers (Rotterdam), 1997, pp18-25.
2 Cited in the abridged version of the Jury Report, *Archis* 12, 1996, pp 8-9.
3 See 'Computer Animisms (Two Designs for the Cardiff Bay Opera House)', *Assemblage* 26, 1995, pp8-37.
4 Greg Lynn, 'The Renewed Novelty of Symmetry', *Assemblage* 26, p14.
5 *Deconstructivist Architecture*, Philip Johnson and Mark Wigley (eds), Museum of Modern Art (New York), 1988, p18.
6 See Jeffrey Kipnis, 'Towards a New Architecture', *Folding in Architecture*:
Architectural Design Profile 102, Academy Editions (London), 1993, p42.
7 See Greg Lynn, *Animate Form* , forthcoming from Princeton Architectural Press.
8 *Anywise*, Cynthia Davidson (ed), MIT Press (Cambridge, Mass), 1996, p 97.
9 Ibid, p112.
10 Peter Eisenman, 'Misreading', *Houses of Cards*, 1987
11 Greg Lynn, 'From Body to Blob', in *Anybody*, Cynthia Davidson (ed), MIT Press (Cambridge, Mass), 1997), p171.
12 Arie de Geus, *The Living Company: Habits for Survival in a Turbulent Business World*, Harvard Business School Press (Boston),1997.

BRIAN MASSUMI

STRANGE HORIZON
Buildings, Biograms and The Body Topologic

Computer-assisted topological design technique in architecture is no longer a novelty. With the required software and hardware becoming more accessible, paperless studios and offices are less the exceptions they once were. With growing familiarity have come inklings of discontent. There is a common drift to many of the reactions voiced at lectures, conferences, and in the classroom. It seems to be widely held opinion that the abstractness of digital space of topology contradicts the spatial reality of bodies and buildings. 'Since we do not live in non-Euclidean space', the objection goes, 'why are you foisting mutant geometries on us that fail to correspond to anything real? Topological architecture is just too abstract. It can't connect to the body as we experience it. Besides, you can animate architectural design practice as much as you like, but you still end up with a building that isn't going anywhere. It's all a sham. Design techniques based on continuity and movement rather than static form betray themselves in the fixity of their final product. If you're so stuck on continuity, where's the continuity between your process and its product? It's all very pretty, but why should we, your public – livers-in and passers-by of your buildings – why should we care?'

But what if *the space of the body is really abstract?* What if the body is inseparable from dimensions of lived abstractness that cannot be conceptualised in terms other than the topological? The objections that topological architecture is too abstract and does not connect at all with the body would dissipate. Conversely, the question of how precisely the process continues in the product would become all the more pressing. Topological architecture would need to do more than it has up to now to develop a response. After all, its very effectiveness as a design method is in the balance. The answer may well disappoint partisan of concreteness incarnate. It may turn out that computer-assisted topological design technique has inadequately addressed the question of its end-effectiveness because *it is not yet abstract enough* to be a fitting match for the abstract resources of 'concrete' experience.

The Argument from Orientation

It is with some chagrin that I confess to having sat contentedly in my temporary office at the Canadian Centre for Architecture, for no less than two months, looking at the wrong street out of the window. I was looking east onto rue St-Marc, when in fact I was looking north onto rue Baille. I am sad to report that there is no resemblance between the two scenes. Something seriously disorienting was happening in the time it took me to get from the side entry of the building to the door of my office. But that's only the half of it. The seriously disorienting thing that was happening as I snaked my way through the corridors overpowered the evidence of my eyes. It was completely overriding the clear-as-day visual cues available to me from the window of my office. The sudden realisation that my north was everyone else's east was jarring. True, I hadn't paid much attention to the scene. But it wasn't only this. When it hit me, I had the strangest sensation of my misplaced image of the buildings morphing, not entirely smoothly, into the corrected scene. My disorientation wasn't a simple lack of attention. I had been positively (if a bit vaguely and absent-mindedly) seeing a scene that wasn't there. It took a moment's effort to replace what positively hadn't been there with what plainly was. When you actively see something that isn't there, there's only one thing you can call it: a hallucination. It was a worry.

Thinking about it, I realised that I could make my way to and from my office to the exit without error, but if I'd been asked to sketch scenes from the corridors or to map the route, I couldn't have done it with any accuracy. I had precious little memory of the way, yet I navigated it flawlessly. Correction: I had precious little *visual* memory of the way. I must have been navigating on autopilot, using some form of basically nonvisual memory. If I put myself mentally through the paces of exiting, instead of seeing passing scenes, I felt twists and turns coming one after the other with variable speed. I was going on a bodily memory of my movements: one of contorsion and rhythm rather than visible form. There is in fact a sixth sense directly attuned to the movement of the body: proprioception. It involves specialised sensors in the muscles and joints. Proprioception is a self-referential sense in that what it most directly registers are displacements of the parts of the body relative to each other. Vision is an exo-referential sense, registering distances from the eye.

It appears I had been operating on two separate systems of reference: a predominantly proprioceptive system of self-reference for the tunnel-like bowels of the building, and a predominantly visual system of reference for the vistas outside. The two systems were not calibrated to each other. Or they hadn't been, until my moment of hallucinatory truth before the window. Their respective spaces of orientation had been noncommunicating, like qualitatively different monads of experience. The idea that this is not as unusual a situation as my initial concern had suggested came to me in the subway on the way home. If you've ever ridden a subway, it's likely that you've had a similarly jarring experience when surfacing at street level.[1]

That must be it. The paucity of visual cues in tunnel-like places such as corridors and subways requires a back-up system to take over from the usual way of orienting: using visible forms grouped into fixed configurations to make what psychologists call 'cognitive maps'. I had a happy ride, until I thought about how I'd got where I was. My memory of getting from the exit of the building to the subway stop just moments before was virtually blank. Not quite (not again!): twists and turns in rhythm. Yes, again, I had been on autopilot. I had gotten to the train by habit and it was evidently my proprioceptive system of reference that seemed to be the habitual one, window or tunnel, vista or no vista. Clear visual images of forms in mapped configurations now seemed the exception. Landmarks I remembered – sporadically – rising into the light from rhythms of movement, as from an unseen ground of orientation, in flux.

Close your eyes and try to make your way to the fridge. Your visual memory of the rooms and the configurations of the furniture will start to fade within seconds. But chances are, you'll 'intuitively' find your way to the food with relatively little difficulty. Especially if you're hungry. If you think about it, we all go about most of our everyday lives on habitual auto-pilot, driven by half-conscious tendencies that gently gnaw at us like mild urban hungers. Orienting is more like intuitively homing in on the food with your eyes closed than it is like reading a map.

Something is rotten on the shelf of spatial-experience theory. Cognitive maps, built on the visual basis of generic three-dimensional forms in Euclidean geometric configurations, aren't all they're advertised to be. As a general explanation of orientation, they're past their use-by date. The way we orient is more like a tropism (tendency plus habit) than a cognition (visual form plus configuration).

Research in spatial orientation has been stumbling in the same direction. Recent studies assumed the traditional cognitive model, based on 'reading' visual cues embedded in the forms and configurations of objects. It was found, however, that the emptier the space, the better the brain's ability to orient. The conclusion was that humans orient more by the 'shape of the space' than by the visual characteristics of what's in it.[2] But what is the shape of empty space? Indeterminate – except for the rhythm of movement through it, in its twistings and turnings. The studies were suggesting that the proprioceptive self-referential system – the referencing of movement to its own variations – was more dependable, more fundamental to our spatial experience, than the exo-referential visual-cue system. Self-referential orientation is called 'dead reckoning', after the nautical term.[3] It is known to be the basis of many animals' ability to orient. It is a key element, for example, in the well-known feats of navigation achieved by homing pigeons. Its role in human orientation has significant implications for our understanding of space because it inverts the relationship of position to movement. Movement is no longer indexed to position. Rather, position emerges from movement, from a relation of movement to itself. Philosophically, this is no small shift.

It takes little reflection to realise that visual landmarks play a major role in our ability to orient. Landmarks stand out, singularly. Most of us would be capable of pasting them together into a visual map. But to do that, you have to stop and think about it. It takes effort – an effort that interferes with the actual movement of orientation. Cognitive mapping takes over where orientation stops.

The way landmarks function in the actual course of orientation is very different from reading a map. They're what you habitually head towards or away from. They trigger headings. Vectors. Landmarks are like magnetic poles that vectorise the space of orientation. A landmark is a minimal visual cue functioning to polarise movement's relation to itself in a way that allows us habitually to flow with preferential heading. The vectorial structuring effected by landmarks gives the space of orientation a qualitative dimension, expressed in tropistic preference. The cognitive model assumes that visual cues are somehow used to calculate distances, as if our brains were computers, preprogrammed in inches and feet. Isn't it more plausible that our bodies are habituated in steps? And that steps relate more directly to other steps than they do to conventional feet? The computational fiction is a natural outgrowth of the assumption that we effectively move through and live in a static, metric or quantitative, Euclidean space. I for one don't count my way around town. A qualitative space of moving, step-by-step self-reference accords better with my navigationally competent (if at times cognitively challenged) sense of where I am.

Landmarks rise up visibly from a nonvisual sea of self-related movement. They refer more directly to the self-referencing of the movements surrounding them than to each other. Fundamentally, each landmark stands alone with its associated coursings. What they mark most directly is a monad of relation, a patch of motion referencing its own self-variations (the multiple headings it carries). Landmarks and their associated patches of qualitative relation can be pasted together to form a map – but only with an additional effort that must first interrupt the actual course of orientation. It is in a second moment, in an added operation, that the quantifiable cognitive product is fed back into the space of movement. This can indeed increase the flexibility and precision of a body's orienting. But it remains true that cognitive mapping is secondarily applied to the experience of space, or the space of experience. This makes it an overcoding – a certain way in which experience folds back on itself. It is very uncommon, a limit-case rarely attained, that we carry within our heads a full and acccurate map of our environment. We wouldn't have to carry maps on paper if we had them in our brains. No matter how consciously overcoding we like to be, our mappings are riddled with proprioceptive holes, threatening at any moment to capsize the cognitive model (like the empty areas filled with sea-monsters on medieval maps). No matter how expert or encompassing our cognitive mapping becomes, the monstrous sea of proprioceptive dead reckoning is more encompassing still. We are ever awash in it.

The very notion of cognitive overcoding implies that we orient with two systems of reference used together. The contradiction between them is apparent. Pragmatically, they co-function. Visual cues and cognitive mappings function as storage devices, allowing us more ready reaccess to less habituated proprioceptive patches. They also serve as useful correctives, when we find ourselves hallucinating buildings that positively aren't there. The reverse is also true: proprioceptive orienting can act as a corrective to visual awareness. When we are momentarily lost, the buildings in front of us are in plain view. They may be strangely familiar, but we still can't place ourselves. Oddly, the first thing people typically do when they realise they're lost and start trying to reorient is to look away from the scene in front of them, even rolling their eyes skyward. We figure out where we are by putting the plain-as-day visual image back in the proper proprioceptive sea-patch. To do that, we have to interrupt vision, in the same way that visual awareness interrupts proprioception. The alarmingly physical sense we feel when we realise we're lost is a bodily registering of the disjunction between the visual and the proprioceptive. Place arises from a dynamic of interference and accord between sense-dimensions.

Our orienting abilities, then, combine the resources of two different dimensions of experience. The places we plainly see as we go about our daily lives are products of a co-operation between two sense systems. A synaesthetic system of cross-referencing supplements a systemic duality, exo-referential and self-referential, positional and moving, Euclidean and self-varyingly monadic. Synaesthetic co-operation links these dimensions to each other, always locally – specifically, where we are lost. Cross-sense referencing forms a third hinge-dimension of experience. This 'lost' dimension of experience is where vision's conscious forms-in-configuration feed back into the vectorial tendency-plus-habit of proprioception, and where proprioception feeds forward into vision.

Where we go to find ourselves when we're lost is where the senses fold into and out of each. We always find ourselves in this fold in experience.

An aside: If the positioned sights we plainly see always result from synaesthetic interference and accord, was there really a difference in nature between the sight I positively saw that wasn't there out of my window, and the one with which I laboriously replaced it? Weren't they just two sides of the same coin: the interference side and the accord side? If every effectively placed experience is a synaesthetic production, it becomes difficult to maintain that there is a difference in nature between hallucination and perception. Isn't it just a pragmatic difference, simply between cross-referenced and not cross-referenced? It would stand to reason that there would be a kind of continental drift naturally affecting proprioceptive experience patches due to their self-referential, monadic operation. Their mode of *reality* demands it. Isn't getting lost, even seeing things that aren't there, just a momentary grounding in an impractical dimension of reality? It is the encompassing reality of what we really experience in a spatial way that gets lost if we try to narrow our understanding of space down to vision in its exo-referential single-sense functioning and the associated Euclidean geometry of form-in-configuration. In Euclidean vision, where we always find ourselves is what gets lost.

Look at things from the proprioceptive side. Its elements are twists and turns, each of which is already defined relationally, or differentially (by the joint nature of the proprioceptors), before entering into relation with each other. That makes the relation entered into among elements a double differentiation. The elements fuse into a rhythm. The multiplicity of constituents fuses into a unity of movement. The resulting patch is a self-varying monad of motion: a dynamic form figuring only vectors. Although effective, the dynamic form is neither accurate nor fully visualisable. It is operatively vague; a vector space not containable in metric space. It is a qualitative space of variation referenced only to its own movement, running on autopilot. It is not a space of measure. To get a static, measurable, accurately positioned visual form, you have to stop the movement. This capsizes the relation between movement and position. Now position arises out of movement. Static form is extracted from dynamic space, as a quantitative limitation of it. Anexact vector space feeds its self-variational results into the limitative conditions of quantitative, Euclidean space, populated placidly by traditional geometric forms plottable into configurations.

Doesn't this sound familiar? Doesn't the proprioceptive experience-patch sound a lot like a topological figure in the flesh? Doesn't the way it all shapes up sound very like the way Greg Lynn describes computer-assisted design – starting with differential parameters that automatically combine to govern unities/continuities of self-varying movement, ending only when the programme stops running, leaving a Euclidean form as a static witness to its arrested dynamism?[4] Doesn't topological design method digitally repeat what our bodies do noncomputationally as we make our way to and from our work stations? Then, when we watch the programme run, aren't we doing it again, slumped before the screen? Are we not, though immobile, repeating our body's ability to extract form from movement? When we stare, barely seeing, into the screen, haven't we entered a 'lost' body-dimension of abstract orientation not so terribly different from the one we go to when we roll up our eyes and find ourselves in the fold?

The proprioceptive dimension of experience was described as one of two experiential dimensions. But the two were also described as

folding into each other. That folding of the Euclidean and non-Euclidean into and out of each other is itself understandable only in topological terms. This hinge-dimension between quantitative and qualitative space is itself a topological figure – to the second degree, since topology already figures in it. It is a topological hyperfigure. The non-Euclidean – qualitative and dynamic – is more encompassing than the Euclidean – quantitative and static – by virtue of this double featuring. Simply, to put the two together, you have to make a move between them. You have to fold experience back on itself. You have to twist one of its dimensions into the other and cross-reference them both to that operation. This means that all orientation, all spatialisation, is operatively encompassed by topological movement – from which it derives in the first nonplace.

The space of experience is really, literally, physically a topological hyperspace of transformation.

Note on Terminology

'Topology' and 'non-Euclidean' are not synonyms. Although most topologies are non-Euclidean, there are Euclidean topologies.[5] A Möbius strip or a Klein bottle are Euclidean figures, of one and two dimensions respectively. The distinction that is most relevant here is between topological transformation and static geometric figure: between the process of arriving at a form through continuous deformation, and the determinate form arrived at when the process stops. An infinite number of static figures may be extracted from a single topological transformation. The transformation is a kind of superfigure that is defined not by invariant formal properties, but by continuity of transformation. For example, a torus and a coffee cup belong to the same topological figure because one can be deformed into the other without cutting. Anything left standing when the deformation is stopped at any moment, in its passage through any point in-between, also belongs to their shared figure. The overall topological figure is continuous and multiple. As a transformation, it is defined by vectors rather than co-ordinate points. A vector is transpositional: a moving through points. Because of its vectorial nature, the geometry of the topological superfigure cannot be separated from its duration. The figure is what runs through an infinity of static figures. It is not itself determinate, but determinable. Each static figure stands for its determination, but does not exhaust it. The overall figure exceeds any of its discrete stations, and even all of them taken together as an infinite set. This is because between any two points in Euclidean space, no matter how close, lies another definable point. The transformation joining the points in the same superfigure always falls between Euclidean points. It recedes, continuously, into the between.[6] The topological superfigure in itself is the surplus passing through between Euclidean spatial coordinates. Logically, it is not sequential, even though it is oriented (vectorial). It is recessively transitional. In this essay, the word 'non-Euclidean' is used as a convenient shorthand for a space of this kind: one that cannot be separated from its duration due to a transitional excess of movement. 'Non-Euclidean' is a good enough nontechnical term for dynamic or durational 'spaces' that do not fit into the classical Euclidean (actually Cartesian) intuition of space as a triple-axis co-ordinate-box containing things. In this view, widely thought to correspond with our everyday experience, time is an independent variable adding a fourth, formally distinct, dimension to the traditional three of space. Topologically speaking, space and time are dependent variables. They are not formally distinguishable. They cannot be separated from each other without stopping

Relational Architecture, *which most of the following images belong to, refers to large-scale interactive installations that create opportunities for buildings to decline their established roles in their particular social performance. The interventions are not 'site-specific' but rather 'relationship-specific', as the public is an actor of the ephemeral transformation. Based on dissimulation and insinuation, relational architecture pieces dematerialise the environment and amplify participants to an urban scale. Contact:* rafael@csi.com

LEFT: Positioning Fear, Relational Architecture 3 - Transformed the Landeszeughaus arsenal in Graz, Austria. *A teleabsence interface projected shadows of passers-by onto the building. Using tracking systems, the shadows were automatically focused and generated sounds. A real-time IRC discussion about fear, involving 30 artists and theorists from 17 countries, was projected inside the shadows. Project web site:* http://xarch.tu-graz.ac.at/home/rafael/fear
Credits: Rafael Lozano-Hemmer (concept, visuals), Will Bauer (audio, programming), Robert Rotman and Conroy Badger (programming), Nell Tenhaaf (IRC moderator).

RIGHT: Piel Capaz, a technological coffin for vampire buildings. *A virtual reality installation that visualises resting sites for emblematic buildings that are not allowed to have a natural death. The participant's motion controls the point of view in the projected environments on the wall and on the floor.*
Credits: Emilio Lopez-Galiacho (concept, visuals), Rafael Lozano-Hemmer and Will Bauer (interaction).

the process and changing its nature (Euclideanising it). The relation of the dimensions of space to that of time is one of mutual inclusion. This mutual inclusion, and the strange logical and especially experiential effects associated with it, is what is termed a 'hyperfigure' or 'hyperspace' for the purposes of this text. It may be noted in passing that even a Euclidean topological figure may generate a surplus effect, although in a more static vein. A Möbius strip is a one-dimensional figure whose twisting creates a two-dimensional effect. A Klein bottle is a two-dimensional figure whose folding in on itself creates a three-dimensional effect. The 'effects' are real, but not part of the formal definition of the figure. They are in the figure as it is really experienced, adding another quality to it, precisely in the way it stands out from its formal limits. They are extra-formal, stand-out or pop-out effects. The word 'hyperspace' may also be applied to experiential surplus-dimension effects of this kind, whatever the geometry. Experience itself may be defined as a hyper-dimensional reality: as the 'being' of the excess of effect over any determinate spatial configuration. As the following argument from synaesthesia asserts, the 'shape' of experience can be considered to be a one-sided topological figure: an abstract (recessive/pop-out) 'surface' for the reception, storage and reaccess of qualitative hyper-effectivity that can only be approached head on.

The Argument from Synaesthesia

The hinging of the proprioceptive to the visual in the movement of orientation is a synaesthetic interfusion. It is not the only one. Each side, for example, enters into its own synaesthetic fusion with the tactile: a determinate, positioned sight is a potential touch; the tropism of proprioceptive twisting and turning is assisted by past and potential bumps, and the tactile feedback from the soles of our feet. There are many other synaesthetic conjunctions, involving all the senses in various combinations, including smell and hearing. Clinical synaesthesia is when a hinge-dimension of experience, usually lost to active awareness in the sea-change to adulthood, retains the ability to manifest itself perceptually. In synaesthesia, other-sense dimensions become visible, as when sounds are seen as colours. This is not vision as it is thought of cognitively. It is more like other-sense operations at the hinge with vision, registered from its point of view. Synaesthetic forms are dynamic. They are not mirrored in thought; they are literal perceptions. They are not reflected upon; they are experienced as events. Synaesthetes who gain a measure of willful control over them still perceive them as occurrences in the world, not contents of their heads. They describe summoning them into perception, then moving toward or around them. Synaesthetic forms can be usefully recombined with an experience of movement. They serve as memory aids and orientation devices. Since they work by calling forth a real movement-experience, they retain a privileged connection to propriocep-tion. This is not cue-based, form-and-configuration vision. Although synaesthetic forms are often called 'maps', they are less carto-graphic in the traditional sense than 'diagrammatic' in the sense now entering architectural discourse.[7] They are lived diagrams based on already lived experience, revived to orient further experi-ence. Lived and relived: *biograms* might be a better word for them than 'diagrams'.

It is worth paying close attention to how synaesthetes describe their 'maps'. The biograms are usually perceived as occupying the otherwise empty and dimensionless plane between the eyes and objects in the world. This liminal nonplace has been characterised as 'peri-personal'. It lies at the border of what we think of as internal, personal space and external, public space. The appearance of the biogram is borderline in time as well. It is accompanied by a feeling of 'portentous' *déjà vu*: an already-past, pregnant with futurity, in present perception.[8] This makes experiencing the biograms, in the words of one synaesthete dubbed MP in the literature, like 'seeing time in space' – a good way of describing an event. They have a feeling of thickness or depth, like a 'flexible moving third dimension'. But the depthlikeness is vague enough that they can still be compared to diaphanous 'slides' projected on an invisible screen. They retain a surface character. The 'maps' MP draws at the researcher's request do not satisfy her. Her biograms are not plainly visible forms. They are more-than visual. They are event-perceptions combining senses, tenses and dimensions on a single surface. Since they are not themselves visual representations, they cannot be accurately represented in mono-sense visual form. Oddly, although they appear in front and in the midst of things, the biograms are to MP, 'larger than my visual range, like looking at the horizon'. They are geometrically strange: a foreground-surround, like a trick centre twisting into an all-encompassing periphery. They are uncontainable either in the present moment or in Euclidean space, which they instead encompass. Strange horizon.

Since they are determinately positioned neither in time nor space, their presence can only be considered a mode of abstraction. They are real – really perceived and mnemonically useful – abstract surfaces of perception. Since they continue indefinitely, in order to bring up certain regions the synaesthete has to move around, into, or away from them. She doesn't *actually* walk, of course. The movement, though really perceived and mnemonically useful, does not measurably take place in Euclidean space. It is an *intensive* movement, occuring in place (as at a workstation, or with rolled-up eyes) – or more accurately out-placed, in the event. This is an abstract movement on an abstract surface.

The synesthete uses her biograms, for example, to keep track of birthdays. On the birthday biogram, each region stores a conjunction between a date, a name, and a colour. When she has to recall a birthday, she will use the colour as a landmark, and when she approaches the right coloured region, the name and date will appear. The shape and sound of the letters and numbers are stored in the colours, diaphanously merged into them as in a dissolve, or like strands 'woven together' in a patch of fabric. They are accessed by a reverse dissolve that is like 'pulling out threads'. Shape, sound and language: of a fabric with colour.

MP has a unique biogram for everything she needs to remem-ber. The biograms are 'not connected in any way'. They are like separate monads of abstract lived experience. Except that in their strange twisting between foreground and horizon, each loops back at a certain point into darkness. Each biogram arcs in multicoloured mnemonic glory from a sea of shadow. What lies in the darkness at the end of the rainbows? The answer comes without the slightest hesitation: 'other people's minds'.[9]

Biograms cannot be described without resorting to topology: centres folding into peripheries and out again, arcs, weaves, knots and unthreadings. Face it. You are always facing it. Wher-ever you are, whoever you are, whatever day or year it is, the biogram is in front of you. The synaesthetic form of experience is faced, in something like the sense in which writing is handed.[10] Except that a left has a right, and this front doesn't have a back (yet it still has shadow?). This means a biogram is a one-sided topological surface – really, strangely, usefully.[11] This is not a metaphor. If there is a metaphor in play, isn't it rather the mathematical representation that is the metaphor for the biogram? The biogram is a literal, graphically diaphanous event-perception. It is what is portented when you remember seeing time in space.

Synesthesia is considered the norm for infantile perception. The theory is that it becomes so habitual as to fall out of perception in the 'normal' course of growing up. It is thought to persist as a nonconscious underpinning of all subsequent perception, as if the objects and scenes we see are all 'threads' pulled by habit from a biogrammatic fabric of existence.[12] Synesthetes are 'normal' people who are abnormally aware of their habits of perception. 'Normality' is when the biogram recedes to the background of vision. Biograms are always in operation. It is just a question of whether or not their operations are remarked.

For all perceivers, the biogram is the mode of being of the intersensory hinge-dimension. Its strange, one-sided topology is the general plane of cross-reference not only for sights, sounds, touches, tastes, smells, proprioceptions; it is also the general plane of cross-reference for numbers, letters, words, even units of grammar. On that plane, the learned forms that are usually thought of as restricted to a 'higher' cultural plane re-become perceptions. Practice becomes perception. The cognitive model has it that 'higher' forms are associative compounds built up from smaller sights and sounds as from elementary building blocks. But the workings of synaesthetic biograms shows that the higher forms feed back to the 'lower' perceptual level. They enter the general dissolve, on a level with the elementary, fused into the surface, interwoven components of the fabric of life. This makes it impossible to apply to 'raw' experience distinctions such as 'higher' and 'lower', 'perceptual' and 'cognitive', or even 'natural' and 'cultural'. There is no 'raw' experience. Every experience takes place in the already taken place of higher and lower, where they join for the future. Every experience is a portentous *déjà vu* at a hinge.

The relevant distinction is between involuntary and elicited. Or rather: this is the relevant connection. Biograms are described as having an odd status: they are 'involuntary *and* elicited'.[13] They retain the surprise of the *déjà vu* even for clinical synaesthetes who can summon them forth and consciously navigate them for future heading. Eliciting with future heading is not the same as willing. Biograms remain their own creatures even for proficient synaesthetes. They maintain a peri-personal autonomy from psychological or cognitive containment. They cannot be entirely owned personally, since they emerge from and return to a collective darkness. But they can be tamed, induced to appear and perform feats of memory. They are less like a static image on a slide screen than a live circus act, performed in a ring that lies centre stage and encircles the tent.

Clinical synaesthetes have trained synaesthesia to perform on signal. They have perfected the trick of consciously eliciting involuntary intersense connection as a way of invoking memory. Vision is typically used as a plane of general cross-reference. It is on the abstract surface of colour that everything fuses, in a way allowing a single thread to be pulled back out as needed, before returning to the fold. All the other senses, and any and every 'higher' form, are gathered into colour, together with the three dimensions of space and time. It is as if all the dimensions of experience were compressed into vision. This is why the topology of the biogram is so strangely twisted. It is not due to any lack, say of cognitive organisation or of Euclidean accuracy. There are simply too many dimensions of reality compressed into vision. It can't hold them all in discrete, determinate, harmonious form and configuration. It buckles under the existential pressure.

The biogram is not lacking in order. It is over-organised, loaded with an excess of reality. It is deformed by experiential overfill. It is a hypersurface. Its hyperreality explains why it is so stubbornly abstract. Since it cannot concretely hold everything it carries, it stores the excess fused in abstraction, ready for useful reaccess. In other words, the hypersurface of synaesthetic experience is 'real and abstract' in precisely the way Gilles Deleuze describes the virtual: as an intense, torsional coalescence of potential individuations. 'Pulling out a thread', or decompressing a differential strand of the fusional weave of experience, involves actualising a virtuality. That is why the synaesthetic perception is always an event or performance pulling determinate form and function out of a larger vagueness, like a rabbit from a one-sided hat.

It was argued earlier that there was no essential difference between perception and hallucination, both being synaesthetic creations. The feedback of 'higher' forms and their associated functions onto the biogrammatic hypersurface expands the list. There is no fundamental difference between perception, hallucination and cognition. It was also argued that the separation between the natural and the cultural was not experientially sustainable. In view of this, is it so far-fetched to call the unseen out of which biograms arc 'other people's minds'? Not particular other people's minds, of course. The other of them all: an other of particular mindedness from which everyone's individuated perceptions, memories and cognitions emerge, and to which they return, in a twisting rhythm of appearance, and dissolve: a shared incipiency that is also a destiny. What is the other of mindedness? From what does all individual awareness arise and return? Simply: matter. Brain-and-body matter: rumbling sea for the rainbow of experience. The synaesthetic hypersurface refracts the activity of matter through many-dimensioned splendour into colour. It is the hinge-plane not only between senses, tenses and dimensions of space and time, but between matter and mindedness: the involuntary and the elicited.

Reaccessing the biogram and pulling a determinate strand of organised experience from it is to reapproach the point where the materiality of the body minds itself. It is to catch the becoming-minded of the movements of matter in the act. It is to re-perform the memorial trick of experience pulling itself rabbit-like out of the black hat of matter. This is a somewhat ontogenetic contorsion. It involves a hyperreal looping between the impersonal and the 'peri-personal'. Any personal strand is pulled out of that non-to-near-personal loop as the grande finale. After which there is nothing to do but introduce the next abstract act.

That the personal is the finale distinguishes this synaesthetic ontogenesis of experience from phenomenological approaches. For phenomenology, the personal is prefigured or 'pre-reflected' in the world in a closed loop of 'intentionality'. The act of perception or cognition is a reflection of what is already 'pre-embedded' in the world. It repeats the same structures, expressing where you already were. Every phenomenological event is like returning home.[14] This is like the *déjà vu* without the portent of the new. In the circus of synaesthesia, you never really know what act will follow. The rabbit might turn into a dove and fly away. Experience, normal or clinical, is never fully intentional. No matter how practised the act, the result remains at least as involuntary as it is elicited. Under the biogrammatic heading, the personal is not intentionally prefigured. It is rhythmically re-fused, in a way that always brings something new and unexpected into the loop. The loop is always strangely open (with just one side, how could it ever reflect itself?).

What if topological architecture could find ways of extending the 'diagrams' it designs into 'biograms' inhabiting the finished product? What if it could find ways of embedding in the materiality of buildings open invitations for portentous events of individuating *déjà vu*? Might this be a way of continuing its topological process in its product?

To do this would require somehow integrating logics of perception and experience into the modelling. Processes like habit and memory would have to be taken into account. As would the reality of intensive movement. Ways would have to be experimented with for architecturally soliciting an ongoing eliciting of emergent forms/functions at the collective hinge of perception, hallucination and cognition. Techniques would have to be found for overfilling experience. The methods would have to operate in a rigorously anexact way, respecting the positivity of the virtual's vagueness and the openness of its individual endings. Never prefiguring.

In a way, architecture could even surpass synaesthetes like MP by finding ways of building-in nonvisual hypersurfaces. There is nothing wrong with colour, light and darkness. Rainbows of experience are good. But imagine the startling effects that might be achieved by using proprioception as the general plane of cross-referencing. Imagine how positively, qualitatively moving that would be. Practices of architecture allied with experimental art, like the 'reversible destiny' architecture of Arakawa and Gins or the 'relational' architecture of Rafael Lozano-Hemmer, might have much to contribute. Technologies could be favoured that can be twisted away from addressing pre-existing forms and functions towards operating directly as technologies of emergent experience. Imagine if these were to become infrastructural to architectural engineering. What better place to start than with the much-touted 'new media', approached not only as design tools but as architectural elements as basic as walls and windows? Could architecture build on the ability of digital technologies to connect and interfuse different spheres of activity on the same operational plane, to new effect? This is a direction in which the work of Lars Spuybroek, among others, is already moving.[15]

TO BE CONTINUED . . .[16]

Displaced Emperors, Relational Architecture 2 - Intervention on the Habsburg Castle in Linz, Austria. *An architect interface consisted of wireless 3D trackers that calculated the direction of the participant's arm and a large projection of a human hand appearing wherever he or she was pointing. 'Touch' transformed the castle into Chapultepec Palace, the residence of the Habsburg emperors in Mexico and trigger a temporary post-colonial override consisting of a huge image of the Atzec head-dress kept at the ethnological museum in Vienna. Credits: Rafael Lozano-Hemmer (concept, visuals), Will Bauer (audio,programming), Susie Ramsay (production). Photos by Dietmar Tollerind.*

Notes

I gratefully acknowledge the assistance of the Australian Research Council and the Canadian Centre for Architecture in supporting this research.

1 Sandra Buckley analyses the differences, cultural and experiential, between ground-level movement through architectural spaces and underground movement in 'Contemporary Myths of the Asian City', in Robert Sergent and Pellegrino D'Acierno (eds), *(In)Visible Cities: From the Postmodern Metropolis to the Cities of the Future*, Monticello Press (New York), forthcoming.

2 See Russell Epstein and Nancy Kanwisher, 'A Cortical Representation of the Local Visual Environment', in *Nature*, vol 392, 9 April 1998. For a popular press account of their work on adult brain functioning during orientation tasks, see 'A Positioning Unit of Sorts in the Brain', *New York Times*, 28 April 1998, pB13: 'The experiments dovetail with work on rats and human infants showing that when they get lost, it is the shape of the space, rather than the objects in it, that are used to get reoriented'.

3 For an overview, see Ariane S Etienne, Joëlle Berlie, Joséphine Georgakopoulos and Roland Maurer, 'Role of Dead Reckoning in Navigation', in Sue Healy (ed), *Spatial Representation in Animals*, Oxford University Press (Oxford), 1998, pp54–68.

4 Greg Lynn, *Animate Form*, Princeton Architectural Press (New York), 1999; and *Folds, Bodies and Blobs: Collected Essays*, La Lettre Volée (Brussels),1998.

5 Bernard Cache provides an excellent account of the topological resources of Euclidean geometry available for architectural design in 'A Plea for Euclid', *ANY (Architecture New York)*, no 24, 1999, pp54–9. The present essay, however, diverges sharply from Cache in its assessment of the importance and usefulness of non-Euclidean conceptions.

6 'Movement in itself continues to occur elsewhere: if we serialise perception, the movement always takes place above the maximum threshold [in the super-figure's passing-through] and below the minimum threshold [recessively] in expanding or contracting intervals (microintervals) . . . Movement has an essential relation to the imperceptible; it is by nature imperceptible', Gilles Deleuze and Félix Guattari, *A Thousand Plateaus*, Brian Massumi (trans.), University of Minnesota Press (Minnesota), 1987, pp280–281. Another word for 'imperceptible' is 'abstract'.

7 Ben van Berkel and Caroline Bos (eds), *ANY (Architecture New York)*, no 23, 1998, special 'Diagram Work' issue.

8 On the peri-personal and *déjà vu*, see RE Cytowic, 'Synaesthesia: Phenomenology and Neuropsychology', in Simon Baron-Cohen and John E Harrison (eds), *Synaesthesia: Classic and Contemporary Readings*, Blackwell (Oxford),1997, pp20, 23.

9 Cytowic, *Synaesthesia: A Union of the Senses*, Springer-Verlag (New York),1989, pp217–27.

10 For diagrammatic renderings of this, see ibid, figs 7.9–7.17, pp202–9.

11 Raymond Ruyer: experience is 'a surface with just one side . . . If the sensible surface could be seen from two sides, it wouldn't be a sensation, but rather an object . . . it's an "absolute surface" relative to no point of view outside of itself: *Néo-finalisme*, PUF (Paris), 1952, pp98–9.

12 See Daphne Maurer, 'Neonatal Synaesthesia: Implications for the Processing of Speech and Faces', in Baron-Cohen and Harrison, op cit, pp224–42.

13 Cytowic, 'Synaesthesia: Phenomenology and Neuropsychology', op cit, p23.

14 The notion of intentionality is often used as a way of establishing an identity between the structure of the world and the structure of the subject in the world. The insistence on such an identity is a tacit assumption of a divide. An objective-subjective split is backhandedly enshrined in this way of thinking. A mediating instance is then required to bring the two realms back into harmony. The senses are assigned to the job. In architectural phenomenology, a building becomes a 'metaphor', 'reflecting' for the senses the identity-structure shared by the subject and the world. Architecture is called upon to express, and reinforce in concrete, that ideal fit. Its 'mission' is to concretise the 'integrity' of being-in-the-world: to close the loop. The whole process revolves around identity and an ultimately normative ideal of authenticity. The ideal is suspiciously domestic (Heidegger's 'house of being' is just around the corner). This is how Juhani Pallasmaa puts it: 'The timeless task of architecture is to create embodied existential metaphors that concretise and structure man's being in the world. Architecture reflects, materialises and eternalises ideas and images of ideal life . . . Architecture enables us . . . to settle ourselves in the world . . . Our domicile becomes integrated with our self-identity . . . Architecture is the art of reconciliation between ourselves and the world, and this mediation takes place through the senses'. The 'mental task' of architecture, Pallasmaa continues, was best formulated by Frank Lloyd Wright: 'What is needed most in architecture today is the very thing most needed in life – Integrity. Just as it is in a human being, so integrity is the deepest quality in a building . . . If we succeed, we will have done a great service to our moral nature.' It all adds up to a high-minded moralism. This is sharply at odds with any form of architectural experimentalism, whose rallying cry would not be to close the loop, but to loop-the-loop; not to ground in the 'authentic' but to dizzy with potential (remembering that position arises from intensive movement, rather than extended movement departing from pre-position). Juhani Pallasmaa, *The Eyes of the Skin: Architecture and the Senses*, Academy Editions (London), 1996, pp50–1. In the perspective of this essay, there is not an identity between the subjective and objective, or between the world and experience: there is a continuity that mutually includes each side of the divide in the same self-differentiating reality.

15 Arakawa and Madeleine Gins, *Reversible Destiny*, Guggenheim Museum (New York), 1997. Take 'reversible destiny' as 're-incipient life' (experience returning to the point of matter-minded ontogenesis). On 'relational architecture', see Rafael Lozano-Hemmer in this volume and at http://xarch.tu-graz.ac.at/filmarc/fest/fa3/fear. Take 'relational' to mean 'intensively cross-referencing disparate planes of experience'. See also Lars Spuybroek, in this publication. For an overview of his work see Spuybroek, *Deep Surface*, NOX (Rotterdam),1999, (exhibition catalogue, Exhedra Gallery, Hilversum). See especially 'Off the Road: 103.8 MHz', a description of a housing project and noise barrier in Eindhoven. The aim of the project is to create a 'zone of transition' (using among other devices a sound-processing feedback loop between the houses and the cars passing by on the highway) that sets up a 'resonance' between 'bits and bricks', '[air]waves and ground'. This activates the in-between as an operator of relation rather than leaving it a passive boundary. The 'zone of transition' is an airborne, abstract holding together in addition to (rather than in opposition to, or simply breaking down) the concrete holding-apart of discrete, down-to-earth divisions demanded by the need for a highway noise barrier.

16 The full text of this essay is available online at http://www.hypersurface.net

BRIAN MASSUMI
SENSING THE VIRTUAL, BUILDING THE INSENSIBLE

The 'virtual', it is hard not to notice, has been making a splash in architecture. Its full-blown entry into the discourse was somewhat belated in comparison to other fields. This has been to architecture's great advantage, for the poverty of prevailing conceptions of the virtual, in its popular compound with 'reality', has become all too apparent. 'Virtual reality' has a short conceptual half-life, tending rapidly to degrade into a synonym for 'artificial' or 'simulation', used with tiresome predictability as antonyms for 'reality'. The phrase has shown a pronounced tendency to decompose into an oxymoron. It was in that decomposed state that it became a creature of the press, a death warrant on its usefulness as a conceptual tool.

There is a countervailing tendency to use 'virtual' without the 'reality' tag – not because the virtual is thought to have no reality but because its reality is assumed, the only question being what mode it takes. It is in the work of Gilles Deleuze and Félix Guattari that this current gains its most elaborated contemporary expression. The advantage of architecture is that the virtual has been introduced into its discourse by theorists and practitioners cognisant of the impasse of earlier appropriations of the concept in other domains, and conversant with the alternative Deleuze and Guattari's work represents.

Deleuze and Guattari, following Bergson, suggest that the virtual is the mode of reality implicated in the emergence of new potentials. In other words, its reality is the reality of change: the *event*. This immediately raises a number of problems for any domain of practice interested in seriously entertaining the concept. If the virtual is change as such, then in any actually given circumstance it can only figure as a mode of abstraction, for what is concretely given is what is – which is not what it will be when it changes. The potential of a situation exceeds its actuality. Circumstances self-abstract to the precise extent to which they evolve. This means that the virtual is not contained in any actual form assumed by things or states of things. It runs in the transitions from one form to another.

The abstractness of the virtual has been a challenge to certain discourses, particularly in the interdisciplinary realm of cultural theory, which make a moral or political value of the concrete. This is not the case with architecture, even though its intimacy with the concrete is quite literal. Architecture has always involved, as an integral part of its creative process, the production of abstract spaces from which concrete forms can be drawn. The challenge that the virtual poses for architecture lies more in its 'unform' nature than its abstractness. How can the run of the unform be integrated into a process whose end is still-standing form?

The answer for many has been topology. Topology deals with continuity of transformation. It engulfs forms in their own variation. The variation is bounded by static forms that stand as its beginning and its end, and it can be stopped at any point to yield other still-standing forms. But it is what happens in-between that is the special province of topology. The variation of seamlessly interlinking forms takes precedence over their separation. Forms figure less as self-enclosures than as open co-dependencies of a shared deformational field. The continuity of that field of variation is inseparable from the forms populating it. Yet it exceeds any one of them, running across them all. When the focus shifts to continuity of variation, still-standing form appears as residue of a process of change, from which it stands out (in its stoppage). A still-standing form is then a *sign*: of the passing of a process. The sign does not in the first instance signify anything. But it does imply something; or better, it implicates. It envelops in its stillness a deformational field of which it stands as the trace: at once a monument of its passing and a signpost of its potential to be repeated. The variation, as enveloped past and future in ceasing form, is the virtuality of that form's appearance (and of others with which it is deformationally interlinked).

Topology has exerted a fascination on certain contemporary architects because it renders form dynamic. This has important consequences for both the design process and the built form to which it leads.

The topological turn entails a shift in the very object of the architectural design process. Traditionally, form was thought of as both the raw material and end product of architecture, its origin and telos. Form bracketed design. Approached topologically, the architect's raw material is no longer form but *deformation*. The brackets swing open. Form falls to one side, still standing only at the end. Form *follows* the design process, far from enclosing it. Far from directing it, form *emerges* from the process, derivative of a movement that exceeds it. The formal origin is swept into transition. Followed by architect.

One thing swept away is the popular image of the architect as autonomous creative agent drawing forms from an abstract space of Platonic pre-existence to which he or she has inspired access, and artfully dropping them into the concrete of everyday existence, which is thereby elevated. The architect's activity becomes altogether less heroic – and the abstract more palpable, for the architect must follow the same process that the form follows. The architect becomes a prospector of formative continuity, a tracker in an elusive field of generative deformation. The abstract field of variation takes on a certain post-Platonic thickness, in and by its very elusiveness, by becoming a field of hands-on exploration and experimentation. New form is not conceived. It is coaxed out, flushed from its virtuality. The architect's job is in a sense catalytic, no longer orchestrating.

Le Corbusier outlines the antithetical position in an early manifesto:

> The goal of art is to put the spectator . . . in a state of an elevated order. To conceive, it is first necessary to know what one wishes to do and specify the proposed goal . . . Conception is, in effect, an operation of the mind which foreshadows the general look of the art work . . . Possessed of a method whose elements are like the words of a

language, the creator chooses among these words those that he will group together to create a symphony . . . One comes logically to the necessity . . . of a logical choice of themes, and the necessity of their association not by deformation, but by formation.[1]

Here, creation consists in the masterful composition of aggregate forms, drawing on a pre-existing vocabulary of combinable elementary forms. Creation is an individual expression of the artist at the same time as it accedes to universality. The 'pure' artist possesses a superior combinatorial logic allowing 'him' to articulate to 'universality' of 'man': a 'capital point, a fixed point'. Forms, in this account, are elementary, and elementary forms are 'words' signifying 'universal' principles of fixity. The completed forms could not be further from the asignifying signs, materially enveloping singular conditions of change and emergence, towards which hands-on topological experimentation moves.

Those hands, of course, are on the computer keyboard. In a most unCADlike way. The computer is not used to prefigure built form, in the sense of presenting an anticipatory image exactly resembling it. The whole point of the topological turn is to catalyse newness and emergence rather than articulating universalised fixation. Of course, topological transformations are just as formalisable, in their own way, as are classical geometric forms. Chance must be added to truly yield change. The computer becomes a tool of indeterminacy. Abstract spaces are no longer neutral screens for imaging what has already been seen in the mind's eye. They must be actively designed to integrate a measure of indeterminacy. As a consequence, the space of abstraction itself becomes active, no longer merely prefiguring. The abstract space of design is now populated by virtual *forces* of deformation, with which the architect must join forces, to which he or she must yield in order to yield newness. The design process takes on a certain autonomy, a life of its own.

From the 'artful genius' perspective, this may seem like a cowardly abdication of creativity to autonomised machinic procedure. In fact, the arbitrary returns. Its first point of re-entry is the way in which the activity of the abstract space is programmed. There is no such thing as pure indeterminacy, certainly not in a programmed environment. Indeterminacy must be designed to emerge from an interplay of constraints. What constraints are set to interact will be an arbitrary decision of the architect, working from a more or less explicitly developed aesthetic orientation, and taking into consideration the functional parameters of the desired end product as well as client preferences on a number of other levels (including cost). The manner in which such 'analogue' traits are translated into topological terms informs the programming, but is not itself preprogrammed. It is the point of entry, into what is nevertheless still an autonomic process, for the architect's decision.

The process does not of itself generate a completed form. It generates a proliferation of forms. The continuity of the deformational

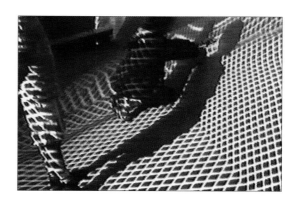

FROM ABOVE: Nox Architects, interior of FreshH₂O eXPO (Water Pavilion) – two views; Le Corbusier, Edgar Varése and Iannis Xenakis, Philips Pavilion, 'Poéme Electronique', Brussels World Fair, 1958

variation can be cut at any point, any number of times. The constraints can be tweaked and set in motion again to experimentally generate whole new series of formal separations. The outcome of any given run cannot be predicted. But a choice must be made: a set of forms must be selected to provide the foundation of the actual design. The second area of arbitrariness is in the selection. The overall process is that of an *analogue*. Such constraints as taste, function, preference and cost are analogically translated into virtual forces, which are then set into variation, and analogically translated back into taste, function, preference and cost *as embodied* in the final, composite sign-form. The movement is not from the simplicity of the elementary to the sophistication of the complex. Rather, it is from one arena of complexity to another. Complexes of complexity are analogically launched into interaction. Each complex is separated not by a self-enclosure, but by an analogical gap that the process must leap. The art of the architect is the art of the leap.

Integrating topological procedures involving indeterminacy does not replace creative freedom of expression with machinic necessity. To begin with, the absolutes of 'freedom' and 'necessity' are endemic to the 'creative genius' approach of the Le Corbusier quote. They do not apply to the topological approach, which works instead with arbitrarity and constraint, dosed rather than absolute and locally co-functioning rather than in Promethean struggle with one another as universal principles. The opposition between the absolutes of freedom and necessity was never, of course, itself absolute. The creative freedom enjoyed by the 'purified' artist was predicated on allying himself with a higher necessity (unchanging, universal, 'primary' order). His 'elevated' activity consisted in giving that necessity formal expression in the 'secondary' world of the dirty, ever-changing, individually varying, everyday. The artist separated himself from the everyday in order to return to it, reorder and re-form it. The world itself was his raw material, as if he himself could freely stand outside and against it as pure, formative activity. This elevating mission might be seen as typical of 'high' modernist approaches to cultural production.

To the topologically inclined, things are very different. Arbitrariness and constraint are internal to the process. They are variables among others, in a process that is all variation, and which separates itself into phases, across analogical gaps, instead of separating the 'artist' from the world, the better to impose order upon it. The 'impurities' of the everyday – personal taste, dirty function, preference enforced in part by social convention, and most vulgar of all, cost – enter the process, across the analogic gaps. The translation into and out of virtual force lays everything out on a single, complex, deformational surface from which form emerges as a certain kind of stoppage. The architect's activity is swept up in that complexity, its triggering and stoppage. It works at a level with it. The architect yields dosed measures of his or her activity to the process. The 'arbitrarity' of the decisions that enter and exit the process are more like donations to its autonomy than impositions upon it. Rather than being used to claim freedom for the architect, decision is set free for the process. The architect lets decisions go, and the process runs with them.

'Arbitrarity' might not be the best term for the decisive activity of the architect as process tweaker and form flusher, since that role requires 'following' the process, which in turn requires having a certain 'feel' for its elusiveness, for its running, for its changeability: a feeling for its virtuality. The old and abused term

of 'intuition' perhaps fits better than terms such as arbitrarity, freedom, inspiration, or genius. 'Intuition' is the feeling for potential that comes of drawing close enough to the autonomous dynamic of a variational process to effectively donate a measure of one's activity to it. Intuition is a real interplay of activities. It is neither a touchy-feely dreamlike state nor an imposition from on high of form on matter, order on disorder. It is a pragmatic interplay of activities on a level. The 'donation' involved should not be construed as an 'alienation' of the architect's activity, because what is donated is returned in varied form, ready for insertion into a different process, or a different phase of the same process (building).

None of this has anything to do with purity. Everything is mixed together at the beginning and comes out just as mixed. Constraint enters as conventional strictures and professional expectations, client preference, cost projections, etc. Each of these involves more or less static forms, as well as their own dedicated matters of variation. Arbitrarity or 'freedom' enters in the way those constraints are set into interaction, and how an end-form is extracted from the interaction. That end-form must in some way accommodate itself to these constraints or it will be 'pure' in a very down-to-earth sense: not built. The success of the exercise is not measured by any god-like ability to create something from nothing. It is the more modest ability to extract a difference from a variation (a standing difference from a running variation). It all depends on what happens in the middle. Cultural production becomes the art of the prevailing middle.

This is not really a 'low' modernism against Le Corbusier's 'high' modernism, since it interactivates those categories as well. Neither is it exactly a postmodernism, since the sign-form is primarily a sign of a material differentiation rather than a citation, and it implicates a process rather then referring intertexturally. The architectural activity associated with the topological turn is not unrelated to such modernist adventures as Cage's experiments with chance, or Burroughs' cut-up and fold-in ventures. It might well be considered a neo-modernism, although it has become more acceptable to refer to it, along with its modern antecedents, as neo-Baroque, defined by Deleuze in terms of the 'fold to infinity' (the mutual processual envelopment, on a single abstract variational surface, of complexes of complexity). It mixes procedures evocative of the modern avant-garde with an admitted complicity with vulgar worldly constraints. It might be recalled that Baroque art was an art of patronage. Today's commercial constraints on architecture are different, but just as strong. Maintaining a stance of 'purity' towards them is not a test of political mettle. It is a test of intellectual honesty. It goes without saying that no architect can build without being in complicity with commerce and industry. The choice is not between complicity and purity, but between a politics that maintains the relevance of the distinction and one that recognises that creation in absolute freedom from constraint was only ever a self-aggrandising myth. An architectural politics that admits 'complicity' – the co-functioning of arbitrarity and constraint in the extraction of a standing difference from a running continuity of mixture – is what Deleuze would call an ethics, in distinction to the heroic moralism of the teleologically fixated.

Labels are of limited value. They tend to stereotype, as 'high' modernism inevitably has been in this account for purposes of exposition. The stereotyping can easily extend to both 'sides'. It is just as important not to group too hastily into one rubric all architects who use techniques akin to the ones described here as belonging to the topological turn (as if they constituted a school) as it is to recognise the simplifications that abbreviated accounts like the present one confer upon the topologically challenged. The ways in which the analogical gaps described above are negotiated by architects who are topologically engaged with the virtual will vary widely. There are no constants. The signature engagement with computers is not even necessarily a constant, since allied processual effects may be produced by other means (as the Cage and Burroughs examples indicate). A fluid typology of post-heroic architecture could be delineated along multiple gap-leaping lines of variation, in what may be an expanding field of futurity already prospecting the architectural present (or what may, alternatively, be just a blip). Whatever the fate of contemporary currents, it is more important to multiply productive distinctions than lump camps.

Although the inherited antinomy of freedom and necessity ceases to be the central problem it once was, the topological turn produces ample problems of its own. The originality of a cultural process is measured by the complexity and productiveness of the new problems it creates, not the neatness of its creative solutions; for in complexity there is life. A good problem is a gift of life, the provision of an opening for others' activities, for uptake by other processual dynamisms, a contribution to the collective surface of continuing variation. By that standard, the topological turn in architecture is already a stunning success.

Foremost among the problems it produces is the nature of the actual relation between the built forms that emerge from its process and the process as it happened. In other words, if the idea is to yield to virtuality and bring it out, where is the virtuality in the final product? Precisely what trace of it is left in the concrete form it deposits as its residue? What of emergence is left in the emerged? If the end form is a sign that does not signify, then what does it do and how does it do it? What is the relation of the asignifying sign to its event?

The problem raised is a semiotic one that neither architecture nor current discourses in cultural theory are well equipped to handle. To be appropriate to its field of application, this semiotic problem must be posed in terms of singular potential, material emergence and event, rather than the tried-and-true terms of universal (or at least general) signifying structure and individual decodings or interpretations variously conforming to it.

The difficulty of the problem is that it points to the continuation of the architectural design process outside of itself, in another process. The outside of architectural design is in a very real sense its own product – the building itself: the life of the building. The building is the processual end of the architectural process, but since it is an end that animates the process all along, it is an immanent end. Its finality is that of a threshold that belongs integrally to the process, but whose crossing is also where the process ceases, to be taken up by other processes endowing the design with an afterlife. The most obvious after-processes are two: looking and dwelling. The exterior of the building takes its place as an object in the cultural landscape, becoming an unavoidable monument in the visual experience of all or most of the inhabitants of its locale. And the building becomes an experienced form of interiority for the minority of those people who live in it, work in it, or otherwise pass through it.

There is resistance from many quarters in architectural discourse to highlighting the experience of the built form. There are very good reasons for this reluctance. Talking about it in signifying semiotic terms of decoding and interpretation clamps the brackets closed again. It re-imprisons the architectural process in pre-existing formal structure, consigning it to intertextural referral, for those who are familiar enough with and care enough about the collective conventions, or to the banality of metaphorical 'free' association on the part of those operating 'below' the structural level of citation, on the local level of 'individualised' variation. The latter is, in fact, entirely prepackaged, since all of the 'individual' variations pre-exist as possible permutations of the general structure of signification. The variation is punctual. It does not emerge. It is 'realised' (conceived) at structurally spaced intervals, at predictable 'positions'. In the end, there really is not such a great a difference between the self-conscious structural irony of the citationalists and the heartfelt 'personal' metaphors of 'naive' associationists. The uptake has been into a process that assumes an opposition between the constant and the variable, and can therefore hope, at best, to achieve a sterile dialectical synthesis between imposed form and 'freely' chosen pre-authorised variations ('discovery' deconstructively unmasked as 'really' being a 'reading'). Quite different is continual variation, in which everything enters the mix and in which there are no constants (even though things may occasionally stand still) and no structural pre-existence (even if there is ample systemic feedback), and thus neither dialectic nor deconstruction (only deformation and emergence). This is the true alienation: when the immanent outside is not only taken up but is taken away by a process so legibly alien to it.

Another receiving-end option is phenomenological. The way of phenomenology posits a 'raw', unprepackaged substrate still perceptible, if only one knows how to 'return' to it, beneath the structure of referral and association. The substrate is construed as 'intentional', or as prefiguring subject-object relations. The experiential substrate, it turns out, is not so much unprepackaged as it is packaged by a structural pre-fit between the body and the world. This has the merits of avoiding imprisonment in signification, and of reconnecting with material processuality. But it consigns everything to function, hypostasised as the ontological ground of lived experience. 'Intentionality' is another word for function, glorified as the ground of all experience. This transcendentalisation of function encloses process in organic form; another difference between 'high' modernism and existential phenomenology, although not so great as it is made out to be. For both, experience is formally prefigured.

The difference is that in the first case the form is purely, otherworldly geometric, and in the second, rawly organic, 'lived' and at one with the world (the world made flesh). The great rallying cry of Deleuze's view of creativity, as a drawing on the virtuality of process by a yielding to it, is the Spinozan slogan that 'we do not know what a body can do'. Phenomenology cannot yield (to) the virtual, whose 'body' is emphatically 'machinic': an autonomised processuality (if not necessarily a high-tech one). It cannot take the machinic indeterminacy of the virtual, even when it takes its own topological turn (as in Merleau-Ponty's last work on folding and gapping, or 'chiasmus').[2] It cannot step over that threshold. It can only stand a 'return' to the well-trodden ground of possibilities for organic functioning. The divergence between Deleuze and phenomenology is summed up in another slogan: to the phenomenologists, 'consciousness is always *of* something' (cognitive prefit).[3] Deleuze responds, 'consciousness always *is* something' (ontological emergence).

The topological turn in architecture must avoid both these directions, and does. But does it live up to the project of drawing on the virtual to draw out the new? The question remains: how could it if its end product is still recognisably standing form? By virtual definition, the built form does not resemble its conditions of emergence. It does not resemble the virtual forces generating it, or the analogical gaps its generation leaps. Unlike a structure of constants and variable realisations of it, the asignifying sign-form does not conform to its own event: there can be no conformity between the product and its process, no one-to-one correspondence between end result's formal features and the steps of its deformational emergence. Virtuality cannot be seen in the form that emerges from it. The virtual gives form, but itself has none (being the unform of transition). The virtual is imperceptible. It is insensible. A building is anything but that. A building is most concrete.

This impasse has led to the frequent complaint that the architecture operating in the topological field is formally indistinguishable from modernism: that there is nothing so 'original' about it, nothing to it but a lot of techno-tricks in the design process that leave no visible trace in the built form, at least none that anyone not directly involved in the design could be expected to notice or care about. Isn't it still a building, to which a style can be attributed, that is recognisable as belonging to a particular category of building, that fulfils the typical functions of its kind? Where is the newness? In the computer gadgetry? In slight variations on existing architectural themes?

There is no way of effectively responding to this criticism as long as there is no serious attention given to the afterlife of the design process in the life of the building. Taking the looked-at, lived-in life of the building into account does not fatally entail a surrender to the structural reduction of the signifying sign, or to the phenomenological apotheosis of organic form and function. There is, perhaps, a way out of the impasse, but only if there is a willingness to reentertain questions about perception, experience and even consciousness that have, for some time now, been anathema to many in architecture, as well as in other domains of cultural theory and production.

Although the virtual, Deleuze explains, cannot itself be seen or felt, it cannot not be seen or felt, as other than itself. What he means is that in addition to residue in static form, the formative process leaves traces still bearing the sign of its transitional nature. These are not virtualities, but populations of actual effects that more fully implicate changeability and the potential for further emergence than self-enclosed forms or ordered agglomerations of forms realising a rigid combinatory logic to produce citations, associations, or most ubiquitously, stock functional cues – formal compositions following laws of perspective and resemblance designed to awaken habitual patterns of recognition and response. In even the most ordered formal composition there are accident zones where unplanned effects arise. Nonperspectival, unresembling, they are just glimpsed, in passing, as anomalies in the planned interrelation between actual forms. They are surprising, perhaps mildly disorientating; sometimes, just sometimes, shocking. They are less perceived than side-perceived; half-felt, like a barely palpable breeze; half-seen, on the periphery of habitual vision. They are *fogs* or *dopplerings*; patches of vagueness or blurrings presenting to the senses an insensible plasiticity of form; flushes of freshness, arun in concretised convention and habit; recalls of emergence, reminiscences of newness.

Fogs: actual traces of the virtual are often light effects. Although we tend to think of the perceptual dimensions of light as clearly distinguishable and almost boringly familiar, they are not so docile on closer inspection. Experimental psychology, even after decades of trying, is still at great pains to set even the most 'obvious' boundaries between different light-related phenomena. What is the relation of white and black to lightness and darkness? Are the shades lying in a continuum between those extremes shadows or achromatic colours, intensities of light or gradations of grey? How can the distinction between chromatic and achromatic colours be maintained in the face of such everyday effects as the coloured shadows so lovingly catalogued by Goethe? Is there a simple relation between colour, light intensity, and illumination? Where for that matter is the boundary between one colour of the familiar spectrum and another? What sets the boundary between glimmer, white and clear? How do reflectance and translucence enter into the equation?[4] The boundaries we set and distinctions we function by are habitual. According to many theorists of vision, they do not replace the infinitely complex perceptual fog that is our originary and abiding experience of light. They occur with them, alongside, in a parallel current or on a superposed abstract perceptual surface, in a perpetual state of emergence from the continuum of light dimensions that one frustrated would-be tamer of visual anomaly termed 'the brightness confound'.[5]

The 'brightness confound' can become a conscious percept, through a concerted effort of unlearning habits of seeing, or through a simple accident of attention. When it does, the confound is contagious. It strikes depth: three dimensionality, argues the 'ecological' school of perceptual theory,[6] is an effect of complex differentials of surface lighting played out in ever-shifting proximities of shadow and colour, reflectance and luminosity, illumination and translucence (it is not, as traditional theories of perception would have it, the product of mysterious calculations of relative size and distance).

Depth is a surface effect susceptible to the brightness confound. When it goes, so does separable form. Not only do the relative size and distance of objects flutter, their boundaries blur. They cease to be separate figures, becoming not entirely localisable zones in a fuzzy continuum. In other words, they cease to be objects, becoming what they always were, in the beginning and in parallel: fluctuations; visual runs; experiential transition zones. The distinctions of habit fold back into the always accompanying level of the more-than-three-dimensioned light concurrence from which they emerged. The fixed boundaries and 'constants' of our habitual perceptions are emergences from an experiential confound to which they can return, and must return, for they are not structural constants at all, but continually regenerated effects, predicated on the variation they follow and emerge from, as its perceptual arrest. They rest entirely on variation.

Architecture, Deleuze will say for this reason, is a distribution of light before it is a concretion of forms.[7] Its basic medium is light. It uses concrete and stone, metal and glass, to sculpt light in ways that either direct the fixations of attention steadfastly away from their confounded conditions of emergence, or on the contrary enable it sporadically to fold-back into them. The separation between 'primary' sensations (ie depth and forms) and 'secondary' sensations (in particular colour and lighting) is untenable. Since perception is a matter of complexes of complexities played out in surface relations, the more useful distinctions are, again, topological (cuts and continua; boundaries and transitions; fold-outs and fold-backs) and processual (aflutter or stabilised; arun or still-standing; refreshed or habitual; functional or eventful). One of the direct implications for architectural practice is that colour need not be dismissed as essentially decorative. As a dimension of the brightness confound, it is as primary an architectural element as the cube – if not more so.

Dopplerings: actual traces of the virtual are always effects of movement. When it was said that the separations between the perceptual dimensions of light were habitual, what that really meant is that they arise from movement. Depth perception is a habit of movement. When we see one object at a distance behind another, what we are seeing is in a very real sense our own body's potential to move between the objects or to touch them in succession. We are not using our eyes as organs of sight, if by sight we mean the cognitive operation of detecting and calculating forms at a distance. We are using our eyes as proprioceptors and feelers. Seeing at a distance is a virtual proximity: a direct, unmediated experience of potential orientings and touches on an abstract surface combining pastness and futurity. Vision envelops proprioception and tactility, by virtue of past multi-sense conjunctions whose potential for future repetition our body immediately, habitually 'knows', without having to calculate. Seeing is never separate from other sense modalities. It is by nature synaesthetic, and synaesthesia is by nature kinaesthetic. Every look reactivates a multi-dimensioned, shifting surface of experience from which cognitive functions emerge habitually but which is not reducible to them. It is on that abstract surface of movement that we 'live' and locate. We cannot properly be said to see, or experience, three-dimensional space and the bounded forms filling it. Rather, it is they that emerge from the abstract surface of experience, as reductive concretions and relative stoppages of it. Our seeing *stops* with perspective and form. We do not see or experience perspectival forms from the outside: they occur to our experience and in it, as arrest events that befall it. We ourselves – as spatially located forms in regular interaction with other forms, as embodied subjects in reciprocity with objects – must be co-occurrences with depth and boundary, co-emergences of concretion and stoppage, companion arrests, fall-out of the befallen. 'We' ourselves are stoppage events in the flow of experience.

The relation between space and movement must be inverted, along with the relation between form and lighting. When the relation between space and movement inverts, so does the relation between ourselves and our experience. Experience is no longer in us. We emerge from experience. We do not move through experience. The movement of experience stops with us and no sooner folds back on itself. It continues, alongside us, in parallel: doubling, as a superposed abstract surface in repeated interaction or intersection with the stoppage we have been. Our existence is an ongoing topological transformation of a complexifying abstract ontological surface: separation, fold-back, doubling, intersection, re-separation, fold-back over again, redoubling, resection . . . confound it.

The confound of light envelops form, and with form it envelops space, at which point everything becomes movement. Didn't Bergson argue in the first chapter of *Matter and Memory* that we are beings of light, effects of its differential movements? That our bodies, or for that matter all of matter, are interactions of light with surface dimensions of itself? That the 'abstract surface' is light in itself, interacting infinitely and absolutely with itself, registering or 'feeling' its own variations as form-effects? Contemporary physics would not disagree.[8]

This essay began with the maxim that the virtuality or changeability of a form exceeds its actuality. The point of the detour

FROM ABOVE: Jean Dubuffet, Villa Falbala, 1969-73, exterior and interior views; Alvar Aalto, Finnish Pavilion, New York World's Fair, 1939; Frank Stella, Hooloomooloo, *1994, acrylic on canvas*

through the existential brightness confound is that if we apply that maxim to our own life forms, our 'experience' onto-topologically exceeds our being. Experience is our virtual reality. It is not something we have. It is a transformability that has us, and keeps on running with us no matter how hard we try to stand still and no matter how concretely we build. It is our continual variation. Our becoming. Our event: the lightning whose thunder we are.

The suggestion here is that the philosophical correlation of the topological turn in architecture is the idea that the streaming of experience exceeds being; or put another way, that feeling conveys potential and change (the corollary being that the feeling is absolute, or that it is immanent only to its own process: the feeling in and of itself of a matter of variation, emergent stabilities of form effectively aside). This philosophical orientation was dubbed a 'radical' empiricism by William James, and a 'superior' empiricism by Deleuze. What it means for architecture and other plastic arts is that they can rejoin the virtual and take experience into account in the same move.

For architecture to rejoin the virtual and take experience into account in the same move would mean its aspiring to *build the insensible*. If in any composition of forms, however rigid, an accident of attention can return experience to its confound, then it must be possible to make a project of building in just such accidents of attention. In other words, built form could be designed to make the 'accidental' a necessary part of the experience of looking at it or dwelling in it. The building would not be considered an end-form so much as a beginning of a new process. Stable forms can be designed to interact dynamically, as bodies move past or through them singly or in crowds, or as sounds mute or reverberate, or as relations of surface and volume change with the time of day or season, or as materials change state with levels of moisture or temperature, or as the connection between inside and outside varies as an overall effect of these variations in concert with the rhythms of activity pulsing the city or countryside as a whole. Forms can be composed to operate as catalysts for perceptual events returning experience to its confound. A building can harbour foci of implicative vagueness, lucid blurs, dark shimmerings, not-quite things half-glimpsed like the passing of a shadow on the periphery of vision. Architecture can locally and sporadically return experience to that part of itself which can never be perceived as being (since it has only becoming) but cannot but be felt (in passing). Architecture can accept as part of its aim the form-bound catalysis of the unform (the deform).

The vagaries in question here have to do neither with *trompe l'œil*, optical illusion, nor ambiguity. *Trompe l'œil* is fully subordinated to formal resemblance. More distorted (anamorphic) or unanchored practices of simulation play on resemblance, but in needing it to play on, hold fast to it.[9] Optical illusion also never leaves the formal level, being an oscillation between two forms, rather than a rhythm of recursion between form and the unform. Ambiguity, for its part, belongs to signifying structure. It is nothing new for architects to build-in ambiguity in order to make an event of standing form. But ambiguity still addresses the conventional function of the sign-form. It activates citation and association in order to push them towards a critical reappraisal. It operates on the level of conventional sign-form in order to deliver it to critique. Building-in ambiguity may succeed in catalysing an event – but the event is still a meaning event.

The asignifying or processual sign-form of the onto-topological turn catalyses experiential potential rather than meaning. It is a sign of material dynamics of variation, pointing in two directions at once. On the one hand, it recalls the elements of indeterminacy and chance of the design process itself. It is an echo of the experimentations of the architect. But it does not resemble or in any way conform to them. Rather than referring explicitly to them, it refers them to another process. The architect's processual engagement with the virtual is taken up in an alien process: the life of the building, the looking and dwelling of those who pass by it or through it. This process continues from the design process' point of cessation. The virtual is fed forward into the final form. But in final form, the way the potential is yielded (to) bears no resemblance to what befell during the design process, from which, it must be remembered, it is separated by analogical gaps. The feed-forward of virtuality delineates a continuity, but it is a leaping continuity of differentiation. The architect, who donated his or her activity to the autonomisation of a process, now lets the product go, into another process. Architecture is a gift of product for process, the sign-form fundamentally means nothing. It is meant to stand at the threshold between processes. The middle prevails.

The aim of onto-topological architecture has no end. The aim may nevertheless involve many ends: critical, citational, associational, functional, profit-making. In fact, it necessarily involves all of these: it involves them with each other. It adds them to the catalytic mix. Like stability of form, pre-operative conventional sign systems feature as constraints added to the complex mix out of whose interaction the new re-arises in the design product. The aim of processual architecture does not stop at any end. It takes everything from the middle again. The product is re-process.

Although there is no formal resemblance between the re-process in which the product is taken up and the process that produced it, there is a certain correspondence between them. Were there not, the leap across the processual gaps would not earn the name 'analogical'. The correspondence in question does not concern the nature of the forms in play, or even the qualities of the event they mix to make. The correspondence is a processual retake. It is the process of generating the new from an intuitive interplay of constraints and the arbitrary that keeps the continuity across the leaps. The correspondence pertains to the conditions of emergence rather than the actuality of the emerged. In other words, it is virtual. The identity stretched analogically across the gaps of differentiation is 'machinic': what is repeated is autonomisation, same process, different at every take.

Philosophy and architecture have always been on intimate terms: from Plato's city of the republic to Augustine's city of god to Leibniz's monad-house to Heidegger's house of being to Virilio's bunkers, to name just a few. Formalist modernism's high-moral attachment to purity and geometric harmony can only be understood as a concerted philosophical sortie waged through architectural means. Conversely, architectural achievements have often stood as exemplars for philosophy. Architecture flourishes with philosophical infusions; philosophy exemplifies in monuments. Architecture and philosophy are drawn towards abstract-concrete symbiosis with each other (which of these contributes more of the abstract, and which more of the concrete, is not as straightforward as it may seem).

The basic question of this essay has been: what philosophy can or might enter into a symbiosis with architectures engaging with the virtual, in particular by topological means? The answer seems to lie in a 'radical' or 'superior' empiricism. For architecture, the effect of such a symbiosis is a willingness to bring into even more pronounced expression its processual dimensions. That in turn means theoretically and experimentally re-evaluating the separation between the 'primaries' of form and depth and 'secondaries' such as colour and illumination. That further entails an inversion in what is traditionally assumed to be the relation of form and movement, subject-object structurings and experience, constancy and variation. Where it all leads is to a semiotic of singular potential, material emergence, and event: a semiotic for which the abstract is really material, and the sign-form's material

appearance is not only seen. Vision, following this path, must be grasped as inhabited directly by the other senses, and the other senses by vision. In such an asignifying semiotic, all perception figures as synaesthetic, and synaesthesia is seen as a creature of movement. Perhaps most controversially, a distinction is maintained between movements in the actual world between fixed forms, and the absolute movement of process self-feeling, from which the world itself emerges. A tall order. A tall, autopoietic order. But the theory is not without precedents, and the experimentations have palpably begun.

Note on tunnelling to the future

Most palpably, this has begun in the integration of digital technology into architecture. Although computerisation is not a necessary condition for topological experimentation in design, its forecast integration into built form may bring us to a new threshold in the sensing of the virtual in built form or the building of the insensible. Proponents of 'ubiquitous computing' look to the day when digital media becomes architectural: no longer furnishings or infrastructure, but an absolutely integral part of the building. When the digital display becomes as structural architecturally as a window, looking and dwelling will be transformed, but not as completely as when digital media learns to forego the display and the analogy of the window and the interface is able to go anywhere, responding no longer only to mouse- or keystrokes anchored to the screen but to gestures, movements and sounds – dedicated, roving or ambient, compounded or uncompounded with visions and information.

Electronic media offers, in principle if not yet in practice, an infinite connectibility of spaces. It is crucial to be clear about this: it is not the abstract informational content of what the media might connectively deliver, or even the abstract space of the 'infosphere' from which it is drawn, that is virtual. Although the virtual is a mode of abstraction, the converse is not true. Abstraction is not necessarily virtual. It was argued earlier that the possible (or the permutational: encompassing information no less than signification) and the simulated (of which *trompe l'œil* and anamorphosis are the simplest examples) are abstract without being virtual: the first because it pertains to a generative matrix whose actual permutations pre-exist in it; the second because it retains in one way or another a fundamental link to formal resemblance. What is virtual is the connect*ibility*: potential (the reality of change). It cannot be overemphasised that the virtual is less the connection itself than its *-ibility*.

The assumption is often made that increasing the sheer number and variety of media connections between locations constitutes a virtualisation. This is to confuse the virtual with the technological thing. If the virtual is not the informational content or its infosphere, neither is it the physical implantation of technology. The distinction between the virtual and technological actualisation is paramount. Comparing two qualitatively different ways of digitally connecting spaces brings out the distinction. 'Windowing' is one. Windowing provides a framed and tamed static perspective from one local space onto another that remains structurally distinct from it. The connection established is predominantly visual, or at most audio-visual. Features from, or of, one locale are 'delivered' into another as information, prepackaged for local understanding and use. Windowing is communicational. What characterises communication is that it is designed to be 'transparent': no conversion is supposed to take

place by virtue of the connection in and of itself. The receiver must be primed to enable the information to make a difference – to interpret or exploit it. Information is a feed. Neutral packets ('data') are consumed on one side of the window (or screen) to feed a process already understood and under way, with known effect and intent. Nothing new. What is on the other side of the window stays on the other side, and is not affected by the consumptive conversion operated on the delivery side. The 'conversion' is not really a qualitative change because it just augments something already primed and in place there. The connection is segregated from the conversion.

It is for this reason that communcation is termed a mediation or 'transaction' (rather than an action). Whether communication ever really lives up to its transparent aspirations is doubtful. But that is not so much the issue here. The issue at hand is rather to think of another way of connecting spaces that doesn't even make the pretence. Call it 'tunnelling'. Tunnelling cuts directly into the fabric of local space, presenting perceptions originating at a distance. Not data pre-packagings: perceptions. The perceptual cut-ins irrupt locally, producing a fusional tension between the close at hand and the far removed. As the distant cuts in, the local folds out. This two-way dynamic produces interference, which tends to express itself synaesthetically, as the body returns vision and hearing to tactility and proprioception in an attempt to register and respond to a structural indeterminacy. Vision and hearing are *transduced* into other bodily modes of activation. Tunnelling is not communicational, but transductive. The connection is unmediatedly a conversion. As a consequence, it takes on a thickness of its own. It is not just a transparent delivery. It *is* something, and its something is a doing: a direct conversion; a qualitative change. Something is happening here: action. But is it here? It is not only bodily modes that transduce. Space itself is converted, from the local-or-distant into a *nonlocal*. Distant cut-in, local fold-out: the irruptive perceptions retain as much 'thereness' as they take on 'hereness'. Distance as such is directly presented, embodied in local interference. Two-way movement, between near and far. Between: unplaceably in the midst.

Architecturally speaking, tunnelling builds in the prevailing middle of the experiential confound. It makes structural the transductive irruption of the structurally indeterminate. The opposition between the structural or formal and the accidental is disabled. The 'fogs' and 'dopplerings' described above are no longer peripheral and adventitious. The periphery becomes central, the adventitious of the essence. Structure opens onto the potential of the not-yet known or intended. Melding connection with conversion, tunnelling builds in-*ibility*. The opening is not onto 'the' new: like a new thing. It is onto new*ness*: the reality of transition, the being of the new, quite apart from any*thing* new. Tunnelling may still yield information and function, interpretation and opportunity to exploit in the service of the augmentation of the already-here, or perhaps its purposeful growth into something new, but it does so in a second phase – after a second conversion: when its interfering stills and the newness settle into things. Settle it will, but first it stirs, unforms; any information-function or even invention that emerges from the unforming, singed or tinged by it, as by the lightning its thunder was.

Since tunnelling catalyses unform conditions of actual emergence, it must be considered ontogenetic. The connection is an onto-topological cut-in/fold-out that builds in a phase-space of indeterminate potential. The potential cut of the distant into the out-folding local can actually combine with communicational deliveries or in-foldings from the 'infosphere', paradoxically expanding the confound itself to include information as such (if not function, which always follows the unform). The only proviso is that the materiality of the signs encoding the information stands out. In other words, that the signs be as insistently blips of light as they are letters, as insistently sound-wave as voice: forces of perception. When the communicational medium ceases to be transparent and perforce stands out in its materiality, information blends into perception. Information then precedes its understanding: it is *experienced* as a dimension of the confound before being understood and used and perhaps lending itself to invention. The understanding and use are then already a repetition. Of something they were, but emerged from, diverged from, with no resemblance: transductive perceptual forces, forced *-iblity*, necessarily sensed virtuality. Information takes on a genetic relation to its confounded and *in situ* self. This is a far cry from communication but it may still be considered citational. Tunnelling information builds in what might be called a vertical mode of citationality, in which the citation has a different ontological status from that which is cited, as emergent actuality to repotentialising confound. The relation of the citation to the cited is asignifying and direct, if divergent. The connection between them is processual, more fundamentally experiential than it is cognitive or functional (which are what the experience becomes when it self-diverges).

This kind of self-differing citationality could do with a name to distinguish it from the 'horizontal' postmodern version, in which everything has already been said (delivered) out there somewhere, and delivering it again over here only leads to the conclusion that nothing new has happened, only repetition (no matter how many new inventions have hit the market in the meantime). The name 'self-referentiality' will do as well as any for the emergent or becoming version, in which something does occur, or 'recur'. 'Recursion' might be a better word than 'repetition', for what happens to information in the process (re-emergence, renewal, tinging with potential). Information transductively 'recurs', across a 'vertical' or *in situ* distance from

itself (a concretely abstract self-distance, or self-emergent nonlocality). A new arena of self-referential artistic activity calling itself 'relational architecture', developing under the influence of figures like Stelarc who set up transductive linkages between the body and the Internet, experiments with this kind of recursive confounding of informed experience in the built environment.

Much of what may come of these experimentations is still the province of science fiction, or at best futurism, but as digital technology develops and slowly integrates with architecture, it may be helpful to keep three points in mind: 1) No technology in itself is virtual or virtualising. It is always possible to window new media, and there will be strong cultural and economic pressures to do so. Windowed, digital technology limits itself to the insufficiently-abstract of communication, falling short of its transductive capacity to concretise the abstract as such, to confoundedly actualise the virtual. Virtuality is a mode (*-ibility*). It is not in the 'what' of the technology (its specifications and implantations) but in the 'how' of its composition with other formations such as architecture (its modal conditioning). 2) The postmodernists were in a way right when they said that nothing ever happens here (or there), because it all happens in the middle. Another way of making the point about the 'how' is to say that newness and new things are not the same. No matter how many inventions there have been, it does not mean that an event or real transition has occurred. If invention grows from a communicational feed, and then gives itself over to communication, qualitative change is neither here nor there. The reality of change is transduction – which may occur with or without invention. And with or without, may be built. 3) What points one and two infer is that technology, while not constituting change in itself, can be a powerful conditioner of change, depending on its composition or how it integrates into the built environment.

Technically, the 'tunnellings' somewhat futuristically evoked here as actualisations of the reality of change require fibre optics. It is no surprise to the Bergsonian that the actualisation of the virtual in built form rides on waves of light. The metaphysical assertion that our body and matter itself is constituted by light interacting infinitely with itself as its own hyperabstract surface, feeling absolutely its own variations, has little or no importance in itself. It can, however, act as a reminder: to bring it all back to perception: to perception understood positively as actually productive of existence, or as virtually preceding existing separations of form; to perception in continuity with the world (unform). The reminder is: do not content yourself with facile negative formulations such as 'distance has been abolished', or with structural descriptions of how already-constituted forms in already-separated spaces technically, even inventively, communicate. Bring it all back: to the abstract concretely. Confound it: transduce it.

Notes

1 Le Corbusier and Amédée Ozenfant, 'Purism' (1920), *Modern Artists on Art*, RL Herbert (ed), Prentice-Hall (Englewood Cliffs, NJ), 1964, p62, pp65-67.
2 Maurice Merleau-Ponty, *The Visible and the Invisible*, Alphonso Lingis (trans), Northwestern University Press (Evanston, Ill), 1968.
3 Maurice Merleau-Ponty, *The Primacy of Perception*, James Edie (trans), Northwestern University Press (Evanston, Ill), 1964, p164.
4 The classic treatise on the perceptual vagaries of light is Johann Wolfgang von Goethe, *Theory of Colours*, Charles Lock Eastlake (trans), MIT Press (Cambridge, Mass), 1970. See also Ludwig Wittgenstein, *Remarks on Colour*, Linda L McAlister and Margarate Schättle (trans), Basil Blackwell (Oxford), 1978. See also Jonathan Westphal's gloss, *Colour: Some Philosophical Problems from Wittgenstein*, Aristotelian Society Series, vol 7, Basil Blackwell (Oxford), 1987.
5 Marc H Bornstein, 'Chromatic Vision in Infancy', *Advances in Child Development and Behavior*, vol 12, Hayne W Reese and Lewis P Lipsitt (eds), Academic

Press (New York) 1978, p132.

6 James J Gibson, *The Ecological Approach to Visual Perception*, Houghton Mifflin (Boston), 1979.
7 Gilles Deleuze, *Foucault*, Paul Bové (trans), Minnesota Press (University of Minneapolis), 1986, p57.
8 In relativity theory, 'it is the light figure that imposes its conditions on the rigid figure.' Henri Bergson, *Durée et simultanéité*, PUF (Paris), 1968, p126. See the discussion in Deleuze, *Cinema 1: The Movement-Image*, Hugh Tomlinson and Barbara Habberjam (trans), Minnesota Press (University of Minneapolis), pp8-61. 'Einstein proposed that the particulate nature of matter may be explicable as concentrations and knots in a fundamental, continuous field', David Bohm and F David Peat, *Science, Order and Creativity*, Routledge (London), 1987, p73. 'Blocs of space-time [whose topological torsions constitute rigid bodies] are figures of light', Deleuze, p60.

Shusaku Arakawa and Madeline Gins, Interaction House, 1997 – 'Body Proper + Architectural Surround = Architectural Body'. In this particular project the radical theorisation of both body and environ and their interrelations as architectural body are significant for hypersurface theory. This project is unique in the artists' oeuvre in its absorption of everyday media graphics, a reference to the world of teletechnology, as it plays over the surface of a doubled and fragmented labyrinth, a reference also to language. The rigour of inquiry into both the graphical and material manifestations creates the possibility for an interplay between the graphics and surfaces, creating a plane of immanence – a hypersurface.

GIOVANNA BORRADORI
AGAINST THE TECHNOLOGICAL INTERPRETATION OF VIRTUALITY

An image, for Bergson, is 'a certain existence which is more than that which an idealist calls a representation, *but less than what a realist calls a* thing – *an existence placed halfway between the "thing" and the "representation."'*
Matter is not out there, in the world, but a mix of self and world, perception and memory.

For the majority of theorists, virtuality describes the totality of effects and mutations brought about by the information and communication network.[1] Virtuality designates not only whatever happens on, or is generated by, the Internet but includes the impact of the media on the way in which we apprehend, represent and consequently build the world around us. By this definition, virtuality concerns the blurring of the distinction between perception and representation, original and copy.

How does such blurring occur? For many, the explanation lies in the fact that in virtual space objects do not appear as self-contained entities, accessible via sensory perception; rather, mediatised technology fabricates objects as irreducibly represented and reproduced. This irreducibility is the characteristic of virtual space, where objects become 'simulacra'.[2]

I believe this definition of virtuality to rely on a reductionist assumption: if virtuality amounts to a technologically generated set of events, it is in fact reduced to physical states of affairs. I want to call this reductionist standpoint 'representationalist'. By contrast, I see the possibility of developing a nonreductive concept of virtuality, in which it reflects technologically generated events, phenomenologically understood as an aspect of our experience of the world. With reference to Nietzsche's definition of perspectivism as the doctrine for which there are no uninterpreted facts or truth, I shall call this nonreductive alternative 'perspectivist'.

These two definitions, the representationalist and the perspectivist, are based on fundamentally different conceptions of space. In my reading, the representationalist understanding of virtuality heavily depends upon the rationalist notion of space, whose origins are to be found in Descartes' mind–body dualism. The perspectivist alternative is, instead, a critique of the rationalist notion of space in terms of what I name 'virtual spatiality'.[3] Diametrically opposed to the objectification of space as alienated and homogeneous 'outside', this kind of spatiality has as its chief features heterogeneity and movement.[4]

Drawing from the philosophical insights of Nietzsche and Bergson, I shall unfold a heterogeneous and dynamic concept of virtual spatiality in which tensions and qualia override oppositional pairs: in virtual spatiality, direction and movement cut transversally across the distinction between subjective and objective; density and rarity replace the opposition between material and immaterial; latency and expression take predominance over presence and absence.

Virtuality De-Technologised

How does the concept of virtuality intersect with the fields of philosophy and architecture? Is virtuality a contingent or a necessary link between these two disciplines? Most architectural theorists interpret virtuality as a change of technological paradigm and in so doing opt for the thematic type of connection. At a determinate point in time, so their claim goes, architecture begins to be reshaped digitally, in terms of both its technology and its object. Since the paradigm-shift has occurred, architectural design has been increasingly produced through digital means; the spaces architecture has been called to design are themselves virtual; and, even more importantly, architecture has been put face to face with a different spatial sensibility, derived and constantly enriched by the experience of cruising the digital highways. This different spatial sensibility goes together with a new range of spatial needs, the identification of which is still under way, as ever-larger portions of our existence are being conducted on line. The role of philosophy is restricted to helping architecture demarcate this sensibility.

While I am by no means attempting to deny the compelling aspect of technological virtuality, I dissent from reducing it to a contingent historical occurrence, both in the architectural and philosophical sense. To me, virtuality designates a necessary connection between architecture and philosophy, provided that virtuality be de-technologised.

The nontechnological interpretation of virtuality concerns, both etymologically and metaphysically, the Latin notion of *vis* (force), which is a *leitmotif* in Nietzsche's philosophy. Diametrically opposed to the rationalist conception of space, as the container of entities and forms, Nietzsche's idea of space is that of an immanent field of forces. If space is conceived as a field, entities and forms are not simply 'contained' by it but produced by the very differential that constitutes the relation between them.[5] If we understand the nature of these forces to be discursive, virtual spatiality will emerge as the experience of a nomadic discursivity that, because it is yet unexpressed, is virtual.[6] If this de-technologisation of virtuality is indeed pursued in the direction of a new phenomenological definition of the virtual, what will an architecture of virtuality look like?

As the de-technologisation of virtuality should not imply, I believe, an opposition or denial of technological virtuality, but an attempt at interpreting it as a specific mode amongst a larger phenomenological spectrum, the architecture of virtuality should be viewed as intertwined with its metonymical correlative: the virtuality of architecture. By this, I mean the constitutive role that architecture plays in the creation of the human subject, which is what makes virtuality a necessary rather than a contingent link between architecture and philosophy.

The virtuality of architecture suggests that the individual is not just 'always already thrown' into existence, as Heidegger would have put it, but 'always already built'.[7] Architecture, from this

point of view, does not elaborate theoretical, aesthetic, functional propositions 'in' space but becomes the condition of possibility for the primary hermeneutical exchange between the individual self, others and the environment. It is this exchange that makes the human subject a being-in-the-world. The virtuality of architecture relies on the premise that, if we come across ourselves as 'thrown' into the world, we do so in the face of the fact that such a world is built or constructed spatially, as well as socially, historically and culturally. From the standpoint of the virtuality of architecture, architecture builds us as much as we build it.

Why is 'Virtual Space' a Representationalist Concept?

Why is the reductionist interpretation of virtuality also representationalist? What is the coincidence between reduction and representation? If an entity can be reduced to its physical and quantifiable components, it can also be faithfully 'represented' in terms of those components. Since the Renaissance, perspective has been the science of representation, the technique used to rationalise, quantify, order and control spatial relationships.[8]

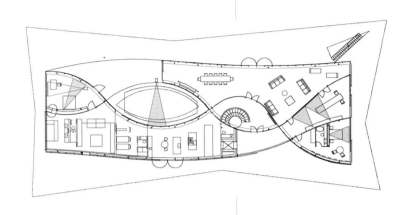

The role of representation in the rationalist lineage is one of the central themes of Heidegger's later philosophy. According to Heidegger, representation can be minimally understood as the relation to a primitive 'presence': the substantial rather than accidental features of an entity.[9] The more representation is granted epistemological transparency, the more the presence of which it is a representation is presumed to be stable, permanent, self-identical. However, stability, permanence and identity cannot exist without that which allows the object to be present: space. Neither reduction nor representation could happen without the homogeneity of the Newtonian and Cartesian space.

Both a reductive and a representationalist apparatus is at work whenever virtuality is understood as the host dimension for simulacra or for effects of simulation. Whenever the blurring of the distinction between perception and representation is justified in technological terms, not only a reductivist but a representationalist position is being offered.

Most of the representationalist positions have a semiological foundation. Simulacra are conceived as infinitely layered compounds of mediated information whose object or reference, assumed as self-contained presence, is ultimately irretrievable. In the vocabulary of poststructuralism, largely influenced by Saussure's linguistics, such an infinite layering of mediated information without a definite object or reference is translated as the endless deferral from signifier to signifier. Whether only simulacra are available, which are neither copies nor originals, or only signifiers are available, which are pointing to each other rather than to a transcendental signified, the categorial framework seems to remain essentially representational.

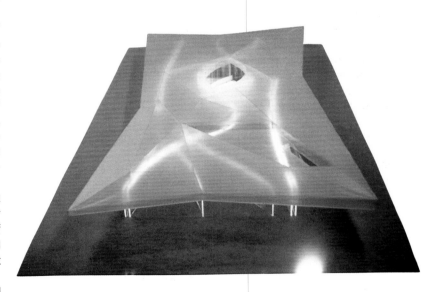

Herzog & De Meuron, Kramlich Residence and Media Collection, California, 1997-2000. FROM ABOVE: elevation; site plan; model.

The Cartesian Theorem

Cartesian theorem about space could be called the underlying sense of space shared by such different architectural experiences as 19th-century historicism and large sections of the Modern Movement. Descartes' conception of space revolves around the central opposition between the empirical dimension, defined as having spatial features, and the transcendent or spiritual dimension, which characterises mental features. We can doubt everything, he writes in the *Meditations*, except that we are thinking beings, because, even if we think that we are not thinking, we are still thinking. Assumed as self-reflection, thought is freestanding, internally justified, autonomous from all sorts of empirical support. In fact, the inescapability of thinking does not prove at all that we are awake or completely sober. All it proves is that thought is absolutely primary and independent of anything that is extended in space.

To make the transition from philosophy to architecture, let us pair what Descartes calls thinking with the notion of form. The Cartesian theorem entails the mutual exclusion between form and space. Any thinking being – or, in our parallel, any form – exists in its own perfection and balance, completely independently from space. The mind injects space with forms and, in turn, the absolute emptiness of space does nothing but receive them.

The extreme polarisation of activity and passivity, in terms of mind and body, form and space, is essential in the history of representationalist architecture.[10] This polarisation is at the root of the obsession with novelty so crucial to the high-modernist visual avant gardes and made programmatic by architectural modernism. The fact that form is located completely beyond space, as well as the empirical sphere, protects it from any mediation, change, obsolescence and fallibility. Conceived in this way, radical novelty can exist only on the condition that it be transcendent. The new is whatever is possible, and therefore not real (otherwise it would no longer be a possibility). As in the Cartesian theorem, form is not immanent to space but transcends it; it is form that represents the possibility of an installation in space from an ageless and mental 'inside'. Such an inside is purely transcendental and spaceless. In this sense, form is structurally utopian. Descartes is the philosophical ancestor of the modernist conception of the new as necessarily utopian. Utopia, however, only in its literal meaning of nonplace, because the modernist utopia is a political project of social emancipation. The modernist utopia is a nonplace in the sense that it is not-yet real but may become so on the basis of conditions found in the real. The utopian side of modernism coincides with a foreseeable possibility; otherwise it could not encompass an emancipatory project, which is one of its essential components.

Two Conceptions of the New

Both in architecture and philosophy, the representationalist approach entails a conception of the new as foreseeable possibility. By contrast, from a perspectivist angle, novelty corresponds to the actualisation of virtual presences: presences virtually contained in the real but not yet actualised. A representationalist notion of novelty is based on the category of possibility: on what is not-yet real but may become so on the basis of conditions found in the real. Perspectivist novelty is the affirmation of submerged and unexpressed forces, virtually contained in the real but not yet actualised. In other words: while representationalism moves within a system of oppositions based on two classical modalities, reality and possibility, the perspectivist

set-up is based on the nonoppositional pair constituted by actuality and virtuality. Moreover, while possibility is larger than reality because it contains whatever could become real on the basis of the conditions found in the real; virtuality is co-extensive with the real, for virtuality is already real, inclusive of the yet unexpressed or non-actualised portion of the real.

Virtual spatiality does not perform the function of space, insofar as it does not provide forms with material and objective stability. While space is the receptor of forms, virtual spatiality is the generator of forms. Virtual spatiality is an active and differentiating dimension rather than a homogenising or alienating one. Forms are not injected into space as if from the outside, but generated within it. While the notion of space implies the installation of the radically new into reality, virtual spatiality implies the affirmation of the yet unexpressed, silent, discursive forces by which reality is constituted. What are these discursive forces? Let us turn to Nietzsche for the answer.

Perspectivism and Force

In Nietzsche's analysis, representation has historically implied the suppression of the notion of force and the dynamics between forces, producing hegemonic outcomes. Instead, representation needs to be looked at as just one of many 'perspectival' alternatives. Perspectivism is the name Nietzsche gives as an alternative to representationalism, that is, to the dogmatic and totalising aspiration of traditional philosophical systems. Why does Nietzsche pick out perspective for this scope? And how does his perspectivism affect architecture?

Perspectivism is laid out as the doctrine according to which there are no uninterpreted facts or truths. Perspective seems thus both a synonym of interpretation and distinguished from knowledge, where knowledge is clearly identified with the detection and rationalisation of some objective dimension. Despite Nietzsche himself using perspective and interpretation interchangeably more than once, there is a subtle difference between them that should not be overlooked by those interested in the contrast between space and virtual spatiality, both from a philosophical and architectural standpoint.[11] While perspective indicates the relativity and uniqueness of our spatial and sensory location within the world, interpretation is an intellectual organisation of perspectives. This is because the juxtaposition of perspectives can be apprehended only at an abstract, intellectual level. Thus, perspective, not interpretation, is the primitive unit of Nietzsche's discourse. Perspectivism reveals the determinacy of our sensory presence within space, assumed by Nietzsche as incompatible with any other. Interpretation is a more constructivist concept, made out of a plurality of perspectives.

Far from naturalising perspective in the representationalist way, as the transparent means of rationalising spatial relationships, Nietzsche attributes to perspective an existential and thoroughly materialistic meaning. In Nietzsche's perspectivist approach, there are as many foci as there are eyes in the world. Perspective is not a technique of representation but the affirmation of one's own actualisation as well as the intuition of the virtual spatiality of others. Perspectivism is both a critical project of displacement of the focus, and an affirmative project consisting in the actualisation of other foci, an actualisation whose scope is to give the undecidable, enigmatic, unpredictable features of existence a new legitimacy. Nietzschean affirmation injects ambiguity into the apparent unity of the actual, opening up fissures of virtuality and becoming.[12] To affirm means to experience the multiplicity of 'perspectives' virtually contained by a present state or form. These perspectives are the virtual lines along which becoming unfolds.

For Nietzsche, becoming affects all facts in the world, whether material, mental or formal. This becoming is the virtual aspect of experience. While form is necessarily actualised, becoming is yet-unformed. The challenge of the architecture of virtuality is diametrically opposed to any formalism. For architecture to be able to connect with perspectivist virtuality, it needs to abandon all formalism, since its challenge would no longer be to simulate or represent existing forms and events but to respond to the yet-unformed. The yet-unformed is pure movement, the movement produced by the pushing of the forces against each other. A movement that, in Nietzsche's philosophy of force, comes before space in the sense that it constitutes spatiality.

The Unformed and the Untimely

The primacy of movement makes perspectivist virtuality available to a thoroughly material, sensory type of experience. But what is movement? How can we 'represent' movement? Can the monumental, archival, memorialising function traditionally attributed to architecture be reconciled with it? The Nietzschean answer would be yes, provided that we shy away from all forms of historicism, including, I suggest, postmodern neo-historicism. Historicism kills movement. History is the first area that architecture has to rethink in its meaning. Next to it, as I shall indicate in relation to Bergson, is memory.

According to Nietzsche, there are two possible connections to history: one is authentic and life-enhancing, and the other is inauthentic and destructive. Inauthentic historiography imposes itself whenever history is taken as a given, as the historicists do by monumentalising and revering it indiscriminately. History has neither determinate meanings nor a unifying scope. Since it is not a self-contained presence, it must be challenged rather than religiously respected. By contrast, authentic historiography depends on the ability to 'make history', which Nietzsche distinguishes from simply 'being in it'. This ability hinges on what Nietzsche names 'plastic power'. Life *is* plastic power, the power to shape new perspectives without becoming self-defensive or losing oneself. Only if this power is affirmed and cultivated, rather than suppressed, will history serve movement and life.

The authentic understanding of history, and of human existence within history, is contingent upon what Nietzsche describes as stepping into the 'Unhistorical'. Such a leap consists in a type of 'creative forgetting', disengaged from the normative power of history, and it is necessary for one's plastic power to strengthen. 'It is possible to live almost without memory, and to live happily moreover, as the animal demonstrates; but it is altogether impossible to live at all without forgetting'.[13] Forgetting means disconnecting from a linear sense of time, described as a series of punctual 'nows', some of which are no-more and some of which are not-yet. This linear description represents selves and cultures as located in time, rather than constituted by it and becoming with it. Switching between the Historical and the Unhistorical, making the present part of becoming, is what secures a healthy, constructive relationship with history, for both philosophy and architecture. What is no-more cannot be objectified as something without an active influence on the present, but needs to be reactivated precisely in terms of these influences. This is the transformative function of time that the Unhistorical is supposed to introduce into the present. Implementing the role

that time, in its transformative function, plays in existence means to implement the contact with a specific ontological modality that is located in reality but is not actualised: virtuality.

The relationship with history opened up by contact with the virtual dimension of experience is neither the radical rejection of the past promulgated by architectural high modernism and the International Style, nor the reverence for the past adopted by the postmodernist appropriation of historical styles. Nietzsche's perspectivist history is not, as it is often all too simplistically interpreted, the generating matrix of an unqualified relativism, that both in architecture and philosophy translates in a neohistoricist kind of sensibility. Perspectivist history presents both the philosopher and the architect with the question of how to interpret the yet-unformed, whether conceptually or spatially. Sensing becoming, responding to movement: these are the new challenges that need to be faced by attempting to capture form as it emerges from the process of its own formation and deformation.

The Tensions of Memory and Perception

Is there a technique of capturing movement, or more precisely, the movement of forms and forces, before their expression? For some, the answer is topology, the digital animation of form, which could lead to 'topological turn'.[14] In contrast to the formalistic orientation promoted by the evolution of modernism into the International Style, topology has pushed architecture to stop viewing form as its ultimate scope but as a by-product of the design process. Topological design no longer consists of a highly polarised activity where the architect injects form and meaning onto an inert, white surface representing space. It has transformed into the interactive experience between a mind and a form, which is interactive because the form emerges from its own generative process. Movement, in other words, exceeds form.

For Bergson, virtuality is the ontological modality of consciousness, or duration. Duration roughly corresponds to what William James, with a famous aquatic metaphor, called the 'stream'. As James's conscious stream is continuous, forward-moving and in constant change, Bergson's duration is the succession of qualitative states of mind, indiscernible as atomic units but only feasible in their interconnectedness and passing. The passing-character is the result of deeper currents that, while remaining submerged, push water towards the surface. Both the deep currents and the superficial motion of the water that they create are real components of our experience. But while the motion on the surface is actual, the submerged currents are virtual.

What does this virtual modality entail? In a word: memory, which Bergson discusses in opposition to perception. Perception and memory are tendencies along which experience 'tends' to organise itself, but do not constitute independent kinds of experience, available separately from one another. Bergson defines perception as the 'abstract' tendency of our experience, referring to what our experience would be like if extrapolated from the effects of time. To stay with the Jamesian metaphor, abstract experience would mean to take the layer of moving water at the surface separately from the deeper currents beneath. This is the kind of experience we tend to produce artificially, when we look at the world objectively, with causal, quantitative, or geometrical models in mind. By contrast, memory embodies the 'concrete' tendency to experience the world as a constant becoming-other than itself. It is experience in terms of the effects of time on it.

Herzog & De Meuron, Kramlich Residence, *California, 1997-2000.*
Interior perspectives.

Here, we need to put aside the aquatic metaphor because Bergson indicates these two tendencies as radically heterogeneous to one another. It is as if deep and superficial could not be measured against each other.[15]

> Whenever we are trying to recover a recollection, to call up some period of our history, we become conscious of an act *sui generis* by which we detach ourselves from the present in order to replace ourselves, first, in the past in general, then, in a certain region of the past – a work of adjustment, something like the focusing of a camera. But our recollection still remains virtual; we simply prepare ourselves to receive it by adopting the appropriate attitude. Little by little it comes into view like a condensing cloud; from the virtual state, it passes into the actual; and as its outlines become more distinct and its surface takes on colour, it tends to imitate perception. But it remains attached to the past by its deepest roots, and if, being a present state, it were not also something that stands out distinct from the present, we should never know it for a memory.[16]

Either we are 'in' memory or 'in' perception. We don't reach the past from the present via the extension of the representational model. Quite the opposite. As we intentionally try to recollect something, we step into the past and its virtuality, and we navigate it, not rationally but intuitively, until we meet the virtual current pushing along the memory we are looking for. In order for us to individuate it and recollect it, that specific memory needs to be actualised and transformed in a perception. But, as Bergson warns in the last sentence of the quotation, part of the memory still remains attached to the past, otherwise we would not be able to discern it is a memory. This explains the sense of uncanniness, otherness, vagueness and suspension that memory entails.

The co-existence rather than integration of perception and memory is key to Bergson's relevance to my discussion of space, virtual spatiality and architecture. Bergson articulates such a co-existence within a peculiar conception of matter defined as the fullest aggregate of images, the sum total of all the past, present and future images available. An image for Bergson is 'a certain existence which is more than that which an idealist calls a *representation*, but less than what a realist calls a *thing* – an existence placed halfway between the "thing" and the "representation."'[17] Matter is not out there, in the world, but a mix of self and world, perception and memory. An example can clarify this point.

Even the most simple perception, like feeling cold or hot, takes time. When I analyse perception and quantify it according to objective scales of measurement, I act as if this time, indispensable to experience, did not exist. In the same way, as I try to recapture a memory long past, I won't be able to revive it without transforming it into a perception. The interesting feature of the differential relationship of memory and perception, virtual and actual, is that perception of actuality is arrived at, according to Bergson, from memory or virtuality. The present is accessed from the past, and not the reverse, so that experience is the constant reassessment of the present in terms of the past.

In concrete experience, as Bergson calls it, form is not injected into space as if from some otherworldly, timeless, geometrical outside, but emerges from the generative process of its own formation and deformation. What contemporary theorists identify as the animation of form, via topological techniques, Bergson illustrated as the infiltration of memory in perception. Such an infiltration provides experience with what Bergson names its 'pictorial' character, which indicates the process-like nature of the world. Paradoxically, it is time itself that constitutes experience pictorially, as a cinematic sequence. Thinking in objective terms implies a conception of matter and space as empty, homogeneous and passive, rather than full, heterogeneous and in constant motion: namely, as an aggregate of images in endless tension and becoming.

Let us go back one more time to the metaphor of virtuality as a range of deep currents that, while remaining submerged, push water to the surface. These submerged currents are virtually present to the stream. It is these virtual movements of duration that determine the emergence, or actualisation, of whatever stretch of the stream of consciousness reaches the surface. Bergson's suggestion is that the virtual currents correspond to what the pure past would be like if it were accessible. The emerged stream taken in isolation from the deep currents corresponds, instead, to what the pure present would be like as a self-contained discrete dimension. However, what is true for the dynamics of aquatic currents is true for perception and memory, present and past, actual and virtual. Experience is the theatre of these dynamics, where the invisible, or deeper layer, is always responsible for the emergence of whatever comes into view.

In contrast to the representationalist interpretation of virtuality, according to which virtuality can be 'represented' as the sum total of the effects of communication and information technology on how we know and build the world around us, I have been trying to elucidate an alternative concept of the virtual by phenomenologically understanding it as an expression of intentionality. My perspectivist definition of virtuality describes a constitutive component of experience, irreducible to physical processes as well as to quantification and formalisation. If this phenomenological interpretation is viable, experience contains a virtual dimension that calls into question a whole range of philosophical categorisations and architectural presuppositions. First of these is the Cartesian notion of space as passive receptor of forms, installed by an active and independent mind. If the hypothesis of a stable and controlled space fails, one of the most enduring bridges between philosophy and architecture is swept away. On its remains, a new concept of virtual spatiality emerges.

The relevance of Nieztsche and Bergson for my project lies in their insistence on the irreducibly passing character of our experience: this is what makes them champions of philosophical anti-Cartesianism and architectural anti-formalism. Cartesian space is incompatible with this passing and becoming feature, which is the greatest challenge of the architecture of virtuality.

Notes

1 I shall limit myself to a few references to indicate different tendencies in recent cybertheory. A utopianist, science fiction-type analysis is represented by Howard Rheingold's *Virtual Reality*, Summit Books (New York), 1991. A more scholarly approach, attempting to bind cybertheory to classical philosophical sources, is Michael Heim's *The Metaphysics of Virtual Reality*, Oxford University Press (Oxford), 1997. A comprehensive theoretical account is Pierre Lévy's *Becoming Virtual: Reality in the Digital Age*, Robert Bononno (trans.), Plenum Trade (New York), 1998. John Beckmann's *The Virtual Dimension: Architecture, Representation, and Crash Culture*, Princeton Architectural Press (Princeton), 1998, is an anthology of essays from a variety of disciplines including architecture.

2 The term was first introduced by Jean Baudrillard. See his *In the Shadow of The Silent Majorities*, Semiotext(e) (New York), 1983; *Fatal Strategies*, Semiotext(e) (New York), 1990; *The Gulf War Did Not Take Place*, Indiana University Press (Bloomington), 1995. In the context of this essay, I use it as emblematic of the 'technological' conception of the virtual, which I critique as 'representational'. Greg Lynn has similar views: 'The term "virtual" has been so debased that it often simply refers to the digital space of computer-aided design. It is often used interchangeably with the term simulation. Simulation, unlike virtuality, is not intended as a diagram for a future possible concrete assemblage but is instead a visual substitute'. *Animate Form*, Princeton Architectural Press (Princeton), 1999, p10.

3 I coin this expression in order to mark the difference between the rationalist concept of 'space' and my nonreductive perspective. In my analysis, the notion of 'space' coincides with the idea of a mutual exclusivity between *res cogitans* and *res extensa*, inaugurated by Descartes. The expression 'virtual spatiality' echoes the Heideggerian 'spatiality', which together with 'temporality' and 'historicity', is at the centre of his phenomenonological and existentialist project as laid out in *Being and Time*. These terms imply a critique of the way in which the tradition of Western metaphysics has 'objectified' space, time and history, which amounts to the inability to posit the meaning of these concepts beyond the oppositional framework set up by the subject-object distinction.

4 The critique of the rationalist concept of space as an alienated and inert 'outside' is one of the steadier themes in Heidegger's philosophy, spanning *Being and Time* to 'Building Dwelling Thinking', 1952. Section III of Part I of *Being and Time*, contains the kernel of his treatment of space. The discussion of spatiality is conducted as a critique of what Heidegger calls 'the Cartesian ontology of the world'. If my perspectivist conception of virtual spatiality draws from Heidegger the opposition to spatial inertia, it draws from Bergson and Nietzsche the further characterisation in terms of movement and heterogeneity.

5 It is difficult to locate a single definition of force in Nietzsche's work, since force is one of the most deeply embedded concepts in his philosophy. In this text, I discuss the idea of force as it is developed in the second of the *Untimely Meditations*, 'On the Uses and Disadvantages of History For Life'.

6 The discursive nature of forces cannot be pursued here. I define discursivity in relation to the all-encompassing notion of textuality assumed as a background for both deconstruction and hermeneutics. Since I derive the notion of force directly from Nietzsche, and the question of the nature of those forces remains problematic in Nietzsche's own writings, I prefer 'discourse' over 'text' because it describes more pertinently what would be the nature of those forces according to a distinctly Nietzschean line of argument. It is no coincidence that Michel Foucault, who coined the term in the mid-1960s and launched it in the postmodernist and poststructuralist context, did so around the time when Nietzsche appeared on the French scene. Deconstruction was not yet born and Heidegger, along with hermeneutics, was still to make his impact on French philosophy. I wish to anchor the term to that context, in which it meant the implicit knowledge that underlies and makes possible specific social practice, institutions or theories.

7 One of the fundamental notions in *Being and Time* is 'throwness' (*Geworfenheit*), which refers to the way in which we find ourselves always already 'placed' in our existence – we are not objectively present in it, but have to make it our own place,
to appropriate it, give it meaning. It seems to me that within this, architecture plays a major role. The world in which we find ourselves thrown is a 'built' world, which has constituted us as what we are in many substantial ways. Some studies have tried to unravel the constitutive role of architecture along Heideggerian lines. A lucid analysis of this theoretical knot is provided by Karsten Harries in his *The Ethical Function of Architecture*, MIT Press (Cambridge, MA), 1997. See also David Farrell Krell, *Architecture: Ecstasies of Space, Time, and the Human Body*, SUNY Press (Albany), 1997 and Edward C Casey, *Getting Back Into Place: Toward a Renewed Understanding of the Place-World*, Indiana University Press (Bloomington), 1993.

8 See Erwin Panofsky, *Perspective as Symbolic Form*, Zone Books (New York), 1991; Hubert Damisch, *The Origin of Perspective*, MIT Press (Cambridge, Mass.); Alberto Perez-Gomez, *Architectural Representation and the Perspective Hinge*, MIT Press (Cambridge, Mass.), 1997.

9 In the Introduction to *Being and Time*, Heidegger first raises the question of presence (*Anwesenheit*) in conjunction with the Greek interpretation of being in relation to time. Assumed as *parousia* or *ousia*, the Being of beings is both ontologically and temporally understood as presence: a definite mode of time (the present). The identification of a specific temporal modality with the way in which beings are, is for Heidegger a meaningful move on the part of Greek thought, since it indicates a fundamental 'repression' of time's becoming quality. Western thought seeks to confirm being in terms of eternal stability (the notion of presence), which is but the abstraction of a specific modality of time: the present.

10 In the history of architectural theory, the concept of 'space' becomes central only from the late 18th century, as the issue of canonical authority, previously identified solely with Vitruvius, is raised in connection with a universal definition of authority, established on human rationality rather than canonical sources. This question is deeply intertwined with the interdependence of the Enlightenment categories of fraternity, humanity and freedom. The paradigmatic example of the role of space in the Enlightenment debate on the foundation of rationality can be found in Siegfried Giedion, *Space, Time and Architecture*, Harvard University Press (Cambridge, Mass.), 1974.

11 A thorough discussion of this point can be found in the excellent chapter on 'Perspectivism, Philology, Truth', in Alan D Schrift, *Nietzsche and the Question of Interpretation: Between Hermeneutics and Deconstruction*, Routledge (London, New York), 1990, pp144–68.

12 On this issue of ambiguity, I disagree with Brian Massumi in 'Sensing the Virtual, Building the Insensible', in Stephen Perrella (ed) *AD: Hypersurface Architecture*, vol 68, no 5/6, Academy Editions (London), 1998, who sees virtuality and ambiguity as incompatible: 'Ambiguity . . . belongs to signifying structure. It is nothing new for architects to build-in ambiguity in order to make an event of standing form, but ambiguity still addresses the conventional function of the sign-form'. I don't see why ambiguity needs to be interpreted in terms of the 'signifying structure'. Why can't it be felt or sensed? Bergson's definition of memory against perception touches exactly on this point. In order for a memory to emerge at the surface of consciousness, it needs to become a perception. However, there is a fraction of memory that remains attached to the past. This is how we know it is a memory and not a perception. Such attachment to the past gives to memory an aura of uncanniness, otherness, and, I claim, ambiguity.

13 Friedrich Nietzsche, *Untimely Meditations*, Daniel Breaseale (ed), trans RJ Hollingdale, Cambridge University Press (Cambridge, Mass.), 1997, p62.

14 See Perrella, *Hypersurface Architecture*, op cit; Lynn, *Animate Form*, op cit.

15 'Deep' and 'superficial' are typical examples of vague predicates and as such, are unmeasurable. I cannot tell, for example, whether 6 feet of water are deep or not, as I cannot tell whether a 3-millimetre cut in my skin is superficial or not. No amount of conceptual analysis or empirical investigation can settle these matters. See, Timothy Williamson, *Vagueness*, Routledge (London), 1994.

16 Henri Bergson, *Matter and Memory*, trans Nancy Margaret Paul and W Scott Palmer, Zone Books (New York), 1988, pp133–4.

17 Ibid, p9.

KAREN A FRANCK

IT AND I

Bodies as Objects, Bodies as Subjects

The body I read about wherever I turn is a strange and contradictory one. It may not be a living, breathing human being at all but rather an idea or metaphor. It may not be a fixed or bounded entity but an expanding and contracting pattern of energies. It may be separate from other things called mind or self; it may contain them, or it may be them. It may be called natural, material, lived, legible, social, medical, architectural, virtual, repressed, absent or obsolete.

Don't be fooled. These are not definitions of *what* the body is – it's too slippery for that – but descriptions of *how* the body is: how it is experienced, conceived or used. Or they may be descriptions of how the body should be experienced, conceived or used. We are always describing and experiencing the body *as* . . . (as metaphor, as separate, as integrated, as lived).

Among all these descriptions, two general approaches are evident. One treats body and self as separate and potentially disconnected. To put it simply, each person *has* a body and sometimes may try not to have one or to have a different one. In this approach bodies are treated as objects, although not necessarily tangible ones. The other approach treats body and self as fully intertwined: each living person *is* a body, always and inescapably. The body as object places the designer or writer, or anyone else, adopting this approach outside the body, looking at or into it. The body as subject positions the writer or designer within the body/self and involves not only looking but also acting and feeling.

Although contrasting, these attitudes are not mutually exclusive, nor is one inherently better than the other. They are both very useful and perhaps necessary. What is troublesome is the dominance of the Western attitude of having a body and the extreme objectification and disdain that follow, enough so that some people feel the body is not necessary for human existence at all and that we would be better off without it. The attitude of being a body recognises the centrality and the value of embodiment to human experience, indeed to life. Being human means being embodied; no other way of being human in this world is possible or even desirable. Propounded in the West by phenomenologists, it is now increasingly endorsed by ecologists, cognitive scientists, feminist philosophers and critics, and architects.

Bodies as objects

The attitude of having a body depends upon a separation between the body and someone or something that has it. At one time it was soul; today it is more likely to be called mind, consciousness, self or subjectivity. In all cases the body is physical, less worthy and possibly disposable, while the not-body is mental, of greater value and essential. The body is often portrayed as inert matter, perhaps a tool or a machine, given life or operated by the not-body.

Once placed in opposition to each other, the body is viewed as resistant to the not-body, an obstacle to its full realisation. Beginning with Plato the body has relentlessly been considered an impediment to achieving something greater or something better, something beyond body and matter. The same references to confinement, imprisonment and the need to escape once made by Plato, Descartes and St Augustine are still frequently made in popular culture and more professional arenas.[1] Nowhere is the burdensomeness of the flesh and the desire for escape more vividly portrayed than in the culture of cyberspace with all its references to 'meat puppets' and 'flesh cage' and its euphoric descriptions of freedom from the physical constraints of the world and one's own body.[2]

Of course the possibility that there is an escape from embodiment in this lifetime predates cyberspace by several centuries. From Descartes the West inherited the belief that the mind can transcend the body's passions and distractions to achieve a purer form of knowledge. What is then exalted as a model of knowing and designing in academic and professional realms and in Western society generally is a mind that is 'free' of the body and thereby of any particular set of experiences or viewpoints, which would be too 'subjective'.[3]

Objectification of the body makes it an extremely rich source of ideas and creations. In architecture, a single objectified body can be idealised and used for deriving proportions and scale, or transformed into a metaphor for a building or for parts of a building. The body as an ideal is a frequent topic in architectural theory.[4] There is no doubt that the body as object is a rich source of insight, design and invention but it is quite remote from active, organic beings with practical, everyday needs and should not be confused with them despite the fact that the word 'body' refers to both.

Those beings – people – who inhabit buildings and cities may receive far less attention from architects than the objectified body. Too often the brief or programme representing particular kinds of bodies engaged in particular everyday tasks with specific needs becomes disconnected from formal manipulations and made secondary to them. Living bodies and their needs seem to be either irrelevant or an obstacle to design, as Colin St John Wilson has pointed out: '. . . the notion of necessity as an unwelcome chore leads in the mind of an aesthete to the relegation of acts of daily living to things to be despised.'[5] Sensory stimulation, other than vision, and spatial experiences, may also be ignored. Juhani Pallasmaa has described the dominance in Modernism of an architecture of the eye which intentionally creates a sensory and mental distance between body and building. 'Modernist design has housed the intellect and the eye, but it has left the body and the other senses, as well as our memories and dreams, homeless.'[6]

What can result is visually compelling buildings that are only to be seen, where the tactile quality of materials and other sources of sensory stimulation are minimised and where orientation may be confusing. The conditions may be actually inimical to the intended use: an art museum in Berlin where the art is best hung in the basement; an opera house in Sydney where large-scale

Marcos Novak, data-driven form

operas cannot be held; and housing in the Bronx for people with developmental disabilities that was hazardous for them to occupy.[7] More recently, the fascination with form and its deconstruction may deny the intended use altogether, so that a fire house in Switzerland must be used instead as a gallery.

And now opportunities for creating highly unusual forms, possibly of great beauty and visual interest, have vastly increased with advances in computer technology and programming; and the designs can be built and met with great acclaim. It seems very likely that these opportunities, afforded by computer technology will increase the propensity that already exists in architecture for form to be disconnected from everyday use and for vision to be the only sensory mode attended to. In its energetic disdain for bodies and materiality, the culture of cyberspace encourages such an attitude. In texts directed at an architectural audience, disparaging references to the body and expressed enchantment with a world without bodies, or with bodies that have been transformed beyond recognition, promote the message to architects that the bodies we (still) inhabit are indeed a burden or a bore, their everyday needs and experiences a drag on inventiveness and progress.[8]

In some ways the body is less of a 'burden' for architects in cyberspace. Elaborate drawings in a wide array of colours, three-dimensional models and interactive CDs can all be made with the small movements of one hand. The architect's body can remain nearly immobile: there is no need for physical manipulation of materials or tools. The sensory experiences of smell and touch that come from interacting with materials are absent as well. And for those architects who design virtual environments that remain in cyberspace to be visited by people but never to be physically inhabited, there is no need at all to consider the practical bodily needs of those visitors and the myriad consequences that follow in physical environments for plumbing, heating, ventilation, emergency egress and so on. So the design of cyberspace fulfils the age-old dream: ' . . . the dream of transcending the physical world, fully alive, at will, to dwell in some Beyond – to be empowered or enlightened there, alone or with others, and to return.'[9]

Bodies as subjects
Cultural critic Vivian Sobchack refers to her own leg with its large scar where a cancerous tumour was removed: 'Even at its most objectified and technologically caressed, I *live* this thigh – not abstractly on "the" body but concretely as "my" body . . . If we don't keep this subjective kind of bodily sense in mind as we negotiate our technoculture, then we . . . will objectify ourselves to death.'[10]

The attitude of being a body encompasses just this 'subjective kind of bodily sense', for it treats body and subject or body and mind as interdependent. The body is our only way of being and a fine way at that, giving us access to rich experiences of the world. The lived body, and the activities, experiences and needs it enables, can be a well-spring of design.

With the insights of Martin Heidegger, Mauice Merleau-Ponty, and now Drew Leder and David Levin, it becomes clear that the relationship of body to space is one of inhabitation and movement, not simple presence. As Merleau-Ponty has written: 'Our body is not in space like things; it inhabits or haunts space.'[11] Movement and imagined movement are key, as research in cognition now demonstrates. As Leder has stated: 'Perception is itself a motor activity. Moreover, that which is perceived is always saturated by the implicit presence of motility. The spatial depth of the perceived world, the experience of objects as *there,* is only possible for a being that moves through space.'[12]

The bodies we *have* are easily treated by architects and others as bounded, passive, entities whose primary, if not singular, sensory mode is vision. The bodies we *are* are moving, changing, permeable and fluid; through the various senses and movement our bodies extend into their surroundings and through the permeability of bodies, the surroundings enter them. The bodies we are require different spatial and physical conditions depending upon the task or activity at hand, depending upon characteristics of age, gender, size and culture, and depending upon the passage of time.

When embodiment is embraced, movement, activities and sensory stimulation can all become sources of design ideas. The alternative that Pallasmaa poses to the Modernist architecture of the eye is an architecture that stimulates all the senses, including the basic orienting system of the body. 'A building is encountered; it is approached, confronted, related to one's body, moved through, utilized as a condition for other things. A building is not an end in itself; it frames, articulates, gives significance, relates, separates and unites, facilitates and prohibits. Consequently, basic architectural experiences have a verb form rather than being nouns.'[13]

Such an architecture of the senses is found in the work of Frank Lloyd Wright, Eileen Gray, Erich Mendelsohn, Hans Scharoun and certainly Alvar Aalto. Colin St John Wilson cites these same Modernists as members of 'the other tradition' of Modernism who practised architecture not as fine art in which use is disdained in favour of aesthetics but as a practical art that seeks to satisfy 'a desire for a certain way of life'.[14] That tradition can still serve as a legacy and inspiration for an architecture that seeks to support and enhance the human condition and experience of embodiment.

While we may readily endorse this goal for architecture, it is possible that we have lost touch with our own embodiment. Many of us live and work in buildings that are temperate cocoons that do their best not to stimulate our senses and are designed for appearance and for some perfectly bland comfort zone. Ever more advanced technologies, such as computers, mediate our corporeal and sensuous relationship to all our surroundings, anaesthetising our senses and reducing bodily movement.[15] The uniformity and standardisation of contemporary spaces contribute as well. As Levin has written: 'We even begin to experience our own bodies as mere "furniture", mere objects in space; we lose touch with our *experience* of embodiment as a dynamic "synergic" process, a perpetual *ek-stasis*, situated in being in a way that could not be more unlike that of a physical thing.'[16]

All of us – architects and clients, teachers and students of architecture alike – may need to rediscover our own embodiment, our own bodily sensations. One place that this can begin to happen is in schools of architecture. In Nadia Alhasani's course on stairs at the University of Pennsylvania students walk up and down different kinds of stairs barefoot, paying attention to the sensations in their feet and their whole body.[17] In her course on the proximate environment, Galen Cranz at the University of California, Berkeley, conducts experiential exercises to increase sensory awareness. She encourages students to design 'from the body outward' which they find empowering because the body conceived as social and physical can be an authentic, experiential basis for design.[18] In my seminar at the New Jersey Institute of Technology on 'Bodies and Matter: The Erotics of Architecture', I have adopted exercises of deep-breathing meditation at the beginning of class, silent and attentive walks through campus, and critiques of buildings from an experiential perspective.

Kim Tanzer's studio courses at the University of Florida in Gainesville assign full-scale projects – drawing and building – to help students make connections between their bodies and architecture and inhabitants' bodies and architecture. When completed, the drawings are unfurled and mapped on to the walls and floors of the school. Neither the students nor the critics can take in the project by looking in one direction with their bodies immobile. They must move and look one way and another, up and down: no longer remote from the architectural object, they now inhabit it. Tanzer reports several consequences of this which suggest a decrease in the objectification of the body and the design and an increase in engagement of the students and the critics.[19]

Our bodies are not naturally given, they are made: they are cultural products. The ways we move and the postures we adopt, even the sensations we have, are all shaped by a particular culture and time period. Despite the persistence of many attitudes and traditions over long periods of time, culture changes and can be changed. Designing for living, active bodies does not mean that architects and other designers should always accept current practices without questioning them.

There is an opportunity to study, analyse and propose modifications to commonly accepted patterns of movement and posture. Cranz's research on the history of the chair and the physiology of the body suggests the need for fairly radical changes in furniture and postures to promote greater health and well being.[20] Bianca Lepori's design for a birthing room also began with physiology; the physiology of giving birth, and with interviews with mothers who had given birth at home. With her design of space and furniture, a woman giving birth can stretch, lean, bend, squat, crouch lie down, sit, or be in a bath.[21] Both Cranz and Lepori adopted a position within the body and so could design *from* the body rather than *for* it. The designs they present encourage a range of movements and support a variety of positions. Choice, activity and change all allow the body to be active, alive, in motion. This is not the body as a burden, an inert object; this is the lived body that gives us access to the world.

Bodies are both objects and subjects; we have them and we are them. But in treating bodies primarily as objects and in dreaming so persistently of transcendence, we neglect bodies as subjects and forget or disdain the bodies we are, both our own and those of others. With the help of computer and other technologies, this can be done with increasing sophistication in many areas including architecture. Fortunately, there is also growing recognition of the pressing need to value human embodiment, to rediscover it and to design in ways that enhance it. Technically there is nothing to prevent architects from adopting this goal and from using all the power and potential of computers to study, simulate, and design the material world for movement, for everyday activities, and for sensuous experience. To do so, however, they must counter the many forces that operate in the opposite direction, forces emanating historically from Western culture and from the dominant tradition in modern architecture. And they must reject the framing of cyberspace as an escape from embodiment and materiality.

Notes

1 For a philosophical and cultural history of the body as a burden, see Susan Bordo, *Unbearable Weight: Feminism, Western Culture and the Body*, University of California Press (Berkeley), 1993.

2 William Gibson, who coined the term 'cyberspace' in *Neuromancer* (1984), was also the first to portray this aspect of cyberspace. Apparently, the connection between the hero's 'bodiless exultation of cyberspace' and the Western dualism of mind and body was intentional on his part: see Mark Dery, *Escape Velocity: Cyberculture at the End of the Century*, Grove Press (New York) 1996, p248. Now embodiment/disembodiment is one of the most frequent themes of movies, novels and commentaries about cyberspace (see *Escape Velocity*, ibid; Anne Balsamo, *Technologies of the Gendered Body: Reading Cyborg Women*; Claudia Springer, *Electronic Eros: Bodies and Desire in the Postindustrial Age*; Allucquere Rosanne Stone, 'Will the Real Body Please Stand Up,' in Michael Benedikt, *Cyberspace: First Steps*; and Scott Bukatman, *Terminal Identity: The Virtual Subject in Postmodern Science Fiction*).

3 See Susan Bordo, *The Flight to Objectivity: Essays on Cartesianism and Culture*, State University of New York Press (Albany, New York), 1987. It has been implicit in Western Culture that it is the male self who will transcend the body while the female manages those functions that require embodiment. While I do not discuss gender in this essay, it is a significant layer in this complex topic of embodied subjectivity, explored by feminist philosophers including Luce Irigaray, Susan Bordo, Elizabeth Grosz, Judith Butler, Rosi Braidotti and Christine Battersby.

4 The idealised figure used to generate proportions in architecture has consistently been a male figure. See Diana Agrest, *Architecture from Without*, 1991; Anthony Vidler, *The Architectural Uncanny*, 1992; and Cynthia C Davidson (ed), *Anybody*, 1997: all MIT Press (Cambridge, Mass).

5 Colin St John Wilson, *The Other Tradition of Modern Architecture: The Uncompleted Project*, Academy Editions (London), 1995, p65. Architects may express an outright arrogance towards people's everyday needs. In November 1996, on a nationally televised discussion in the USA of Peter Eisenman's design for the Aronoff Center for Design and Art in Cincinnati, several very well-known American architects dismissed people's difficulty in locating the door to the building, asserting that 'people need to learn about buildings'.

6 Juhani Pallasmaa, *The Eyes of the Skin: Architecture and the Senses*, Academy Editions (London), 1996, p10.

7 For more detailed information on some cases see Thomas Mitchell, *Redefining Designing from Form to Experience*, Van Nostrand Reinhold (New York), 1993.

8 See previous *AD* articles, including Stelarc, 'Towards the Post-Human: From Psycho-body to Cyber-system,' *AD* 11/12 1995; Neil Spiller, 'Leaving Nadir: Cyborgian Mutation and Architecture' and Rachel Armstrong, 'The Body as an Architectural Space – From Lips to Anus', *AD* 9/10, 1996.

9 Michael Benedikt, 'Cyberspace: Some Proposals', in Michael Benedikt (ed), *Cyberspace: First Steps*, MIT Press (Cambridge, Mass), p131.

10 Vivian Sobchack, 'Baudrillard's Obscenity', *Science-Fiction Studies*: 18(55): 327; cited by Mark Dery, *Escape Velocity*, op cit, p311.

11 Maurice Merleau-Ponty, *The Primacy of Perception*, 1963, p5; cited by Elizabeth Grosz, *Volatile Bodies: Toward a Corporeal Feminism*, University of Indiana Press (Bloomington, Indiana), 1994, p90.

12 Drew Leder, *The Absent Body*, University of Chicago Press (Chicago, Illinois), 1990, p17. Drew Leder, Elizabeth Grosz and Michael David Levin draw upon the ideas of Merleau-Ponty to describe human embodiment; as does Juhani Pallasmaa in his description of an architecture of the senses. For a discussion of embodiment that was inspired by Merleau-Ponty but also draws upon Buddhist philosophy and practice see Francisco J Varela et al, *The Embodied Mind: Cognitive Science and Human Experience*, MIT Press (Cambridge, Mass), 1991.

13 Juhani Pallasmaa, *The Eyes of the Skin*, pp44-45.

14 Colin St John Wilson, *The Other Tradition of Modern Architecture*, p55.

15 For descriptions of more sensory-rich experiences of architecture see Lisa Heschong, *Thermal Delight in Architecture*, MIT Press (Cambridge, Mass), 1979; Kent C Bloomer and Charles W Moore, *Body, Memory and Architecture*, Yale University Press (New Haven, Connecticut), 1977. For an interesting explanation of how written language contributed to a loss of sensual experiences with nature see David Abram, *The Spell of the Sensuous: Perception and Language in a More-than-Human World*, Pantheon Books (New York), 1996.

16 Michael David Levin, *The Body's Recollection of Being: Phenomenological Psychology and the Deconstruction of Nihilism*, Routledge & Kegan Paul (London) 1985, p345.

17 Nadia Alhasani, 'Defying Dreams and Gravitation: On the Making of Stairs', *Triangulating the Bodies of Architecture: Proceedings of the 1996 ACSA Northeast Regional Meeting*, Buffalo (New York), 1996.

18 Galen Cranz, *The Chair: Rethinking Culture, Body and Design*, WW Norton (New York), 1998.

19 Kim Tanzer, 'Scale Problems', paper presented at West Central Regional Meeting of Associate of Collegiate Schools of Architecture, Illinois Institute of Technology, 1991.

20 Galen Cranz, *The Chair: Rethinking Culture, Body and Design*.

21 Bianca Lepori, 'Freedom of Movement in Birthplaces', *Children's Environments*, 1994:11.

Nicholas Goldsmith (FTL Happold), Art on the Beach

REBECCA CARPENTER

FORCE AFFECT

An Ethics of Hypersurface

This essay investigates motion as an ethic within architecture. Three different examples are described: blobs, events-space and hypersurfaces.

It can be argued that architecture is capable of activating a set of relationships as reciprocal presuppositions in the form of time. To present this argument, I will invoke some existing ideas including those set forward by Gilles Deleuze, Félix Guattari and Brian Massumi.

We can say that architecture has the potential to express a 'virtual–actual' system. In using the term 'virtual–actual', I mean to indicate reversible intensities. That is to say, the virtual–actual pairing produces a co-resonating system. This does not mean that the virtual and the actual are simply inverse images of one another with the present occuring in the middle. Immanent here is a transformational time structure producing a topological transformation. The term 'virtual' should be understood as employed by Brian Massumi: as a nonspatial element of 'pure exteriority . . . every point of the virtual is adjacent to every point of the actual even if those points are not adjacent to each other'.[1] In other words, a system of exchange is achieved, which when physically constituted as the present, is the dynamic deformation of the space of one set of points into the adjacent set of points in the production of the *new*.

We will also draw on the terms 'form of expression' and 'form of content', as deployed by Deleuze and Guattari, and on Henri Bergson's notion of duration embodied in 'difference in kind'. In Bergson's discussion, the present is an image produced within a successive time construct set up in one's consciousness. 'Difference in kind' refers to an embodiment of time in each individual existence as a momentum towards a perfection of the space–time relationship. For Bergson, duration is set up in memory, creating a virtual co-existence of the past and present. In other words, we construct time and space through experience. Brian Massumi describes an interface of exchange between function and quality as a reciprocal presupposition: 'The term "form of expression" refers to an organisation of functions such as being an architect. The term "form of content" refers to an organisation of qualities such as brickness.'[2] The relationship between architect and brick takes place as an interface between the 'form of expression' and the 'form of content'. These relationships are presented here to describe memory and meaning as forces that are connected up in experience – for example, in the experience of making architecture. If we connect up the virtual–actual function to this idea, memory and meaning take on the form of a topological transformation, a figural diagram of flickering duration.

The potential to express the virtual–actual transformation in architecture requires that we rewind to the old architectural binary articulation: form and function. Such discrete articulations can become a conflation and inflation of the function: the actual form can constitute an incorporation of virtual functions, and actual functions can constitute a virtual experience. This conflation and inflation is really a two-point separation of form and experience. Whether we look through the discrete constitution of a form, or the abstraction of effects, we can join form and function as points on a moving curve. This transformation can be seen as an indication of their mutual blurring. In this sense, architecture can produce time.

Productive time in architecture has been introduced before in terms such as 'virtuality', 'novelty', 'transformations', 'perturbations' and a 'new pragmatism'.[3] These all suppose, in line with this argument, that architecture can integrate the structure of time by assuming its form. I am interested in the structure of time described by Gilles Deleuze as the process of becoming. In this process, the present has a plural structure. That is to say, any event has that strange plural dimension: past–future–presence. Incorporating this time structure in the construction of space is to join experience and form as a continuously transforming figure: a topological transformation where experience becomes the curve of space.[4]

Greg Lynn and Bernard Tschumi are two architects who take this approach. Each attempts, in their own way, to remove form from a static relationship to function; they reinvent form/function, idea/space, space/experience, opening up to a completely new kind of relationship. They construct what Massumi has called a 'reversible function, in the mathematical sense, a diagrammatic curve joining two points'.[5]

The methods used by these architects to construct this line should not be reduced simply to analytic integration or resistance. Lynn brings a new term to the form–function relationship. By deterritorialising two discrete areas – internal organisations (form) and external influences (function) – he produces a new term – 'blobs' – meaning a productive behavioural system of differentiation and integration. Tschumi also brings a new term to resist a dialectical notion of form and function. 'Event–space' is a concept expressing mutual resistance and heterogeneity but also accessibility.[6] We can describe these two terms, 'blobs' and 'event–space', as constructed differential relationships. However, it can be argued that the problem with both terms is that they rely on either side of the two-point structure of the function rather then the exchange between the two.

Expressing Form

We can speak about the work of Greg Lynn as existing within an ethic of movement. He calls this ethic 'anorganic vitalism'.[7] The term 'anorganic' is meant to indicate a position of differential integration, both organic and inorganic. That is, the incorporation of life science and technology into a mutual construction. This construction is an attempt to create an 'abstract machine' for producing novelty.[8] The emphasis on 'novelty' indicates an attempt to create productive time. Complex conditions create the

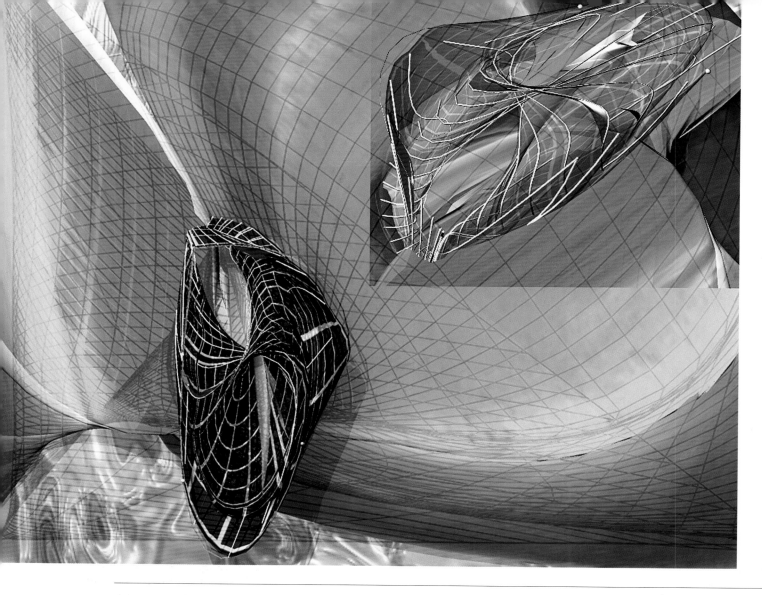

Stephen Perrella and Rebecca Carpenter,
Möbius House Study, 1998

forces determining the internal constitution of form and the external cultural influences of production. Lynn describes this 'concept of order and difference':

> Novelty, rather than some extrinsic effect, can be conceived as the catalyst of new and unforeseeable organisations that proceed from the interaction between freely differentiating systems and their incorporation of external constraints.[9]

The idea expressed by Deleuze and Guattari that language is an evolving body informs Lynn's concept of geometry. The term 'geometry' is a relative one and does not refer to a specific type of geometry; it is a general assemblage of analytic and differential geometry. D'Arcy Thompson's science of related forms and concern for the simplicity of the transformational grid inform Lynn's animate deformations. Thompson's ideas are a complex hybrid of classics, mathematics and zoology. We should note his emphasis on the diagram and Lynn's incorporation of this into his idea of form as the geometry of complexity:

> The form, then, of any portion of matter, whether it be living or dead, and the changes of form which are apparent in its movements and in its growth, may in all cases alike be described as due to the action of force. In short, the form of an object is a 'diagram of forces', in the sense, at least, that from it we can judge of or deduce the forces that are acting or have acted upon it: in this strict and particular sense, it is a diagram – in the case of a solid, of

the forces which *have* been impressed upon it when its conformation was produced, together with those that enable it to retain its formation; in the case of a liquid (or of a gas) of the forces which are for the moment acting on it to restrain or balance its own inherent mobility.[10]

Lynn's notion of form can be understood to be a complexity of forces, interacting over time, that have no single 'idea' operating over them. Form is a system of internal and external forces, an incorporated behaviour over time. All form with such complex behaviour can be said to act like a 'blob'. Blobs are a set of complex behaviours. Going back into architectural theory, Lynn integrates models of complexity to form an aggregate idea about form. He incorporates a reductive approach (top down to arrive at form) and an emergent approach (bottom up to arrive at form). Complexity is seen as 'irreducible and multiple', simplicity as 'reducible and singular', hence the reductive and emergent approaches.[11] By creating an assemblage of these ideas, he generates a third idea:

> Similarly, one approach to a theory of complexity might be to develop a notion of the composite or the assemblage which is understood as neither multiple nor single, neither internally contradictory nor unified. Complexity involves the fusion of multiple and different systems into an assemblage which behaves as a singularity while remaining irreducible to any single simple organisation.[12]

Lynn's idea of complexity resolves the problematic geometry existing in these two approaches. This suggests a way of organising form based on a completely different understanding of geometry, which is diagrammatic and mobile. Isomorphic polysurfaces (blobs) are examples of an alternative geometry. They were developed within animation software to model characters and other supple forms in motion. This geometry is a freely differentiated form (a diagram for complex behaviour over time) and hence not a prescriptive geometry in the sense that it is reductive or emergent, like the previously noted models. Isomorphic polysurfaces are known as 'meta-balls' (or 'clay'), which are defined by a centre, surface area, a mass and two zones of influence (negative and positive). The form of the clay is determined by the interaction of zones of influence, that is, variables of mass, centre locations and surface areas. When forces are applied to the blobs, since they already have their own internal set of forces, the assemblage becomes a highly complex set of interactions that cannot be attributed simply to the force applied to the blob. This is a system that introduces the possibility for form to evolve within the relationship of form and function in an integrated manner.

This may not be intended to be a prescription for a 'methodology of form', but it could certainly be read as a prescription indicating that radical form produces time. The 'anorganic methodology' includes philosophy (meaning has force), life science (study of form and growth), and technology (a culturally situated method of production; a machine that is a double 'content of expression'). This 'methodology of forms' is not intended to create forms that signify a particular subject or source. Form is doubled as continuous transformation and growth, continuity and difference, in a system of forces both past and future (present). Past, because the actual form can be attributed to a system of virtual forces, and future, because the unforeseeable organisations produced by the virtual form will produce forces that affect the actual form. In this sense, the modernist separation of form and function is interrupted. Meaning, where the form signifies a subject, has been interrupted and opened up in an attempt to exclude this direction from exchanging force actualised as form.[13] It could be argued that formal constitution is the function here.

Expressing Effect

The work of Bernard Tschumi can be said to exist within an ethic of movement. This ethic can be called 'linguistic transpositions'. Architecture exists as a transposition of text through the introduction of different texts. Through interdialectics, effects are sought in architecture as an artistic narrative. The narrative is an inaccessible space moving between points – the subjective space of art. One can only access the narrative of architecture by becoming it. The exploration of the subjective space in the narrative of art is itself a new form of knowledge for architecture.

By establishing his practice in New York and Paris, Tschumi transposes the context of production as a means to access this space. Put another way, event–space is the meeting of two exclusive terms: spatial structure and dynamic movement, and this meeting can only be actualised through another event–space; architecture is in the exchange of experience:

> Take for example the buildings of Paul Andreu. We often talk about the buildings of Mies, Palladio, or van Berkel, which we have occasionally seen in person but mostly know through photographs. I've only spent a few hours in buildings by Mies but I've spent approximately a thousand times that time in Andreu's building in the last 25 years. I would even object to his point about pleasure. [Andreu has claimed that function is an 'incentive to prepare pleasure']. The greatest pleasure I had was once when I went from the taxi to the plane in two minutes in a major international airport. [He is probably referring to Charles de Gaulle Airport, Roissy] Congratulations to you; Palladio never gave me that![14]

Architecture exists as 'movement, space and event'; transformations of earlier ideas 'conceived space, perceived space, erotic space (purely subjective)'. These ideas have been moved from their original context – literature, philosophy and art – into architecture. They arrive through linguistic models to solve the problem of form and idea. Tschumi introduces a third point to subvert their duality – event–space – a concept similar to Georges Bataille's notion of deep interior experience.[15] This third point renders the duality indifferent and inaccessible. Spatial structure and dynamic movement are held apart as irreducible and mutually exclusive. They have no relationship without the abstract space of chance encounters: event–space. Event–space aims to 'maintain these contradictions in a dynamic manner, in a new relation of indifference, reciprocity and conflict'.[16] Event–space exists as movement. It is the subjective space of motion, the motion of a narrative and also the intrusion of bodies, free from the problems of consumption implicit in the dialectics. Within this context, form is not worked, event–space does the work of ensuring its noninterpretation as a signification: an unknowable potential of effects. 'Architecture ceases to be a backdrop for actions, becoming the action itself'.[17]

This system of effects introduces the possibility for effects to function against each other as a system existing outside form. The space between structure and movement keeps architecture from annihilation. It keeps chance encounters, forcing effects and resisting consumption. In this space of experience, normative descriptions of movement as geometric (you can't draw it as a form) have no real meaning. Tschumi struggles to find a word for this geometry between space and time:

> Architecture is about the meeting of mutually exclusive terms: concept and experience, virtual and real, envelope and body. That meeting takes place in an in-between, an interstitial space is . . . not geometric, not merely physical. I have no name for it yet.[18]

This resistance to name indicates that the space–time connection cannot be figured; that is to say, it is not a formal analytic; it is an synthetic border of sense:

> At the border of architecture are attitudes about space, geometry and sensuality that often tell more of architecture's nature than the textbooks of architectural orthodoxy.[19]

Tschumi's resistance to formal methodology is expressed as linguistic transposition. This includes philosophy (language as a grid to be mastered through experience), art (subjective space) and culture (culturally situated between cultures). In Tschmu's case, effects are doubled as the impossible-to-grasp potentiality of dynamic movement both past and future (present). Future, because the force of virtual moving bodies can affect the actual form, and past, because the actual form and actual effect will have forces that affect virtual moving bodies. It is in this sense that the modernist separation of form and function is interrupted. Meaning, where the form signifies a subject, has been interrupted and opened up in an attempt to exclude this direction from exchanging effect actualised as event–space. It can be argued that the abstraction of effect is the function here.

Expressing Form is Effect Expressing

Topological transformations are in the form of the virtual–actual function; the experience of the space is the form of the space. In topology, a topological transformation is one in which the function of transformation is biunique and bicontinuous. A form can be deformed into another form without cutting, tearing or otherwise violently altering the original. Geometry usually brings to mind points, circles and squares. This takes us backwards to another time. We expect geometry to change constantly under the influence of new theories and new technologies. Topology is general geometry (general does not mean simplistic). Terms such as 'line', 'circle' and 'triangle', even 'size' and 'shape' have no real meaning in topology. Topological figures are described in terms of 'properties' that exist in relation to other figures. These properties might include having a hole (nonclosed curve), not having a hole (closed curve), having an edge (a surface), and having a homeomorphic relationship to another form determined by deforming, transforming, knotting and linking. Because these are transformations between neighbourhoods with duration they are in effect already the space of experience. The duration of the transformation is the space of experience. 'The invariance of incidence relations provides a basis for the concept of topology as geometry based primarily upon continuity and invariance of neighbourhoods'.[20]

The term 'blob' can be redefined with new emphasis. The surfaces and their boundaries are in fact responsive and effectual and have a distinct relationship to 'nurbs' (nonuniform-rational bsplines). A blob can be considered as a collection of three-dimensional nurbs. A nurb is really just a two-dimensional

Steven Holl, Art Museum

diagram for a potential curved (closed or nonclosed) surface (edge). It is a topological diagram for potential topological space. It is a spline that acquires three dimensions within its own duration. That is to say, potentialising its third dimension is transforming the two dimensions through an exchange of force, really a kind of experience space.

The Möbius House Study was an attempt to construct an experience space curve.[21] In this study, Stephen Perrella and I combined a potential topological space with an arrested topological space. We made a Möbius strip out of a nurb (arrested topological space with the property of one curving surface) and constrained co-ordinates of another nurb (potential topological space) with its own internal set of forces (magnitude – weight, rotation, size – and position), over time. The relationship between the strip and the 'nurb' is a kind of variation on a topological deformation. The Möbius strip was chosen as the figure for the production of a new home. We did this because it can be argued that domestic culture has moved outside the familiar form of the home and onto our screens, where the familiar is already in the form of a strange accelerated repetitive one-sided surface. This is a space of experience already topological, already in a process of continuous deformation both in form and experience,

both in terms of the making and the inhabiting. We have some considerations here: an accelerated experience–space of continuous transformation where the actual is already the virtual, and a technologically driven topological transformation between topological forms (experience–spaces that are already actually virtual): an arrested topological space and a potential topological space. In this study, we argue that the form is the space of experience that forces: each line of the actual is in the line of the virtual. This system is in the form of the curving line of time; it is a hyperspace.

The idea of the Möbius strip is introduced in intuitive topology. If we take a surface and we twist it and then reconnect it, it has some interesting properties. Moving along the surface can produce the mirror image of that thing, a new thing. If we fold the surface in on itself and connect it back to itself we get a Klein bottle. The single-sided surface (the surface is really an edge) can in its transformation produce difference. A Möbius strip is an arrested topological space with the property of one edge. We do not want to build the arrested form. We might say the challenge of inhabiting the flatness of this figure is really a topological transformation between experience and space. We can call this kind of ethic a hypersurface. Hypersurface is an ethic of motion.

Notes

1 Brian Massumi, *A User's Guide To Capitalism and Schizophrenia, Deviations from Deleuze and Guattari*, MIT Press (Cambridge, Massachussetts), 1995, p67. For a description of the virtual and actual system, see p170.

2 Ibid, p15.

3 'Virtuality' and 'topological transformations' as described by Brian Massumi; 'novelty' as described by Greg Lynn (a 'catalyst of new and unforeseeable organisations'); 'perturbations' as discussed by Reiser + Umemoto, 'Yokohama Port Terminal', in Stephen Perrella (ed), *AD: Hypersurface Architecture*, vol 68, no 5/6, Academy Editions (London), May–June 1998, p22-3; 'new pragmatism' as discussed by John Rajchman, 'A new Pragmatism?', *Anyhow*, vol 7, Anyone Corporation, 1998, p211.

4 For a discussion of Built Time see Andrew Benjamin's essay 'Not to Shed Complexity', *Fisuras 3 1/4*, December 1995.

5 Massumi, op cit.

6 I am discussing blobs and event–space as a reinvention of the architectural dialectic form, and experience as a moving diagram – a diagram with time. We can argue that the contextual relevance of this comparison exists within the evolution of organic and dialectic architectures. Gregg Lynn's methodology can be called a formalist continuation of the work of Peter Eisenman. Bernard Tschumi's resistance to an ideology of form and function can be called structuralist. The technique of transposition was typical in 1960s post-war structuralist theories; the historical precedents of this technique belong to the Russian Formalists' approach. The difference in their approach to the problem of incorporating time in architecture can be found within these historical contexts. Lynn incorporates idea and form into a system in which time is imbedded into the form. Tschumi's approach is an attempt to understand the experience through a grid that can be mastered, where experience is linked to language as the primordial symbolic material. See Louis Martin, 'Interdisciplinary Transpositions: Bernard Tschumi's Architectural Theory', in *The Anxiety of Interdisciplinarity*, vol 2, Backless Books, 1998, p81.

7 Greg Lynn, 'Geometry in Time', *Anyhow*, vol 5, Anyone Corporation, 1998.

8 Greg Lynn, 'The Renewed Novelty of Symmetry', in *Books by Architects: Greg Lynn, Folds, Bodies and Blobs: Collected Essays*, La Lettre Volée (Bruxelles), 1998.

9 Ibid, p64.

10 D'Arcy Wentworth Thompson, *On Growth and Form*, Cambridge University Press, 1961, p11.

11 Greg Lynn, op cit.

12 Greg Lynn, 'Blob tectonics or Why Geometry is Square and Topology is Groovy', ibid, p173.

13 For a structuralist analysis of meaning in architecture see Rosalind Krauss, 'Death of a Hermeneutic Phantom, The Materialisation of the sign in the work of Peter Eisenman', *The Anxiety of Interdisciplinarity*, vol 2, Backless Books, 1998.

14 Bernard Tschumi quoted from a panel discussion on infrastructure and distribution, *Anyhow*, Anyone Corporation, 1998, p101.

15 This argument is formally similar to Roland Barthe's paradox of the avant-garde. Louis Martin describes Tschumi's theory of eroticism (pleasure) as a 'perversion of Bataille's position' in 'Interdisciplinary Transpositions: Bernard Tschumi's Architectural Theory', *The Anxiety of Interdisciplinarity*, vol 2, Backless Books, 1998, p71.

16 Tschumi, 'Index of Architecture', in *Questions of Space, Lectures on Architecture*, Architectural Association (London), 1990, p100.

17 Tschumi writes, 'I do not think it is very important to discuss "what buildings look like". It is what they do that is important.' 'Through A Broken Lens', *Anyhow*, vol 7, Anyone Corporation, 1998, p240.

18 Ibid, p242.

19 Tschumi, 'Episodes of Geometry and Lust', *Questions of Space*, op cit.

20 Bruce Meserve, *Fundamental Concepts of Geometry*, Dover Publications Inc, (New York), 1983, p291.

21 Stephen Perrella and Rebecca Carpenter, 'The Möbius House Study', in Stephen Perrella (ed), *Hypersurface Architecture*, op cit.